Pike Place Public Market
Seafood Cookbook

Pike Place Public Market
Seafood Cookbook

Braiden Rex-Johnson

Illustrations by Spencer Johnson

TEN SPEED PRESS
BERKELEY, CALIFORNIA

Once again, to Spencer and Bo-Bo, with all my thanks and love.

Copyright © 1997 by Braiden Rex-Johnson
Illustrations © 1997 by Spencer Johnson

Cover design by Catherine Jacobes and Nancy Austin
Text design by Nadja Lazansky and Sarah Levin
Interior illustrations by Spencer Johnson

Bibliography is on file with publisher. Write to: Ten Speed Press, P.O. Box 7123, Berkeley, CA, 94707.

Permissions:
"Hot Honeyed Halibut" and "Crab Louis" reprinted by permission from *Joy With Honey* by Doris Mech.
    Copyright © 1995, by Doris Mech, St. Martin's Press, Inc., New York, NY.
"Cold-Smoked Salmon with Corn Bread Pudding, Shiitake Relish, & Fried Basil" reprinted by permission from
    A Harvest Celebration: Delectables from Distinguished Northwest Chefs. Copyright © 1995, The Market Foundation,
    Seattle, WA.
"Bronzed Tuna" and "Salt-Baked Trout" reprinted by permission from *Short Cuts to Great Cuisine* by Carol Foster.
    Copyright © 1994, The Crossing Press, Freedom, CA.
"Sole with Grapes and Champagne" from the Spring 1993 issue of *Simply Seafood* Magazine.
"Smoked Chilean Sea Bass with Thai Vinaigrette" reprinted by permission by G. P. Putnam's Sons, from
    Graham Kerr's Kitchen, by Graham Kerr. Copyright © 1994, The Treena & Graham Kerr Corporation.

Pike Place Public Market is a licensed trademark of the Pike Place Market Preservation and Development Authority,
85 Pike Street, Room 500, Seattle, WA 98101, (206) 682-7453.
The cover of this book is based on the 1990 commemorative anniversary poster produced by the Pike Place Market
Merchants Association. The poster is available by contacting the Merchants Association at 93 Pike Street, #312,
Seattle, WA 98101, (206) 587-0351.

Library of Congress Cataloging-in-Publication Data
Rex-Johnson, Braiden. 1956-
        Pike Place public market seafood cookbook/ Braiden Rex-Johnson;
    illustrations by Spencer Johnson.
            p.   cm.
        Includes index.
        ISBN 0-89815-872-9
        1. Cookery (Fish) 2. Cookery (Seafood) 3. Pike Place Market (Seattle, Wash.) I. Title.
    TX747.R56 1997
    641.6'92--dc21   97-3447
                                                            CIP

Printed in the United States of America
First Printing, 1997

1 2 3 4 5 / 01 00 99 98 97

Contents

·Part 1·

A FISH-LOVER'S PRIMER FROM
THE SOUL OF SEATTLE

·Part 2·

FINFISH

Halibut · 61

Hot Honeyed Halibut

Halibut Soup (Aïgo Boulido)

Pepper-Glazed Halibut Cheeks

Poached Halibut with Spicy Mashed Potatoes

Plank-Roasted Halibut with Sour Cream Sauce

Lingcod · 70

Lingcod with Gremolata Braised Vegetables

Lingcod Nuggets with Hazelnut Crumb Crust

Baked Lingcod with Tarragon Pesto

Marlin · 74

Caribbean Marlin with Orange-Black Bean Sauce

Marlin à la Sicilienne

Monkfish · 77

Baked Monkfish Fillets with Fines Herbes Bread Crust

Monkfish in Curried Carrot Broth

Stir-Fried Monkfish

Rockfish · 82

Baked Whole Rockfish with Vietnamese Dipping Sauce

Yelloweye Rockfish Salad with Light Gazpacho Sauce

Blackened Rockfish Fillets

Sablefish (Black Cod) · 89

Sablefish with Chukar Cherry Sauce

Sablefish with Kasu Marinade

Smoked Sablefish Poached in Milk

Salmon · 94

Salmon Loaf

Yoko's Barbecued Salmon

Baked Whole Salmon with Crab-and-Shrimp Stuffing

Balsamic-Glazed Salmon

Richard's Copper River Salmon Croquettes

Twice-Baked Potatoes with Salmon-Basil Stuffing

Steamed Salmon Cantonese Style

Sephardic Salmon

Cold-Smoked Salmon with Corn Bread Pudding, Shiitake Relish, and Fried Basil

Alaska Salmon with Warm Blackberry and Shallot Compote

Seared Salmon with Thai Curry Peanut Sauce

Salmon Cakes with Yellow Corn Relish

Spicy Smoked Salmon with Wasabi Dipping Sauce

The Odd Skillet of Finfish · 120

Sautéed Shad Roe with Sorrel Sauce

Broiled Northwest Shad

Sautéed Skate with Georgian Walnut Sauce

Pan-Fried Smelt with Lemon Butter

Applewood-Smoked Sturgeon with Corn Salsa, Tomatillo Syrup, and Anaheim Chile Oil

Poached Sturgeon with Sorrel and Wild Mushroom Sauce

Swordfish · 134

Swordfish Teriyaki

Grilled Swordfish Spinach Salad

Trout · 138

Salt-Baked Trout

Wild Rice-Stuffed Trout

Steelhead Fillets in Basil Rice Paper

Tuna · 144

Braised Tuna with Pike Place Fish Secret Sauce
Bronzed Tuna
Tuna Escabèche
Yin and Yang Tuna

·Part 3·
SHELLFISH

Clams · 152

Basic Steamed Clams
Daisy Sage's Clam Chowder
Northwest Clambake in the Oven
Boston-Style Clam Chowder
Stir-Fried Clams
Smoky Clam Chowder
Manhattan Clam Chowder
Baked Razor Clams with an Asian Accent
Geoduck Fritters

Crab · 167

Basic Cooked Crab
Chandler's Crab Cakes
Cold Crab Cakes with Fresh Chive Aïoli
Crab Veneto
Crab-Stuffed Peppers
Hood Canal Crab Cakes with Honey-Yogurt Salsa
Herb Crepes with Dungeness Crab, Sweet Peppers, and
Crème Fraîche
Crab Soufflé Cakes with Sweet Pepper and Corn Relish
Spicy Crab Boil

Tarragon Crab Boil
Hot Crab and Artichoke Dip
Crab and Cheese Canapés

Mussels · 187

Cinchy Steamed Mussels
Roasted Mussels
Gingery Mussels
Moules à la Marinière
Mussel, Potato, and Tomato Salad
Mussels and Millet in Curried Yogurt Sauce
Mussels Provençal
Mussels in Pinot Noir Butter
Five-Spice Rice with Mussels
Saffron Mussel Bisque

The Odd Kettle of Shellfish · 200

Golden Abalone
Crawfish Boil
Cooking a Live Lobster
Lobster Medallions and Couscous Salad with
Ginger Vinaigrette
Boiled Octopus

Oysters · 211

Baked Oysters
Oyster and Corn Casserole
Oysters on the Half Shell with Mignonette Ice
Margaret's Oyster Stew
Fried Oyster Caesar Salad
Oysters Chez Shea
Oyster Fritters Shelton Style

Scallops · 228

Scallops St. Jacques

Sea Scallop and Snow Pea Bisque

Singing Scallops Steamed with Fresh Fennel

Thai Curry Scallops

Blue Sea Scallops

Coconut Soup with Sea Scallop Medallions

Shrimp and Prawns · 237

All-American Shrimp Boil

Shrimp Gumbo

Herb-Crusted Alaskan Spot Prawns with
Warm Mushroom-Potato Salad

Stir-Fried Prawns with Sour Sauce

Scandinavian Open-Face Bay Shrimp Sandwich

Prawns in Red Lentil Purée

Alaskan Spot Prawn Wonton Salad

Shrimp-n-Vegetable Quiche

Shrimp with Porcini Mushroom Glaze

Vietnamese Shrimp Rolls with Hoisin Dipping Sauce

Alaskan Spot Prawns with Vanilla Beurre Blanc

Squid · 254

Boiled Squid

Calamari Napoli

Crisp-Fried Calamari with Three Sauces

Vietnamese-Style Squid

Red Hot Chile Pepper Squid

Calamari Fillets with Ground Almonds

Florentine Stuffed Squid

· Part 4 ·

CANNED AND SMOKED SEAFOOD, SEAFOOD COMBINATION DISHES, AND SEAFOOD SIDEKICKS

Canned and Smoked Seafood · 268

Smoked Salmon Pasta Salad

Smoked Salmon Dutch Baby with Dill Sauce

Smoked Salmon and Wild Rice Cakes with Paprika
and Green Onion Aïoli

Smoked Salmon Ravioli with Lemon-Cream Sauce

Southwestern Smoked Scallop Chowder

Scandinavian Pasta

The Shinbos' Cherry-Applewood Smoked Salmon

Tuna and White Bean Salad

Seafood Combination Dishes · 284

Seafood Chili

Mariage Oleronais

Seafood Pasta in Parchment

Sailboat Salmon Pasta

Pike Place Market Seafood Stew

Paella à la Navarra

Country French Fish Soup

Fiesta Brew Fish Stew

No-Bake Seafood Lasagne

Shellfish Risotto

Seafood Sidekicks · 300

ASIAN SAUCES 300

Sake Sauce

Black Bean Vinaigrette

Acknowledgments

A BOOK OF THIS magnitude is never a solo project. I want to thank all those in the field of seafood cookery for their wisdom, in particular A. J. McClane, Shirley King, Mel and Sheryl London, Jane Brody, James Peterson, and Susan Herrmann Loomis, without whose knowledgeable voices my book could never have been written.

Particular thanks to Cynthia Nims, Jon Rowley, Graham Kerr, Kathy Casey, and all the chefs and restaurateurs who shared their recipes and thoughts with me.

On the mind-boggling scientific side, I would like to thank Andy Lamb and Phil Edgell, and Robin Milton Love for their insightful books. Also, my gratitude goes to Paul Dunn, Harry Yoshimura, the Catfish Farmers of America, Clear Springs Foods, *Simply Seafood* magazine, Washington Sea Grant, and the Alaska Seafood Marketing Institute for freely sharing information of all sorts with me. Once again, many thanks.

My colleagues at the Pike Place Market constantly amaze me with their knowledge and enthusiasm, in particular Roy Feiring, Shelly Yapp, Sue Gilbert Mooers, John Turnbull, and Scott Davies. Heartiest thanks.

My humble appreciation to the friendly faces behind the farm tables, highstalls, the creamery, and the cheese shop—Sue Manzo, Frank Genzales, Nancy Nipples, Nancy Rentschler and Pearl Linteau, the Duff family, Sue and Mike Verdi, Eugene and Ivonne Brown, Doris and Don Mech, and Clarissa and Doug Cross. Thank you for sharing your lives and smiles with me.

Of course, without quality seafood this book would have been impossible to write, and for that I thank the owner of Pure Food Fish, Sol Amon, and his expert crew—Richard, Harry, John, Jack, Walt—you guys are the greatest day in and day out. Also thanks to Jack Mathers, Jack's Fish Spot; Johnny and Dick Yokoyama, Pike Place Fish; and Jon and Sara Daniels and Gary Cobb, City Fish, for additional counseling and guidance.

To Ten Speed Press, especially my editors, Lorena Jones and Kathryn Bear, publisher Kirsty Melville, publicist Cynthia Traina, and special sales director and vice president Jo Ann Deck, more thanks than you will ever know.

On the personal side, I want to thank my husband, illustrator of my books and faithful taste-tester, Spencer Johnson, and our cat Beauregard (Bo-Bo) Johnson, who sat by the side of my computer purring contentedly many a late night. My parents, Julie and Gene Rex, and in-laws, Sue and Colon Johnson, are great supporters as well.

Finally, my heartfelt thanks to my astute agent, oftentimes editor, and always friend—Anne Depue—who came up with the idea for this book. I owe it all to you.

Introduction

I HAVE ALWAYS BEEN DRAWN to bodies of water and the good foods that come from the sea. My office and kitchen overlook Seattle's Elliott Bay, the West Coast's second busiest port. Ferryboats glide in and out, their horns weaving a melancholy tune. Cargo ships from exotic places such as Suriname and Panama slip into port, ready to be unloaded by towering cranes that look like huge prehistoric birds.

Elliott Bay teems with activity below the surface, too. Sometimes I sit at my computer and daydream about the schools of native Northwestern fish that frolic in the cold water, perhaps colliding with the world's largest octopus or snared by the largest burrowing clam in the world, the geoduck (pronounced "GOOEY-duck").

Besides having proximity to the water, I'm also fortunate to live just half a block from the Pike Place Public Market (the Market), the longest continuously operating farmers' market in the United States. The Market, which is gearing up to celebrate its ninetieth anniversary on August 17, 1997, is home to some of the freshest, most varied seafood available in the United States. It was at those fish stalls that I received my baptism into Northwest seafood. Like many residents of this region, my husband, Spencer, and I are transplants, or Northwesterners by choice.

Almost ten years ago, on our first trip to Seattle as wide-eyed tourists, I remember walking through the Market and marveling at the various types of salmon available. I thought a salmon was a salmon and knew nothing of the creature's different species or seasons. Every evening during our all-too-brief visit, I ordered the hallowed fish for dinner. Spencer joked that if I wasn't careful, I might sprout gills!

I had never before seen scallops in the shell and I so enjoyed discovering pink singing scallops. Dungeness crabs, with their huge, meat-filled bodies, were so different from the soft-shell crabs I knew as a child growing up on the East Coast. They tasted so wonderful; their flavorful flesh didn't even need melted butter for dunking.

It was after many such food epiphanies that Spencer and I promised each other that if we could ever move to the Northwest, we would. One midlife crisis and two years later, we were back for good, living the Market lifestyle and savoring Northwest cuisine, which begins with the freshest local ingredients foraged or grown in season—morels, mussels, crab, salmon, berries, apples, lamb, pears, lettuces, and greens. These are prepared using traditional cooking techniques, many attributed to Native Americans—smoking, grilling, broiling, and steaming. A mixture of traditional European cuisines (French, Scandinavian, and Mediterranean) often spiced with Pacific Rim flare

(Chinese, Japanese, and Thai), Northwest cuisine is a melting pot of flavors and textures from around the world.

As my Northwest palate became educated, little did I know what an important part the region's cuisine, and particularly its seafood, would come to play in my life. Over the years, Spencer's and my love of seafood has grown so much that neither of us eats red meat anymore, and chicken only rarely. We are not alone: Per capita seafood consumption in the United States is on the rise, hitting 15.2 pounds in 1994, up from 15 pounds in 1993. And like a growing number of Americans (so-called "pesco-vegetarians"), our family has chosen fish as the main source of pure animal protein in our diets.

My almost daily visits to the fish stalls in the Pike Place Public Market serve as my informal seafood classroom. I often shop without any particular recipe or type of fish in mind, and just buy what the fishmongers suggest is freshest. They usually offer up a recipe or two to go along with my daily catch.

In this voyage through the seas, you will learn about each type of seafood available throughout the year at the Pike Place Public Market. In an easy-to-use alphabetical format, the book covers everything from abalone to tuna, along with seafood combination dishes, canned and smoked seafood recipes, and more than thirty seafood sauces. Recipes following each seafood profile include my own and those of regional chefs and food professionals, fishmongers and fishers, talented home cooks, and other "a-fish-ionados" who use the Market as a resource and point of inspiration. Recipes range from simple to gourmet, classic to con-temporary, homey to fit-for-company, low-calorie to scandalously rich.

They cover the many ethnic cuisines represented in the Market. The longer chapters include at least one light-and-healthy and one quick-and-easy recipe. You'll find recipes from many Market and Market-area restaurants, from the high-and-mighty with international reputations to humble haunts that nourish the locals.

Read the recipes and consider them blueprints. I am hopeful that after learning about the Market's seafood bounty, you'll feel confident enough to substitute types of fish, cooking techniques, and flavorings as desired, based on what's fresh at your seafood market the day you shop.

Being flexible—using what's fresh and in season—is the secret to good cooking and, in that respect, Northwest cooks are blessed. We live close to nature and the sea, understanding their rhythms, their annual regeneration. We know when the salmon are running and when the oysters are spawning, and we use the ocean's riches as they become available, cooking them in the most progressive ways.

And thanks to advances in cooling technology and transportation systems across the United States, even cooks outside the region can experience Northwestern seafood or easily substitute their own area's native fish and shellfish. Indeed, the technique of shopping and cooking with the seasons to use your region's unsurpassed fresh fish in creative, innovative dishes is one of life's simple pleasures. Enjoy this seafood celebration!

Part 1

A FISH-LOVER'S PRIMER
FROM THE SOUL OF SEATTLE

A Brief History of Pike Place Fish Markets

SEAFOOD HAS ALWAYS been a hot commodity along Seattle's Pike Place. During the 1920s and 1930s, there were eleven fish stalls inside the Market. They were small and compact, tucked into every level and area of the old Market, and often shared space with grocery stores and butter and egg shops. With names such as American Fish, State Fish Market, and Olympia Fish and Oyster Company, the businesses were resolutely New World, while the fishmongers who ran them were largely Sephardic families who had come from the Mediterranean to Seattle in the early 1900s. Employees with surnames of Calderon, Bensussen, Ovadia, Cohen, Amon, and Levy were common.

Today, the number of fish stalls is fewer, but the stalls are larger and better stocked. The four fresh fish stores and one smoked fish store in the Market each has its own specialties, "personality," and unique history. Locals in search of dinner rub elbows with tourists seeking the freshest Northwest salmon or other goodies to take with them or to ship to the folks back home. Longtime customers shop with the appropriate fishmonger based on their needs and desires.

Pure Food Fish was one of the original fish stores in the Market, opened in 1917. Present owner Sol Amon has been in charge since 1959, when he took over from his father, Jack, who began working at Pike Place fish markets in 1911. Look for the blackboard behind the counter for the ever-changing list of fresh fish and shellfish, then ask for recipe suggestions when buying from the helpful fishmongers at Pure Food Fish.

Pike Place Fish is nicknamed "the home of low-flying fish" because its vociferous fishmongers entertain the crowds with sea chanties and acrobatic throws of everything from huge whole salmon to bags of singing scallops. Established in 1930, Pike Place Fish has been owned since 1965 by Johnny Yokoyama, who started in the Market at the age of eight working at his parents' fresh produce stall.

Jack's Fish Spot stands out as the only fish stall in the Market boasting both fresh shellfish tanks and a small seafood bar; it's a good place to sit down to a bowl of cioppino, a shrimp cocktail, or a platter of fried seafood. Owner Jack Mathers has been in the Market since 1982, although the space was once home to Philadelphia Fish Market, one of the original Pike Place Market fish stores, which closed in 1969.

Totem Smokehouse is the only store in the Market devoted exclusively to smoked seafood, such as hot-smoked salmon, oysters, rainbow trout, and albacore tuna, and cold-smoked Nova lox. It was created after owner Don Fleming quit his day job, moved to the Northwest, and spent years researching and perfecting the seafood smoking techniques of the Northwest Coast Indians. Jane and Fred Poole, Rebecca Petre, and Mark Zenger bought the business from Don in early 1995.

City Fish lays claim to the most intriguing fish tale in the Market. It was started by the city council of Seattle in 1918 when the price of salmon had skyrocketed to a whopping twenty-five cents per pound. Although city intervention helped bring the price of a pound of salmon down to just ten cents, the city decided to bail out after several years of marginal profits. David Levy, nicknamed "Good Weight Dave" by his appreciative customers, bought the business in 1922 and turned it into a Market institution symbolized by the bright neon fish atop its roof. It was always a family-run enterprise; at one time, five Isaac Levys worked there. Market regulars used to enjoy calling out, "Hey, Isaac," and watching five heads turn in their direction! Good Weight Dave's descendants continued to run City Fish until February 1995, when former Alaska fisherman Jon Daniels, a strapping young man with eyes as blue-gray as the ocean and a vise-like handshake forged by years at sea, took over the business.

And while owners may change and fishmongers come and go, the essence of the Pike Place Public Market fish stalls stays the same—to sell fresh Northwest seafood with a bit of the old, hard sell; a sense of artistry and showmanship; and a plethora of expertise and dedication—all of which are treasured by tourists and locals alike.

FUN FACT

- Fresh fish at the Market is displayed on ice in open trays. When the City of Seattle threatened to force the fishmongers to put their wares behind glass to meet health code requirements, a special ordinance was passed by the Health Department in 1979 to keep the fish on ice and out in front.

A Word About Using This Book

LIKE MANY OF YOU, I am a good home cook who has taken lots of cooking classes, read many cookbooks and cooking magazines, and spent years working and experimenting with different foods. However, I have no formal culinary training as a chef, nutritionist, or dietitian; therefore, I have no biases in any of these areas.

My kitchen is nothing fancy; measuring just 7 by 10 feet, it barely holds the inexpensive electric stove over which I test all my recipes, a well-worn refrigerator, and the melange of pots and pans, knives, and gadgets I have collected over the years. I use my food processor, hand mixer, and blender occasionally but much prefer to chop, dice, and mince by hand whenever possible. I have tested all the recipes myself under these normal, everyday (some would say battlefield!) conditions and modified them to reflect the same.

Before beginning to cook, read through the recipe a couple of times to familiarize yourself with the cooking techniques, steps involved, and ingredients required. Thoroughly understanding the road map of a recipe before diving in can save lots of wasted effort and poor results later on. Knowing the timing in advance also enables you to always preheat the oven, which is required for more even cooking. Where recipes do not specify options, use the following:

- Fresh herbs
- Freshly ground black and white pepper
- Fruits and vegetables are medium size, unless stated otherwise
- Granulated (white) sugar
- Kosher or sea salt, not table salt (which contains chemicals and additives that give it a harsh, cloying taste)
- Large white eggs
- "Softened butter" means butter softened to room temperature
- Unsalted butter or margarine
- Unsifted, all-purpose (white) flour
- Whole milk
- Whole-milk yogurt
- White baking potatoes

The recipes in this book are designed to yield 4 servings unless otherwise noted. Four was chosen as an average number, and the serving size is considered average, although it may provide more or less than you would like. If you are cooking for two, almost all of the recipes can be cut in half and cooked as directed (if this is not the case, I indicate so). If cooking for six or eight, most recipes can be doubled or tripled, although slight adjustments in cooking times or the addition of increased amounts of seasonings will sometimes be necessary.

The recipes rarely require more than basic cooking techniques and terms. However, I do use a few techniques and terms that are less common and warrant some description. Here are the ones that might be unfamiliar.

Chiffonade: Pull basil leaves from stem, stack neatly one on top of the other, and roll tightly like a cigar. Using a very sharp knife, cut into thin slivers. Unroll basil slivers, fluff, and measure.

Clarifying butter (ghee): Melt unsalted butter in a nonstick skillet over low heat. As white foam rises to top, skim and discard. The clarified butter is the heavy yellow liquid that remains in the bottom of the pan.

Deglazing: After you sauté or roast a food, a flavorful residue of browned juices and food particles sticks to the bottom and sides of the pan. To make a delicious sauce from these caramelized pan juices, add a small amount of liquid (such as wine, broth, or water) to the hot pan and heat on the stovetop over medium-high heat. With a wooden spoon or spatula, scrape the bottom and sides of the pan to loosen the browned particles and crusted juices. The sauce can be served as is, or additional ingredients may be added.

Degreasing: For health and/or aesthetic reasons, it is sometimes preferable to remove excess fat from the surface of sauces, soups, stocks, or stews before serving. Several times as the liquid cooks, simply draw a large spoon over its surface, removing a thin layer of fat and discarding it. After the dish is cooked, remove the pan from the heat and let it sit for 5 minutes. Any remaining fat will rise to the surface, where it may be removed by drawing a paper towel across the surface. Another way to degrease (if time permits) is to chill the food in the refrigerator or freezer until the grease congeals on top, then remove it with a spoon.

Making unseasoned soft bread crumbs: Tear a slice of white or whole wheat bread into chunks and place in a food processor. Process until crumbs of the desired size form. Fresh bread crumbs can be stored in the refrigerator for up to a week; in the freezer, tightly wrapped, they keep for about six months.

Making unseasoned dry bread crumbs: Place a layer of white or whole wheat bread slices on a baking sheet and bake at 300° for 10 to 15 minutes, or until the bread turns light brown and dries completely. Allow bread to cool, then place in a food processor or blender and process until you have the desired texture.

Making unseasoned dry bread cubes: Remove crusts from several slices of white or whole wheat bread. Cut slices into 1/4-inch cubes. Place a single layer of bread cubes on a baking sheet and bake at 300° until the cubes turn light brown and dry completely, about 10 to 15 minutes. Toss during cooking. Allow cubes to cool and use immediately, refrigerate for up to a week, or freeze, tightly wrapped, for up to 6 months.

Mise en place: This French cooking term (pronounced "MEEZ ahn plahs") refers to having all of the ingredients prepared and ready to combine before starting to cook. It is useful for any dish, but particularly for seafood sautés, stir-fries, or other dishes that are cooked over high heat in a very short amount of time.

Peeling and seeding a tomato: Cut a shallow "X" in the bottom end of the tomato and drop into boiling water for 15 to 20 seconds.

Remove and transfer to a bowl of ice water. Remove, pat dry, and slip off skins with a sharp knife. To seed, cut each tomato in half horizontally and gently squeeze the halves over a bowl to force out the seeds. Fingers or a small spoon work well to remove any remaining seeds.

Plumping dried fruits: Add fruits to a small saucepan and cover with water, stock, or liqueur. Bring to a boil, cover, then remove pan from heat. Allow to stand for 20 minutes, or until fruit is plumped. To speed the plumping process, put $1/2$ cup water in a microwave-safe glass dish. Add fruit and microwave on HIGH for 30 seconds. Stir and repeat. When fruit begins to plump, remove from microwave and cover. Let rest for 5 minutes, drain water, then use fruit as directed.

Reducing sauces: Reducing, or cooking down liquids of a sauce concentrates the flavors and thickens the sauce to the right consistency. Do not further salt a liquid or sauce that is to be reduced, or the final sauce may end up oversalted. Season to taste after the sauce has been reduced.

Roasting garlic: Preheat oven to 375°. Slice $1/2$ inch off the top of the garlic bulb, wrap in aluminum foil, and bake for 35 minutes.

Roasting bell peppers: Roasting peppers can be done in one of four ways. Char the skin of whole peppers with a propane blowtorch until the skin is black; roast the peppers over a gas burner on high heat, turning frequently with kitchen tongs until well charred on all sides; broil the peppers under a broiler several inches from the heat until brownish black blisters form; or roast the peppers in a 400° oven for 10 to 15 minutes until dark blisters form.

Put roasted peppers in a paper or plastic bag, close the top, and let stand for 10 minutes. Remove peppers from bag and scrape off skin, then cut in half and remove seeds and ribs. Wipe away any remaining black particles with a damp cloth, then slice or chop as needed. If desired, use latex or rubber gloves to protect your hands while preparing the peppers.

Toasting hazelnuts: Place nuts on a baking sheet in a single layer and toast in a 375° oven for 10 minutes. Remove from oven and allow to cool slightly. Place nuts between two rough kitchen towels and rub off as much of the brown skins as you can, or rub a handful of nuts between your palms, or a single difficult-to-skin nut between your forefinger and thumb. Alternately, use the seed toasting method.

Toasting sesame seeds, mustard seeds, coriander seeds, cumin seeds, Szechwan peppercorns, and nuts: Place seeds, peppercorns, or nuts in a dry nonstick skillet over medium heat, shaking the pan often until they begin to turn light brown or become aromatic, or both (mustard seeds will also begin to pop), about 3 to 5 minutes. Let cool, and grind as directed or add to your recipe.

From Sea to Shore: How Fish Are Caught and Seafood Availability

THE WAY THE FISH YOU BUY at the store was caught and handled immediately after its death directly affects its quality. A conscientious fisher chooses fishing techniques that allow the fish to undergo a "good" death, even though that seems like the ultimate oxymoron! A "good" death is one that causes the least amount of trauma to the fish, for when a fish dies under stress, it pumps enzymes through its system, which can lead to a loss of flavor. Even when the fish is not stressed, natural bacteria begin to multiply when a fish dies and eventually cause the fish to spoil. That is why holding seafood just above freezing to slow bacterial growth or flash-freezing within hours of landing the fish is such an important factor in seafood quality.

Commercially caught fish are harvested in three ways: gillnetting, purse seining, and trolling. Commercial fishing boats called trollers are equipped with overhead stainless steel lines, with several hooks attached to each line. As the boat moves, the hooks sweep through the water at different levels. When a fish strikes, the line is pulled in by hand and the fish are taken off the hook one at a time.

To ensure the best quality, conscientious fishers immediately stun, bleed, gut, and ice each fish on board as soon as it is caught and before rigor mortis has a chance to set in. Removing the organs, intestines, and blood gives a much whiter appearance and far cleaner taste to the flesh than fish left ungutted. Ungutted fish can suffer from belly burn, a discoloration and foul odor caused when enzymes contained in the stomach break down the belly walls. The fish is covered with lots of ice, which ensures a slow, cold passage through rigor mortis. Moving slowly through rigor mortis preserves good texture and develops the best flavor in the fish flesh. Alternately, just after the fish is bled and gutted, it can be flash-frozen, which also preserves its quality. This process is both time- and labor-intensive. So troll-caught fish are usually more expensive than fish caught by other means.

In gillnetting, the fish simply swim into nets that are hung like curtains behind a drifting boat. Their gills become entangled as they try to escape, and the catch is then hauled on deck. In purse seining, huge nets encircle fish in a bag of webbing. Once a purse seine net has surrounded the fish, the net is closed, much like a drawstring purse. Although in the hands of skilled fishers gillnetting and purse seining can produce quality results, both methods cause more stress to the fish than trolling. Gillnetting often results in scale and fin loss, while purse seining can cause bruises and puncture marks.

So, when buying seafood, ask the seller how the fish was caught, and understand and appreciate why prices for the same type of seafood can vary so dramatically. The troll-caught king salmon served in your favorite up-scale seafood restaurant has most likely died a much more pampered and civil death than the gillnetted pink salmon you buy as an end-of-summer supermarket special.

Seafood Availability

When I began this book, I envisioned writing an encyclopedic text explaining Northwest fish and shellfish, to the exclusion of seafood from other parts of the United States and the world. After only a short period of research, I learned that because of the marvels of air transport, "fresh-frozen" fish, and farmed fish, much of the seafood sold at the Pike Place Market and throughout the region is available year-round from waters sometimes half a world away. Therefore, you will note that among the types of seafood listed and discussed within these pages, some species are captured or farmed outside of Northwest waters. These include catfish, Chilean sea bass, marlin, monkfish, and yellowfin tuna.

Seasonality

As the world becomes a smaller place, many people are losing sight of seasonality in their foods. While summer used to be synonymous with strawberries, autumn with apples, and winter with acorn squash, nowadays these foods are available year-round, flown to market from far-flung places such as New Zealand, Mexico, or South America. Likewise in seafood: Whereas salmon used to be available fresh only during the 4 or 5 months of the year when it was running, today farm-raised salmon from Canada and Chile make salmon available in stores year-round.

The advent of refrigerated trucks and overnight air shipping has also changed our perceptions about seasonality and regionality in seafood. Mississippi catfish, hybrid striped bass raised in Chile, and rainbow trout grown in Idaho line supermarket seafood shelves year-round. In defining what is seasonally available at the Pike Place Market, I first specify what is always available, and then list the wild species that are available only at certain times of the year.

FISH AVAILABLE AT THE PIKE PLACE PUBLIC MARKET YEAR-ROUND

Catfish
Chilean Sea Bass
Clams (hard shell)
Cod (Pacific Cod, Alaska Cod, Alaska
    Pollock, Walleye Pollock, Hake)

Crabmeat
Dungeness Crab
Flounder/Sole (Petrale Sole, Dover Sole,
   English Sole, Rex Sole, Pacific Sanddab)
Gaspergoo (Buffalo Fish)
Halibut
Hybrid Striped Bass
King Crab Legs
Lingcod
Lobster
Marlin
Monkfish
Mussels
Oysters
Rockfish (Rock Cod, Pacific Snapper, Red
   Snapper, Alaska Snapper, Black Sea Bass,
   Ocean Perch, Pacific Ocean Perch, or
   Yelloweye Rockfish)
Salad or Popcorn Shrimp
Salmon
Scallops (bay and sea varieties)
Shrimp
Squid
Swordfish
Tilapia
Trout
Tuna

FISH AVAILABLE AT THE PIKE PLACE PUBLIC MARKET ON A SEASONAL OR OCCASIONAL BASIS

Clams (Butter, Razor, Geoduck)
Crawfish
Herring, Salted (December)

Mackerel
Mahimahi
Orange Roughy
Sablefish (Black Cod)
Scallops (Pink)
Shrimp (Alaskan Spot, Hood Canal Spot,
   Rock)
Shad (fish and roe)
Shark
Smelt (Eulachon and Surf Smelt)
Steelhead
Sturgeon

Shipping Fish

Any of the fish stalls in the Market, as well as most specialty seafood shops, will pack seafood in leakproof, odorproof containers lined with blue gel "ice" packs. The containers are guaranteed to keep the contents fresh up to 48 hours. They are designed to carry on the plane or check as luggage, or can be shipped by overnight air express. The Market's fishmongers take their air-freight business very seriously, shipping tens of thousands of orders per year, mainly within the United States and to Japan. In spite of long distances, inevitable airline delays, and a highly perishable product, less than $1/2$ of 1 percent of these orders go awry. Because of the extraordinary care that must be taken when shipping fresh seafood, the quality of air-shipped fish rivals that of fish just out of the case at the local seafood market.

The Cold, Hard Facts:
Fresh vs. Frozen Fish

WHEN SHOPPING FOR seafood, we invariably look for fish that is fresh. When we think of fresh seafood, we usually think of fish that has never been frozen. That "fresh" salmon in the fishmonger's display could have been sitting in the hold of a fishing boat for two weeks and then at the fishmonger's stall for a couple of days, but we clamor to buy it in lieu of the flash-frozen Alaska pollock in the next tray; in our minds, the salmon is fresher than the frozen pollock.

Instead of the "F" word, we should be using the "Q" word—for QUALITY—with our fishmongers and restaurateurs. "Is the seafood good QUALITY?" we should ask, meaning does the finfish or shellfish possess that just-caught odor, flavor, and texture, whether it was pulled from the water hours before or flash-frozen at sea months ago.

Today, with advances in modern freezer technology and transportation systems, much frozen fish compare in quality to fish directly out of the water. Seafood that was good quality to begin with and that has been handled throughout its journey from the ocean to your table will possess fine flavor and texture even if it has been frozen. Captured far from polluted waters by factory trawlers that are like huge processing plants, fish are gutted, flash-frozen within hours of being caught, and carefully stored in sub-freezing conditions until the boat returns to port. Weeks or months later, when the fish are delivered to seafood counters across the country, they are (ideally) slowly and carefully thawed so they are in prime condition when you buy them.

Some fish and shellfish frozen at sea goes to supermarkets in its frozen state, is unwrapped at the store, and set in the seafood case to thaw gradually. It is labeled "fancy" at the Pike Place Market and "previously frozen" or "fresh frozen" at other seafood markets. Some seafood is flash-frozen and has never been thawed. You can find flash-frozen seafood in the freezer case of most supermarkets.

The tests for quality seafood—fresh or flash-frozen—should be the same. Check the fish before you buy it. Find out whether it smells like the ocean, whether the flesh is firm and springy, and whether the skin is moist and shiny with most of the scales intact.

Buying and Storing Frozen Seafood

As with all seafood, when buying frozen finfish and shellfish, look for a reputable seafood vendor to ensure you get the highest quality product. When buying frozen seafood, keep in mind the following guidelines:

- The wrapping on frozen fish should be tight fitting (no holes or abrasions) and free of frost buildup.

- Breading on breaded fish should be crisp, not soggy.

- Make sure there are no open, torn, or crushed edges on the packages.

- Avoid packages that are kept above the frost line in the store's display freezer.

- There should be no signs of frost or ice particles inside the package. If ice crystals are present, the fish has either been stored for a long period or thawed and refrozen. There should be no liquid, frozen or thawed, in the package.

- Whole fish should be free of ice crystals, with no discoloration.

- Fish steaks or fillets should be frozen hard.

- The flesh of frozen fish should be bright. White "cottony" patches, yellow spots, dark spots, or discoloration or fading of red or pink flesh indicate dehydration or freezer burn.

- Individually quick-frozen seafood (IQF) is identifiable because each piece of seafood will be loose in the package. IQF seafood that has been thawed and partially refrozen will have clumps of seafood and should be avoided. (The exception is very small shrimp, which may clump even when properly handled.)

- Packaged frozen seafood may have an expiration date stamped on the label—always use the seafood before the expiration date.

- Do not allow frozen seafood to thaw until you are ready to use it.

- Once you get flash-frozen seafood home, leave it in its original packaging and freeze immediately unless you are ready to thaw and cook it within 24 hours.

Freezing Seafood at Home

Freezing seafood at home is not recommended; residential freezers simply cannot get down to temperatures low enough in a short enough amount of time without damaging the flavor and texture of fish and shellfish. However, if you are sure your seafood is freshly caught (not previously frozen and thawed) and must, for whatever reason, freeze fish at home, here are some general guidelines:

- A chest-style freezer unit set at 0° or below is recommended.

- Rinse the fish under cold water and pat it dry with paper towels.

- Wrap the fish tightly in heavy-duty freezer paper or heavy plastic wrap for the freezer, squeeze out all the air, then wrap tightly in aluminum foil or a heavy-duty freezer bag.

- Store frozen fish and seafood at 0° or below (check your freezer compartment with a freezer thermometer).

Once again, because home freezers do not get cold enough to freeze fish properly, and because the freezer door is opened and closed often, the quality of seafood stored in the residential freezer suffers greatly. Therefore, while many cookbooks recommend keeping fatty fish three months and lean fish six months in the freezer, I prefer to err on the side of less freezer time for top-quality results.

- Frozen fillets and steaks from lean fish (cod,

flounder/sole, lingcod, monkfish, octopus, pink and chum salmon, Alaska pollock, rockfish, sand dab, skate, squid, haddock, halibut, catfish, swordfish, tuna, and red snapper) keep two to three months.

- Fillets and steaks from moderately fatty to fatty fish (Chinook, sockeye, and coho salmon, sablefish, mackerel, mahimahi, gaspergoo, eel, shad, smelt, sturgeon, trout, swordfish) can be frozen up to one month.

- Store-bought frozen breaded fish keeps up to three months. Previously cooked fish keeps up to three months in the freezer.

- Raw shellfish, scallops, cooked and raw shrimp, cooked crab, shucked clams, cooked crawfish, cooked lobster, shucked mussels, shucked oysters, and squid keep up to three months in the freezer. Previously cooked shellfish lasts about two months in the freezer.

- As with all seafood, the sooner you use frozen seafood, the better the quality. For best flavor and texture, use frozen seafood within one month.

Thawing Frozen Seafood

Frozen seafood maintains its flavor and texture best when allowed to thaw slowly.

- Thaw seafood overnight in the coldest part of the refrigerator (usually the bottom back shelf). Place the wrapped package on a plate or shallow pan to catch any liquid that drips out. Allow 8 to 10 hours of thawing time. Check the fish occasionally, and pour out any liquid that accumulates.

- Never defrost seafood at room temperature or in warm water. These methods not only

result in a loss of texture and flavor but encourage the growth of bacteria.

- To defrost seafood quickly, leave the seafood in its original wrapper and place it in a plastic bag. Submerge the bag in a basin of cold water and change the cold water periodically. Check the seafood often and cook or refrigerate the fish as soon as it is thawed.

- Fish can also be thawed quickly in the microwave. Just select the lowest defrost power (usually 30 percent) and follow manufacturer's instructions for thawing. A 1-pound portion of seafood will normally take about 5 minutes to thaw. Continue to cook the fish completely once you start the microwave-defrost process.

- Thawed seafood is extremely perishable and should never be refrozen.

- In a pinch, seafood that is to be baked, poached, or broiled without first adding a coating, marinating, or stuffing can be cooked straight out of the freezer by doubling the cooking time.

Cooking Frozen Fish

Fish that has been frozen responds to heat differently than a never-frozen product. Because frozen fish can cook up to 70 percent faster than a fresh product, it needs to be cooked at a lower temperature to keep it from drying out. Grilling frozen fish is particularly tricky. Do not subject the fish to direct heat; instead raise the grill or lower the heat.

AN ANCIENT FARMING METHOD
COMES OF AGE (AQUACULTURE)

ON TIMES PAST, fishers were hunters. The fishing industry was subject to the whims of nature, as sea and sky often conspired to prevent fishers from doing their jobs. Nowadays, aquaculture (also known as fish farming) is creating a more level playing field for fishers, as well as stable prices and a steady supply of safe, high-quality fish and shellfish.

An ancient Egyptian bas-relief depicting pond-reared tilapia (African freshwater fish) is the oldest physical evidence of aquaculture, but experts believe that fish farming began even earlier, probably in Asia. For most cultures over the centuries, eating seafood has meant hunting seafood on the open seas. And up until the past decade, this has been relatively easy, particularly with advances in technology.

In recent years, world fishery production has leveled off. Some fish stocks have been depleted, fewer new fish resources have been discovered, and some nations are becoming territorial about their fish stocks. With fewer wild fish to catch, aquaculture has gained popularity as a practical way to supplement a fisher's income as well as to supply seafood to the consumer.

Aquaculture is the culturing of fish, shellfish, and aquatic plants. It can be conducted indoors or outdoors, in fresh water, brackish water, or salt water. The "farm" can be a constructed pond or a large container of water on dry land. Alternately, fish farming can take place in a pen or a cage that holds the fish, shellfish, or plants in a natural body of water.

Catfish, tilapia, hybrid striped bass, rainbow and golden trout, shrimp, blue mussels, Pacific oysters, clams, bay scallops, and Atlantic salmon are among the types of seafood that are commonly farmed.

Farmed salmon deserves a special mention because it accounts for one-third of the world supply of salmon. Farmed salmon are grown in sea ponds and floating cages and are never released to the ocean. Because the farm-raised variety swim and struggle less than salmon in the wild, many people claim their flesh is milder in taste and less firm.

Aquafarmed seafood is a consistent source of protein and is definitely the wave of the future. Farm-raised mollusks, particularly Northwest oysters, mussels, and Manila clams, are plumper, better tasting, and safer to eat than their wild counterparts. Farm-raised shrimp (which account for more than half the shrimp sold in the United States) and bay scallops are the norm in the seafood industry nowadays.

There can be health concerns associated with farm-raised fish, including the use of antibiotics, steroids, and red food coloring although these are regulated by the U.S. Food and Drug Administration. If any of these additives is a health concern to you, you might seek out wild fish rather than farm-raised.

Nutritionally, both farmed and wild fish are above-average sources of protein, low in saturated fats, and rich in unsaturated fats. Farm-raised fish are generally fattier and therefore contain more calories than seafood caught in the wild.

Murky Waters:
Common Misconceptions

EOPLE HAVE A MILLION excuses for not eating seafood, some based on outdated perceptions, others based at least in part on fact. Take a minute to consider the facts and put many of these concerns to rest.

Seafood Is Difficult to Prepare at Home

Seventy percent of the seafood purchased in the United States is eaten away from home. Many people don't purchase seafood for home use because they believe it is difficult to cook, requires special equipment to prepare, or will smell up the house. Nothing could be further from the truth. Fish is nature's answer to fast food. It is quick and easy to prepare, perfect for today's fast-paced lives.

Because the protein in seafood is much more delicate than that found in other types of protein food, no fish dish I can think of takes over 1 hour to cook. Baking a whole 5- or 6-pound fish only takes 10 to 15 minutes of prep time and just over 30 minutes to bake or barbecue.

Seafood even gives you visual cues when it is ready to eat: Shrimp turn pink and their tails just begin to curl, the shells of lobsters and hard-shelled crabs turn red, fish fillets just turn opaque and begin to flake. It isn't essential to prepare an elaborate sauce for a fish; the natural juices from the fish are often enough to flavor and moisten the fish. Not having to prepare sauces eliminates time in the kitchen. Nothing could be easier—or quicker—to serve than dishes that draw on nature's glorious bounty from the sea.

Seafood Is Plain

Many home cooks think fish cookery is a piece of broiled fish, but if you are looking for versatility in your diet, fish is a perfect choice. From halibut and tuna to mussels and oysters, seafood offers a vast array of flavors and textures. With a diverse variety of fish from freshwater lakes and rivers and from the sea, supplemented by fish from faraway places, in both fresh and frozen form, cooking seafood offers endless opportunities for gustatory exploration and delight.

The variety of seafood, range of cooking techniques (from steaming to smoking), and the many different ethnic preparations of seafood mean you never have to repeat a dish if you don't want to. For example, in this book alone, eighteen types of finfish and eleven types of shellfish are featured. Add to this the twenty-plus techniques you can use to cook them, plus all the ethnic twists and flavors, and you have an exponential number of preparations for many different types of seafood.

Adaptability and flexibility are watchwords when working with seafood: If your recipe calls for shrimp, you can often use scallops; if it calls for flounder, you can often use another whitefish, such as cod or halibut. Even many chicken and red meat recipes can be adapted to fish, such as pizza, chili, or tacos. These "disguised" seafood dishes are good to try with reluctant seafood eaters or children.

Seafood Is Expensive

There is no arguing that certain types of seafood, such as swordfish, lobster, and tuna, are usually more expensive per pound than like amounts of poultry or beef. There is a reason for this. Seafood caught in the wild is a very different food resource than poultry, beef, and lamb. Fishers face the expenses of a boat and a crew. Unlike chickens that can be raised in cages or cows that are kept on a feedlot, the movement of fish populations is erratic and can never be counted upon.

Luckily, there are several ways to enjoy seafood at a reasonable price. One way is to buy fish in season. When large quantities of a fish or shellfish are available, they are often sold at bargain prices. For example, Dungeness crab can be expensive in summer, but when they are caught by local fishers in winter, they are much more reasonably priced.

Certain types of seafood cost less because they are less well known or less popular. These include squid, skate, and often bottomfish such as sole or flounder. Farm-raised fish, because they are raised in controlled conditions, are also priced more moderately than seafood that is caught in the wild. Flash-frozen seafood is often moderately priced.

Because seafood is a lean, pure protein and there is very little waste, consider serving it in smaller portions than you might chicken or beef. Four to six ounces of seafood is more than enough for an adult for one meal; a family of four can get their fair share of protein from only 1 to $1^{1}/_{2}$ pounds of seafood. Alternately, serve seafood as a supporting part of a meal. When combined with an extender such as potatoes, pasta, grain, or vegetables (see "Seafood Combination Dishes", page 284), much less seafood per person is needed.

I Could Be Eating the Last Fish

The media enjoy dispensing sensational stories about disappearing stocks of seafood (particularly salmon), so much so that some people cannot sit down to a fish dinner without being racked by guilt. Alaska has even started a publicity campaign to persuade people it's all right to eat salmon without feeling guilty.

It's true that certain stocks of fish are or have been almost fished out and only diligent rebuilding will make them strong again. However, some runs of fish, such as Alaska salmon, which enjoyed a record catch of 214 million wild and hatchery-raised salmon in 1995, are incredibly healthy and well managed and they will stay strong for the future.

Farm-raised fish, particularly shrimp, scallops, catfish, trout, and salmon, have made many more types of seafood available to the American public. In 1995 Norway, Chile, and several other countries exported more than 100 million pounds of fresh or frozen farm-raised salmon to the United States alone. The abundance of farm-raised salmon has meant reliable stocks of salmon are available year-round, which was unheard of just a decade ago.

Seafood Isn't Safe to Eat

When compared to poultry and beef, seafood has an amazingly clean track record. According to the Food and Drug Administration, fishery products are implicated in less than one percent of all foodborne illnesses in the United States. Specifically, seafood is responsible for one illness per 250,000 servings; chicken is ten times more risky. If you exclude bivalve mollusks (primarily clams and oysters), which are commonly eaten raw, fish causes one illness per five million servings.

When cooked, seafood is the safest muscle protein we can eat. However, eating raw seafood can pose health problems, particularly for those with certain health conditions, which include liver disease (cirrhosis or chronic alcohol abuse), diabetes mellitus, immune disorders (AIDS or cancer), or gastrointestinal disorders. Raw shellfish accounts for 85 percent of all illnesses caused by eating seafood.

Among the culprits in seafood illnesses are *Vibrio vulnificus*, a bacteria that can multiply rapidly in raw seafood. The bacteria can cause food poisoning, with symptoms such as sudden chills, fever, nausea, vomiting, stomach pain, and even blood poisoning. *Vibrio* is completely killed when seafood is thoroughly cooked. The Norwalk virus can cause severe diarrhea in people who eat undercooked or raw shellfish, although the virus is killed when shellfish is cooked.

Naturally occurring algae blooms called red tides can cause paralytic shellfish poisoning (PSP) in humans. This type of poisoning is rarely a problem in commercial fish because when the red tides occur, commercial fishing grounds in the affected areas are closed. Sport fishers who gather their own shellfish should observe all beach closures or call local PSP hotlines for detailed information on where to harvest shellfish (see page 21).

Some fish and shellfish are harvested in areas where waters contain low levels of toxic chemicals. Some types of fish and shellfish may build up large amounts of toxic chemicals in certain parts of their bodies such as the eyes, liver, gills, brain, and viscera, which are normally not eaten anyway. Exposure to high levels of some of these chemicals is associated with an increased risk of cancer in humans. Eating a wide variety of fish and shellfish will ensure against ingesting too much of any one type of toxin or contaminant.

Raw fish dishes, such as sushi and sashimi, are safe for most healthy people to eat if they are made with very fresh fish, commercially frozen (home freezers simply do not get cold enough to do the job) for at least three days at −4°, and then thawed before they're eaten. The freezing kills any parasites that are present, although it will not kill bacteria. For this reason, people with any of the risk factors outlined and pregnant women should not eat raw fish.

On a more positive note, most seafood is low in calories, sodium, saturated fats, and cholesterol and high in vitamins, minerals, protein, and omega-3 fatty acids. Omega-3 fatty acids can help thin the blood and lower cholesterol to combat heart disease, and have been linked to the prevention and treatment of arthritis, migraine headaches, multiple sclerosis, diabetes, skin disorders, and certain types of cancer. One study showed that eating just one fatty fish meal (such as salmon, herring, mackerel, and sardines) a week reduced the risk of cardiac arrest by 50 percent.

Seafood can be a boon to people who are watching their weight. According to Anne M. Fletcher, R.D., author of *Eat Fish, Live Better*, "Compared with other protein-rich foods, including red meat, pork, and cheese, most types of fish have a low-calorie, low-fat edge. In other words, fish is naturally "light." A three-and-a-half-ounce cooked serving of meat, poultry, or fish provides well over a third of the daily recommended amount of protein for a man or woman. Eating fish means eating fewer calories to get the same amount of protein as in other kinds of meat."

Eating a variety of fish and shellfish can ensure you are getting many health benefits.

PSP (RED TIDE) HOTLINES

Contact the following organizations or call local PSP (paralytic shellfish poisoning) hotlines for up-to-date information about PSP and shellfish harvesting closures.

Alaska: Check with the local Department of Environmental Conservation Office.

British Columbia: Fisheries and Oceans' Shellfish and Red Tide Update, (604) 666-3169.

Washington: Washington State Department of Health PSP Hotline, (800) 562-5632.

Oregon: Oregon Department of Agriculture's Shellfish Information Line, (503) 986-4728.

California: California Department of Health Services' Shellfish Information Line, (510) 540-2605.

Seafood Basics 101:
Choosing, Storing, and Cleaning Fish

SEAFOOD IS ONE OF THE most perishable of all fresh foods and must be handled with great care. Following are general guidelines for seafood selection and storage. More detailed instructions (particularly for idiosyncratic shellfish) are given within individual chapters.

Finfish

Fish you buy in the market will come in one of several forms. "Whole" or "round" is the fish just as it comes from the water. A "drawn," or "head-on" fish, is one that has been gutted or had its entrails removed. A "dressed" fish is one with its entrails, scales, and gills removed (and often its fins, as well). "Pan-dressed" is a fish that has had entrails, scales, gills, head, and fins removed, and its tail is trimmed. "Fillets" are the sides of a fish removed from the backbone and ribs. Fillets are usually boneless, with or without skin. "Steaks" are cross-section slices of fish with the backbone and ribs attached. A fish that has been "butterflied," "book-filleted," or "split" is one that has been split open and boned out or not, producing two sides of the fish joined by the belly skin or the back so that the halves lie flat. "Cheeks" are the portion of a large fish right behind the mouth. They can be removed and cooked separately, or when cooking the fish whole, can be scooped out at the table. "Chunks" (roasts) are cut from the heaviest part of a large fish that usually weighs between 5 and 10 pounds. Chunks themselves can weigh from $1\frac{1}{2}$ to 4 pounds or more.

Selecting a Seafood Market

Perhaps the most important decision when buying fresh seafood is the place you purchase it. Jon Rowley, Seattle's "sultan of seafood," suggests considering the following factors when deciding where to buy your seafood.

- First, smell the place—it should not have a fishy odor.

- Look at the number of customers; the faster the turnover of product, the fresher the fish.

- The labeling on the fish should be clear and specific. "Sockeye salmon steaks" is much more helpful than merely "salmon."

- Finfish should be displayed separately from shellfish, and raw separately from cooked, to avoid contamination.

- The ice in which the fish is displayed should be clean and white. Whole fish should be in plenty of fresh, clean ice. Cut fish should not sit directly on ice, but rather in trays placed over ice. A fish sitting in its own juices suffers from drip loss, a sign that the fish is deteriorating and will be dry when cooked.

- The market should cut its own fish.

- The staff should be able to answer questions knowledgeably and offer good culinary recommendations.

General Shopping Tips

- When shopping, purchase seafood last and take it home immediately. Don't stop to run a few additional errands on the way home or the seafood will suffer in quality.

- Never let seafood sit unrefrigerated for long, especially in a hot car. If it is over 30 minutes from your seafood shop to your home, ask that your seafood be packed with a separate bag of ice or frozen gel packs (also known as "blue ice" packs), or bring along a cooler filled with ice or frozen gel packs.

- Make friends with your fishmonger. A friendly face behind the seafood counter may be your best insurance of sparkling fish on the plate. Let your fishmonger know you want and can discern the highest quality fish; good fishmongers respect and appreciate knowledgeable clients.

- Call ahead with special orders and requirements; when a fish market delivers the goods, call back and express your thanks.

- Ask questions and share your knowledge and recipes with your fishmonger.

- If a fish doesn't meet your expectations, take it back immediately and explain why it is less than perfect. A good fishmonger will be glad to replace the questionable product with something to your liking.

Purchasing Whole Fish

- The old rules suggested that clear, bright eyes in a whole fish meant a fresh fish. Unfortunately, the eyes of some species go cloudy very quickly, while others stay clear long past the time that the fish is fresh. Eye condition is not infallible and should be considered as just one of several indicators of freshness.

- Flesh should be firm, springy, and shiny; dull flesh may mean the fish is old. The flesh should be plump, not separating from the bones. A very fresh fish will have a bright, reflective slime on its surface.

- The gills, if still in the fish, should be vivid red or pink and free of mucous. Brownish or grayish gills are a sign of age. However, if the fish has been bled, the gills will have lost their bright color.

- The intestinal cavity should be clean and pink. If you are allowed to pick up the fish before buying it, sniff the stomach cavity and gills for "off" odors. High-quality fish should smell clean, fresh, and almost sweet.

- The fish should have most of its scales. Avoid fish with bruises, puncture marks, or ragged fins, for these telltale signs of mishandling mean the fish will deteriorate more rapidly.

- Headless fish should not have brown edges.

Purchasing Cut Fish

- When purchasing fish fillets or steaks, look for a clear, bright, translucent glow and a luminous, shimmering color in the flesh, which should not be milky.

- The flesh should be moist, firm, and elastic to the touch, with no darkening around the edges of the fish, brown or yellowish discoloration, a dull or opaque color, blood spots, or dry or mushy areas.

- Circulatory system markings in swordfish, shark, marlin, and tuna should be bright red or pink; a brownish color indicates age.

- Smell the fillets or steaks—they should have no fishy, ammonia, or chemical odor.

- The knife work should be sharp and even—steaks cut with sloping sides (known as shingle cuts) or fillets with jagged edges cook unevenly and should be avoided. Steaks should be cut to an even thickness, depending on the type of species and the way it cooks.

- If the fish has been prepackaged (placed in a styrofoam tray and overwrapped in plastic), it should be tightly wrapped with little or no air and no liquid in the packaging.

Preparing Whole Fish

When purchasing fresh seafood, most of us buy our fish cut to order or select precut fish fillets or steaks. However, selecting a whole fish and butchering it yourself can be a more economical alternative. When choosing a whole fish to butcher at home, be sure to follow the purchasing suggestions described on page 23 to ensure a high-quality fish. The following general rules apply to most finfish. You will need a sharp 10- or 12-inch chef's knife, a paring knife, and a boning or filleting knife with a flexible or rigid 6- to 8-inch-long blade.

- To scale, rinse the fish and place it on a flat surface or in the kitchen sink. Holding the fish by the tail, use the back of a knife, a spoon, or a fish scaler, and scrape from the tail toward the head in short, assured strokes. Scale the whole fish, then rinse well.

- To remove fins, use a boning or paring knife to make a $1/8$-inch-long cut on each side of the fin. Cut on an angle, so that the cuts form a "V" with the fin in the middle. With your hands or using a pair of pliers, pull out the fin and bones that attach the fin to the fish.

- To gut, cut a slit from the fish's anal opening to the gill openings with a sharp, small knife. Pull out the innards with your fingers. With a spoon or a knife, scrape out any viscera that remains, then rinse the fish.

- To behead, make a cut on either side of the fish's head above the pectoral fin. Using the palm of your hand or a rubber mallet, hit the back of the knife handle to cut through the fish's thick neck bones.

- To remove the gills (which is unnecessary if beheading), snip them at the bottom with a knife or scissors, then snip at the top and remove. Be careful: The gills can be very sharp.

- To make steaks, cut off the fish's tail. Then, using a sharp, heavy knife or a cleaver, cut through the body of the fish to make steaks of desired thickness (usually $3/4$ to 1 inch). Be sure to make even, clean cuts.

- To fillet, lay the fish on its side and make a top-to-bottom cut behind the gill cover. Next, with the back of the fish toward you, make a long cut along the back from the gill cover to the tail. Follow the line of the central bone, lifting the flesh as you cut to reveal the central bone. Turn the fish so the belly is toward you and make a long cut from gill to tail. The fillet should be released when the tip of the knife meets the first cut at the central bone. If the thin belly flap contains a row of bones, cut underneath them from each side, forming a "V" shape, then lift out the "V" and remove.

- Remove pin bones with a fish-bone puller, a strawberry huller, or needle-nose pliers.

- To skin, make a small cut at the tail end of the fillet and grab the skin. Hold a sharp knife parallel to the skin and run the knife between the skin and fish flesh.

Portion Size

In years past, the standard American rule in both restaurant and home cooking has allowed about 8 ounces ($^1/_2$ pound) of trimmed, usable seafood flesh per dinner serving, about 5 to 6 ounces per luncheon serving, and about 4 ounces ($^1/_4$ pound) for appetizer portions. Shellfish, because it is considered richer, is often served in smaller portions.

However, under the new U.S. Food and Drug Administration guidelines, half of that amount will provide the needed protein in most diets. Since many modern cooks add vegetable proteins to each meal, less pure protein is required per meal.

For this reason, and because seafood is a gift from the sea to be treasured with every bite, in general the recipes in this book allow about 5 to 6 ounces of usable flesh per serving for main courses and 4 ounces when the seafood is combined with other ingredients.

As a general rule, purchase $^3/_4$ to 1 pound of whole fish per entrée-sized serving; $^1/_2$ pound of pan-dressed (cleaned) fish or fish steaks per portion; and $^1/_3$ pound of skin-on or skinless fish fillets per serving. About $^1/_2$ pound of shellfish meats makes 1 serving; $1^1/_4$ to $1^1/_2$ pounds of live lobster, crab, or crawfish per entrée portion; $1^1/_2$ to 2 pounds of live mussels or clams per serving; $2^1/_2$ to 3 pounds of live oysters per serving; 1 pound of whole, head-on shrimp per serving; or $^1/_2$ to $^3/_4$ pound of shrimp with the shells on and heads removed per serving.

Storage

- Refrigerate seafood as soon as possible at 32°. Although this temperature is cooler than most home refrigerators, it can be achieved by placing whole fish, fish fillets, or steaks in resealable plastic bags. Press out as much air as possible from each bag, seal the bag, and roll up the fish in the remaining portion of the bag. Place a layer of ice in a container large enough to hold the plastic bag without crowding. Place the bag over ice, then cover with more ice. Set the container in the coldest section of the refrigerator (usually the bottom back shelf), drain ice as it melts, and refresh with new ice as needed. A nice alternative is to store the plastic bags between layers of blue ice packs. Fresh fish stored in this way will keep for one to two days, twice as long as fish stored at 37°. However, if you cannot use the fish within a day or two, freeze it immediately, provided it has not been previously frozen.

- Cooked fish will keep for 3 or 4 days in a tightly sealed container in the refrigerator. Raw shellfish keeps 1 day in the refrigerator; cooked shellfish lasts 3 or 4 days.

- Before cooking fresh seafood, rinse under cold water and pat dry with paper towels.

- Do not leave raw or cooked seafood unrefrigerated for more than 2 hours, including preparation time and time on the table.

Seafood Cooking: An Overview of the Methods

SEAFOOD IS SURELY THE original convenience food: it is easy to prepare for cooking, it cooks quickly, and it even gives you visual cues when it is done. Despite such attributes, many people are intimidated by fish because they have experienced dry, overcooked fish, tough shrimp, or rubber bandlike squid rings. This section will dispel many of the myths associated with fish and shellfish cookery and open up the bounty of the seas to you. The instructions given for each cooking method are general. More detailed, specific cooking directions are given in the recipes.

The 10-Minute Rule

When cooking finfish, follow a handy guideline to follow when baking fish at 450°, broiling, sautéing, steaming, grilling, or poaching; it does not apply to fish that is microwaved or deep-fried. The "10-minute rule," developed by the Canadian Department of Fisheries and Oceans, advises measuring the fish (whole, steaks, or fillets) at its thickest point and cooking 10 minutes per inch, turning the fish halfway through the cooking time. (If the fish is stuffed or rolled, measure it after stuffing or rolling.) For example, a 1-inch-thick fish steak should be cooked 5 minutes on each side.

Pieces of fish less than $1/2$-inch thick do not have to be turned over. Add five minutes to the total cooking time if cooking the fish in aluminum foil or parchment or in a sauce, and double the time for frozen fish that has not been thawed.

Experiment with the rule and adjust cooking times depending on the type of fish and your personal tastes; perhaps you prefer fish cooked 8 or 12 minutes rather than 10. To my taste, and perhaps due to my oven, I prefer to bake fish at 425° rather than 450°—again the "10-minute rule" is a guideline rather than an edict. In any case, it is always a good idea to check the fish a few minutes before the end of the estimated cooking time. Don't cook fish until it flakes easily and falls apart, as outmoded cooking instructions have suggested, or the result will be tough, dry, and overcooked fish. Seafood continues to cook even after it is removed from the heat, so it is better to slightly undercook and rely on retained heat to finish the job.

Generally speaking, fish is done when the flesh is opaque and just begins to flake when tested at its thickest point with the tip of a small, sharp knife, or when it is easily pierced with a bamboo skewer. On an instant-read thermometer, fish is ready when its internal temperature reaches 145°, although many people prefer their fish cooked medium-rare, which would be 130° to 135°.

Dry-Heat Methods

Most fish and shellfish are naturally lean, with little internal fat to keep them moist when cooked using dry heat. For this reason, it is best to marinate lean fish before cooking or baste during cooking so it will not lose its moisture, or choose fish higher in fat when using any of the following dry-heat cooking methods.

BAKING (OVEN ROASTING)

Baking, or oven roasting, is a simple dry-heat method. Arrange small fillets or fish pieces (skin side down and seasoned with salt and pepper, if desired) or shellfish in a shallow baking pan or dish that has been lightly oiled or sprayed with nonstick cooking spray. Place pan in a preheated 450° oven until the fish tests done, 8 to 12 minutes per inch of thickness, or until the fish is just opaque throughout. It is not necessary to turn the fish during baking. For large pieces of fish and whole fish, cook for a longer period in a 350° oven so the fish will be completely cooked in the interior. For example, a whole 5-pound fish will cook in a 350° oven in 25 to 35 minutes.

BLACKENING/BRONZING

Blackening was popularized in the 1980s by world-famous New Orleans chef Paul Prudhomme. Fish fillets (Prudhomme used red fish) are dredged on both sides in a Cajun spice mix, then quickly cooked in a castiron skillet or on a griddle that is almost smoking hot.

The coating burns onto the surface of the fish, creating an extra-crispy crust (as well as lots of acrid smoke in the kitchen—be sure to turn on the overhead vent before employing this cooking method!). Bronzing is a milder form of blackening in which fish is cooked in a cast iron skillet at a lower heat (about 350°) with much less resulting smoke.

BROILING

Broiling is a version of grilling, except that the food is cooked directly under a gas or electric heat source, rather than from below. Arrange pieces of fish that are $1/4$ to $1^{1}/4$ inches thick on a rimmed baking sheet or on a rack set over a pan. Adjust oven rack so the top of the fish is 3 to 4 inches from heat. Preheat broiler. If desired, season seafood on both sides with salt and pepper, then place on broiler pan skin side down, allowing at least 1 inch between pieces. If using an electric range, leave oven door partially open and broil until fish is opaque in the center, 8 to 10 minutes per inch of thickness. Fish fillets or steaks under 1 inch thick can be cooked without turning; fillets or steaks thicker than 1 inch should be turned halfway through. To broil unthawed frozen fish, double the cooking time and turn the fish over halfway through broiling.

BROIL/BAKE

The broil/bake method, a favorite of Julia Child, cooks the top of the fish to a nice brown while keeping the underside moist and tender. To broil/bake, set one oven rack 3 to 4 inches from the broiler and a second rack in the center of the oven, then preheat the broiler. Season the fish with salt and pepper and place in an oiled baking dish. Broil 1 to 2 minutes, or until the top of the fish is browned. Set oven temperature to 375°, pour $1/8$ inch dry white wine or dry vermouth (or fish or chicken stock) around the fish and place the pan on the center oven rack. Bake until the fish just turns opaque, 5 to 7 minutes, depending on thickness. Do not turn the fish.

SEAR/BAKE

A technique common in restaurant kitchens that is not well known to home cooks is the sear/bake method, in which a teaspoon of oil or butter is added to an ovenproof pan over medium-high heat, the seafood is seared (cooked briefly) skin side up, turned, then immediately placed in a hot oven (450°) to finish cooking. Searing creates a flavorful seal and beautiful brown exterior, which helps the fish remain moist and tender on the inside. Meanwhile, the indirect heat of the oven penetrates the fish to finish cooking it in a more gentle way than the direct heat of a skillet. I have had very good luck with this method and appreciate the small amount of fat it requires.

GRILLING

Grilling is similar to broiling except the heat element is located under the fish rather than over it. Oily fish, fish with a sturdy texture, and crustaceans (when skewered for easy handling) are the most likely candidates for grilling. Delicate fish such as sole and flounder can be grilled if placed on a small-grid grill or piece of aluminum foil that has been punctured to allow air flow.

A wood, charcoal, gas or electric barbecue,

stovetop grill, or grill pan all work well. About 10 minutes before cooking, preheat to the hottest setting, rub cleaned rack lightly with oil and position adjustable grills 4 to 6 inches above hot coals or heating element. Brush both sides of seafood with oil, mayonnaise, or butter (most of which will melt away during cooking). Set fish skin side up on hot grill and cook, turning only once, until done, 8 to 10 minutes per inch of thickness.

During grilling, if desired, baste seafood several times with oil or basting sauce. To infuse seafood with a smoky flavor, cover the grill during cooking. When skewering seafood for the grill, use bamboo skewers (soaked in water for 30 minutes) or metal skewers, or use herb stems such as rosemary, tarragon, and mint. The stems are not only attractive, they also impart a subtle flavor to the fish or shellfish.

PLANKING

Planking is a variation of grilling that has been around since ancient times. Nowadays, planking means oven-roasting foods directly on a plank of aromatic fresh wood (cedar and alderwood are commonly used in the Northwest), which creates a moist, subtle flavor that is remarkable yet not overpowering. Commercially produced planks are available in a range of sizes, or a lumberyard can cut an untreated piece of alder or cedar to your specifications. A useful size is 16 x 8 inches.

Before using the plank, lightly oil the cooking surface. Arrange seafood on the plank and place in a 450° preheated oven on the top or center oven rack. (Never place the plank on the bottom rack or it could crack.) Immediately turn heat down to 375° and cook 10 to

16 minutes per inch of thickness, turning once, or until seafood just turns opaque and reaches an internal temperature of 130° (for medium rare). Serve immediately right on the plank, then handwash the plank in warm water and allow it to air dry. Periodically sand the plank to restore its natural oils.

SMOKING

Smoking is a dry-heat cooking method that has been used for centuries to preserve food. In modern times, smoking is used mostly to impart distinctive flavors and textures. There are two main types of smoke cure: cold-smoking, which smokes but does not cook the fish, and hot-smoking, which smokes and cooks the fish at the same time. See "Canned and Smoked Seafood" (see page 268) for additional information on smoking fish and shellfish.

SAUTÉING (PAN-FRYING)

Sautéing, or pan-frying, is a method of cooking a food in a pan in a small quantity of melted fat until the food is golden brown. About 1 to 2 teaspoons of a fat with a high smoking point, such as clarified butter, pure olive oil (not extra virgin), vegetable, peanut, canola, sunflower, safflower, or corn oil, or unclarified butter mixed with a few tablespoons of one of the high-temperature oils, should be added to a pan placed over medium-high heat and the oil well heated before the food goes into the pan. Make sure the seafood is patted absolutely dry, then add the seafood in small batches (lightly floured or breaded, if desired) so that the pan is not crowded. Cook the seafood on one side until lightly browned and the edges turn opaque about halfway up, 4 to 5 minutes for 1-inch-thick pieces. Turn fish over and cook until done, 4 to 5 minutes more.

After sautéing, a simple sauce can be made by removing the fish, draining any remaining fat, adding stock, wine, or cream, and cooking for a few minutes over high heat. Scrape the bottom of the pan to dissolve any browned particles of food or juices, enhancing the flavor of the sauce (this is called deglazing).

STIR-FRYING

Stir-frying is a Chinese method of sautéing that calls for small, uniformly sized pieces of food cooked quickly in a small amount of oil (traditionally peanut or corn oil) over high heat. Because stir-frying is such a rapid method of cooking, make sure all ingredients are prepared, measured, and arranged in accessible containers before cooking. Heat a wok or a large flat-bottomed skillet over medium-high to high heat. When the pan is hot, add a portion of the total amount of oil called for in the recipe (1 to 2 tablespoons per pound of seafood) and swirl to coat bottom. Add a small amount of fish (about $1/3$ to $1/2$ pound) and toss, turn, and flip every 15 seconds to keep the morsels moving. If too much seafood is added at one time, the oil cools and juices seep from the fish, resulting in simmering rather than frying. When the fish is cooked, remove it from the pan, drain, and repeat procedure with any remaining fish.

DEEP-FRYING

Deep-fried foods are totally immersed in fat during cooking, but unlike sautéed dishes or stir-fries, the fat is not served with the final dish. To deep-fry, fill a deep, heavy frying pan or wok one-third to one-half full of oil (canola, sunflower, safflower, peanut, pure olive, corn, or solid vegetable shortening work well) and heat to 375°, or until a haze appears on the surface of the oil. Use fish pieces that are less than 2 inches thick. Coat fish pieces with breading or batter of your choice. Add only a few pieces of fish at a time to the hot oil and fry 3 to 4 minutes, turning once, or until the fish is golden brown. Drain fried fish on paper towels, then keep warm in a warm oven (200°) until all of the fish is cooked. Allow the oil to reheat between batches.

OVEN-FRYING

Oven-frying, or "Spencer hot-oven baking," was devised in 1934 by Mrs. Evalene Spencer of the U.S. Bureau of Fisheries. Oven-frying crisps and browns seafood similar to deep-fat frying, but with much less fat. To oven-fry, preheat oven to 475° and lightly oil a baking sheet or spray with nonstick cooking spray. Dip boneless, skinless fish fillets or shellfish (such as peeled and deveined shrimp) in beaten egg or beaten egg whites mixed with milk, then dredge in bread crumbs or a similar coating. Place on the prepared baking sheet and drizzle with melted butter or margarine. Cook 8 to 10 minutes per inch of thickness, or until fish just turns opaque.

Wet-Heat Methods

Moist-heat cooking methods use liquid as a cooking medium, providing a gentle means of cooking that is suitable for many types of fish and shellfish.

BRAISING (PAN POACHING)/STEWING

Braising, or pan poaching, is traditionally defined as a process of slow cooking that is used for tenderizing and concentrating flavor in less tender cuts of beef, veal, pork, and lamb. But because fish is a delicate protein that cannot withstand long cooking time, braising takes on a whole different meaning in seafood cookery. To braise fish fillets, steaks, a whole fish, or shellfish (browned or not), place in a covered pan with a dense, concentrated liquid or sauce (not enough to cover) and cook on top of the stove or in the oven until done. Stewing involves gently simmering seafood in a larger quantity of liquid (usually a sauce flavored with herbs and aromatic vegetables) than is required for braising.

POACHING/STEEPING

Poaching refers to cooking food submerged in liquid (water, court bouillon, or fish or chicken broth) that is barely simmering (170° to 180°); there should be tiny bubbles breaking at the bottom of the pan. Poaching is second only to steaming in respect for the natural flavor and texture of the fish. The fish should be at least 1/2 inch thick. Choose a pan that will hold the fish in a single layer. For whole fish, lay fish in the pan and add cold liquid to cover fish by 1 inch. Bring the liquid with the fish in it to a simmer, cover pan, and simmer gently until the fish tests done, about 8 minutes per inch of thickness. For fish fillets, fish steaks, or shellfish, lay fish in the pan and add cold liquid to cover fish by 1 inch. Remove fish, bring liquid to a simmer, return seafood to the pan, and proceed as above.

Steeping is a variation of poaching in which a poaching liquid twice as high as the thickest part of the fish is brought to a rolling boil (212°). The seafood is added, then the pan is covered and immediately removed from the heat. After 8 to 10 minutes, 1-inch-thick pieces of fish will be cooked and the water temperature will have dropped to 165° to 170°. Seafood can be left in the steeping liquid up to 20 minutes without overcooking. Steeping works best with fish fillets or steaks less than 1 1/2-inches thick, shell-on or shelled shrimp, scallops, or squid. This method also works well for reheating cooked crab, lobster, clams, or fish.

STEAMING

Steaming is the process of cooking food in a closed vessel with just enough liquid to generate steam (water, broth, wine, beer, or a combination of these, along with aromatics, herbs, and spices to flavor the liquid, if desired). Because food is cooked in steam rather than immersed in liquid, steamed foods retain their natural flavor and most of their soluble nutrients. The three pieces of equipment necessary for steaming include a cooking vessel with a tight-fitting lid, a small amount of cooking liquid, and a rack to elevate the food at least 1 inch above the liquid. Arrange seafood on the rack and set the rack over simmering water. Cover the pan and cook until done, 8 to 10 minutes per inch of thickness.

Other Cooking Methods

EN PAPILLOTE

Cooking *en papillote*, a French term for cooking in a paper case, is a method of steaming in which pieces of fish or shellfish up to 1 inch thick and are securely wrapped in parchment paper and cooked over boiling water or baked in a 400° oven about 10 to 15 minutes per inch of thickness. The fish's own juices create the steam and cook the fish without added oils or fats. In the modern kitchen, aluminum foil or banana leaves sometimes substitute for the traditional parchment paper.

MICROWAVE COOKING

I am not a fan of the microwave oven, although many people rave about its value for cooking seafood. That said, if you want to microwave a piece of fish or shellfish, use a round or oval shallow microwavable casserole dish and place the seafood around the inside edge of the dish with the thicker parts facing outward. Cover the dish with plastic wrap, turning the plastic wrap back at one corner so steam can vent. Cook fish on HIGH (except for small whole fish, which should cook on MEDIUM) 3 minutes per pound of boneless fish. Move, turn, or stir seafood halfway through cooking time. Remove dish from the microwave when the edges of the fish are firm and opaque and the center is slightly translucent and allow to stand, still covered, 2 to 3 minutes to finish cooking. It is best to undercook at first, then add more cooking time in 30-second intervals, if needed.

Raw Fish

Japanese cooks are especially skilled in the preparation of raw fish in dishes such as sashimi (raw fish or shellfish cut into artful forms or served on the half shell with condiments) and sushi (vinegared rice garnished with pieces of fish, shellfish, or vegetables and served with condiments). Certain other cuisines include what is essentially raw seafood that has been marinated in salt and acid (citrus juice or vinegar) so that the connective tissues in the fish break down and the protein firms up, "cooking" the fish. Examples of these include Scandinavian gravlax, in which salmon fillets are layered with a dry rub of sugar, salt, dill, and sometimes spices, and Latin American ceviche, in which shrimp, scallops, and pieces of whitefish are marinated in lemon or lime juice, salt, and hot peppers.

There are health concerns in eating raw fish (see page 20), which is why many health professionals recommend eating raw seafood only if it is selected and prepared by an expert, such as a sushi master or professional chef.

HANDY COOKING HINT

The late Gilbert LeCoze, founder and chef of Le Bernardin in New York City, had a useful method for testing fish for doneness. He would insert a thin metal skewer, such as a turkey lacer, into the flesh of cooked fish, leave it there for 2 seconds, and then touch the skewer to his lower lip. Cool meant raw, warm signaled rare, very warm meant perfectly done, and uncomfortably hot indicated overdone fish flesh.

The Well-Equipped Galley: Essential Equipment and Pantry Items

WHEN PEOPLE THINK OF cooking seafood, they often picture narrow copper poaching pans, hinged fish baskets, and huge stockpots for making fish stock. While this equipment is useful, it can be expensive, and many people have neither the space to store it, nor the time to polish it. There are a few moderately priced pieces of equipment that are relatively small in size and make seafood cooking a joy. Following are some of my favorites.

Must-Have Equipment

Broiler pan with rack

Citrus zester

Crab/lobster cracker: Better suited to lobster claws than crab.

Crab/lobster mallet: Very useful when picking Dungeness crab and easier to control than a crab/lobster cracker.

Fine-meshed strainer: Necessary for sauce and stock preparations.

Ginger grater

Kitchen shears/scissors: Numerous uses, but one of my favorites is to cut the backs of shrimp shells and devein the shrimp. Cooking in the shell holds in the flavor during cooking, while the narrow cut allows for easy peeling once the shrimp are cooked.

Knives: A good-quality boning or filleting knife (6- or 9-inch for very large fish) allows you to easily remove skin from fish fillets, slice raw and cooked fish, and stay close to the fish's bone as you remove the flesh.

Metal tongs: Over the years, my metal tongs have become like a second set of hands. I use them to turn scallops as they sauté, snatch mussels out of the pot as they steam open, and stir seafood soups.

Nonstick cookware: A 10-inch, good-quality skillet is a must; 2- and 4-quart saucepans are also useful.

Oyster knife: Protects your hands when shucking oysters; if you eat clams, a clam knife is useful, too.

Parchment paper: Indispensable when making preparations of seafood *en papillote* (in a paper case).

Pastry brush: Many uses, but I particularly like to brush a small amount of oil or butter in a skillet before sautéing.

Rimmed baking sheets

Seafood forks: Useful for picking crabmeat from shells and wonderful for seafood soups and stews that contain mussels, clams, or in-shell shrimp.

Shrimp deveiner: I recommend the stainless-steel model even though it costs a few dollars more because it is more durable than the plastic type.

Six-inch plastic or stainless-steel ruler: Indispensable when using the "10-minute rule" (see page 26).

Slotted spoon(s): Great for fishing out small pieces of shellfish from a soup or stew.

Strawberry huller, fish-bone puller, large tweezers, or needle-nose pliers: With a bit of practice, any of these devices works wonders for pulling out elusive pin bones from fish fillets.

Wide, perforated spatula: I must admit that I never owned one of these before I started working on this book. Now I couldn't live without it—because it supports more surface area of fish fillets and steaks, it's much simpler and less worrisome to turn them.

Optional Equipment

Cedar or alder plank: Planked foods cook quickly and cleanly with little added fat, and the plank can be taken directly to the table for a dramatic presentation. Easy cleanup is yet another bonus.

Food processor or blender: The food processor is the more useful piece of equipment because it chops and slices. However, a blender is better for making purées and sauces. Mini-chop food processors are very useful too and

inexpensive. Immersible food processors are great for puréeing soups and sauces.

Grilling equipment: If you grill, a charcoal or gas grill, oval grilling basket, skewers (wood or metal), wide spatula, grilling grate, and assorted types of wood chips are all important to own.

Instant-read thermometer: Great for checking internal temperatures of fish and shellfish; especially valuable when cooking *en papillote* (in paper casing).

Large roasting pan: This piece of equipment can easily substitute for a fish poacher. Simply cut the tops and bottoms out of clean tuna cans, place a rack over the cans, and place the whole fish on the rack. The same setup can be used to steam whole large fish over water or an aromatic liquid.

Salad spinner or microwave vegetable steamer: Either of these devices works well for seafood storage.

Small electric coffee grinder: Used exclusively to grind whole spices for the freshest tastes and aromas imaginable.

Steaming apparatus: Stainless-steel steaming inserts that fit snugly atop one another and rest inside a cooking vessel with a tight-fitting lid are my steaming implements of choice, although bamboo steaming baskets placed atop a wok, stainless-steel steaming racks, or stainless-steel steaming baskets (less useful because they can tip over when filled with food) are alternatives.

Stovetop grill pan: I use a 10-inch, round, nonstick grill pan with ridges that create beautiful grill marks, but many sizes and shapes are available.

Stovetop smoker: The stovetop smoker is a

godsend for its ease of use indoors and its compact size. However, if you intend to smoke lots of seafood, an outdoor smoker (either electric or charcoal) may prove more practical.

The Pantry

Seafood is one of the most versatile foods available; with just a couple of different types of finfish or shellfish (fresh or frozen) and some of the pantry ingredients suggested here, you could eat for weeks without ever duplicating menus. Do not be intimidated by the length of this list or the breadth of these ingredients; add to your pantry slowly and become comfortable with new ingredients at your own pace.

FRESH FOODS

Bell peppers: Green, yellow, red, orange
Citrus fruits: Lemons, limes, oranges, blood oranges
Fresh herbs: Parsley, thyme, basil, oregano, rosemary, chives, cilantro, dill, tarragon
Garlic
Gingerroot
Green (white, yellow, and red) onions
Kaffir lime leaves (may be frozen for longer storage)
Leeks
Shallots

FROM THE REFRIGERATOR AND FREEZER

Butter or margarine
Cheese: Parmesan, Parmigiano-Reggiano, feta
Commercially prepared frozen fish stock
Frozen vegetables: Peas, corn, spinach, carrots, mixed vegetables, stir-fry vegetables
Nonfat, lowfat, or whole milk, depending on dietary preferences
Plain yogurt and sour cream
Whipping cream

DRIED FRUITS AND VEGETABLES

Dried fruits: Cranberries ("craisins"), cherries
Dried mushrooms: Shiitakes, porcini, morels
Fermented black beans
Sundried tomatoes: Dehydrated and oil-packed

HERBS AND SPICES

Crushed red pepper flakes
Dried herbs: Thyme, basil, oregano, marjoram, rosemary, dill, tarragon, bay leaf, mint
Kosher or coarse sea salt
Old Bay seasoning
Spices: Ground cumin, coriander, curry powder, garam masala, ground cayenne pepper, paprika (sweet and hot), dry mustard, five-spice powder, turmeric, saffron threads, white pepper, chile powder, ground ginger
Whole peppercorns: Black, white, green, pink, assorted, Szechwan
Whole spices (used in small quantities or mixed with other spices): Allspice, cloves, cardamom, cinnamon, nutmeg

Oils

Corn, canola, safflower, sesame, toasted sesame, vegetable, mustard, avocado

Hot chili oil

Nonstick cooking spray: Regular, olive oil, garlic-flavored

Nut oils: Macadamia, hazelnut, walnut, peanut, almond

Olive oil: Pure, virgin, extra virgin

Nuts and Seeds

Nut butters: Peanut, sesame (tahini), almond

Seeds: Black and white sesame, black mustard, poppy seeds

Whole, chopped, slivered, sliced, and crushed nuts: Almonds, peanuts, macadamias, pecans, hazelnuts

Bottled Foods

Capers

Clam juice

Marinated artichoke hearts

Olives: Black, green, kalamata, niçoise

Canned Foods

Coconut milk

Evaporated skim milk

Peppers: Whole and diced green chiles, chipotle peppers in adobo

Seafood: Clams, oysters, mussels, salmon, tuna

Stocks: Chicken, Asian-style (miso), and vegetable

Tomato products: Tomato paste, whole tomatoes, stewed tomatoes, tomato sauce

Prepared Condiments, Sauces, and Seasonings

Black bean sauce

Bouillon cubes: Chicken, fish, vegetable

Chili garlic sauce

Cocktail sauce

Curry pastes: Yellow, green, red

Dashi-no-moto (Japanese instant soup stock made with dried bonito tuna flakes and dried kelp)

Fish sauce: Thai (*nam pla*) or Vietnamese (*nuoc nam*)

Hoisin sauce

Horseradish: Prepared horseradish, wasabi (Japanese horseradish powder)

Jerk sauce or paste

Ketchup

Liquid smoke

Mango chutney

Mayonnaise

Mustard: Dijon, stone-ground, country-style, sweet-hot

Oyster sauce

Pesto

Pickled sliced ginger

Plum sauce

Salad dressings (to use as seafood marinades): Italian, red wine vinegar, and others as desired

Salsa: Mild and hot, plus various flavors

Seafood marinades

Soy sauce: Light, dark, low-sodium, tamari, shoyu

Stir-fry sauce

Sweet-and-sour sauce

Tabasco sauce: Red and jalapeño
Tartar sauce
Teriyaki sauce
Vinegars: Red wine, balsamic, rice wine,
  raspberry or blueberry, white wine,
  tarragon
Worcestershire sauce: White and dark

PASTA, RICE, BEANS, AND GRAINS

Asian noodles: Soba, rice vermicelli, *udon*
Beans: Kidney, black, garbanzo, cannellini
Fresh or dried pastas: Plain, whole-wheat,
  spinach, tomato, or other flavored pasta in
  various shapes including penne, angel hair,
  spaghetti, corkscrews, bowties, butterflies,
  seashells, lasagne noodles, orzo
Grains: Yellow cornmeal, polenta, millet,
  quinoa, couscous
Lentils: Green, brown, red
Rice: Arborio, basmati, brown, jasmine, long-
  grain white, short-grain white, wild

BREAD PRODUCTS

Bread crumbs: Unseasoned, Italian, *panko*
  (Japanese bread crumbs)
Flour, whole-wheat, and corn tortillas
Prepared pizza crusts
Taco shells

WINES AND LIQUEURS

Liqueurs: White dry vermouth, anise-
  flavored, orange-flavored, dry sherry, rice
  wine (sake or mirin)
Wines: Dry white wine, sweet white wine,
  dry red wine

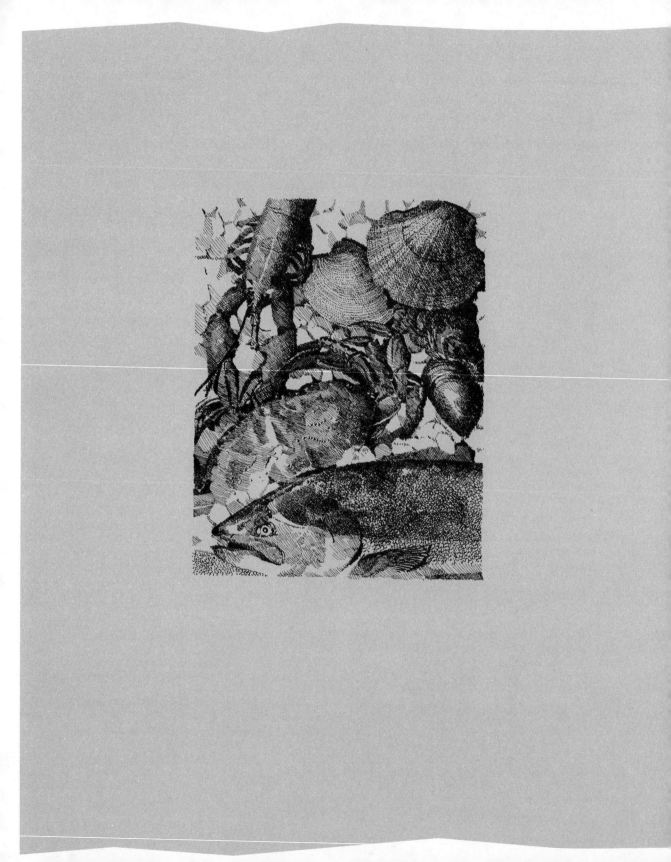

Part 2

FINFISH

The Types of Fish in the Sea

FISH ARE VERTEBRATES with backbones, fins, and gills. Most fish can be divided into two distinct groups—flatfish and roundfish—depending on their anatomy.

Flatfish

Members of the flatfish family resemble long, dark pancakes with a crooked smile and two eyes on top of their heads, but they do not begin life that way. As newborns, flatfish larvae resemble roundfish, with a symmetrical body and an eye on each side of their heads. But within a time period that is specific to each species, two dramatic changes occur: one of a flatfish's eyes migrates (either left or right, depending on the species) until it is beside the second eye, and the skull undergoes a corresponding and necessary twisting. As these dramatic anatomical changes take place, the strange-looking fish swims with an ever-increasing sideways tilt to compensate. After the eye migration process is complete, the young fish's body becomes darkly pigmented, almost always on its "eyed" side, and its body flattens and lengthens.

From this point on, the adult fish spends the rest of its life lying flat on the surface of the sand or swimming horizontally near the ocean bottom, propelled by undulating body movements. Its darker, mottled side faces upward, blending into its habitat and camouflaging it from enemies; its pale eyeless side faces the ocean floor, safely away from predators. Ichthyologists believe all flatfish originally descended from an ancient, symmetrical, perch-like ancestor that began lying on its side.

Flatfish include flounder, sole, and halibut.

Roundfish

Roundfish have thicker, more bullet-shaped bodies than flatfish, and their spines lie deeper within their rounded forms. Roundfish have eyes on both sides of their heads and swim in a vertical position. When you cut a roundfish crosswise, the steaks are oval or circular. When cut lengthwise, roundfish form two fillets. Roundfish include salmon, rockfish, and trout.

Other Shapes of Fish

Fish whose bone and body structure are unusually shaped (such as tuna, swordfish, and monkfish) and fish that have skeletons made of cartilage rather than bone (such as skate or shark) do not fit into either the flatfish or roundfish categories. However, since they are usually cut into fillets, steaks, or loin pieces (and skinned, if necessary) before sale, their unusual body shapes should not prove an obstacle to the home cook.

Catfish

THERE ARE 2,500 SPECIES of catfish around the world and at least 39 species in North America alone. Most live in fresh water, although some inhabit the oceans and are often referred to as "hogfish." A fish called the "ocean catfish" is frequently marketed as true catfish, although it is actually a wolffish—a large, very firm-fleshed ocean fish that dines on shellfish.

The catfish gets its name from the eight long, razor-sharp, whiskerlike barbels (feelers) which dangle around its mouth. The catfish's bluish-gray to black skin is scaleless and very tough. Its head is massive, its body streamlined, and its tail deeply forked.

Catfish are bottom feeders, but their natural habitats have become muddy and polluted, which has led to aquafarming of 99 percent of the catfish in today's retail markets. The species most widely farmed and eaten, the channel catfish (*Ictalurus punctatus*), is the most important species of aquatic animal commercially cultured in the United States. Native to North America, the channel catfish is found in the wild from the Great Lakes south to Virginia and west to Mexico. Weighing from 1 to 10 pounds, the channel is also considered the best eating.

The farmed catfish industry began in the 1960s as one farmer's experiment in supplemental income; catfish has since become the number one farmed finfish in America. About 95 percent of the nation's farm-raised catfish is raised in four states: Mississippi, Arkansas, Alabama, and Louisiana, where catfish ponds cover approximately 140,000 acres.

Farm-raised catfish grow up in clay-based ponds averaging 10 to 20 acres each. The ponds are built above ground from rich, southern soils that have been compacted and divided by levees (embankments), which are filled with 4 to 6 feet of pure, fresh water pumped from underground wells.

Controlled for quality as well as weight, baby catfish are harvested when they reach 1

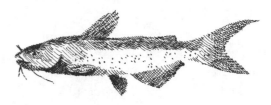

Channel Catfish

to 1½ pounds in size. The smaller ones are skinned and left whole, much like the farm-raised trout you'll often find in seafood markets, while the fillets of the larger fish are shipped fresh-frozen to markets across the country, including the large supermarket chains.

Quality control of farm-raised catfish is stringently regulated by the U.S. Food and

Drug Administration and the departments of agriculture and commerce. Every crop of catfish must pass its first taste test at the side of the pond it was grown in. After the live catfish are loaded aboard aerated tank trucks and delivered to processing plants, they are tested a second time. Any fish that don't pass muster are returned to the grower. Those that do pass are processed within 30 minutes, then put in refrigerated trucks for shipment all over the United States.

Farmed catfish have a mild flavor (as opposed to the "muddy" flavor of wild fish many of us remember from twenty years ago) because of what and how they eat. Instead of dredging the bottom of the pond for their meals like fish in the wild do, farm-raised catfish eat puffed, high-protein food pellets that float at the top of the pond. The food pellets—a mixture of soybeans, corn, wheat, vitamins, and minerals—give the fish a mild, almost sweet taste and help avoid "off" flavors in the fish's flesh.

Catfish come to market most commonly as boneless, skinless fillets, although sometimes they are available whole (skinned, head removed, and weighing about 12 ounces), as steaks, strips, or nuggets, or marinated and breaded or precooked in frozen dinners and entrées. The flesh should be white but may have subtle pink hues. A gray-white band of fat that sometimes appears on the skin side may be cut away before cooking if desired. Catfish is best when cooked within 2 days of purchase. When properly wrapped, catfish keeps a maximum of 3 months in the home freezer set at 0° or below.

Catfish fillets weighing 4 to 6 ounces serve 1 generously; one whole catfish weighing ¾ to 1 pound will serve 2.

Today's farmed catfish have a sweet, mild flavor and fine, firmly textured flesh that flakes and remains tender when cooked. Because of these traits, the versatile fish is complemented by strong flavorings as well as mild ones. It is well suited to any cooking method, including baking, blackening, broiling, frying, deep-frying (the classic method), stir-frying, oven-frying, poaching, smoking, grilling, microwaving, sautéing, steaming, braising, or adding to chowders or stews.

Good news for the cook is that, unlike most fish, catfish can tolerate a bit of overcooking or overhandling without suffering any loss in taste. Undercooked catfish, on the other hand, is tough. To test catfish for doneness, insert a fork or the tip of a small, sharp knife in the thickest part of the fillet. It should feel tender, while the flesh should be completely opaque.

Farmed catfish are available year-round.

FUN FACT

• Mississippi produces about 70 percent of the catfish consumed in the United States, and most of that comes from Humphreys County, the "Catfish Capital of the World."

Catfish Bombay

Catfish is normally associated with the South, where it is traditionally deep-fried and served with hush puppies, balls of deep-fried cornmeal dough studded with chopped scallions. In this recipe, a spicy yogurt marinade helps create a flavorful new breed of "fried" catfish, which is actually pan-fried rather than deep-fried to save time, trouble, and perhaps a few calories. Broccoli or cauliflower florets, sautéed with a bit of curry powder, and rice pilaf would make perfect accompaniments.

1/2 CUP PLAIN NONFAT YOGURT

2 TABLESPOONS TOMATO PASTE

2 TABLESPOONS RED WINE, WHITE WINE, OR CHICKEN STOCK

2 CLOVES GARLIC, MINCED

1 TEASPOON GRATED GINGERROOT, OR 1/2 TEASPOON GROUND GINGER

1/2 TEASPOON GROUND CORIANDER

1/2 TEASPOON GROUND CINNAMON

1/2 TEASPOON GROUND CUMIN

1/2 TEASPOON GROUND CURRY POWDER

1/2 TEASPOON GROUND TURMERIC

1/4 TEASPOON CRUSHED RED PEPPER FLAKES

1 1/2 POUNDS CATFISH FILLETS, SKINNED, RINSED, DRAINED, PATTED DRY, AND CUT INTO 4 (6-OUNCE) FILLETS

1/2 CUP ALMOND SLICES, FINELY CHOPPED

1/2 CUP HOMEMADE OR STORE-BOUGHT DRY UNSEASONED BREAD CRUMBS

1/2 TEASPOON GROUND SWEET PAPRIKA

1/4 TEASPOON SALT

2 TABLESPOONS MUSTARD SEED OIL OR VEGETABLE OIL

1. In a nonreactive baking dish large enough to hold catfish fillets in one layer, stir together yogurt, tomato paste, wine, garlic, gingerroot, coriander, cinnamon, cumin, curry powder, turmeric, and red pepper flakes. Add catfish fillets and turn several times to coat each side well with marinade. Cover and refrigerate at least 30 minutes and up to 2 hours, turning fish occasionally.

2. On a flat plate or piece of waxed paper, mix together almonds, bread crumbs, paprika and salt. Remove fish fillets from marinade, retaining as much marinade as possible. Pat crumbs on both sides of each catfish fillet and place on one of two baking sheets. Repeat until all of the fillets are coated with crust.

3. Preheat oven to 200°.

4. Heat oil in a large skillet over medium-high heat. When oil is very hot, add fish fillets without crowding, cooking in two batches and adding more oil if necessary. Cook fish fillets 5 to 7 minutes, turn carefully, and cook another 5 to 7 minutes, or until fish just flakes (cut into the middle of one of the fillets to test for doneness). The fish should cook a total of 12 to 14 minutes per inch of thickness.

5. Transfer cooked fish fillets to second baking sheet and place in oven to keep warm. When all of the fillets are cooked, divide among individual plates and serve immediately to keep the crust from becoming soggy.

SERVES 4

Smothered Cajun Catfish

The Cajun "holy trinity"—a combination of chopped onions, celery, and green pepper—forms the base for a spicy tomato sauce spiked with Worcestershire and Tabasco, in which catfish fillets are gently braised. A side dish of long-grain white rice and lots of crusty bread will complete this one-skillet dish in proper Louisiana style.

2 TABLESPOONS VEGETABLE OIL

1 ONION, CHOPPED

2 CLOVES GARLIC, MINCED

1/2 CUP CHOPPED CELERY

1/2 CUP CHOPPED GREEN PEPPER

1 (14 1/2-OUNCE) CAN STEWED TOMATOES,
    WITH JUICE

1 1/2 TABLESPOONS CAPERS

3/4 CUP FISH STOCK OR CLAM JUICE

1 TABLESPOON WORCESTERSHIRE SAUCE

1/2 TEASPOON TABASCO SAUCE

1 1/2 POUNDS CATFISH FILLETS, SKINNED,
    RINSED, DRAINED, PATTED DRY, AND CUT
    INTO 4 (6-OUNCE) FILLETS

1. In a large skillet with a lid, heat vegetable oil over medium-high heat. Add onion and garlic and cook 2 minutes, stirring occasionally. Add celery and green pepper and cook 3 minutes, stirring occasionally.

2. Add tomatoes, capers, fish stock, Worcestershire sauce, and Tabasco sauce. Bring to a boil, decrease heat to a simmer, and cook 7 to 10 minutes, or until vegetables are tender-crisp, stirring occasionally. Lay catfish fillets over sauce, then spoon sauce over tops of fillets. Cover and cook 5 minutes, then turn fillets. Spoon sauce over fillets, cover skillet, and cook 7 to 10 minutes, or until fillets are just opaque.

3. Transfer catfish to a large plate and cover with aluminum foil to keep warm.

4. Reduce sauce until thickened, then place catfish fillets on individual plates and "smother" with thickened sauce.

SERVES 4

FUN FACTS

- The Loyal Order of Catfish Lovers, of Belzoni, Mississippi, offers a membership card and button, a bumper sticker, and a secret handshake with a finger wiggle, along with an annual Catfish Festival. The fan club's motto is, "Sic Semper Whiskers!"

- Hush puppies, small cornmeal dumplings that are the traditional accompaniment for fried catfish, got their name from Southern cooks. To keep hungry dogs from begging for food while dinner was being prepared, the cooks tossed scraps of the fried batter to the pets with the admonition "Hush, puppy!"

Catfish Fillets Orientale en Papillote

This elegant recipe uses a classic French technique, en papillote (in paper), to cook catfish fillets and seasonal ingredients. It is best made in late spring and early summer, when asparagus (affectionately referred to as Yakima grass because it grows so abundantly in eastern Washington's Yakima Valley) and morels (native Northwestern mushrooms with a pleasantly chewy texture and earthy taste) are at their peak of freshness and flavor.

2 TABLESPOONS BUTTER

1 CARROT, CUT INTO 1 1/2-INCH LENGTHS
    AND JULIENNED

1/2 GREEN, YELLOW, OR RED BELL PEPPER,
    STEMMED, SEEDED, AND JULIENNED

1/2 POUND ASPARAGUS, TOP 3 INCHES ONLY,
    CUT INTO 1-INCH PIECES

2 GREEN ONIONS, CUT INTO 1 1/2-INCH
    LENGTHS AND JULIENNED

2 MOREL OR SHIITAKE MUSHROOMS, DICED

SALT AND FRESHLY GROUND BLACK PEPPER

1 1/2 POUNDS CATFISH FILLETS, SKINNED,
    RINSED, DRAINED, PATTED DRY, AND CUT
    INTO 4 (6-OUNCE) PIECES

1. Preheat oven to 400°.

2. Cut four 12-inch squares of parchment paper. Fold in half to form four 6-inch squares, then cut into half-heart shapes. (When parchment is opened, you will have symmetrical heart shapes.) Set aside.

3. Melt 1 tablespoon of the butter in a large skillet over medium-high heat. Add carrot and cook for 1 minute, stirring often. Decrease heat to medium, add bell pepper, and cook for 1 minute more. Add asparagus pieces and cook for 2 minutes, stirring occasionally. Add green onions and morels and cook for 1 minute more, stirring often, or until vegetables are tender-crisp. Remove from heat and set aside.

4. Melt the remaining 1 tablespoon butter in a microwave oven or on the stovetop. Open one piece of parchment paper so that it forms a full heart. Using a pastry brush, coat the heart with the melted butter. Lightly sprinkle catfish fillets with salt and pepper, then place a fillet in the center of one side of the heart closest to the fold. Spread one-quarter of the vegetable mixture over the top of the fish fillet, covering as evenly as possible. Do not overstuff parchment; the fish and vegetables need room to expand during baking.

5. Fold half the parchment over fish and vegetables, then fold over and roll edges of parchment every inch or inch and a half to seal tightly. It is very important to form a tight seal all around or the parchment could open during baking and the contents will not cook properly. Repeat with remaining ingredients.

6. Place parchment packets on 2 baking sheets and cook until slightly puffed and lightly browned, 10 to 15 minutes. To gauge cooking time, measure fish at the thickest part and cook for 10 minutes per inch of thickness, then add 3 to 5 minutes to allow heat to penetrate parchment paper.

7. To serve, place parchment packets on individual plates and, with a sharp knife or kitchen shears, cut packets open in an X-shaped pattern.

SERVES 4

Chilean Sea Bass

A MEMBER OF THE Noto-theniidae family, **Chilean sea bass** (*Dissestichus eleginoides*) is one of the most misunderstood fish in the sea. Neither a true sea bass, nor a grouper, nor a cod (all fish for which it is sometimes mistaken), Chilean sea bass is similar in texture to the sablefish (black cod) that inhabits Northwest waters. Originally, Chilean sea bass was found only in the southwestern Pacific; now, its grounds have been extended to much of the Southern Hemisphere. In its native waters it is called *bacalao de profundidad*, or cod of the depths, for it lives in deep water between 1,600 and 3,200 feet and resembles cod in color and texture.

Chilean Sea Bass

Once you start looking for this fish, you will notice it on many restaurant menus and in many seafood markets. The fish is quite popular among Pike Place Market fishmongers during the winter months, when salmon isn't at its best and customers want something with a richer flavor and firmer texture than the ubiquitous bottomfish.

The flesh of Chilean sea bass is almost whiter than white, so look for fish that is clear and bright white in color. It should have a firm, not soft or gelatinous, texture.

Because Chilean sea bass has a high oil content, the fish does not dry out as quickly as leaner fish but should never be overcooked. The large pin bones that are often left in the fillets can be removed before cooking. Because the fish has big, tender flakes after cooking, be sure to cut Chilean sea bass into pieces at least 1 to 1½ inches wide to prevent it from falling apart. Favored cooking methods for the fish include broiling, baking, poaching, braising, steaming, grilling, smoking, and sautéing.

With its unique flavor and texture, Chilean sea bass can be prepared with only minimal seasonings or sauces. However, it also holds up to bold flavors; one of my favorites is Chilean sea bass with black bean sauce.

Chilean sea bass is available year-round, with heaviest catches and least expensive prices between November and February.

Middle Eastern Sea Bass with Garbanzo Bean Sauce

~~◆~~

I got the idea for using falafel mix, a combination of ground garbanzo beans or fava beans and spices, as a crust for fresh fish from Elisabeth Rozin's wonderful book, Ethnic Cuisine. *I took the idea a step further by adding freshly ground* achiote *(ah-chee-OH-tay), the rusty-red, triangular seed of the tropical annato tree. Used primarily as a coloring agent in Indian, Caribbean, Spanish, and Latin cooking, the ground achiote seeds also give the fish fillets a mild, musky, peppery flavor. They are available at Mar-ketSpice in the Pike Place Market and gourmet and ethnic markets. The garbanzo bean sauce, reminiscent of Middle Eastern hummus but with a more pro-nounced lemony flavor and gingery bite, creates a beautiful color and textural contrast to the sautéed fish. Serve with basmati rice or pita bread to scoop up any leftover sauce.*

3 TABLESPOONS FRESHLY SQUEEZED
   LEMON JUICE
1 TABLESPOON TAHINI (GROUND SESAME
   SEED PASTE)
1 TABLESPOON SHIRO (WHITE) MISO
2 TEASPOONS LOW-SODIUM SOY SAUCE
1 TEASPOON MINCED PEELED GINGERROOT
1 CLOVE GARLIC, MINCED
1/8 TEASPOON TABASCO SAUCE
1 CUP SALT-FREE CANNED GARBANZO
   BEANS, DRAINED, LIQUID RESERVED
1/4 CUP FALAFEL MIX

1 TEASPOON ACHIOTE SEED, GROUND TO
   A FINE POWDER IN A SPICE MILL OR
   ELECTRIC COFFEE GRINDER (OPTIONAL)
1 1/2 POUNDS CHILEAN SEA BASS FILLETS,
   RINSED, DRAINED, PATTED DRY, AND CUT
   INTO 4 (6-OUNCE) PIECES
1 TEASPOON EXTRA VIRGIN OLIVE OIL
FRESH MINT LEAVES, FOR GARNISH

1. Place lemon juice, tahini, miso, soy sauce, gingerroot, garlic, Tabasco, and garbanzo beans in a food processor or blender and process until smooth. Add 1 to 2 tablespoons reserved gar-banzo bean liquid until mixture forms a thick sauce. Spoon into a nonreactive dish, cover, and allow to sit at room temperature while preparing fish.

2. Stir together falafel mix and achiote seed on a plate or piece of waxed paper. Gently press fish fillets into crust mix, coating both sides of fish completely and evenly.

3. Heat a nonstick skillet large enough to hold fish fillets without crowding over medium heat. Add oil. When oil is hot but not smoking, add fish fillets and cook 3 to 5 minutes. Turn and cook fillets another 4 to 5 minutes, or until fish just turns opaque.

4. To serve, spoon a circle of garbanzo bean sauce on individual plates and place fish in cen-ter of circle. Garnish with fresh mint leaves.

SERVES 4

Smoked Chilean Sea Bass with Thai Vinaigrette

Like many of us who live in the Northwest, Graham Kerr has adopted and embraced this area as his home because of the wonderful array of foodstuffs here and its invigorating yet casual lifestyle. Renowned as public television's "Galloping Gourmet" for more than a decade in the 1960s and 1970s, in recent years Graham has been the worldwide ambassador for healthy cooking. His philosophy relies on cooking with kindness by enhancing aroma, color, and texture in everything he cooks. I particularly liked this recipe from Graham Kerr's Kitchen because it illustrates tea-smoking, a technique which can be used with many different fish and shellfish to impart a delicate, smoky taste and golden brown color. As Graham says, if you have a taste for the exotic, you'll love this smoky dish.

Sea Bass

1 POUND CHILEAN SEA BASS FILLETS, SKIN REMOVED AND CUT INTO 4 (4-OUNCE) PIECES

2 TABLESPOONS UNCOOKED LONG-GRAIN WHITE RICE

4 WHOLE CLOVES

TEA LEAVES REMOVED FROM 2 EARL GREY TEA BAGS

1/4 TEASPOON LIGHT OLIVE OIL

DASH OF TOASTED SESAME OIL

Couscous

1/2 TEASPOON LIGHT OLIVE OIL

DASH OF TOASTED SESAME OIL

1/4 CUP COARSELY CHOPPED FRESH LEMON-GRASS

2 TABLESPOONS FINELY CHOPPED GINGER-ROOT

1/4 CUP CHOPPED GREEN ONION, WHITE PART ONLY

GRATED ZEST OF 1/2 LIME

3 3/4 CUPS SEAFOOD STOCK (SEE PAGE 319)

1/8 TEASPOON FRESHLY GROUND SEA SALT

1 (10-OUNCE) BOX INSTANT COUSCOUS

Thai Vinaigrette

1 CUP RESERVED SEASONED FISH STOCK

1 TABLESPOON THINLY SLICED GINGERROOT

1/4 CUP THINLY SLICED FRESH LEMONGRASS

3 TABLESPOONS FRESHLY SQUEEZED LIME JUICE

1 TABLESPOON LOW-SODIUM SOY SAUCE

2 TABLESPOONS LIGHT OLIVE OIL

1/4 TEASPOON TOASTED SESAME OIL

2 TABLESPOONS CILANTRO LEAVES

12 FRESH MINT LEAVES

2 TEASPOONS ARROWROOT MIXED WITH 4 TEASPOONS RESERVED VINAIGRETTE (SLURRY)

Raw Vegetable Garnish

1 (5- TO 6-INCH) PIECE GINGERROOT, SLICED LENGTHWISE INTO 4 FLAT PIECES

2 GREEN ONIONS, SLICED LENGTHWISE INTO PAPER-THIN PIECES

1 RED BELL PEPPER, FINELY JULIENNED

1/2 ENGLISH CUCUMBER, JULIENNED

1 CARROT, JULIENNED

MINT LEAVES, THINLY SLICED

1. To make the sea bass and tea smoke, rinse and pat the fish fillets dry with a paper towel. Cut 3 sheets of heavy-duty aluminum foil into 15-inch squares. Roll the edges under to form a circle that fits in the bottom of a Dutch oven. (The pot should not be made of a light alloy or alloy bonded to other metals. Cast iron and cast aluminum both work fine.) You should have an aluminum foil saucer approximately 5 inches in diameter. When the edge is rolled to about 1 inch high, stop and flatten the foil. Depress the center to hold the smoke ingredients.

2. Sprinkle the rice, cloves, and contents of tea bags in the depression of the aluminum foil saucer. Place saucer in bottom of Dutch oven, cover pan tightly, and cook over high heat until ingredients in the foil start smoking, about 5 minutes.

3. Brush a long-legged steamer basket with the olive and sesame oils. Place the sea bass on the steamer platform and set in the Dutch oven over the smoke ingredients. Cover and continue smoking over high heat until cooked through, about 8 minutes. Remove from heat and let cool.

4. To make the couscous, pour the olive oil and sesame oil into a medium saucepan over medium heat and fry the lemongrass, gingerroot, green onion, and lime zest for 2 minutes. Add the stock and bring to a boil. Decrease heat and simmer for 10 minutes to allow for infusion and reduction. Strain into a large measuring cup. You should have 3 cups of liquid. Reserve 1 cup for the vinaigrette. Pour remaining 2 cups back into the saucepan and return to a boil. Stir in the salt and couscous, cover, remove from heat, and let stand for 5 minutes.

5. To make the vinaigrette, in a medium saucepan, combine reserved stock, gingerroot, and lemongrass and boil until reduced to $1/2$ cup, about 10 minutes. Strain into the jar of a blender. Add lime juice, soy sauce, olive oil, sesame oil, cilantro, and mint leaves and blend for 2 minutes to emulsify. Reserve $1^1/2$ tablespoons. Pour remainder into a small saucepan and bring to a boil. Remove from heat, stir in arrowroot slurry, return to heat, and bring to a boil to thicken and clear, about 30 seconds.

6. To serve, place a mound of couscous on each plate and place a smoked fillet on top of couscous. Arrange the raw vegetables, reserving mint, around the plate. Ladle vinaigrette on top of the sea bass and garnish with slivers of mint.

SERVES 4

Grilled Chilean Sea Bass with Citrus-Anaheim Salsa

———— ❧ ————

QUEEN CITY GRILL, SEATTLE, WASHINGTON

The Queen City Grill is a favorite hangout in the hip Belltown section of downtown Seattle. The restaurant is known for its perfectly grilled meats and seafood, grilled portobello mushroom salad, and bustling bar. Chef Paul Michael, the steady hand behind this lively ship, likes to let food stand on its own with simple but respectful treatment featuring lots of fresh herbs, marinades, and grilling. The Louisiana-born chef doesn't completely forgo his roots however. Chicken "wild rice" gumbo, a mixed grill with andouille, and crab cakes with roasted pepper and garlic aïoli are Queen City Grill favorites.

1/2 CUP DRY SHERRY

1/4 CUP OLIVE OIL

1 TABLESPOON TOASTED SESAME OIL

1/4 CUP RICE VINEGAR

1/4 CUP SOY SAUCE

1 TABLESPOON CHOPPED GARLIC

1 TABLESPOON CHOPPED GINGERROOT

1 1/2 POUNDS CHILEAN SEA BASS FILLETS, RINSED, DRAINED, PATTED DRY, AND CUT INTO 4 (6-OUNCE) PIECES

LEMON WEDGES, FOR GARNISH

CITRUS-ANAHEIM SALSA (RECIPE FOLLOWS)

1. In a nonreactive baking dish large enough to hold fish in one layer without crowding, mix together sherry, olive oil, toasted sesame oil, rice vinegar, soy sauce, garlic, and gingerroot. Add sea bass and turn to coat both sides thoroughly with marinade. Cover, place in refrigerator, and marinate 30 minutes.

2. Ten minutes before cooking, preheat grill or broiler. If broiling, take out a baking sheet and oil lightly or spray with nonstick cooking spray. Place fish fillets on baking sheet and position under broiler 3 to 4 inches from heat source. If grilling, spray grill with nonstick cooking spray, then place fish fillets on grill. Grill or broil 10 minutes per inch of thickness of fish, about 3 to 5 minutes per side, turning once.

3. Divide fish and lemon wedges among individual plates and top fillets with salsa.

SERVES 4

Citrus-Anaheim Salsa

1 CUP CHOPPED TOMATOES

3 GREEN ONIONS, CHOPPED

1/4 CUP CHOPPED CILANTRO

1 CLOVE GARLIC, PRESSED

1/2 CUP CHOPPED ANAHEIM CHILES, STEMMED, SEEDED, AND DERIBBED

2 TABLESPOONS SHERRY VINEGAR

2 TABLESPOONS FRESHLY SQUEEZED LIME JUICE

1 TABLESPOON OLIVE OIL

In a medium nonreactive mixing bowl, stir together all salsa ingredients. Cover and refrigerate at least 1 hour, or preferably overnight, to allow flavors to blend.

MAKES 1 CUP

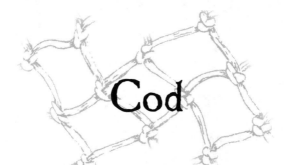

Cod

OD HAS BEEN an important source of food in this country since the early days in New England. Cod is the most widely consumed finfish in the United States, with 400 million pounds of cod eaten every year. It is a very versatile, lean fish—characteristics that have earned it a reputation as the workhorse of the seafood menu.

The cod family includes many common American white-meat fish, such as Atlantic cod, haddock, hake, and scrod on the East Coast and Pacific cod and Alaska pollock on the West Coast. Although they are called cod, lingcod (see page 70), rock cod (see page 82), and black cod, also known as sablefish (see page 89), are not members of the cod family.

Pacific Cod (*Gadus macrocephalus*), also known as true cod, Alaska cod, or gray cod,

Pacific Cod

ranges from California to northern Alaska. Similar to the Atlantic cod in anatomy, appearance, and cooking characteristics, it is a lightweight version of its East Coast cousin,

averaging 20 inches long and weighing 5 to 10 pounds. The Pacific cod is brown to light gray and its back and sides are covered with brown spots. The fish has a distinctive chin barbel that is about as long as the diameter of its eye.

The flesh is snowy white, lean, tender, firm, flaky, and mild-flavored, though not as sweet as the Atlantic variety. It has a natural affinity for herbs and light sauces. Preferred cooking methods include baking, steaming, poaching, sautéing, braising, frying, and broiling.

Pacific cod is fished year-round and is nearly always sold as skinless, boneless fillets, either fresh, frozen, or thawed and ready to use. If properly wrapped, Pacific cod fillets can be stored in the freezer at 0° for up to 3 months. For optimum quality, store thawed cod in the refrigerator for no more than 1 day.

Alaska Pollock (*Theragra chalcogramma*) is one of the most abundant whitefish in the market. As of the late 1980s, the commercial fishery for pollock was the largest single-species fishery in the world. More widely distributed than the Pacific cod, it is also known as walleye pollock, Pacific pollock, or bigeye pollock, and ranges from central California to northern Alaska. Generally weighing less than 2 pounds, it is distinguished from the Atlantic pollock, which is darker, oilier, and has a stronger flavor.

Alaska pollock has white, lean meat. In the past, was often ground into fish meal or used to feed minks. Today, because of newfound uses for the fish, the pollock fishery has expanded. Part of the fishery, which is centered in the Bering Sea, targets the species only for its roe, *tarako*, which is popular among the Japanese. A second part of the catch is made into *surimi* (fish paste) and later processed into

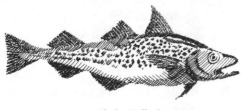

Alaska Pollock

surimi seafood (see page 182). The remaining portion of the pollock catch is cut and processed to make frozen fish fillets and fish sticks.

Skinless, boneless fillets are available year-round. Fillets cook more quickly than other cuts and also have a more distinctive flavor. They are best suited to baking, sautéing, poaching, deep-frying, and simmering. Alaska pollock fillets may be stored in the home freezer at 0° or lower for up to 3 months. For optimum quality, use the thawed fish within 1 day.

(see page 182)

FUN FACTS

- The largest Pacific cod is recorded at 50 pounds and 46 inches. Some may live as long as 13 years. Females produce as many as 3,350,000 eggs each time they spawn.

- The Alaska pollock can grow to 3 feet in length and live at least 14 years.

- It is estimated that 1 out of every 3 fish fillets and steaks eaten in the United States is cut from codfish.

- McDonald's sells more than 100 million Filet-O'-Fish sandwiches a year and recently switched from using Atlantic cod to Alaska pollock because it cost less and most customers couldn't tell the difference between the two fish. Among seafood fast-food restaurants, Alaska pollock and New Zealand hoki have surpassed Atlantic cod as the choices for deep-frying.

Cod Roll-Ups with Sorrel Pesto

—⚬—

IVACCO FOODS,
PIKE PLACE MARKET

Paupiettes, roll-ups, roulades, and turbans are all fancy names for thin slices of meat or fish that are seasoned or stuffed, rolled jelly-roll fashion, then fried, baked, or braised in wine or stock. In this inspired rendition of roll-ups, Ann Magnano, former owner of Ivacco Foods, a health food store in the Market, uses fresh sorrel rather than the traditional basil to make a pesto stuffing for cod fillets. The fillets are then gently simmered in a mixture of white wine, butter, and olive oil. Lightly steamed baby zucchini and yellow squash, along with lots of good, crusty bread to sop up the savory juices, make pleasing accompaniments.

6 TABLESPOONS EXTRA VIRGIN OLIVE OIL

2 BUNCHES FRESH SORREL OR BASIL
   LEAVES, STEMS REMOVED (ABOUT 4 CUPS
   FIRMLY PACKED LEAVES)

4 SPRIGS FLAT-LEAF PARSLEY, STEMS RE-
   MOVED AND DISCARDED, LEAVES TORN
   INTO PIECES

2 TABLESPOONS PINE NUTS

2 TABLESPOONS FRESHLY GRATED PARME-
   SAN CHEESE

1/4 TEASPOON SALT

1 1/2 POUNDS COD FILLETS, 1/4 TO 1/2 INCH
   THICK, SKIN AND BONES REMOVED,
   RINSED, DRAINED, PATTED DRY, AND CUT
   INTO 4 (6-OUNCE) FILLETS

1 TABLESPOON BUTTER

1/4 CUP DRY WHITE WINE OR CHICKEN STOCK

1. Place 4 tablespoons of the olive oil (1/4 cup), the sorrel, parsley, pine nuts, and cheese in a food processor or blender and process until the mixture forms a paste. Remove from food processor and set aside.

2. Place cod fillets on a large plate or piece of waxed paper and brush tops with 1 tablespoon of the olive oil. Divide pesto among fillets, spreading evenly over the top of each piece of fish. Starting at the shorter end, roll the fillets loosely, jelly-roll style.

3. Melt the butter and the remaining 1 tablespoon olive oil in a large skillet over medium heat. Place rolled fillets in pan seam side down. Pour white wine around cod rolls, cover pan, and simmer 15 to 20 minutes, or until cod just turns opaque throughout. To test, cut one of the rolls in half to make sure that inside layers are cooked.

4. To serve, transfer roll-ups to individual plates. Stir sauce, then spoon over roll-ups.

SERVES 4

FUN FACT

- The Pacific cod fishing industry is the oldest on the Pacific Coast, dating back to the 1880s when fishing fleets traveled as far as Siberia in their three-masted schooners.

Cod with Miso Sauce

———✠———

Delicately steamed cod comes alive when dressed with an Asian sauce flavored with miso (fermented soybean paste), wasabi (fiery green Japanese horseradish), and black sesame seeds. The sauce tastes rich and creamy, even though it contains only a hint of toasted sesame oil for a powerful punch of flavor. Steamed brown or white rice and stir-fried shredded green cabbage and carrots make a delicious accompaniment.

1 1/2 POUNDS COD FILLETS, SKIN AND
    BONES REMOVED, RINSED, DRAINED,
    PATTED DRY, AND CUT INTO 4 (6-OUNCE)
    FILLETS
1/4 CUP SHIRO (WHITE) MISO
2 TABLESPOONS PLUS 2 TEASPOONS
    UNSEASONED RICE VINEGAR
2 TABLESPOONS MIRIN OR SWEET SHERRY
1 TABLESPOON SUGAR
1 1/2 TEASPOONS WASABI, DISSOLVED IN 1
    TABLESPOON WARM WATER
2 TEASPOONS BLACK SESAME SEEDS
1/4 TEASPOON TOASTED SESAME OIL

1. Prepare a steaming rack large enough to hold cod fillets in one layer. Bring water to a boil no higher than 1 inch below rack and place fish fillets on rack. Cover and steam 10 minutes per inch of thickness or until cod just flakes.

2. While fish is steaming, combine miso, rice vinegar, mirin, sugar, and wasabi mixture in a small saucepan. Place over medium heat and stir until sugar is dissolved, about 2 to 3 minutes. Do not allow mixture to come to a boil. Remove from heat and stir in sesame seeds and toasted sesame oil.

3. When fish is ready, divide the sauce among individual plates, then place fish fillets on top. Serve immediately.

SERVES 4

FUN FACTS

- Atlantic cod, also known as the beef of the Atlantic, is so much a part of the heritage of New England that a huge wood carving of the fish hangs in the Massachusetts House of Representatives. Throughout the history of Colonial America, the cod appeared on coins, stamps, legal documents, corporate seals, and weather vanes.

- Because revenues from cod helped pay for the sea war against England, the Revolutionary War is sometimes called the "cod war."

Alaska Pollock with Sundried Tomato Tapenade

Tapenade is a thick paste traditionally made of capers, anchovies, ripe olives, olive oil, lemon juice, and seasonings. My bright, lemony version offers a bold contrast in color, taste, and texture to mild-flavored, simply broiled pollock. Using a mini-food processor helps cut down on preparation time, although the ingredients can also be minced by hand. Any leftover tapenade can be served with other finfish, vegetables, or chicken.

1 CUP OIL-PACKED SUNDRIED TOMATOES,
    DRAINED AND COARSELY CHOPPED
1/2 CUP PIMIENTO-STUFFED GREEN OLIVES,
    COARSELY CHOPPED
1 TEASPOON CAPERS
1 CLOVE GARLIC, CUT IN HALF
ZEST OF 1 LEMON
JUICE OF 1 LEMON
TABASCO SAUCE
1 1/2 POUNDS ALASKA POLLOCK FILLETS, 1/2
    TO 3/4 INCHES THICK, SKINNED, BONED,
    RINSED, DRAINED, PATTED DRY, AND CUT
    INTO 4 (6-OUNCE) FILLETS
SALT AND FRESHLY GROUND BLACK PEPPER
1 TABLESPOON OLIVE OIL

1. Preheat broiler. Lightly coat a baking sheet with oil or nonstick cooking spray.

2. Place sundried tomatoes, olives, capers, garlic, and lemon zest in a mini-food processor and process until minced, or mince the ingredients by hand. Place minced vegetables and lemon juice in a small nonreactive mixing bowl and stir well. Season to taste with Tabasco, cover, and set aside at room temperature.

3. Sprinkle pollock fillets lightly on both sides with salt and pepper. Place fillets on prepared baking sheet and brush lightly with olive oil. Place fish 3 to 4 inches under broiler. Broil 5 to 7 minutes, depending on thickness of fillets, or just until they turn opaque.

4. When fillets are done, divide among individual plates. Spoon 2 tablespoons of the sundried tomato mixture beside each fillet.

SERVES 4

FUN FACTS

- More Alaska pollock is caught each year than all of the other species of Alaska seafood combined. In 1993 the Alaska pollock catch weighed in at around 3.3 billion pounds. When Alaska pollock are netted and brought on board a fishing boat, the catch is so large it is measured in metric tons.

- In 1995 Alaska pollock maintained its Number Three position among Top Ten seafoods, following canned tuna and fresh shrimp.

Flounder (Sole)

THERE ARE TWO FAMILIES of bottom-dwelling flatfishes. About two hundred recognizable living species make up the large Bothidae family, popularly known as the left-eye flounders. Approximately one hundred known species make up the Pleuronectidae family, or right-eye flounders. About a dozen species from among both families are commercially harvested in the United States; about half a dozen are commercially harvested in Northwest waters.

Common names for flatfish create confusion for fishmongers and consumers alike because there are so many of them, and they are called different names in various parts of the world. For example, the highly prized Dover sole (the best known of the "true soles") is found only in European waters. Dover sole on America's West Coast is a completely different fish that is really a flounder, not a true sole at all. In fact, in the United States, no true sole is commercially caught or sold—all of the fish called "sole" (except for imported European Dover sole) are varieties of flounder. Even within the United States the nomenclature is inconsistent. In the Southeast, flounder is called flounder, while in the Northeast and Northwest, flounder is called sole.

The confusion between sole and flounder came about because sole was, and is, a revered species of fish in Europe. In response to

European immigration to the United States, enterprising fishmongers attached the name "sole" to various species of flounder, its less well-known American cousin, and the incorrect moniker stuck.

To this day the name "sole" is used interchangeably with "flounder" in the United States. Luckily for those of us who cook, American flounders, with their firm white flesh, fine texture, and delicate flavor, are close enough in taste and texture to stand in for European soles in classic recipes. Within the flounder family itself, most species are interchangeable, with only subtle differences in texture and taste.

Dover Sole (*Microstomus pacificus*) is the common name of the flounder found from Baja California to Alaska. Unless it is imported from Europe, this sole is not the famed Dover sole, which is an entirely different species, revered by gourmets.

Dover sole is light to dark brown on the eyed side, gray on the blind side, and ranges in weight from 2 to 10 pounds, although 2½ pounds is average. Dover sole is a major part of the Western U.S. sole landings and the least expensive of Pacific flounders. The entire catch is sold in fillet form because the fish is especially slimy, which accounts for two of its nicknames—slime sole or slippery sole.

While the quality of Dover sole is generally good and the white, flaky meat normally cooks up tender and delicate, it is sometimes inconsistent. According to Dr. Robin Milton Love, "As Dovers age and they move into deeper waters, their body water content increases and they develop what commercial fishermen refer to as a 'jellied' condition. The relatively high water content makes their muscle tissue very flaccid and gelatinous." Upon cooking, this unpleasant gelatinous texture causes the fish to turn mushy in the pan. Since there is no way to tell beforehand if this will happen, it is best to substitute other species of sole or flounder when available. The fish is best suited to steaming, sautéing, frying, and baking. Because they produce long, narrow fillets, Dover sole lend themselves especially well to stuffing and rolling.

English Sole (*Parophrys vetulus*) is a small (15-inch) flounder sometimes known as lemon sole, and is found from Baja California to Alaska. Although generally of good quality, its white, lean meat sometimes has an iodine-like odor. Frying, sautéing, baking, and steaming are the preferred cooking methods.

Petrale Sole (*Eopsetta jordani*) is a large flounder found from Baja California to Alaska. It resembles a small halibut, with gray top skin and white bottom skin. It ranges in weight from 2 to 8 pounds, with 4 the average. The flesh is white with a pale pink stripe running the length of the fillet.

Petrale is larger flaked than most sole, tender and lean. Next to the renowned Pacific halibut, the petrale sole has always rated as the number one flounder in the Northwest because of its thicker flesh and sweeter flavor. It is well suited to poaching, sautéing, baking, broiling, and steaming.

Rex Sole (*Glyptocephalus zachirus*) is a small Pacific flounder found from Baja California to Alaska. Its bright white flesh, fine texture, and sweet, distinctive flavor make it prized among connoisseurs. Because Rex sole are less numerous than other flatfishes, they command a higher price.

Rex sole are generally marketed whole and pan-dressed, because their smaller size makes them too thin to fillet properly. They are best lightly coated with seasoned flour, then sautéed whole. They also can be baked, broiled, or poached.

Pacific Sand Dab (*Citharichthys sordidus*), a miniature but delectable flounder, is found from Baja California to northwestern Alaska. It is brown with orange, yellow, or reddish brown spots on the eyed side. Weighing up to 2 pounds, dabs average $1/2$ to $3/4$ pounds. Despite its very small size, the sand dab's lean

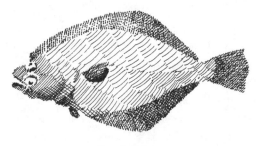

Petrale Sole

white meat is sweet and finely textured. This tasty fish is best prepared by baking, deep-frying, or sautéing whole. Dabs are no less venerated by many Western gourmets than petrale and Rex sole and are caught year-round.

Whether fresh or frozen, the larger species of flounder are almost always found in fillet form. Fillets may be marketed with the skin on, particularly if they're from the preferred white side of the fish. Fillets should be moist and of consistent color throughout, with no dry spots or brown edges. The flesh should be firm and elastic, with a fresh, mild odor. Among the smaller species, whole, dressed fish make frequent appearances at fishmongers' counters.

Purchase $1/4$ to $1/3$ pound skinless fillet per person, and $3/4$ to 1 pound of whole-dressed fish per person. Generally, a whole $1^1/2$- to $1^3/4$-pound fish will serve 2; a whole $2^1/2$- to 3-pound fish will serve 4.

The mild, delicate flavor and fragile texture of flounder and sole are amplified by sauces, herbs, spices, fruits, and vegetables, as well as contrasting seafoods. Recipes that work well with sole and flounder are those that enhance rather than overpower them. The flatfish are often stuffed.

Because sole and flounder are very lean fish, usually containing less than 1 percent fat, the fillets are fragile and tend to break apart during cooking. The best cooking methods require minimal handling of the fish while protecting the thin fillets from drying out. Most traditional cooking methods—pan-frying, deep-frying, baking, broiling, poaching, microwaving, steaming, stuffing, oven-frying, sautéing, or cooking *en papillote* (see page 31) —work well, while grilling and stir-frying are usually too harsh. Nonstick or well-oiled cookware help avoid breakage, too.

Before cooking, pat fillets with paper towels to dry thoroughly. To ensure even cooking, fold thin fillets in half or tuck thin ends under to form an even thickness. Do not over-cook sole and flounder: The fish is cooked when the flesh just begins to change from translucent to opaque or white.

Cooking "on the bone" is reputed to be the absolute best method because the bones impart a fuller flavor to the meat while the skin holds in moisture and flavor. The result is more tender, flavorful sole or flounder.

FUN FACTS

• Paleontologists have determined that flounders have flourished in the world's seas for at least 50 million years, since lower Eocene time. One-million-year-old otoliths (calcified ear bones) from both English sole and Pacific sand dabs have been found in Pliocene deposits in Long Beach, California.

• Dover sole as long as $2^1/2$ feet have been hauled in. Females live at least 53 years and some males live to 58 years.

• Sole was a popular fish among the ancient Romans, who called it *solea Jovi*, or Jupiter's sandal.

Banana Leaf–Baked Chipotle Sole

‒‒⟑⟑‒‒

This dish will transport you to the tropics with its sweet-hot sauce and dramatic presentation in a banana-leaf packet. Canned chipotle peppers in adobo sauce, kaffir lime leaves, and frozen banana leaves are available in the Pike Place Market at El Mercado Latino or most Latin markets (see Note). If banana leaves are unavailable, substitute parchment paper or aluminum foil, although the flavor and texture of the fish may not be as good.

1 TABLESPOON ADOBO RESERVED FROM
   CANNED CHIPOTLE PEPPERS IN ADOBO
1/4 CUP UNSWEETENED PINEAPPLE JUICE
1 TABLESPOON FRESHLY SQUEEZED LIME
   JUICE
1 TEASPOON OLIVE OIL
1 CLOVE GARLIC, MINCED
1 1/2 TEASPOONS MAPLE SYRUP
2 GREEN ONIONS, CUT INTO 1/4-INCH
   ROUNDS
2 TEASPOONS MINCED CILANTRO
4 FROZEN BANANA LEAVES, DEFROSTED
1 1/2 POUNDS DOVER, PETRALE, OR ENGLISH
   SOLE FILLETS, SKIN REMOVED, RINSED,
   DRAINED, AND PATTED DRY
4 KAFFIR LIME LEAVES, OR 1/2 TEASPOON
   MINCED LIME ZEST

1. Preheat oven to 350°.

2. In a small mixing bowl, stir together adobo, pineapple juice, lime juice, olive oil, garlic, maple syrup, green onions, and cilantro. Set aside.

3. Wash banana leaves under cold running water, then dry with paper towels, leaving a bit of moisture on the leaves. Lay leaves out flat and cut into 16 x 8-inch rectangles. Spread out a banana leaf rectangle and place 1/4 of the fish fillets in the center. It may be necessary to trim fillets to form even portions or fold under thinner edges to create an equal thickness of fish. Pour 1/4 of the adobo over top of fish, then place a kaffir lime leaf on fish or sprinkle fish with 1/8 teaspoon minced lime zest.

4. Fold top and bottom flaps of banana leaf over center of fish, overlapping ends, then repeat with side panels. Place banana leaf bundle folded side down on a baking sheet (smooth side facing upward). Repeat procedure with remaining fish fillets and banana leaves.

5. Bake fish 10 to 15 minutes, or until banana leaves turn a dull brown color. To check doneness, undo one bundle and test fish. If more cooking time is needed, refold banana leaf and continue cooking. Remove from oven, place banana leaf–wrapped bundles on individual plates seam side up, and allow everyone to open bundles themselves.

SERVES 4

Note: *Banana leaves* come from cultivated banana trees, which can grow up to 30 feet high. The leaves are so large they are often sold in folded sections. *Chipotle chiles* are dried, smoked jalapeño peppers that are available pickled or canned in adobo. *Kaffir lime leaves* are glossy, dark-green leaves with a sweet limelike aroma. Grown in Southeast Asia and Hawaii, they are available fresh but can be frozen for up to a year.

Sole with Grapes and Champagne

———⊰⊱———

My good friend Cynthia Nims, a La Varenne-trained chef and editor of Simply Seafood *and* Spa *magazines, has been an invaluable help in writing this book and has graciously allowed me to reprint this sole recipe. It is an easy and delectable variation on the French Véronique preparation, which is a dish garnished with seedless white grapes. As Cynthia says, "The delicate, tender flesh of sole is perfect with the refined flavors of the sauce.... True Champagne is by no means a requisite for this recipe; indeed, any domestic sparkling white wine will do."*

1 ½ POUNDS SOLE FILLETS, RINSED,
     DRAINED, AND PATTED DRY
SALT AND FRESHLY GROUND WHITE PEPPER
2 CUPS CHAMPAGNE OR SPARKLING WHITE
     WINE
2 WHOLE STEMS FRESH TARRAGON
½ CUP HEAVY WHIPPING CREAM
¼ POUND SEEDLESS GREEN OR RED
     GRAPES, CUT IN HALF

1. Preheat oven to 350°. Lightly butter a shallow baking dish and a piece of aluminum foil just large enough to cover the dish. Lay sole fillets in the dish, folding thin tail ends under for even thickness. Season to taste with salt and pepper.

2. In a small saucepan, combine Champagne and tarragon stems. Bring the liquid to a boil and simmer for 1 minute. Carefully pour the hot liquid over the sole fillets, cover with the buttered foil, and bake 2 to 5 minutes, or until the fillets flake easily at the thickest part.

3. Using a spatula, carefully remove fillets from the liquid and transfer to paper towels. Cover with aluminum foil to keep fish warm. Pour liquid back into saucepan, add whipping cream, and bring to a boil. Cook 5 minutes, or until sauce turns pale gold in color and thickens slightly. Discard tarragon stems, stir in grapes, taste and adjust seasoning.

4. Arrange sole fillets on individual plates, spoon sauce over fish, and serve immediately.

SERVES 4

FUN FACT

- By the end of the eighteenth century, the demand for sole was so great that wholesalers hired carriages hitched to speedy horse teams to rush the fish from the English port of Dover, where it was caught, to market in London, where it was sold. Thus, Dover sole came to mean the freshest fish of the highest quality.

Halibut

THE HALIBUT IS RELATED TO soles, sand dabs, and other flatfish and shares many common characteristics, such as eyes on top of its head, mottled greenish to dark brown or gray skin on its top side, and snow-white skin on its underbelly. However, the *Hippoglossus*, or "hippo of the sea", claims one distinct feature—it far outweighs its relatives. Halibut are the largest of all flatfish and are among the larger species of fish in the sea. The biggest specimens in the Atlantic and Pacific have been rumored to weigh 700 pounds and stretch over 9 feet in length, although these reports have not been thoroughly documented and may be entertaining folk tales.

The two main species of true halibut are the Atlantic halibut and the Pacific halibut, with the Pacific vastly more plentiful. Nearly all Pacific halibut are caught in the North Pacific, with over 90 percent coming from Alaska. Halibut meat, whether Atlantic, Pacific, or California, is pure white, with a dense texture and firm flake; its heavy texture makes it more versatile in the kitchen than its relative the flounder. Its meat is also more flavorful and distinctive tasting than other flatfish and a bit on the sweet side. Like all flatfishes, halibut is low in fat.

In 1995 the Alaska halibut fishery changed to an individual quota system, which allows fishers to catch their quotas on a more flexible schedule rather than in only four 24-hour openings per year. As a result, fishing boats go out from March through November and fresh halibut is available almost year-round. Most halibut are hook-caught, and bled, cleaned, and iced within minutes of being landed, which assures the highest quality fish.

Pacific Halibut (*Hippoglossus stenolepis*) is a right-eyed flounder found in cold waters from central California to the Bering Sea and north to Japan. It is brown to black on the eyed side, with a slightly indented tail. Market sizes run from 10 to 200 pounds.

Considered one of the finest of Northwest seafoods, it cooks up white, tender, and large-flaked. The lean white meat has a delicate flavor and appears as steaks, fillets, or (more rarely) as cheeks, a gourmet specialty. Pacific halibut is best poached, steamed, baked, fried, grilled, and sautéed.

California Halibut (*Paralichthys californicus*) is found from Baja California to Washington and is similar in shape to the Pacific halibut. The fish measures 2 to 5 feet long and is usually caught at weights between 4 and 12 pounds. They are usually brown or blackish with various blotches on the eyed side, which can be either the right or left side of the head. Unlike other Pacific flatfish, the California halibut has small, sharp teeth.

The California halibut is sold mainly as fresh boneless fillets rather than as steaks unless the fish is exceptionally large. The meat is somewhat comparable to Atlantic or Pacific halibut but less choice. California halibut is best suited to steaming, poaching, baking, and frying.

Halibut flesh should be glossy white and translucent, with a moist surface. While fresh is best, frozen halibut is a good alternative if it has been properly frozen at sea and carefully

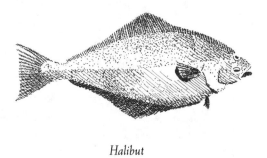

Halibut

thawed. Frozen halibut should have the same translucent look of fresh halibut. Signs of poor handling include flesh with a milky, opaque white color, blotches, or a yellowish tinge.

Fresh halibut is available from spring through fall, and frozen halibut (generally a very suitable alternative) is available year-round.

Halibut meat is firm, lean, and white. It has a sweet, delicate taste and is suitable for a variety of preparations and any number of sauces, from a mild herb butter or a rich cream to a hot and spicy marinade. Although it has a distinctive flavor, halibut is still mild enough to adapt to a wide variety of flavor combinations.

Because its firm flesh holds together well, halibut may be prepared using all cooking methods. It can be baked, grilled, sautéed, poached, broiled, microwaved, fried, barbecued, steamed, and stir-fried. It also keeps its firm texture in soups and chowders. Marinating before cooking enhances its mild flavor.

Previously frozen halibut becomes overcooked more quickly than fresh and should be removed from the heat before you might normally think it is done. When grilling thicker halibut cuts (those exceeding 1 inch in thickness), place halibut over medium coals or indirect heat and baste frequently, turning once. When broiling, add $1/8$ inch of water to the pan and turn the fish when half-cooked to help keep it moist.

Cook halibut steaks with the bones left in. Along with the skin, the bones tend to add flavor and moisture to the flesh and hold the fish together while it cooks. Plus, the large bones are easier to remove after cooking.

When purchasing halibut fillets, allow 4 to 6 ounces per serving; for steaks, allow 6 to 8 ounces per serving.

Fresh or frozen and defrosted halibut keeps in the refrigerator for 1 to 3 days. Properly packaged halibut will keep in the home freezer for up to 3 months, although its quality is best if used within 2 months. Thaw frozen halibut in the refrigerator 8 to 10 hours, or thaw overnight in a covered container. Halibut can also be thawed in a microwave oven according to manufacturer's instructions for thawing fish.

Hot Honeyed Halibut

MECH APIARIES, PIKE PLACE MARKET

The inspiration for this recipe comes from Doris Mech's delightful book, Joy With Honey. *It's an easy, quick, healthy recipe in which the special ingredient, honey, coats snow-white halibut fillets with a gorgeous golden glaze. Doris and her husband, Don, are beekeepers in Maple Valley, Washington, where they founded Mech Apiaries in 1973. Doris, who brings some of the finest honeys in the state to the North Arcade of the Market on Saturdays throughout the year, suggests using maple blossom honey for this recipe.*

2 TABLESPOONS HONEY

1/2 TEASPOON TABASCO SAUCE

2 TABLESPOONS LOW-SODIUM SOY SAUCE

1 TABLESPOON FRESHLY SQUEEZED LEMON JUICE

1 TABLESPOON VEGETABLE OR CANOLA OIL

1 1/2 POUNDS HALIBUT FILLET, BONES REMOVED, RINSED, DRAINED, PATTED DRY, AND CUT INTO 4 (6-OUNCE) PIECES

1. In a small bowl, stir together honey, Tabasco, soy sauce, and lemon juice. Reserve for later use.

2. Heat oil in a large skillet over medium-high heat. Add halibut fillets flesh side down (skin side up) and cook 3 to 5 minutes. Turn and cook 3 to 5 minutes more, or about 10 minutes per inch of thickness. During last 2 minutes of cooking, drizzle reserved honey mixture evenly over fillets.

3. When fillets just turn opaque, divide among individual plates and serve immediately.

SERVES 4

HANDY HALIBUT TIP

Diane Zell, specialty food broker and a Market resident, suggests this easy tip for outstanding broiled halibut: Simply blend key lime juice and softened butter for a terrific fish topping. Brush halibut fillets or steaks with the key lime butter several times while cooking. Key limes are available at El Mercado Latino in the Market, where owner Lulu Babas says that appearances may be deceiving; even when the limes turn brown, they are still very juicy.

Halibut Soup
(Aïgo Boulido)

―❧―

PIROSMANI,
SEATTLE, WASHINGTON

Laura Dewell is head chef and co-owner of Piros-mani, a sophisticated restaurant that highlights the cuisines from the Republic of Georgia (in the former Soviet Union) and the Mediterranean. Chef Dewell explains aïgo boulido *(boiled water) is one of the oldest culinary traditions from the region of Provence in southwestern France. The original recipe calls for nothing more than garlic and herbs boiled in water, with an egg yolk beaten in for thickening, all served over slices of bread sprinkled with olive oil. Chef Dewell's incarnation features a garlic-infused broth served in shallow bowls along with poached fish, veg-etables, and a drizzle of walnut oil.*

3 CUPS FISH BROTH (RECIPE FOLLOWS)

1 ½ POUNDS HALIBUT FILLETS, SKIN AND
    BONES REMOVED, RINSED, DRAINED,
    PATTED DRY, AND CUT INTO 4 (6-OUNCE)
    PIECES

SALT AND FRESHLY GROUND WHITE PEPPER

2 CARROTS, CUT INTO 1 ½-INCH LENGTHS
    AND JULIENNED

ASSORTED SEASONAL VEGETABLES, SUCH
    AS 8 ASPARAGUS TIPS, 1 BELL PEPPER
    (THINLY SLICED), 1 LARGE PARSNIP
    (CUT INTO ⅛-INCH ROUNDS), AND/OR
    ½ BULB FENNEL (JULIENNED)

2 GREEN ONIONS, THINLY SLICED

⅓ POUND WILD MUSHROOMS (SUCH AS
    CHANTERELLES OR PORTOBELLOS),
    THINLY SLICED

½ POUND FRESH MIXED GREENS (SUCH AS
    CURLY ENDIVE, FRISÉE, AND/OR
    ARUGULA), WASHED, DRIED, AND TORN
    INTO BITE-SIZED PIECES

1 TABLESPOON WALNUT OIL

1. In a saucepan or deep skillet that will hold all of the fish in a single layer, add fish broth, cover, and bring to a boil. Decrease heat to medium-low so stock just simmers. Sprinkle fish fillets lightly with salt and pepper. Add to simmering stock, cover, and cook 3 to 5 minutes, or until fish is partially cooked.

2. Uncover saucepan and add carrots, seasonal vegetables, green onions, and wild mushrooms. Cover and cook 2 to 3 minutes more, or until fish is just opaque. Remove saucepan from heat and add greens, stirring gently just to wilt.

3. Divide broth, vegetables, and fish among soup bowls. Drizzle each with ¾ teaspoon wal-nut oil.

SERVES 4

Fish Broth

2 BAY LEAVES

2 WHOLE CLOVES

LARGE PINCH OF SAFFRON THREADS

4 CUPS SEAFOOD STOCK (SEE PAGE 318)

PINCH OF SALT

PINCH OF FRESHLY GROUND WHITE PEPPER

2 TABLESPOONS WALNUT OIL

3 CLOVES GARLIC, MINCED

4 SHALLOTS, THINLY SLICED

FRESHLY SQUEEZED LEMON JUICE TO TASTE

1. In a large saucepan, bring bay leaves, cloves, saffron, stock, salt, and white pepper to a simmer. Cover and cook 20 minutes.

2. Toward the end of cooking time, heat walnut oil in a large saucepan over medium-high heat. Add garlic and shallots and cook 3 to 5 minutes, or until shallots are tender, stirring occasionally. Do not allow to brown.

3. When stock has finished cooking, strain through a fine-meshed sieve and add to sautéed garlic and shallots. Stir well, then season to taste with lemon juice and additional salt and white pepper.

4. If using immediately, proceed with recipe. If using later, let stock cool, then refrigerate for up to 2 days (which yields a richer stock as the flavors meld). Alternately, the stock can be frozen until ready to use.

MAKES 4 CUPS

FUN FACTS

- Halibut is one of the oldest commercial fisheries on the West Coast, dating back to 1888, when three sailing schooners rounded Cape Horn from New England and began fishing off Cape Flattery on the Washington coast. The catch was then shipped from Tacoma to Boston on the newly completed transcontinental railroad. Big companies took over, the fleet expanded, and eventually the fishery moved to Alaska.

- Fishers with names such as Rotten Robert, Long and Narrow, and Blood Poison Bill searched for halibut in schooners, which carried up to twelve dories, each of which was operated by two men. They were paid by the number of halibut they caught, exchanging the fish tongues for their pay at the end of the day.

- The commercial halibut fishery was pioneered by fishers of Norwegian ancestry. Many of the original immigrants had fished halibut in Norway and came to North America in the late 1880s intent on earning their living in the Pacific halibut fishery. Once established, relatives followed, and many second-, third-, and fourth-generation Norwegians work in the Pacific halibut industry to this day.

Pepper-Glazed Halibut Cheeks

———✥———

Halibut cheeks are considered a delicacy by West Coast gourmets because of the fish's crablike taste and consistency. This easy yet exotic recipe uses Asian spices to subtly enhance the natural flavor and texture of this rare, expensive cut of fish. Serve with steamed brown rice and sautéed baby bok choy.

1 TABLESPOON BUTTER

¼ CUP MAPLE SYRUP

2 TABLESPOONS LOW-SODIUM SOY SAUCE, OR 1 TABLESPOON REGULAR SOY SAUCE PLUS 1 TABLESPOON WATER

¼ TEASPOON FIVE-SPICE POWDER

1 ½ POUNDS HALIBUT CHEEKS, RINSED, DRAINED, AND PATTED DRY

2 TABLESPOONS SZECHWAN PEPPERCORNS, TOASTED AND FINELY GROUND IN A SPICE MILL OR ELECTRIC COFFEE GRINDER (SEE PAGE 34)

1. Preheat broiler. Lightly coat a baking sheet with oil or nonstick cooking spray.

2. In a small saucepan, melt butter over medium heat. Add maple syrup, soy sauce, and five-spice powder and stir well. Bring to a boil and stir occasionally until glaze thickens. Remove from heat.

3. Place fish fillets on baking sheet and brush lightly with glaze. Place fish 3 to 4 inches under broiler. Broil 2 minutes, then remove from oven and brush lightly with glaze. Broil 2 minutes more, then brush lightly with glaze. Broil 2 to 3 minutes more, depending on thickness of cheeks, which should just turn opaque when done.

4. Remove fish from broiler and sprinkle heavily with the ground Szechwan peppercorns. Divide fish among individual plates.

SERVES 4

HALIBUT CHEEKS

Here's a quick-and-easy recipe for halibut cheeks suggested by Scott Mallard, former fishmonger at Pure Food Fish: Preheat oven to 375°. Butter the bottom of a 10 x 8-inch baking dish and cover with an even layer of spinach leaves. Splash with white wine and place 1 pound of halibut cheeks evenly over spinach leaves. Cover halibut with a second layer of spinach leaves so halibut is completely covered. Bake 8 to 12 minutes, depending on thickness of cheeks. Discard spinach leaves and serve halibut cheeks with wild rice or baked potatoes and steamed asparagus.

Poached Halibut with Spicy Mashed Potatoes

———✦———

Mashed potatoes have become all the rage in upscale restaurants across the country, with each chef serving his or her variation of this simple, rustic food. I add Asian elements to my rendition and like to top a heaping mound of my spicy potatoes with a tender poached halibut fillet.

1 POUND BAKING POTATOES, PEELED AND
    CUT INTO 1 ¹/₂-INCH CHUNKS

2 CLOVES GARLIC, PEELED AND CUT IN
    HALF, PLUS 2 CLOVES GARLIC, PEELED
    AND CRUSHED

1 TEASPOON TOASTED SESAME OIL

¹/₄ TEASPOON THAI RED CURRY PASTE

¹/₂ CUP FAT-FREE, ¹/₃-LESS-SODIUM
    CHICKEN STOCK (SEE NOTE)

2 TEASPOONS SOY SAUCE

1 CUP WATER

1 CUP WHITE WINE

1 ¹/₂ POUNDS HALIBUT FILLETS, SKIN AND
    BONES REMOVED, RINSED, DRAINED,
    PATTED DRY, AND CUT INTO 4 (6-OUNCE)
    PIECES

STEAMED BRUSSELS SPROUTS, BROCCOLI
    FLORETS, OR ¹/₄-INCH-THICK CARROT
    COINS (OPTIONAL)

1. To make mashed potatoes, place potatoes and the 2 cloves peeled and halved garlic in a saucepan and cover with several inches of water. Bring to a boil and cook 15 to 20 minutes, or until potatoes are tender. Drain well, then put potatoes and garlic through a ricer, or mash with a fork.

2. In a small bowl, mix toasted sesame oil, red curry paste, chicken stock, and soy sauce until smooth. Add to potatoes, mix well, cover, and keep warm.

3. To poach fish, bring water, wine, and crushed garlic to a boil in a skillet large enough to hold fillets without crowding them. Remove pan from heat, add halibut fillets, return pan to heat, reduce heat to low, partially cover (set lid slightly askew so that steam can escape), and simmer 5 to 10 minutes, or until fish just turns opaque. Do not allow water to boil. Remove fish fillets and place on several layers of paper towels to drain well.

4. To serve, place a mound of mashed potatoes in the center of individual plates and place a halibut fillet in the center. If desired, arrange steamed vegetables in a circle around mashed potatoes.

SERVES 4

Note: If fat-free, ¹/₃-less-sodium chicken stock is unavailable, substitute defatted chicken stock and omit the 2 teaspoons soy sauce.

HANDY HALIBUT TIP

Sue Gilbert Mooers, communications specialist with the Pike Place Market Preservation and Development Authority, recommends making this easy recipe for halibut cheeks after a busy workday: Simply dip the cheeks (after rinsing and patting dry) in beaten egg, then in bread crumbs, then fry in olive oil.

Plank-Roasted Halibut with Sour Cream Sauce

⚓

PALISADE RESTAURANT, SEATTLE, WASHINGTON

Planking, or oven-roasting foods directly over a plank of aromatic fresh wood, has become one of my favorite cooking techniques since I took a class from senior executive chef John Howie III, the man behind the cedar planks at the exotic Palisade Restaurant, located in the Elliott Bay Marina. In his Cedar Plank Cookbook, *chef Howie shares fifteen recipes, from appetizers to desserts (and lots of wonderful seafood, naturally), that are cooked using the planking technique. You will need two cedar planks to prepare this dish for four people; one plank for two. The planks and cookbook are available at the restaurant or by mail order (see page 329).*

1 1/2 POUNDS HALIBUT FILLET, 3/4-INCH THICK, SKIN AND BONES REMOVED, CUT INTO 4 (3 X 5- TO 6-INCH) PIECES

2 TEASPOONS DILL DRY RUB (RECIPE FOLLOWS)

1/2 ENGLISH CUCUMBER, SLICED PAPER-THIN

1 CUP SOUR CREAM SAUCE (RECIPE FOLLOWS)

FRESH DILL SPRIGS, FOR GARNISH

LEMON WEDGES, FOR GARNISH

1. Sprinkle each halibut fillet with 1/2 teaspoon of the Dill Dry Rub. Cover and refrigerate at least 1 hour.

2. Ten minutes before cooking, arrange oven racks in top and center positions and preheat oven to 375°. If using the plank for the first time, pour 1 tablespoon of olive or canola oil in the center of it and, using a paper towel, wipe oil on top and bottom surfaces until evenly distributed. If plank is already seasoned, decrease oil to 1 to 2 teaspoons and rub only in center depression. Place 2 of the halibut fillets side by side on the plank. Arrange cucumbers on tops of fillets, overlapping from front to back to resemble fish scales. Repeat with remaining halibut fillets and cucumber slices.

3. When oven is hot, place planks on top and center oven racks. Cook halibut for 10 to 15 minutes, or until just opaque and fish reaches an internal temperature of 120° to 130°.

4. To serve, transfer halibut fillets to individual plates and pour Sour Cream Sauce over fillets. Garnish with fresh dill and lemon wedges. Serve immediately.

SERVES 4

Dill Dry Rub

5 TABLESPOONS DRIED DILL

2 TABLESPOONS KOSHER SALT

1 1/2 TEASPOONS DRIED TARRAGON

1 TEASPOON FRESHLY GROUND WHITE PEPPER

1/2 TEASPOON GROUND SWEET PAPRIKA

Place all of the ingredients in an electric coffee grinder or spice mill and process until mixture forms a fine powder. Remove dry rub from grinder and reserve.

Sour Cream Sauce

2 TABLESPOONS BUTTER

¼ CUP MINCED RED ONION

¼ CUP DRY WHITE WINE

3 TABLESPOONS VEGETABLE STOCK, FISH
STOCK, OR CLAM JUICE

PINCH OF FRESHLY GROUND WHITE PEPPER

⅛ TEASPOON DRIED DILL

½ CUP LOWFAT OR REGULAR SOUR CREAM

1. In a small saucepan, melt butter over medium heat. Add onion and cook 3 to 5 minutes, or until translucent. Increase heat to medium-high, add wine, and stir. Decrease heat to medium, add stock, pepper, and dill, and reduce to ½ cup.

2. Remove pan from heat and add sour cream, stirring continuously. Return to low heat and stir until heated through. Reserve over very low heat until ready to serve.

MAKES 1 CUP

FUN FACTS

- A "chicken" is a halibut weighing under 20 pounds. A "whale" is anything over 100 pounds. Most fall into the 40- to 60-pound range, and are called "mediums," although 200-pounders are fairly common. Occasional "monster" halibut of 400 pounds or heavier are landed. The maximum recorded size was 105 inches (almost 9 feet) and 495 pounds. Only the females reach the larger sizes because they live longer than males.

- The age of a halibut is determined from the otolith, a stone-like tissue in the inner ear that serves as a balancing organ. The otoliths grow as the fish grows, so that the size of halibut can be estimated from the otolith's length or weight. Each year, alternating opaque (summer) and translucent (winter) rings are deposited on the otolith. These annual growth rings are counted to determine the age of the fish. The oldest age recorded for a halibut is 42 years for females and 27 years for males. Most halibut in North America are 8 to 15 years old.

Lingcod

VEN THOUGH IT IS found from Baja California to Alaska, Lingcod (*Ophiodon elongatus*) is most commonly commercially fished in Washington, Alaska, and British Columbia. Neither a ling nor a cod, the lingcod is a member of the greenling Hexagrammidae family. This small family of fishes contains only thirteen known living species, of which the lingcod is the largest.

The lingcod's slender body can grow to 5 feet and 50 or 60 pounds in weight, although 5 to 40 pounds is average. With a mottled brownish black to bluish green body, a large protruding mouth filled with caninelike teeth, double nostrils, and a long, moderately notched dorsal fin, the fish has a fierce appearance.

The flesh of the lingcod, although usually white in color, sometimes has a greenish cast, particularly in younger fish. No matter what the color is to begin with, the flesh turns bright white when cooked, with a mild taste, large flakes, and a firm texture.

Lingcod is available either fresh or frozen whole, or as fillets and steaks. It is also sometimes available hot-smoked or "kippered." It may be prepared in almost any manner, including poaching, steaming, baking, deep-frying, sautéing, broiling, or grilling. Chunks of lingcod are a good addition to soups and stews because of their firm texture, and whole lingcod can be stuffed and baked.

Because of its relatively dense flesh, lingcod may take a bit longer to cook than other lean fish. For best results, check it carefully throughout the cooking process. The fish is available year-round, although as with many other bottomfish, winter season is the best.

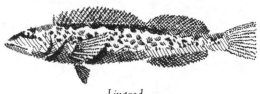

Lingcod

FUN FACT

- The largest recorded size for a lingcod is 60 inches and 100 pounds.

Lingcod with Gremolata Braised Vegetables

—◆—

Lingcod, like all bottomfish, is at its peak quality and least expensive during the winter months. The mild-flavored fish really comes alive when braised over winter harvest vegetables that have been seasoned with the sprightly essence of gremolata. A mixture of garlic, lemon, and parsley, gremolata is traditionally used to season osso buco, or braised veal shanks.

1 TABLESPOON BUTTER

1 TABLESPOON OLIVE OIL

1 RED BELL PEPPER, STEMMED, SEEDED, AND CUT INTO $1/4$-INCH STRIPS

1 LEEK, WHITE PART ONLY, WELL-RINSED TO REMOVE ALL GRIT, AND THINLY SLICED

1 BULB FENNEL, WHITE PART ONLY, QUARTERED AND CUT INTO $1/4$-INCH SLICES

2 CLOVES GARLIC, MINCED

$1/4$ POUND BRUSSELS SPROUTS (ABOUT 5 SPROUTS), STEMS AND OUTER LEAVES REMOVED, RINSED, DRAINED, AND QUARTERED

$1/4$ CUP CHICKEN STOCK OR WATER

$1/2$ TEASPOON FRESHLY GRATED LEMON ZEST

1 TABLESPOON FRESHLY SQUEEZED LEMON JUICE

1 TABLESPOON MINCED FRESH FLAT-LEAF PARSLEY LEAVES

$1/2$ TEASPOON FRESH THYME LEAVES STRIPPED FROM STEMS, OR $1/4$ TEASPOON DRIED THYME, CRUMBLED

$1 1/2$ POUNDS LINGCOD FILLETS, SKIN AND BONES REMOVED, RINSED, DRAINED, PATTED DRY, AND CUT INTO 4 (6-OUNCE) PIECES

SALT AND FRESHLY GROUND BLACK PEPPER TO TASTE

1. Preheat oven to 425°.

2. Over medium-high heat, melt butter and oil in an ovenproof skillet large enough to hold lingcod fillets without crowding. Add bell pepper and cook 2 minutes, stirring occasionally. Add leek, fennel, and garlic and cook 3 minutes, stirring occasionally. Add brussels sprouts, chicken stock, lemon zest, lemon juice, parsley, and thyme, and stir well. Decrease heat to simmer, cover, and cook 10 to 12 minutes, or until vegetables are tender, stirring occasionally. Season to taste with salt and pepper.

3. Lightly sprinkle lingcod fillets on both sides with salt and pepper. Arrange fillets in middle of vegetables, pushing vegetables to side of pan. Bake uncovered 10 to 15 minutes, or until fillets just turn opaque.

4. To serve, mound vegetables in the centers of individual plates and place lingcod fillets atop vegetables.

SERVES 4

Lingcod Nuggets with Hazelnut Crumb Crust

～❧～

Luscious hazelnuts, from Washington and Oregon orchards, elevate chunks of lingcod to new heights in this easy recipe. The hazelnuts from Holmquist Hazelnut Orchard, the largest-producing hazelnut orchard in Washington state, are my favorites for cooking. The DuChilly species, which the Holmquists have cultivated since 1928, is less fatty and sweeter than the conventional round hazelnut, with a shape and taste more like an almond-hazelnut hybrid. Holmquist hazelnuts are available in the North Arcade of the Market, or by mail (see page 330).

2 TABLESPOONS DIJON MUSTARD

2 TABLESPOONS SOY SAUCE

2 TABLESPOONS BUTTER, MELTED

1 TABLESPOON HONEY

1/4 CUP PANKO BREAD CRUMBS OR DRY
    UNSEASONED BREAD CRUMBS
    (SEE PAGE 9)

1/4 CUP FINELY CHOPPED HAZELNUTS

2 TEASPOONS MINCED CILANTRO PLUS
    EXTRA SPRIGS FOR GARNISH

1 1/2 POUNDS LINGCOD FILLETS, SKIN AND
    BONES REMOVED, RINSED, DRAINED,
    PATTED DRY, AND CUT INTO 16 PIECES

SALT AND FRESHLY GROUND BLACK PEPPER
    TO TASTE

3 CUPS COOKED JASMINE OR BASMATI RICE

1. Preheat oven to 450°. Lightly coat a baking sheet with oil or nonstick cooking spray. Set aside.

2. In a small mixing bowl, stir together mustard, soy sauce, butter, and honey. In another small bowl, mix together bread crumbs, hazelnuts, and cilantro.

3. Lightly sprinkle lingcod pieces with salt and pepper. Dip the top of each lingcod nugget in honey-mustard mixture, allow excess to drain off, then dip in hazelnut-crumb mixture. Place nuggets on the baking sheet without crowding.

4. Bake lingcod nuggets for 8 to 12 minutes, or 10 minutes per inch of thickness. Fish should just turn opaque. To test for doneness, cut into the center of one nugget with the tip of a small, sharp knife and pull apart slightly.

5. To serve, divide rice and mound in center of individual plates. Place nuggets in a symmetrical pattern over rice mounds and garnish with cilantro sprigs.

SERVES 4

Note: Panko bread crumbs are a lightly colored, coarsely textured crumb used in Japanese cooking to coat fried foods. They are available in Asian markets and the Asian section of most grocery stores.

Baked Lingcod with Tarragon Pesto

———⚬———

Tarragon is my favorite herb, and pesto is such a popular sauce that I decided to merge the two in this savory topping for sturdy lingcod fillets.

1 ½ POUNDS LINGCOD FILLETS, SKIN AND BONES REMOVED, RINSED, DRAINED, PATTED DRY, AND CUT INTO 4 (6-OUNCE) PIECES

½ CUP LIGHTLY PACKED FRESH TARRAGON LEAVES, MINCED, PLUS EXTRA SPRIGS FOR GARNISH

6 TABLESPOONS FINE, UNSEASONED DRY BREAD CRUMBS (SEE PAGE 9)

3 TABLESPOONS OLIVE OIL

1 ½ TABLESPOONS TARRAGON VINEGAR OR WHITE WINE VINEGAR

2 CLOVES GARLIC, MINCED

¼ TEASPOON SALT

⅛ TEASPOON CRUSHED RED PEPPER FLAKES

LEMON WEDGES, FOR GARNISH

1. Preheat oven to 400°. Lightly coat a baking sheet with oil or nonstick cooking spray. Place fish fillets on baking sheet, skin side down, evenly spaced without crowding. Set aside while preparing pesto.

2. In a small bowl, mix tarragon, bread crumbs, olive oil, vinegar, garlic, salt, and red pepper flakes. Spread evenly over tops of lingcod fillets, pressing down with the back of a spoon to help topping adhere to fish.

3. Place fish in oven and cook 8 to 12 minutes, depending on thickness of fillets, until fish just turns opaque.

4. To serve, divide fillets among individual plates and garnish with lemon wedges and tarragon sprigs.

SERVES 4

FUN FACT

- According to A. J. McClane in *The Encyclopedia of Fish Cookery*, "The lingcod was a favorite food of coastal Indian tribes in British Columbia who caught them with a 'hee-hee.' This device, much like a shuttlecock made of wood and fibers, was pushed toward the bottom with a long three-tined spear. When the spear was suddenly withdrawn the hee-hee spun slowly toward the surface followed by a curious lingcod. When the fish came within range it was easily dispatched."

Marlin

THE MARLIN IS A MEMBER of the family Istiophoridae, along with the sailfish and the spearfish. This common, large fish is found in temperate and tropical waters worldwide. The West Coast species, the **striped marlin** (*Tetrapturus audax*), ranges as far north as Winchester Bay, Oregon, although it is most plentiful from central California southward to Baja California and beyond.

The striped marlin is dark blue on its back and silver on its belly, with 15 to 25 light blue bars or vertical rows of spots on its sides and a very high dorsal fin. Because of its long "spear," or bill, the marlin looks like the swordfish, although the two belong to different families.

The marlin used to be primarily hunted for sport and released by fishers after the catch, but it has recently made an appearance at West Coast fish markets, most likely as a result of the popularity of tuna, swordfish, and shark, which it resembles in taste and texture. The marlin is a full-flavored fish, with very sturdy meat and a circular flake similar to yellowfin or albacore tuna. The flesh of the marlin is pink to pale red when raw and turns white after cooking.

Marlin is available as fresh or frozen boneless, skinless fillets. It is best for baking, broiling, sautéing, smoking, or grilling and lends itself to preparations that include sauces or marinades. When grilling, be sure to marinate the fish first, then baste while cooking so it can absorb more oil. Marlin can substitute for swordfish, tuna, and shark in any recipe, although it cooks a bit differently. Its high-protein, lowfat composition makes it prone to drying out if overcooked even slightly, and it is best when prepared medium-rare (still pink in the middle), lest it resemble home plate. When in doubt, it is better to undercook than overcook marlin and allow the fish to finish cooking off the heat. Follow recipe times precisely and check the fish often while cooking to avoid drying out or toughening it.

FUN FACTS

- Striped marlin reach about 13½ feet in length. Females produce between 11 million and 29 million eggs when they spawn.

- Striped marlin are harvested by long line and gillnet throughout much of the Pacific and Indian oceans. Worldwide, the fish have major commercial value.

Caribbean Marlin with Orange–Black Bean Sauce

—◆—

Since the marlin enjoys tropical waters, I like to marinate it in the flavors of the Caribbean—orange, dark rum, and allspice—for a taste of the islands. And adding black beans to the sauce emphasizes the theme, while complementing the meaty, firm texture of the fish. Long-grain rice cooked in chicken broth and a bit of turmeric to add a warm yellow color makes a good accompaniment, as would a fresh batch of piña coladas or tequila sunrises. (Tiny paper umbrellas are encouraged!)

1 CUP FRESHLY SQUEEZED OR FROZEN
    ORANGE JUICE

1 TEASPOON LOW-SODIUM SOY SAUCE

1/2 TEASPOON GRATED GINGERROOT

1 CLOVE GARLIC, MINCED

1 CANNED CHIPOTLE CHILE IN ADOBO

2 TABLESPOONS DARK RUM

1/4 TEASPOON GROUND ALLSPICE

1 1/2 POUNDS MARLIN FILLETS, RINSED,
    DRAINED, PATTED DRY, AND CUT INTO 4
    (6-OUNCE) PIECES

1 TEASPOON SESAME OIL

2 TEASPOONS CANOLA OIL

1 TABLESPOON PURE MAPLE SYRUP

1/2 CUP CANNED BLACK BEANS, DRAINED,
    RINSED, AND DRAINED AGAIN

2 TABLESPOONS MINCED CILANTRO, FOR
    GARNISH (OPTIONAL)

1. Place 1/2 cup of the orange juice, the soy sauce, gingerroot, garlic, chipotle chile, 1 tablespoon of the dark rum, and the allspice in a food processor or blender and pulse until smooth.

2. Pour marinade into a nonreactive bowl and place fish fillets in marinade, turning to coat both sides. Cover and place in refrigerator 20 minutes to 1 hour.

3. Heat sesame oil and canola oil in a large skillet over medium-high heat. Remove marlin from marinade and pat dry. Reserve marinade. When oil is hot, add marlin and cook 2 minutes, or until fillets are opaque about halfway through. Turn marlin and cook 3 to 5 minutes more, about 7 minutes total per inch of thickness, or until fillets are opaque on the outside but still slightly translucent through the center. Immediately remove skillet from heat, remove marlin fillets from pan, set aside on a large plate, and cover to keep warm. Do not overcook or marlin fillets will become dry and tough.

4. Return skillet to medium-high heat. When pan is hot, add the remaining 1/2 cup orange juice and cook 1 minute, stirring up any bits of fish that have accumulated on bottom of pan. Add 1 tablespoon of the reserved marinade, the remaining 1 tablespoon dark rum, and the maple syrup and stir well. Cook 2 to 3 minutes, or until reduced slightly. Add black beans and stir well. Cook 1 minute, or until black beans are warmed through.

5. Divide marlin fillets among individual plates and spoon sauce and black beans on top of fillets. Sprinkle with cilantro, if desired.

SERVES 4

Marlin à la Sicilienne

I must admit I've had mixed luck with cooking marlin. The first time it was perfectly cooked, but the second and third times, the fish was so tough, I had to resort to a sharp knife to cut through it. Marlin flesh is structured differently than other fish so I knew my problems were caused by a lack of understanding of the fish, not bad fish. Finally my trusty fishmonger advised me to think of marlin like a filet mignon and to cook it the same way—medium-rare in the middle— or similar to the "new" way to cook tuna fillets in which the tuna is seared on the outside but still raw on the inside. I never had trouble cooking marlin again.

1 TABLESPOON OLIVE OIL

1/4 CUP OIL-PACKED SUNDRIED TOMATOES,
    DRAINED AND CHOPPED, PLUS 2
    TABLESPOONS OF THE RESERVED OIL

1 1/2 POUNDS MARLIN FILLETS, RINSED,
    DRAINED, PATTED DRY, AND CUT INTO 4
    (6-OUNCE) PIECES

SALT AND FRESHLY GROUND BLACK PEPPER
    TO TASTE

1 ONION, CUT IN HALF AND JULIENNED

3 CLOVES GARLIC, MINCED

4 PLUM TOMATOES, CORED AND COARSELY
    CHOPPED, OR 1 (14 1/2-OUNCE) CAN
    WHOLE TOMATOES, DRAINED AND
    CHOPPED

1/2 CUP DRY WHITE WINE

1/2 CUP DEFATTED CHICKEN STOCK

2 TABLESPOONS MINCED FRESH BASIL
    PLUS EXTRA LEAVES FOR GARNISH,
    OR 2 TEASPOONS DRIED BASIL

2 TABLESPOONS MINCED FRESH OREGANO,
    OR 2 TEASPOONS DRIED OREGANO

1. In a small mixing bowl, combine olive oil and reserved sundried tomato oil. Lightly brush marlin fillets on both sides with the oil mixture and sprinkle both sides with salt and pepper. Reserve remaining oil mixture.

2. Heat a nonstick skillet large enough to hold marlin fillets without crowding over medium heat. When pan is hot, add reserved oil mixture. When oil is hot, add onion slices and cook 3 to 5 minutes, or until onions are tender-crisp, stirring occasionally. Add garlic and cook 2 minutes more, stirring occasionally. Add plum tomatoes and cook 2 to 3 minutes, or until tomatoes begin to lose their juices, stirring occasionally.

3. Add wine, stock, sundried tomatoes, half of the basil, and half of the oregano. Bring the mixture to a boil, stir well, and cook 5 minutes, or until sauce thickens slightly. Season to taste with salt and freshly ground black pepper.

4. Turn down heat to medium-low, place marlin fillets in skillet, and spoon sauce over top of fillets. Cover and cook 3 minutes, or until fillets are opaque about halfway through. Turn fillets and cook 3 minutes more, or until fillets are opaque on the outside but still slightly translucent through the center. Immediately remove skillet from heat, remove marlin fillets from sauce, and set aside on a large plate. Do not overcook or marlin fillets will become dry and tough.

5. Return skillet to heat and stir the remaining basil and oregano into sauce. Stir well and cook 1 to 2 minutes, or until heated through.

6. To serve, place marlin fillets on individual plates. Divide tomato sauce among the plates, spooning it over tops of fillets. Garnish with basil leaves.

SERVES 4

Monkfish

THE ONLY MEMBER OF THE family Lophiidae, the monkfish (*Lophius americanus*), ranges from Maine to Virginia. Besides the name monkfish, this creature is known by many colorful monikers, including goosefish, sea devil, anglerfish, frogfish, lawyerfish, bellowsfish, devilfish, abbotfish, bullmouth, allmouth, and bellyfish, among others.

Some of the names undoubtedly came about because of the fish's frightful appearance—it has a huge head with beady eyes, a gaping mouth with rows of caninelike teeth, and a long, eellike tail. Its upper body is mottled dark brown or gray-black, with a light underside.

Other names are a result of the monkfish's unique method of catching prey. As the monkfish lies on the bottom of the ocean, long filaments with fleshy tabs resembling bits of food dangle from atop its head over its open mouth. The fish waves these thin antennae like a lure, and captures baitfish, crustaceans, water birds, and just about anything else that wanders into its path, even the occasional ray or shark.

Monkfish weigh from 2 to 50 pounds. Only the tail, which weighs from 1 to 10 pounds, is marketed, with the huge head almost always discarded at sea. The monkfish has long been popular in Europe, where it is known as *lotte* in France, *coda di rospo* in Italy, and *rape* in Spain.

The fish first gained notoriety in the United States thanks to Julia Child's cookbooks and television show. Nonetheless, up until the 1980s, when upscale restaurants in New York City started featuring monkfish on their menus as *lotte*, it was considered a trash fish. Now the public has embraced it and can't get enough of it.

Monkfish play an important part in the fish displays at Pike Place Fish Market, also known as "the home of the low-flying fish." Here, a whole monkfish is displayed over ice, its huge mouth propped open so that row upon row of sharp, triangular teeth are exposed to view. Unbeknownst to the unsuspecting, the monkfish's tail is attached to a string that runs across the tiled floor and behind the fish counter. When curious tourists move in to inspect the ugly monstrosity more closely, the fishmongers pull the string so that the fish leaps up from its bed of ice. Screams ring out and some tourists have been known to run out of the Market! Of course, the locals and the fishmongers love the show.

Those tourists don't know what they're missing, because monkfish is a superior specimen. The two fillets that come from the tail of the fish possess an unusually dense, firm, and meaty texture with a lobsterlike springiness. The nonflaky flesh turns bright white after cooking, with a sweet, delicate taste that has been compared to lobster, thus the nickname "poor man's lobster".

Monkfish is almost always sold as skinless tail pieces or fillets, but a layer of pinkish-purplish tissue covering the white flesh may still remain. Even though edible, this dark membrane (which resembles plastic wrap) must be removed before cooking because it turns an unappealing dark gray and shrinks around the fish, distorting its shape. To remove the membrane, puncture it with the tip of a small, sharp knife. Peel it away, cutting close to the flesh as you pull the membrane away with your fingers and discard.

Once the monkfish has been prepared (the purple membrane cut away), it can be cooked whole or cut on the diagonal into medallions (thick slices), scallops (thin slices), or cubes. To cube monkfish, cut fillets horizontally into slices 1 to 1¼ inches thick, then cut slices into bite-sized cubes. Keep in mind when cutting monkfish fillets or cubes that monkfish shrinks when cooked, so cut the portions or cubes larger than usual to compensate.

Monkfish shrinks and loses quite a bit of moisture as it cooks, so you must buy a greater quantity of fish to begin with. On the bright side, since the fillets are boneless and skinless, there is little waste. Fillets or sliced monkfish weighing 8 to 10 ounces is considered one entrée-sized portion, while 6 to 8 ounces of cubed monkfish for grilling or broiling per serving is adequate.

Monkfish can be cooked in almost any way imaginable—baked, poached, steamed, sautéed, smoked, braised, fried, roasted, broiled, or grilled. Monkfish cubes can be stir-fried with vegetables, skewered for kebabs, featured in soups and stews, and they are a classic addition to bouillabaisse. The flesh of monkfish cooks differently than other fish, however; it must be cooked gently but thoroughly or it will be tough. Monkfish also takes longer to cook than most fish; "medium-rare" monkfish is definitely a no-no. Timing is everything—watch the fish carefully and check it often as it cooks.

Monkfish makes a suitable substitute in some recipes calling for lobster and works well in any dish that calls for scallops or firm, white fish. If monkfish is mixed with lobster or shrimp it will assume their taste, thus stretching seafood dollars.

Monkfish flesh absorbs flavors readily, so you can use many delicious ingredients, such as garlic, tomatoes, fresh herbs, wine, and stocks, to flavor it. Light sauces and marinades also enrich the mild flavor of monkfish.

Monkfish is found in most fish markets year-round.

FUN FACTS

- The monkfish will eat nearly anything, and its appetite is insatiable. Flounders, shark, skates, eels, herrings, cod, and sea bass are only a few of the fishes in its diet. Sea birds (such as cormorants, gulls, and ducks) are part of its regular fare. Lobsters, crabs, squid, and other assorted invertebrates make up a large part of the monkfish's diet and give the fish its lobsterlike taste. Wooden buoys from lobster pots have also been found in the stomachs of monkfish, although it is questionable how much lobster flavor the lobster pots impart to the taste of the fish! There are even documented reports of monkfish grabbing swimmers' feet.

- Monkfish liver is considered a great delicacy in France and Japan.

Baked Monkfish Fillets with Fines Herbes Bread Crust

———⚓———

KASPAR'S,
SEATTLE, WASHINGTON

Since moving to the Northwest in 1989, Swiss-born and trained chef Kaspar Donier has been pairing classical international cooking styles with the freshest Northwest ingredients to great success and acclaim, including four nominations for the James Beard Best American Chef: Northwest award. Since 1994, Chef Donier, his wife Nancy, and brother Markus have presided at Kaspar's on lower Queen Anne hill. In this recipe, Kaspar uses a fines herbes blend (chopped parsley, tarragon, chervil, and chives) with a Northwest twist by substituting fresh chopped dill for the chervil and chives.

2 TABLESPOONS UNSALTED BUTTER,
    SOFTENED
2 POUNDS MONKFISH FILLETS, RINSED,
    DRAINED, PATTED DRY, AND PURPLE
    MEMBRANE REMOVED
1 ¼ TEASPOONS SALT
2 SLICES WHITE BREAD, CRUSTS REMOVED
    AND TORN INTO PIECES
1 CLOVE GARLIC, PEELED AND CUT IN HALF
½ CUP LOOSELY PACKED, COARSELY
    CHOPPED PARSLEY
1 ½ TEASPOONS MINCED FRESH TARRAGON
    LEAVES
2 TABLESPOONS SNIPPED FRESH DILL
1 TABLESPOON OLIVE OIL
1 CUP WHITE DRY VERMOUTH

1. Preheat oven to 425°. Butter the bottom of a baking dish large enough to hold monkfish fillets without crowding. Lightly sprinkle monkfish fillets on both sides with 1/4 teaspoon of the salt. Place monkfish fillets in baking dish and set aside.

2. Place bread, garlic, parsley, tarragon, dill, olive oil, and the remaining 1 teaspoon salt in a food processor or blender and pulse until finely chopped.

3. Sprinkle bread mixture evenly over fillets. Pour vermouth around fillets. Bake fish for 12 to 16 minutes, or until monkfish is opaque throughout.

4. Divide monkfish fillets among individual plates and drizzle a little butter/vermouth broth over each fillet. Serve immediately.

SERVES 4

Note: It is important to use kosher or sea salt in this recipe, as common table salt makes the crumb topping too salty and strong in taste.

FUN FACTS

- The name "monkfish" has a couple of possible roots. During the Middle Ages, European fishers frequently found monkfish in their nets when fishing for cod. As they sorted their catch, they discarded the monkfish to die on the beach. Local townspeople and hungry monks collected the discards, and thus the name "monkfish" came to be. Others say the name comes from the hooded appearance of the monkfish's huge head.

Monkfish in Curried Carrot Broth

In addition to supplying our daily source of vitamin C, juicers are good for other culinary purposes, such as juicing savory vegetables that form the basis for simple broths and sauces. Because they are light and healthy, these sauces and broths work especially well with seafood, as shown in this appetizer recipe, which uses carrot juice as a soup stock. Don't worry if you don't have a juicer; many grocery stores and health food stores carry canned and even freshly squeezed carrot juice nowadays.

2 CUPS FRESH OR CANNED CARROT JUICE

1 TABLESPOON UNSALTED BUTTER

1 ONION, DICED

2 CLOVES GARLIC, MINCED

1 GRANNY SMITH OR GRAVENSTEIN APPLE,
    PEELED AND DICED

1 1/2 TEASPOON CURRY POWDER

2 TABLESPOONS WATER

2 TABLESPOONS HEAVY WHIPPING CREAM

SALT TO TASTE

FRESHLY GROUND WHITE PEPPER TO TASTE

1 1/2 TEASPOONS OLIVE OIL

1 1/2 POUNDS MONKFISH FILLETS, RINSED,
    DRAINED, PATTED DRY, PURPLE
    MEMBRANE REMOVED, AND CUT IN THIN
    SLICES ON A DEEP DIAGONAL INTO
    SCALLOPS

1 TABLESPOON FRESHLY SQUEEZED LIME
    JUICE

2 TABLESPOONS MINCED CILANTRO,
    FOR GARNISH

1. Bring carrot juice to a boil in a medium saucepan and cook 5 minutes. As carrot solids rise to the top of the pan, skim and discard until carrot juice is clear. Remove pan from heat and pour juice through a fine-meshed sieve lined with several layers of dampened cheesecloth. Reserve broth.

2. Heat a large nonstick skillet over medium heat. When pan is hot, melt 1 1/2 teaspoons of the butter in pan. Add onion and garlic and cook 5 minutes, or until onion is tender-crisp, stirring occasionally. Add apple and curry powder and cook 2 minutes, stirring continuously. Add water and cook 3 minutes more, stirring frequently.

3. Add reserved carrot broth and stir well to blend. Bring to a boil, decrease heat, and simmer 5 minutes, stirring occasionally. Remove from heat and ladle half of the broth and vegetables into a food processor or blender. Process until smooth, return purée to skillet, and place over medium-low heat. Add whipping cream and stir well. Season to taste with salt and white pepper. Cover broth and keep warm over very low heat.

4. Heat a large nonstick skillet over medium heat. When pan is hot, add the remaining 1 1/2 teaspoons butter and the olive oil. When butter melts, add monkfish and cook 2 minutes, then turn and cook 2 to 3 minutes more, or until monkfish scallops are opaque throughout. Remove from heat.

5. To serve, divide carrot broth among four shallow soup bowls. Divide cooked monkfish scallops among bowls, then drizzle 1/4 teaspoon lime juice over monkfish. Sprinkle with cilantro and serve immediately.

SERVES 4 AS AN APPETIZER

Stir-Fried Monkfish

In this recipe, the spices and fish pair in a new and delicious way. As with all stir-fried dishes, be sure to have all the ingredients prepped and close at hand before you start cooking.

Marinade

4 CLOVES GARLIC, MINCED

1 1/2 TABLESPOONS SWEET PAPRIKA

1 TABLESPOON GROUND CUMIN

1/4 CUP DRY SHERRY

2 TABLESPOONS SOY SAUCE

1 TABLESPOON SESAME OIL

1/8 TEASPOON HOT CHILE OIL

Stir-Fry

2 TABLESPOONS MIRIN

2 TABLESPOONS WATER

1 TABLESPOON ARROWROOT OR
   CORNSTARCH

1 TABLESPOON PEANUT OIL OR SESAME OIL

1/8 TEASPOON TOASTED SESAME OIL

SEVERAL DASHES OF HOT CHILE OIL

1 1/4 POUNDS MONKFISH FILLETS, RINSED,
   DRAINED, PATTED DRY, PURPLE
   MEMBRANE REMOVED, AND CUT INTO
   1-INCH CUBES (SEE PAGE 78)

1 YELLOW OR WHITE ONION, CUT IN HALF,
   THEN CUT INTO PAPER-THIN SLICES

4 CLOVES GARLIC, MINCED

1 1/2 TEASPOONS MINCED GINGERROOT

1 RED PEPPER, CUT IN HALF HORIZONTALLY,
   THEN CUT INTO PAPER-THIN SLICES

2 CUPS SNOW PEAS OR SUGAR SNAP PEAS,
   RINSED, DRAINED, AND CUT IN HALF

3 TABLESPOONS WATER

3 CUPS COOKED RICE, PASTA, OR SOBA
   NOODLES

CHOPPED CILANTRO, FOR GARNISH

1. To make marinade, combine all of the ingredients in a large nonreactive bowl and stir well to mix. Divide marinade in half, add monkfish chunks to half of marinade, and toss with a spoon to coat. Cover dish and let sit at room temperature for about 20 minutes. Add mirin, water, and arrowroot to remaining half of marinade, stir well to blend, and reserve for later use.

2. To make stir-fry, place a large, well-seasoned wok or skillet over medium-high heat. When pan is very hot, add peanut oil, toasted sesame oil, and hot chile oil. Add monkfish cubes and stir-fry 3 to 4 minutes, stirring frequently, or until fish turns opaque throughout and is tender when pierced with the tip of a small, sharp knife. Remove fish and set aside.

3. Add onion, garlic, and gingerroot to pan and stir-fry 1 minute, stirring continuously. Add red pepper and snow peas and cook 1 minute, stirring constinuously, then add water, cover, and steam vegetables 2 to 3 minutes, or until tender-crisp.

4. Remove pan from heat and add reserved marinade. Stir-fry vegetables to coat completely with marinade, then return pan to heat and stir-fry vegetables 1 to 2 minutes more, or until sauce is thickened. Add monkfish and toss well to coat with sauce. Stir-fry about 1 minute more. Remove pan from heat.

5. To serve, divide cooked rice among individual plates and top with stir-fry. Sprinkle with cilantro.

SERVES 4

Rockfish

ROCKFISH BELONG TO the family Scorpaenidae, of which there are 330 or more species worldwide, including the tropical stonefishes, scorpionfishes, and lionfishes, as well as the North Pacific thornyheads and rockfishes. Rockfish are the largest and most common family of Pacific Coast fishes used as food and one of the most important fish families in Northwest waters.

With so many species, it is hard to generalize, but the basic body shape of all rockfish is similar, with a large head and mouth, a single spiny dorsal fin, and heavily armored gill covers. Colors and patterns vary wildly, however, depending on the species. Blue, black, copper, brown, vermillion, and yellow rockfish are all part of the clan. Spots, mottling, stripes, and multi-colored and dramatically shaped dorsal fins are other distinguishing features.

Because of the sheer number of rockfish, there is a great deal of confusion over the names given to the different species available in local fish markets. This misleading nomenclature came about because the rockfish was scorned in early times. Perhaps due to its negative-sounding name and to the availability of higher-quality fish—salmon, halibut, and flounder (sole)—the lowly rockfish was renamed rock cod, Pacific Ocean perch, Pacific snapper, black sea bass, and red snapper to try to upgrade its flagging image.

Among the many species of rockfish, those with rosy, red, orange, or reddish-orange skin are considered the highest quality, are fished the hardest, and are the most expensive. Brown rockfish are next in line, with darker colors at the bottom of the ladder. Particular confusion has arisen among the red rockfish varieties, which are often referred to as Alaska snapper or red snapper even though there are no true snappers on the West Coast. Keep in mind that the red snapper in the Pike Place Market is not even remotely related to the renowned red snapper from the Gulf of Mexico. Nonetheless, Northwest red snapper makes for uncommonly good eating.

Yelloweye Rockfish (*Sebastes ruberrimus*), is also known as red rockfish, goldeneye rockfish, red snapper, red rock cod, red cod, drum, rasphead rockfish, and turkey red rockfish. It is found from Baja California to the Gulf of Alaska, but is particularly important off southeastern Alaska, where it is particularly sought after for its vibrant orange color and large size. With bright yellow eyes, numerous spines on head and cheeks, and golden yellow to orange bodies, the adult yelloweye cuts an impressive figure. This species of rockfish can reach 3 feet in length and weigh up to 10 pounds, but usually comes to market weighing between 1 and 4 pounds. With a lower oil content than other rockfishes, its lean white meat is considered the highest quality of all Northwest species.

Yellowtail Rockfish (*Sebastes flavidus*), alias yellowtail rockcod, green snapper, bass, yellow bass, or yellowtail bass, is found from southern California to the Gulf of Alaska. The fish is predominantly olive green, with brown or gray backs and sides, silvery bellies, and yellow to yellow-orange fins. It reaches a maximum size of 26 inches long, weighs between 1 and 4 pounds, and lives at least 64 years.

Canary Rockfish (*Sebastes pinniger*), alias orange rockfish, yellow or red snapper, red rock cod, fantail, or swallowtail, ranges from Baja California to Alaska. The canary rockfish is thick-bodied with orange-gray skin, light orange fins, and gray lateral lines. Its maximum size is 30 inches, and the fish can live to be 75 years old.

Other rockfish commercially fished in the Northwest include the quillback (also known as speckled rockfish, orange-spotted rockfish, yellow-backed rockfish, brown rockfish, gopher rock cod, and rock cod), widow (alias soft brown, brown bomber, browny, widow rockcod, rock cod, rockfish, Pacific snapper, and bass), black (sold as black rockfish, bass, bass rockfish, black bass, black sea bass, black rock cod, black snapper, sea bass, and bluefish), bocaccio (also known as salmon rockfish, brown bomber, rock salmon, salmon grouper, grouper, rock cod, and tomcod), and redstripe (alias red-striped rockfish and rock cod).

Rockfish are usually sold at weights ranging from 1 1/2 to 5 pounds, although they can weigh up to 15 pounds. They are sold as fillets or as whole dressed or whole undressed fish. When purchasing whole undressed rockfish, allow 3/4 pound per entrée-sized serving; for whole dressed rockfish, allow 1/2 pound for each serving; for fillets, allow 6 ounces per serving.

No matter what species of rockfish you purchase, they all feature lean, white flesh that is solid and firm, yet tender. The meat is mild and delicate in flavor, although more flavorful than flounder and cod. The flesh turns snow white when cooked and is sweet and flaky without being overpowering. When purchasing rockfish, talk to your fishmonger about the specific species available, then ask for cooking tips and the best uses for that particular type.

Rockfish can be broiled, fried, poached, sautéed, steamed, baked, microwaved, grilled (whole fish), or used in fish soups, stews, and fishcakes. The skin is very tough and should

Yelloweye Rockfish

be removed before cooking. Rockfish makes a tasty and often less expensive substitute for flounder (sole), with the added bonus that it is less likely to fall apart when cooked.

Because there are so many species, some type of fresh rockfish is available year-round. However, like all bottomfish, it is of highest quality and least expensive during the fall and winter months. Fresh-frozen rockfish is available year-round.

Baked Whole Rockfish with Vietnamese Dipping Sauce

SAIGON RESTAURANT, PIKE PLACE MARKET

There's something ceremonial and celebratory about serving a whole baked fish, and this classic Vietnamese interpretation from Saigon Restaurant in the Soames-Dunn Building of the Market is one of the easiest and best. The Saigon, one of the oldest Vietnamese restaurants in Seattle, is favored by chefs and other locals for its expertly prepared, quick, and inexpensive seafood dishes. The no-frills atmosphere is more than made up for by owner/chef Vinh Pham, who greets her regular customers by name and knows which are their favorite dishes.

¹/₂ TEASPOON SALT

¹/₄ TEASPOON FRESHLY GROUND WHITE PEPPER

¹/₄ TEASPOON MONOSODIUM GLUTAMATE (OPTIONAL)

2 TABLESPOONS LOW-SODIUM SOY SAUCE

2 TABLESPOONS DRY WHITE WINE OR CHICKEN BROTH

1 WHOLE 4-POUND YELLOWEYE (OR OTHER TYPE) ROCKFISH (SEE NOTE)

4 CLOVES GARLIC, THINLY SLICED

2 QUARTER-SIZED SLICES GINGERROOT, SMASHED WITH THE FLAT PART OF A KNIFE BLADE AND JULIENNED

6 TO 8 GREEN ONIONS, WHITE PART JULIENNED, GREEN PART CUT INTO ¹/₄-INCH SLICES AND RESERVED

3 TABLESPOONS PEANUT OR SESAME OIL

VIETNAMESE DIPPING SAUCE (RECIPE FOLLOWS)

1. Place a sheet of aluminum foil lengthwise across a baking sheet, extending foil 8 to 10 inches beyond ends of sheet. Place a second sheet of foil widthwise across baking sheet, again allowing 8 to 10 inches of excess foil on each side. Set aside.

2. In a small mixing bowl or glass jar with a lid, combine salt, white pepper, monosodium glutamate, soy sauce, and white wine to make seasoning mix. Stir or shake well to combine and set aside.

3. Rinse fish under cold running water, being especially careful to remove any blood remaining in stomach cavity. Pat dry inside and out with paper towels. Place fish on foil-lined baking sheet.

4. With a sharp knife, make 6 to 8 diagonal scores from top to bottom on both sides of the fish, about ¹/₄-inch deep. Rub seasoning mix into sides of fish and into stomach cavity. Stuff cuts with garlic, ginger, and green onion julienne. Sprinkle fish with any remaining garlic, ginger, and green onion julienne. Carefully fold sides of foil over fish to seal fish tightly. Let foil-wrapped fish sit at room temperature for 20 minutes.

5. Ten minutes before you are ready to cook, preheat oven to 400°. Place the baking sheet in the center of oven and bake for 20 minutes, or until flesh is firm and white, but still juicy at the base of the cuts. Remove from oven and fold back top ends of foil to expose top of fish. Return fish to oven and bake an additional 10 minutes, or until fish just flakes. Remove fish from foil and transfer to a large serving platter.

6. Heat peanut oil in a small skillet over medium-high heat. Add the reserved green onion slices and cook for 5 to 10 seconds, stirring continuously. Remove skillet from heat and pour flavored oil over fish.

7. Serve whole fish at the table with dipping sauce.

SERVES 4

Vietnamese Dipping Sauce

¹/₄ CUP VIETNAMESE FISH SAUCE
   (NUOC NAM)

1 CLOVE GARLIC, CRUSHED

1 THAI CHILE, SEEDED AND MINCED

2 TEASPOONS SUGAR

1 TEASPOON FRESHLY SQUEEZED LEMON
   JUICE

Place all the ingredients in a small bowl and stir until sugar dissolves. Cover and set aside if using immediately, or refrigerate until ready to use.

MAKES ABOUT ¹/₄ CUP

Note: Whole hybrid striped bass or tilapia can easily substitute for yelloweye rockfish. Hybrid striped bass, a cross between wild ocean striped bass and freshwater white bass, is a farmed fish (the majority are grown in California). They are mild-flavored, white-fleshed fish available fresh and frozen year-round, although they are expensive. Tilapia, originally from Africa, are now raised all over the world, including in Taiwan, Thailand, the United States, Colombia, and Costa Rica. This mild, tender white fish is available in skinless fillets, whole undressed, and whole dressed fish both fresh and frozen year-round. Because the farmed fish are often harvested when they weigh between 1 and 2 pounds, you will need to buy two of the larger fish to prepare this dish.

Note: The technique of using a hot seasoned oil over steamed or baked fish is known as flavor smoothing and helps force the flavors of the seasonings into the fish. You can vary the flavor of the seasoned oil by substituting minced garlic, chopped fresh basil leaves, or chopped cilantro.

HANDY BAKED FISH TIP

For special occasions, Vinh Pham suggests substituting a whole 4- or 5-pound salmon for the rockfish, increasing cooking time as needed. The baked salmon (or baked salmon leftovers) can also be wrapped in rice paper to form appetizers. To do this, dip sheets of rice paper in warm water until pliable. Line rice paper sheets with lettuce leaves, then sprinkle on chopped cucumber and shredded carrots or sautéed green onions, and top with bite-sized chunks of the baked salmon. Roll the rice paper to enclose the filling, then dip salmon rolls in Vietnamese Dipping Sauce. For more detailed information on rice paper, see page 143.

Yelloweye Rockfish Salad with Light Gazpacho Sauce

Over twenty years ago, I spent one college semester in Madrid improving my language skills and soaking up the culture. During that time, I sampled gazpachos in many different parts of Spain and was always surprised by their diversity—various combinations of garden-grown vegetables, fruity olive oil, and a splash of dry red wine or sherry. My experiences there inspired the sauce for this recipe, whose pale pink color and spicy taste work well with the premier rockfish in West Coast waters—yelloweye rockfish. However, I am sure any Spanish chef worth his or her tapas would prepare it with European hake, or, merluza, which is similar to a flavorful, coarsely textured cod, and Spain's most highly prized fish. Try this recipe in winter, when the bottomfish are running, for a little shot of springtime.

1 CUP DRY WHITE WINE

2 CUPS WATER

1 SHALLOT, COARSELY CHOPPED

1 BAY LEAF

4 WHOLE PEPPERCORNS

1 WHOLE CLOVE

SALT TO TASTE

1 1/2 POUNDS ROCKFISH FILLETS, RINSED, DRAINED, AND PATTED DRY

LIGHT GAZPACHO SAUCE (RECIPE FOLLOWS)

1 POUND SALAD GREENS, RINSED, DRAINED, AND WELL DRIED

1 RIPE PLUM TOMATO, DICED, FOR GARNISH

1 CUCUMBER, DICED, FOR GARNISH

1. In a skillet large enough to hold rockfish fillets without crowding, bring wine, water, shallot, bay leaf, peppercorns, and clove to a boil. Cover and boil 15 minutes, then season to taste with salt.

2. Remove pan from heat, add rockfish fillets, decrease heat to low, partially cover (set lid slightly askew so that steam can escape), and simmer 5 to 10 minutes, depending on thickness of fillets or until fish just turns opaque. Adjust heat if water simmers too fast or too slowly. Do not allow water to boil. Remove fish and place on several layers of paper towels or a clean kitchen towel to drain. When fish is cool enough to handle, remove any skin or bones.

3. To serve, divide greens among individual plates and sprinkle with tomato and cucumber pieces. Divide rockfish fillets and place in center of plates. Drizzle fish and greens with sauce.

SERVES 4

Light Gazpacho Sauce

2 RIPE PLUM TOMATOES, CORED AND CHOPPED

1 CUCUMBER, PEELED AND CHOPPED

1 CUP LOWFAT OR NONFAT MAYONNAISE

1 TABLESPOON EXTRA VIRGIN OLIVE OIL

1/4 TEASPOON GROUND CAYENNE

1/4 TEASPOON GROUND CUMIN

2 TEASPOONS BALSAMIC VINEGAR

JUICE OF 1/2 LEMON

1. Place tomato in food processor or blender and process until smooth. Pour tomato purée into a fine-mesh sieve over a medium mixing bowl, and press purée through sieve with the back of a

wooden spoon. Measure out $1/2$ cup tomato juice and reserve. Discard tomato solids and remaining juice.

2. Place cucumber in same food processor or blender (you don't have to rinse it out) and process until smooth. Pour cucumber purée into the fine-mesh sieve over the medium mixing bowl, and press it through with the back of the wooden spoon. Measure out $1/2$ cup cucumber juice and reserve. Dispose of cucumber solids and remaining juice.

3. Place mayonnaise in the medium mixing bowl. Add olive oil, cayenne, and cumin and whisk until well blended. Add reserved tomato juice, reserved cucumber juice, balsamic vinegar, and lemon juice and whisk until well blended.

4. Pour sauce into a small mixing bowl or jar, cover, and refrigerate 2 hours or overnight to allow flavors to blend.

MAKES 1 $2/3$ CUPS

FUN FACTS

- Young yelloweye rockfish look nothing like their parents. Juveniles start out red with two white stripes and black-edged fins. As the fish grow, they lose the stripes and their bodies turn golden yellow to orange. So different is the yelloweye's appearance in youth than in maturity that it was thought to be two different species of rockfish for many years.

- Yellowtail rockfish have a very strong natural homing instinct. In Alaska, when researchers captured and released them at various distances from their original reef, some yellowtails traveled as far as $12^1/2$ miles to return home.

- The oldest known yelloweye rockfish lived to be 114 years old.

- Members of the scorpionfish family are so named because they carry sacks of venom in their spines. Fortunately, the poison in Northwest rockfishes is not very potent, as compared with the strong venom of the beautiful yet dangerous lionfish, which lives in tropical waters. Nonetheless, a jab from the spine of a rockfish can result in pain, swelling, and even a fever, so watch out!

- The stomach of the widow rockfish is lined with a black pigment, possibly because the fish sometimes feeds on fish or invertebrates that produce light. If the fish's body cavity were not lined in black, the widow rockfish might glow after eating the luminescent fish, which would be a dead giveaway to predators!

Blackened Rockfish Fillets

———— ⚓ ————

MARKETSPICE,
PIKE PLACE MARKET

Blackening is a cooking technique made famous by Louisiana chef Paul Prudhomme in which meat or fish is coated with Cajun spices, then cooked in a smoking-hot cast-iron skillet. The poker-hot skillet combined with a blackening mix made of varying amounts of cayenne, black pepper, white pepper, dried thyme, dried rosemary, garlic salt, garlic powder, onion powder, chile powder, paprika, and/or dried oregano gives food an extra-crispy crust. When blackened foods were the rage several years ago, stocks of redfish (the most popular food for blackening) were seriously depleted and blackened dishes even appeared on menus at fast-food restaurants. Today, the technique isn't as common, but it is still fun to try from time to time as long as you turn on your stovetop vent, disconnect the smoke alarm, and open lots of windows. Blackened Redfish Seasoning is available from MarketSpice in the Market (see page 330), although most grocery stores stock commercial blends.

1 1/2 POUNDS ROCKFISH FILLETS, SKIN AND BONES REMOVED, RINSED, DRAINED, AND PATTED DRY

1/2 CUP UNSALTED BUTTER, MELTED

BLACKENED REDFISH SEASONING

1. Heat a large cast-iron skillet over high heat until very hot. Dip rockfish fillets in melted butter, then sprinkle seasoning mix generously on both sides of fish.

2. Place fish fillets in skillet and pour a small amount of remaining butter on top of each fillet. Cook 3 to 4 minutes, or until fish turns black and crusty. Turn fillets and cook 3 to 4 minutes more, or until underside of fish turns black and crusty. Do not overcook or coating will burn and fish will be overdone.

3. To serve, divide rockfish fillets among individual plates and serve immediately.

SERVES 4

HANDY ROCKFISH TIP

John Peterson, a longtime fishmonger and manager of Pike Place Fish, shares this simple recipe for yelloweye rockfish fillets: When barbecuing, dot the fillets with butter and sprinkle with freshly squeezed lemon juice, then cook directly over hot coals for fish that browns on the outside, tastes like lobster, and is absolutely wonderful.

Sablefish (Black Cod)

ONLY TWO MEMBERS OF the family Anoplopomatidae exist and both are found in the Northwest. The large skilfish is an offshore creature rarely seen by naturalists, while the more common sablefish is popular on Northwest tables. The sablefish (*Anoplopoma fimbria*), is often called blackcod (also spelled black cod), Alaska blackcod, coalcod, or coalfish. Sometimes it is even misnamed blue cod, bluefish, skil-fish, skil, or candlefish. In California, after the sablefish has been filleted, it is also sometimes sold as butterfish. Smoked sablefish is frequently marketed under the name smoked Alaska black cod.

Caught off the Pacific Coast from Baja California to the Bering Sea in Alaska, the highest concentrations of the fish occur in the Gulf of Alaska, where the active fishery harvests sablefish by otter trawl, fish trap, or long line. As an adult, the sleek, slim-bodied sablefish is dark gray, greenish gray, or blackish, although yellow ones and albinos have been reported. The fish averages between 3 to 7 pounds but can reach up to 40 pounds in weight.

Sablefish is sold as fresh steaks, fillets, chunks, and smoked fillets. For optimum quality, keep fresh sablefish in the refrigerator for no longer than 1 day because of its high oil content. Properly wrapped, frozen unflavored or smoked sablefish may be kept in the home freezer at 0° up to 1 month. It should be defrosted 8 to 12 hours or overnight in the refrigerator and used within 1 day.

Buy 4 to 5 ounces of fresh fillets, 6 ounces of fresh steaks, and 8 ounces of whole dressed sablefish per entrée-sized portion. Because of its very rich flavor and oily texture, 4 ounces of smoked sablefish is sufficient as a main-dish serving.

Sablefish is distinguished for its high oil content, soft white flesh, and large flaky texture. Its flavor is rich and distinctive, yet delicate. Preferred cooking methods include smoking, steaming, microwaving, poaching, broiling, baking, grilling, or sautéing.

Sablefish

Even though it is sometimes called blackcod, sablefish does not lend itself to true cod recipes because of the difference in oil content between the two fish. Unlike cod, the sablefish's moist flesh does not dry out easily when cooked, and its distinctive flavor and texture do not need to be masked by flavorful sauces, as is often the case with the milder and more coarsely textured cod.

Fresh sablefish is available on and off

throughout the year depending on fishing restrictions and weather conditions. Fresh-frozen sablefish and the smoked product are available year-round.

Fun Facts

- A large portion of the sablefish catch goes to Japan, where the oil-rich fish is a favorite ingredient in sashimi. Sablefish for the Japanese market is graded by its oil content, with deeper-dwelling sablefish having more oil in their bodies.

- The largest sablefish of recorded size measured 42 inches and over 126 pounds. Sablefish can live to at least 55 years old.

- Orca whales have a real preference for silky sablefish; they have been known to take them off long lines, ignoring less delectable species.

Handy Sablefish Tip

At Ray's Boathouse, Seattle's venerable seafood restaurant, the freshest fish is at its best with the plainest preparations. This holds true for their treatment of smoked sablefish, which is labeled "smoked black cod fillet" on the menu. The noble, oily fish is simply steamed, then left altogether alone, unsauced. The result is moist fish suffused with smoke, and served with steamed new potatoes and vegetables of the season. For the home cook, Portlock brand smoked sablefish (labeled as "Pacific Sable Fish" and "Smoked Black Cod Pieces") is available frozen at Port Chatham Smoked Seafood outlets in the Seattle area.

The product can be defrosted in the refrigerator overnight and used within 1 day. To steam sablefish, prepare a steaming rack large enough to hold sablefish fillets in one layer. Bring water to a boil no higher than 1 inch below rack and place 1 pound of sablefish fillets cut into four 4-ounce pieces skin side down over rack. Cover and steam 10 minutes per inch of thickness, or until sablefish just flakes. Remove from steamer, divide among individual plates, and serve with steamed potatoes and vegetables and lemon wedges.

Sablefish with Chukar Cherry Sauce

—⁂—

CHUKAR CHERRY COMPANY, PIKE PLACE MARKET

Pam and Guy Auld were successful real estate and management professionals in Seattle before suffering a classic case of urban flight in the mid-1980s. In search of a better life for their family, the Aulds moved east of the mountains to a small town, Prosser, Washington, and purchased a 350-acre farm with a cherry orchard. They soon realized that fresh cherries have a very short season and shelf life, and they searched for a way to market their crop throughout the year. The result was the Chukar Cherry Company, which has a stall in the Market and sells all manner of dried cherry and berry products across the United States, Canada, Australia, and parts of Asia. This cherry sauce is a worthy complement to lush sablefish; it would also pair well with smoked sablefish (see page 93) for a real contrast in rich, distinctive flavors.

1 1/2 TABLESPOONS BUTTER

1 TABLESPOON OLIVE OIL

1/3 CUP DRIED BING OR RAINIER SWEET
   CHERRIES, CUT IN HALF

1/2 CUP RED SWEET VERMOUTH

3 TABLESPOONS NONFAT, LOWFAT, OR
   REGULAR SOUR CREAM

1 TEASPOON CRACKED BLACK PEPPERCORNS

1 1/4 POUNDS SABLEFISH FILLETS, ABOUT
   1/2 INCH THICK, RINSED, DRAINED,
   PATTED DRY, AND CUT INTO 4 (5-OUNCE)
   FILLETS

1. Melt 1 tablespoon of the butter and 1 1/2 teaspoons of the olive oil in a small saucepan over medium heat. Add cherries and vermouth and cook 3 to 5 minutes, or until cherries become soft and plump, stirring occasionally. Remove pan from heat and stir in sour cream and peppercorns. Return to heat and keep warm over very low heat while preparing fish.

2. Heat a large nonstick skillet over medium heat. When hot, add remaining 1 1/2 teaspoons butter and 1 1/2 teaspoons olive oil and swirl pan until butter melts. Alternately, spray skillet with nonstick cooking spray. Add sablefish fillets flesh side down and cook 2 to 3 minutes. Turn fish and cook 2 to 3 minutes more, or until fish is opaque on both sides, but still slightly translucent in the middle.

3. To serve, divide fish fillets among individual plates and spoon sauce over each fillet.

SERVES 4

Sablefish with Kasu Marinade

———✦———

Kasu is a fragrant, doughy sediment left over after rice is fermented to make sake, much like the lees, or dregs, that remain after winemaking. Strongly flavored finfish marinated in kasu before cooking has become standard on many Seattle-area menus, but this wasn't always the case. Although kasu-marinated finfish is a classic in Japanese cuisine, it wasn't popular in Seattle until 1982 when Tom Douglas, then a young chef at Café Sport, "discovered" the dish and put it on his menu. The dish proved so popular that many chefs followed with kasu-marinated sablefish, halibut, and salmon. Chef Douglas, now co-owner with wife Jackie Cross of Etta's Seafood, Dahlia Lounge, and The Palace Kitchen, still features kasu-marinated sablefish as an appetizer at his restaurants, another testament to the dish's enduring popularity.

5 TEASPOONS SALT

1 QUART WATER

1 ¼ POUNDS SABLEFISH, RINSED,
     DRAINED, PATTED DRY, AND CUT INTO
     FOUR (5-OUNCE) FILLETS

1 POUND KASU

2 TABLESPOONS SHIRO (WHITE) MISO

¼ CUP MIRIN, SAKE, OR WATER

1 CUP SHREDDED SPINACH LEAVES OR ¼
     POUND OCEAN SALAD (OPTIONAL)
     (SEE NOTE)

1. In a large nonreactive baking pan that will hold sablefish fillets in one layer, combine salt and water and stir until salt is dissolved. Add sablefish, turn to coat both sides, cover, and refrigerate. After 30 minutes, remove pan from refrigerator, drain fillets, and pat dry. Rinse out pan and dry.

2. In a mixing bowl, stir together kasu, miso, and mirin. Add sablefish fillets to baking pan and spread the kasu mixture evenly over the fish. Cover sablefish with mixture, turning to coat all sides, cover pan, and refrigerate 1 to 2 days, depending on strength of flavor desired (marinating for 1 day gives a more subtle flavor that may work best for first-timers).

3. When ready to cook, preheat broiler. Oil a baking sheet lightly or spray with nonstick cooking spray.

4. Scrape the kasu mixture off the fillets, leaving just a light film on the surface. Arrange fish fillets on baking sheet and place fish 3 to 4 inches under broiler. Broil 10 to 12 minutes per inch of thickness, or until fish just turns opaque.

5. Divide spinach among individual plates and top with fish fillets.

SERVES 4

Note: Kasu is available at Japanese markets, which also sometimes offer premarinated sablefish. All you have to do is open the package, sauté, grill, or broil, and enjoy. Ocean salad is a mixture of seaweed, kelp, and other ocean-floor greens. It is usually available fresh or frozen in seafood stores and Asian markets or specialty grocery stores. While it adds a salty taste, and crunchy texture, it is not essential.

Smoked Sablefish Poached in Milk

—⁂—

Sometimes it is fun to look through old cookbooks and see how our predecessors in the kitchen cooked native Northwest seafood. While flipping through Ameri-can Cooking: The Northwest, published in 1970, I read that even back then sablefish was often known as "black cod." Particularly in Alaska and British Columbia, it was often smoked, poached in milk, and served in golden flaky pieces, with melted butter glistening in the crevices. After a description like that, I rushed to the kitchen to give it a try. Here is my rendition of this traditional method, which is North-west comfort food at its best, and would be good served with nothing more than a green salad with a good-quality vinaigrette for a very special late-night treat.

2 CUPS MILK

2 BAY LEAVES

¹/₄ TEASPOON SALT

¹/₈ TEASPOON FRESHLY GROUND WHITE
    PEPPER

1 POUND SMOKED, UNCOOKED SABLEFISH
    FILLETS, THAWED IF FROZEN, CUT INTO 4
    (4-OUNCE) FILLETS

4 SLICES GOOD-QUALITY WHITE BREAD,
    TOASTED AND CUT DIAGONALLY IN
    QUARTERS

2 TABLESPOONS UNSALTED BUTTER

FRESHLY GRATED NUTMEG, OPTIONAL

1. In a skillet large enough to hold the sablefish fillets without crowding, add milk, bay leaves, salt, and white pepper. Place over medium heat and cook, stirring occasionally, until milk just begins to simmer. Add sablefish fillets flesh side down, cover, and cook 10 minutes per inch of thickness, or until fish just flakes. Adjust heat if milk simmers too quickly or too slowly. Do not allow milk to boil.

2. Place 4 toast wedges in each of four shallow soup bowls. Remove skin from fish fillets and place one fillet in center of toast. Ladle enough milk to cover toast, but not to completely sub-merge fish. Place 1¹/₂ teaspoons butter on top of each fish fillet, sprinkle with additional white pepper and nutmeg, and serve immediately.

SERVES 4

HANDY SABLEFISH TIP

Sablefish is easily pan-seared. The resulting flaky, golden fish opens the door to many possi-bilities, such as layering the fish over a mound of Asian-inspired mashed potatoes (see page 67) or couscous (see page 209) for an incredible mixture of strong flavors and contrasting textures. To pan-sear, in a large skillet, heat 2 tablespoons olive oil over medium-high heat. When oil is hot, add 1¹/₄ pounds sablefish fillets flesh side down and cook 4 to 5 minutes. Turn and cook 4 to 5 minutes more, or until fish just flakes.

FUN FACT

• Native Northwest Indians used to sun-dry oily sablefish; today, enterprising fishers smoke and sell it as smoked Alaska black cod.

Salmon

NO FISH SYMBOLIZES THE Northwest as perfectly as the Pacific salmon. Through the centuries, the salmon's magical journey has been an elemental part of the mythology and religion of Northwestern Native Americans. In more modern times, the salmon has been the most highly prized and commercially important fish in the Northwest. The figures are impressive. The United States is the largest salmon producer in the world, producing about one-third of the total world supply. Alaska produces 90 percent of the U.S. salmon catch.

The yearly run of Pacific salmon begins in May with the Chinook salmon. Considered by many experts to be the best variety of salmon, the return of the Chinook is the first glimmer of hope that spring has arrived after the long drizzle of winter. Northwesterners know that if we have made it this far, we are well on our way to milder temperatures and summer sun.

During those (usually) sunny summer months, life in the Pike Place Market seems to revolve around salmon. Tourists marvel at the salmon-throwing ritual performed by the Pike Place fishmongers, and usually end up taking a pink-and-silver slice of Northwest nirvana home to Nebraska or Tokyo to share with fortunate family and friends. Locals discuss the culinary distinctions among various salmon runs like some people discuss the differences among wine varietals.

A cookbook author should probably remain impartial, but I will unblushingly go on record as saying that I consider salmon the king of all fish, not only because of its unique flavor and luscious texture but because of its forgiving nature when cooked. I've tried pink salmon (most of which is canned and not considered one of the best eating salmon) that had been frozen for over a year, and it was still surprisingly tasty. This just shows that even the salmon species of lesser quality are good. Even if overcooked a bit, salmon flesh still remains relatively moist and flavorful.

Because of my passion for salmon, the first time I visited the Northwest, I ate it every night for dinner and was lucky enough to taste not only red, but also white Chinook. Since then, I've had salmon wrapped in rice paper, simmered in soup, brushed with lemon butter, crusted with hazelnuts, served with pesto, baked on a bed of fennel tops, and alder-planked. The range of these preparations shows the versatility of this fish, its many moods and forms.

Considering all that salmon go through in their lives, it is a wonder they arrive on our plates in edible condition at all. Wild salmon start life in freshwater streams and rivers, then undergo smoltification, a physiological process in which the fish change shape, color, and most important, begin to excrete salts, which allows them to go from fresh to salt water. Once they swim to the ocean, salmon spend their adult lives eating so they can grow strong and healthy for the trip back upriver. This method of using different habitats during different times of the fish's life has allowed the salmon to overcome the food and space limits of the freshwater environment.

After one to four years at sea, the fish return en masse to their freshwater birthplace to mate and produce offspring. This unique characteristic of the fish—mass spawning—means that salmon of one stock spawn together. This makes individuals within a given stock genetically strong because it reduces the chance that genes from other stocks will be introduced by crossbreeding.

The latest scientific theory about salmon spawning hypothesizes that salmon find their way back to fresh water by using an inner magnetic map and a strong sense of day length. The theory holds that a given fish usually knows approximately where it is in relation to its home stream. As a change in season is signaled by changing day length, the fish

THE FATE OF THE SALMON

SADLY, THE WILD SALMON population has dropped precipitously since the early 1900s because of overfishing, logging, the damming of rivers, and other environmentally damaging factors that prevent the fish from reaching its breeding grounds. To counteract the decline in the numbers of salmon, commercial and recreational salmon fishing along the West Coast has been curtailed and, in some cases, completely shut down. In another bold measure, utility companies have vowed to reduce the number of dams on Northwest rivers to encourage the salmon to return to their spawning grounds.

Though many Americans think the salmon is an endangered species, thankfully, this is not true. While some Northwest runs of wild salmon are endangered, in Alaska stringent management programs have resulted in record salmon harvests during the 1990s. Farmed salmon harvests have more than doubled during the past five years, with salmon farmers now producing about 40 percent of the world's total salmon harvest.

According to a 1996 article in the *Seattle Times*, the worldwide supply of farmed, wild, and ranched (hatchery raised) salmon has increased by 37 percent in 5 years, from 1.05 million to 1.43 million metric tons. Worldwide, salmon is in oversupply, partly because of farmed fish from Norway and Chile. To help use the glut of salmon, new products are being developed and marketed, such as salmon ham, salmon-flavored bagel spreads, and salmon sausages.

moves toward the river mouth. During its final approach, the salmon depends on its sense of smell to filter out the water smells it remembers from the early stages of its life.

Once they arrive at the mouth of the river where they were born, salmon never eat again. Using only the energy stored in their bodies from their years in the sea, their journey upriver can last several months and cover up to 600 miles. Only the fastest and strongest salmon survive as they travel up to 30 miles a day, sometimes jumping 10 feet in the air to get over a waterfall. When the obstacle is a dam, the fish must clear a fish ladder—a series of pools arranged like steps at the side of a dam so the fish can jump up from one to the next.

The best-quality salmon are caught in the ocean or just prior to entering the river. Their firm, plump bodies are bright silver, and in perfect condition for the rigors of migration. As they move upriver, their fat and protein reserves are gradually absorbed. During their final days, salmon become bruised and deformed, their muscular bodies soften and change color, their scales are absorbed as nourishment, and white fungus may grow on open sores or over their eyes. Nonetheless, they overcome these physical limitations to fulfill their final act: Spawning. After propagating the species, they die.

Some understanding of the salmon life cycle is important to the cook when shopping for the best quality salmon, for the taste and texture of salmon depends not only on the genetic makeup of each species but on its fat content. Fat content is determined by the length of time the fish spends in the ocean and the distance it must cover to reach its spawning grounds. The longer the distance the salmon must travel in fresh water to spawn, the more body fat the fish produces in the ocean, which leads to better flavor and texture.

In her book, *Eat Fish, Live Better*, Anne M. Fletcher, R.D., says that even though most people tend to think of salmon as fatty fish, only Chinook salmon falls into the oily category, and contains the highest number of calories of all the salmon at 180 per serving. Atlantic, coho, and sockeye are all medium-fat fish, which average around 150 calories per portion. In the lowfat group are chum and pink salmon—they're the lowest in calories at 120 and 116, respectively.

Because of the great length of the salmon's freshwater runs, some Northwest rivers have become famous for the high-quality salmon they produce. Salmon from these sources are marketed under the names of their river of origin, such as Copper River or Yukon River.

Many different species of salmon run throughout the year, each with attributes worth celebrating. Like the trout and char, salmon are members of the Salmonidae family, which comes from a Latin word meaning "the leaper." Six major species of salmon are sold in the United States; five from the Pacific, and one from the Atlantic.

The **Atlantic salmon** (*salmo salar*) differs from the Pacific salmon because it doesn't die after it reproduces and can return to fresh water as many as four times. Sadly, very few Atlantic salmon are left in the wild, so the Atlantic salmon that grace our tables are always farm-raised, often in Maine, Canada, Norway, Chile, and Iceland. Locally, the fish is even aquacultured as close as Bainbridge Island, a

30-minute ferry ride from downtown Seattle.

Although Atlantic salmon has its proponents, in my opinion it is inferior to wild Pacific salmon. The flesh is pale orange in color, large of flake, watery, and less firm than fish in the wild. Because farm-raised fish are more docile, the flesh of the Atlantic salmon is milder and duller in flavor than a wild fish and has a uniform flavor because the farmed fish eat a standard diet. Nonetheless, when wild salmon are not available, Atlantic salmon make a suitable substitute in recipes. Atlantic salmon is best baked, poached, braised, grilled, broiled, or sautéed. It is also very good when cold- or hot-smoked.

Chinook, sockeye, coho, pink, and chum are the five types of salmon found in Pacific Coast waters from California to Alaska. A sixth Pacific salmon, the cherry salmon (*Oncorhynchus masou*), is found in fresh waters in Korea and Japan to the Kamchatka Peninsula. Weighing between 4 to 8 pounds, this small fish resembles the coho and is not available in our markets.

Chinook salmon (*Oncorhynchus tshawytscha*), also known as king, blackmouth, spring, or tyee (although the latter term, from the Chinook Indian language, is usually reserved for fish weighing 30 pounds and more), is found from southern California to the northernmost waters of Alaska. Trollers harvest Chinooks for the fresh fish trade using hook and line rigs, while gillnetters and seiners supply the catch for canning or freezing. The Chinook is the least abundant of the North American Pacific salmon, and the catch accounts for less than 5 percent of North American salmon production.

The Chinook is a solid, thick fish, and the largest of the Pacific salmon, measuring 3 feet and averaging between 15 and 25 pounds, although fish more than 50 pounds are not uncommon. The fish grows to 58 inches in length, can weigh at least 126 pounds, and lives from 4 to 8 years. At sea, the fish is deep green, blue, grayish, or black on its back, with

SALMON WINES

SALMON IS AN OILY FISH with fairly strong flavors. Whether farm-raised or wild, salmon has enough oil, body, and texture to stand up to a wide array of wines, everything from a full-bodied white (such as a chardonnay) to a lighter, less overbearing red wine (such as merlot or pinot noir). Wild salmon, in particular, is a rich, meaty fish with multiple dimensions of flavor described as "nutty," "woodsy," and "gamelike," that pairs well with pinot noir. Pinot noir, characterized by delicacy and subtlety in both flavor and texture, ranges from light and fruity when young to full-flavored and complex as it ages. Other wines, such as melon, fumé blanc, sauvignon blanc, pinot gris, or pinot grigio, are good with salmon.

a silver belly. Irregular black spots on the fish's back and tail and black gums distinguish this species from others.

The Chinook has the highest fat content of all the Pacific salmon species; consequently, it boasts the most intense flavor of any salmon, as well as a rich, buttery texture. Its flesh ranges from ivory to deep red, is firm and luxuriant, and separates into large, creamy flakes when cooked.

Pale, almost white-meat salmon comes from the white Chinook, although it is a rarity, accounting for only about 1 in 500 fish. More common in Alaska and British Columbia than in Washington, Oregon, and California, white Chinooks look the same as red Chinooks from the outside and the taste and texture of the two fish are virtually identical. Nonetheless, even though flesh color is not an indicator of quality, consumers prefer darker

Chinook Salmon

meat in salmon, so red-fleshed Chinooks command a higher price. Variations in flesh color among Chinooks are due to genetic factors, rather than differences in diet.

A blackmouth is simply an immature Chinook salmon. It is named for the characteristic black gumline that distinguishes Chinooks from the other Pacific salmon. A blackmouth becomes a Chinook when it reaches maturity and feels the primal urge to return to its natal stream to spawn. Blackmouth range in size from 3 to more than 20 pounds, averaging from 6 to 8 pounds.

The Chinook can be cooked in almost any way, including grilling, broiling, poaching, steaming, sautéing, baking, or smoking.

The Chinook runs May through October, and the fish is also available fresh-frozen year-round, while farmed Chinooks from Canada (which weigh between 4 and 7 pounds) are available year-round. Chinook and sockeye, the other spring-run salmon, combine perfectly with the vegetables and herbs of the season—asparagus, peas, new potatoes, dill, chives, and tarragon.

Sockeye salmon (*Oncorhynchus nerka*) is also known as blueback or red salmon. The name red salmon came about because sockeye meat is the most vivid red of any salmon species, and also because when the fish returns to its home river to spawn, the outside of its body turns deep red.

The sockeye, which is found from southern California to Alaska, is the most important commercial fish in the Pacific Northwest. The third most abundant species after pinks and chum, the sockeye is taken by seine and gillnet. In years past, most of the catch was exported to the Japanese (who prize the bright red flesh in sushi), but in recent years more sockeye has become available to American consumers at reasonable prices.

The sockeye is the slimmest of Pacific salmon, a long bluish black to silvery fish. It averages 2 feet long and 6 pounds, with weights up to 12 pounds. Some stocks of sockeye, known as kokanee, remain in fresh water throughout their lives. They weigh only 1 pound when mature and are good broiled, baked, deep-fried, or pan-fried for breakfast.

The sockeye is less fatty than the Chinook but is equally prized by many experts for its intense flavor, fine-flaked texture, and bright red flesh. Sockeye is best when steamed, broiled, grilled, baked, sautéed, braised, and smoked. Because its bright color holds up through the cooking process, it is the most beautiful type of salmon to poach for use in hot dishes, or particularly for use in salads or on the buffet table. A limited number of sockeyes are canned and sold at premium prices; the high-quality, brightly colored product is definitely worth the extra expense.

Sockeyes are not farmed and are therefore available fresh only during the summer or fresh-frozen year-round.

Coho salmon (*Oncorhynchus kisutch*) is also known as silver salmon. The fish ranges from Baja California to Alaska but is most abundant from Oregon to southeastern Alaska. It is a major commercial fish, taken by trollers for the fresh market, and purse seining and gillnetting for canning, smoking, or freezing. At sea, its back is bluish-green and its belly silver. Black spots dot the fish's back and upper tail, and its gums are white. The fish averages 2 feet long, weighs 6 to 12 pounds, and lives for 3 years. The longest coho measured over 38 inches, with an unofficial weight record of 31 pounds.

Coho salmon flesh is red to pale orange with a medium oil content and fine flake. Coho can be baked, braised, poached, steamed, grilled, broiled, or sautéed.

Wild coho run from July to September; farmed coho, often weighing 1/2 to 1 pound apiece, are available year-round.

Pink salmon (*Oncorhynchus gorbuscha*), also known as humpback, humpy, or humpie salmon, are the smallest, yet most abundant, species of salmon in the North Pacific. Ranging from southern California to Alaska, in

Pink Salmon

some years they make up half the U.S. salmon catch. Most are gillnetted or purse seined, and because so many are caught at one time, they are most often canned or frozen.

The silvery fish has large oval spots on its back and tail. Pinks average 20 inches and 4 pounds. Because of the prominent cartilaginous hump on the back of male pinks during spawning season, the fish is sometimes called the humpback. It can grow to 30 inches, weighs a maximum of 15 pounds, and live about 2 years.

With its pale to light pink flesh and low fat content, the pink salmon has historically rated poorly in comparison with other salmon. Broiling or grilling may dry out these lowfat fish more quickly than other methods, so it is best to baste with an herb butter or marinade during cooking. Whole fish are also often baked in a flavorful sauce or pan-fried, although steaming and poaching also work well.

Pinks are not farmed and are available fresh only in early fall.

The **Chum salmon** (*Oncorhynchus keta*) is sometimes called the dog, keta, fall, calico, or silverbrite, not to be confused with the silver (coho) salmon. The fish ranges from southern California to Alaska. Second in abundance to pink salmon, this little-loved species is canned, smoked, frozen, or harvested for its eggs for export to Japan.

The silver, thick-bodied fish averages 2 feet, weighs 9 pounds, and lives 3 to 5 years. The white tip on the anal fin and faint gridlike shading on the sides are distinguishing features of the species. The name "dog" was given to the fish by the Athapaskan Indians of the Yukon, who feed the chum salmon to their dogs, while keeping the choicer species for themselves. Chums are also known as dogs because of the large, fanglike teeth that are present during the spawning season.

The fish have pale pink meat that is coarse in texture and low in fat. The quality of chums is more variable than most salmon. They are sometimes graded as silverbrites, semibrites, and darks, silverbrites being the most desirable. Chum are the species of fish often featured in supermarket advertisements for summer salmon "specials" and, if you choose carefully, they can be a good value.

Preferred cooking methods for chum include smoking, grilling, broiling, or pan-frying. Lower cooking temperatures are needed for chum salmon after initial high-heat searing to prevent overcooking.

Chums, the last salmon fishery of the year, are sometimes called fall salmon. The fish are not farmed and are available fresh only from July through October.

When looking for a high-quality whole salmon, you should follow the general rules for selecting any finfish, but with a couple of additional guidelines. Feel the outside of the fish for firmness—it should have no soft spots, sponginess, bruising, fin tears, or bloody holes. Softness along the rib bone or spine bone also indicates a fish of lesser quality. Check the body cavity; it should be thick, with lots of fat. The cuts where the fish was gutted should be smooth, with no blood or membranes in the belly. While there is always some scale loss in salmon due to the shock of the fish being pulled from the water, for the best-quality fish, scale loss should cover no more than 10 to 20 percent of the body. When buying salmon steaks or fillets, follow the general guidelines for all finfish.

Fresh or freshly thawed salmon can be stored in the refrigerator for 1 to 3 days. Thaw salmon in the refrigerator 8 to 10 hours or overnight in a covered container, or thaw in a microwave oven according to manufacturer's instructions. Don't refreeze previously frozen salmon. If purchased frozen, properly packaged pink and chum salmon may be stored in the home freezer at 0° or lower for up to 3 months, although Chinook, sockeye, and coho, because of their high fat content, are best used within 1 month.

Salmon has rows of pin bones within its flesh. To find them, run your fingers along the surface of the salmon's flesh, then pull out with clean tweezers, pliers, or a strawberry huller before cooking.

Salmon is sold in several forms—whole dressed, salmon roast (the center cut of a whole salmon), salmon steak, and salmon fillet. It is also available canned, pickled, smoked, and salted. Allow about 4 to 6 ounces for each serving, although many people can eat much more simply because it is so delicious.

Depending on the variety and cut you select, you can bake, poach, sauté, broil, steam, grill, braise, or microwave salmon. It can also be cooked in chowder or cold- or hot-smoked. Many people eat salmon uncooked (in sashimi, ceviche, or gravlax). Others like their salmon cooked medium-rare, which means the salmon is still a bit raw in the center; flakes will separate, but with some coaxing.

Eating raw or undercooked salmon is fine as long as it has been farmed or commercially frozen. However, experts recommend cooking wild salmon well-done if it has not been commercially frozen, since wild salmon can carry parasite larvae that cause stomach upset in humans. Salmon is well-done when it is cooked beyond the point of just turning opaque in the center and measures 140° on an instant-read thermometer. This results in a drier, paler piece of fish with flakes that are firm and separate easily. In my opinion, this is fish that is overcooked. And although I know I am bucking common-sense advice, I prefer to eat my wild salmon cooked medium-rare and risk the consequences.

Personal preference dictates the "best" way to prepare salmon. Many argue that salmon is so flavorful in and of itself, it should be cooked simply, without spicy ingredients to overpower its natural taste. Others suggest that because of the salmon's assertive flavor, it takes well to strong flavors, such as Asian-style marinades and sauces made with flavorful additions of fresh ginger, garlic, crushed red pepper, black beans, soy sauce, and sesame oil. Some favor bright, acidic sauces, claiming that lemon, capers, sorrel, tomatoes, and fruit vine-

gars cut through the fish's natural oils. Still others amplify the natural richness of salmon with heavy sauces made of butter, cream, crème fraîche, sour cream, or nuts.

However you flavor it, in most cases, cook salmon with the skin on; the skin is easier to remove after cooking and helps hold together the flakes when turning or moving the fish. The Alaska Seafood Marketing Institute explains that Alaska salmon isolates a layer of fat just under the skin. To ensure maximum moisture and flavor when cooking salmon, place the flesh side over the heat (skin side up) for the initial phase of cooking. This draws the fat into the flesh of the fish, rather than letting it render into the pan. The exception to this rule is baking. Since you do not flip the fish during baking, the flesh side (presentation side) should be placed face up in the pan.

Salmon availability is plentiful. Some type of fresh, farm-raised, or fresh-frozen salmon is available to cooks year-round across the United States and is of excellent quality.

FUN FACTS

- Before Alaska became a state, the salmon canning industry there produced 75 percent of the territory's tax revenues.

- *Quenelles*, delicate, egg-shaped pillows made of ground salmon and cream, were the gastronomic rage during the late 1700s in the court of Louis XV.

Salmon Loaf

⚓

PURE FOOD FISH,
PIKE PLACE MARKET

Salmon loaf, like salmon croquettes, is a dish that takes me back to childhood, when my mother used canned salmon in dishes smothered with cream sauce. This recipe modernizes the 1960s version by using freshly cooked salmon and brown rice, which improves taste and texture greatly. This loaf is good served warm or at room temperature and makes a great lunch item, Sunday brunch dish, or offering on the buffet table.

1 TEASPOON CANOLA OR VEGETABLE OIL

1/3 CUP MINCED ONION

1/3 CUP MINCED CELERY

3 CLOVES GARLIC, MINCED

2 EGGS

1/3 CUP SOUR CREAM

JUICE OF 1 LEMON

PINCH OF SALT AND PINCH OF FRESHLY
    GROUND BLACK PEPPER

1 1/2 CUPS COOKED BROWN OR LONG-GRAIN
    WHITE RICE

1 (13 3/4-OUNCE) CAN ARTICHOKE HEARTS
    PACKED IN WATER, DRAINED, RINSED,
    DRAINED AGAIN, AND COARSELY CHOPPED

1 1/2 CUPS POACHED OR LEFTOVER COOKED
    SALMON, SKIN AND BONES REMOVED,
    BROKEN INTO CHUNKS (ABOUT 3/4 POUND)
    (SEE PAGE 30)

SWEET PAPRIKA TO TASTE

1/2 CUP PLAIN YOGURT OR SOUR CREAM, FOR
    GARNISH

1 TABLESPOON FRESH MINCED DILL, OR 1 1/2
    TEASPOONS DRIED DILL, FOR GARNISH

1 CUCUMBER, PEELED AND CUT INTO
    1/8-INCH SLICES

1. Preheat oven to 325°. Grease a 9 x 5-inch loaf pan lightly with butter or spray with nonstick cooking spray.

2. Heat a small nonstick skillet over medium heat. When pan is hot, add canola oil. When oil is hot, add onion, celery, and garlic, and cook 3 to 5 minutes, or until vegetables are tender-crisp, stirring occasionally. Remove from heat and allow to cool.

3. In a large mixing bowl, lightly whisk eggs, then add sour cream, lemon juice, salt, and pepper. Whisk to blend thoroughly, then add sautéed vegetables and whisk to blend.

4. With a large spoon, stir in rice and artichoke hearts. Add salmon chunks, stirring thoroughly but gently without breaking up salmon. Place salmon mixture in loaf pan, smoothing top with the back of a spoon.

5. Cook 40 to 45 minutes, or until salmon loaf pulls away from sides of pan, loaf is firm, and top is lightly browned. Loaf should still be a bit moist when the blade of a small, sharp knife is inserted in center. Remove salmon from oven and allow to cool in the pan 5 minutes.

6. To serve, invert salmon loaf onto a large serving plate, cut into 4 slices (or 8 slices if serving for a buffet), and divide among individual plates. Sprinkle slices with paprika, spoon a dollop of yogurt to the side of slices, and sprinkle yogurt with dill. Surround salmon loaf with cucumber slices, and serve warm or at room temperature.

SERVES 4

Yoko's Barbecued Salmon

PIKE PLACE FISH,
PIKE PLACE MARKET

This recipe comes from Dick Yokoyama, one of Pike Place Fish's dedicated fishmongers. Except for brief stints in the U.S. Army and at a local grocery chain, Dick has worked in the Market since he was eight years old. Dick's preferred methods of cooking fish include broiling or barbecuing, as in this simple mayonnaise-based recipe. John Peterson, another familiar face and the manager of Pike Place Fish, uses a similar formula. When cooking king salmon, he stuffs the fish with a blend of mayonnaise, dill, and lemon, then barbecues the salmon, covered, over indirect heat. Take a cue from these well-seasoned (no pun intended) fishmongers, and add your own creative touches, such as a pinch of blackening mix, lemon pepper, five-spice powder, or Pike Place Fish's Northwest Seafood Seasoning (see page 146) to personalize this basic recipe.

1 WHOLE SALMON, BUTTERFLIED (ABOUT
   5 POUNDS)
1 CUP MAYONNAISE
2 CLOVES GARLIC, CHOPPED
SALT AND FRESHLY GROUND BLACK PEPPER
   TO TASTE

1. Heat electric grill to 350° (medium-high) and grease grill rack lightly or spray with nonstick cooking spray. Alternately, preheat oven to 350° and lightly coat a baking sheet large enough to hold salmon without crowding with oil or nonstick cooking spray. Rinse salmon with cool water inside and out, pat dry with paper towels, and set aside.

2. In a small mixing bowl, stir together mayonnaise and garlic. Open salmon so inside flesh is exposed, and lightly sprinkle with salt and pepper. With a spoon or spatula, spread mayonnaise-garlic mixture evenly over salmon.

3. Leaving salmon open so that the flesh is still exposed, carefully transfer to grill. Close cover and cook 20 to 25 minutes, or until salmon just begins to flake. If baking in oven, place the open salmon on the prepared baking sheet and cook 15 to 20 minutes, or until fish just turns opaque and begins to flake.

4. To serve, cut salmon into 6-ounce servings and place on individual plates.

SERVES 8 TO 10

FUN FACT

- The Native Americans' favorite way to cook salmon was to place an opened, cleaned fish between two tree branches fastened with small lateral twigs to hold the fish spread open before the fire. They also liked to plank their salmon on driftwood or sandwich it between alder wood, which was then laid over a bed of glowing embers. Clams, mussels, oysters, and barnacles were cooked in a similar fashion (they were never eaten raw). They were then strung on buckskin or cedar bark for winter storage. Today, you can experience salmon cooked in the traditional Native American way at Tillicum Village, a short boat ride from Seattle on Blake Island.

Baked Whole Salmon with Crab-and-Shrimp Stuffing

CITY FISH, PIKE PLACE MARKET

Jon Daniels, the young, energetic owner of the Market's City Fish, and Gary Cobb, his outgoing manager, make a dynamic duo that is hard to beat. Jon is a second-generation commercial fisher in Alaska, and Gary worked in Seattle-area restaurants for ten years before joining City Fish when Jon acquired the business in early 1995. This recipe, devised by Gary, was served at a barbecue for employees, family, and friends of City Fish, where it received wide acclaim. It has the added advantage of combining two of the Northwest's favorite foods—salmon and Dungeness crab—and can be cooked either in the oven or on the barbecue. Gary suggests serving it with a true French classic— béarnaise sauce.

OLIVE OIL

2 EGGS

1 TEASPOON GARLIC POWDER

1/2 TEASPOON GROUND CAYENNE PEPPER

1/2 POUND DUNGENESS CRABMEAT, SHELLS AND CARTILAGE REMOVED

1/2 POUND COOKED PINK (BAY OR SALAD) SHRIMP, RINSED, DRAINED, AND PATTED DRY

3 STALKS CELERY, DICED

1 ONION, DICED

1 CUP UNSEASONED DRY BREAD CRUMBS (SEE PAGE 9)

1 WHOLE SALMON, BUTTERFLIED (ABOUT 5 POUNDS)

1. Preheat oven to 375°. Line a large baking sheet with aluminum foil, placing one sheet of foil lengthwise across baking sheet, allowing enough excess foil on both sides to be folded across fish. Run another sheet of foil from top to bottom, again allowing enough foil to fold over fish. Brush foil with olive oil and set aside.

2. To make stuffing, in a medium mixing bowl, stir together eggs, garlic powder, and cayenne until completely mixed. Add crabmeat, shrimp, celery, onion, and bread crumbs, and stir gently, being careful not to break up crabmeat. Set aside.

3. Rinse salmon with cool water inside and out and pat dry with paper towels. Place salmon, skin side down, on prepared baking sheet. Open salmon so inside flesh is exposed, and spread stuffing evenly over half of fish. Fold top of fish over stuffing and press ends of fish together to seal. Bring ends of foil up around head and tail, fold down neatly to seal fish, then repeat with other ends of foil. Place in oven and bake for 30 to 35 minutes, or until fish is opaque throughout but still very moist. Remove from oven and let rest 10 to 15 minutes.

4. To serve, unseal foil, place fish on a warmed large platter, and allow everyone to serve themselves at the table.

SERVES 8 TO 10

Note: This can also be cooked on a grill. Place foil-wrapped salmon directly on grill rack and cook 12 minutes with grill uncovered, then turn fish over and cook an additional 12 minutes. Roll back upper layer of foil to expose top of fish, cover grill, and cook 8 to 10 minutes more, or until fish is opaque.

Balsamic-Glazed Salmon

IL BISTRO,
PIKE PLACE MARKET

The musky, yet sweet taste of balsamic vinegar pairs perfectly with the fatty flesh of salmon. This dish, which has been a daily feature at Il Bistro for over twenty years, was devised by Frank D'Aquila, the original chef and co-owner. He passed it along to his son, Dino, who also worked as a chef at the popular Market haunt. The balsamic glaze is good on other types of seafood as well, particularly on sablefish or scallops.

2 TABLESPOONS OLIVE OIL

1 1/2 POUNDS SALMON FILLET, BONES RE-
   MOVED, RINSED, DRAINED, PATTED DRY,
   AND CUT INTO 4 (6-OUNCE) PIECES

1 CLOVE GARLIC, CHOPPED

2 PLUM TOMATOES, CORED AND SLICED
   1/4 INCH THICK

2 TABLESPOONS FRESHLY SQUEEZED
   LEMON JUICE

1/4 CUP BALSAMIC VINEGAR

1/2 CUP SEAFOOD STOCK (SEE PAGE 318)
   OR CHICKEN STOCK

2 TABLESPOONS BUTTER

3 TABLESPOONS BASIL CHIFFONADE

1. Preheat oven to 425°. Lightly coat a baking dish large enough to hold the salmon fillets without crowding with oil or nonstick cooking spray.

2. Heat olive oil over medium-high heat in a skillet large enough to hold salmon fillets without crowding. (Alternately, use two skillets or cook salmon in two batches.) When oil is hot but not smoking, add salmon fillets flesh side down and cook 3 minutes, or until fish is golden brown outside, but still rare inside. Place salmon in reserved baking dish skin side down and place in oven for 8 to 10 minutes, or until fish just turns opaque.

3. Return skillet to medium-high heat and add garlic, tomatoes, lemon juice, balsamic vinegar, and fish stock. Cook until reduced to 3 to 4 tablespoons, stirring occasionally. Remove from heat and add butter and basil, swirling to blend.

4. To serve, divide salmon fillets among warmed individual plates and drizzle with glaze.

SERVES 4

FUN FACTS

- The technology to farm salmon in a captive environment from egg to adult was developed at the University of Washington, in Seattle.

- Salmon swim an estimated 14 miles per hour, compared to the tuna's rate of 50 miles per hour.

Richard's Copper River Salmon Croquettes

⚮

PURE FOOD FISH, PIKE PLACE MARKET

Richard Hoage, a close friend and trusted fish expert, has patiently and knowledgeably answered many of my questions while I was writing this book. Across the counter at Pure Food Fish, we compare notes on our finicky felines (Bo-Bo and Caribe), share Market gossip, and exchange recipes. In May and June, when Copper River kings are running, Richard occasionally saves some meaty bones as a special treat. I take them home and scrape away the succulent nubbins of flesh, then use Richard's recipe to make salmon croquettes. Sometimes I add my own flourishes, such as diced red or green peppers or the kernels from an ear of fresh corn, depending on what strikes my fancy. The croquettes can be served with Honey-Yogurt Salsa (see page 177), Sweet Pepper and Corn Relish (see page 180), or even Hoisin Dipping Sauce (see page 252).

1 EGG

PINCH OF SALT

PINCH OF FRESHLY GROUND BLACK OR
    WHITE PEPPER

2 CLOVES GARLIC, MINCED

$1/2$ ONION, DICED

2 TABLESPOONS MINCED FLAT-LEAF
    PARSLEY, OR 1 TABLESPOON MINCED
    CILANTRO, PLUS ADDITIONAL SPRIGS
    FOR GARNISH

1 POUND COPPER RIVER SALMON MEAT, OR
    1 POUND SALMON FILLET, SKIN AND
    BONES REMOVED, MINCED BY HAND OR
    FOOD PROCESSOR

1 TO $1 1/2$ CUPS UNSEASONED FRESH BREAD
    CRUMBS (SEE PAGE 9)

1 TABLESPOON OLIVE OIL, OR $1 1/2$
    TEASPOONS OLIVE OIL AND $1 1/2$
    TEASPOONS UNSALTED BUTTER

LEMON WEDGES, FOR GARNISH

1. In a large mixing bowl, stir together egg, salt, pepper, garlic, onion, and parsley. Add salmon and stir gently until egg mixture is well incorporated. Add 1 cup of the bread crumbs and stir again. If salmon mixture is still too sticky to handle, add remaining bread crumbs and stir again. Divide salmon into 4 portions and form into patties. Do not handle salmon any more than absolutely necessary.

2. Over medium heat, place a nonstick skillet large enough to hold patties without crowding. When pan is hot, add olive oil. When oil is hot but not smoking, add patties and cook 5 minutes, or until lightly browned. Turn and cook 3 to 5 minutes more, or until patties just turn opaque in middle. Alternately, the patties can be baked on a lightly greased baking sheet in a 400° oven for 6 to 8 minutes on each side, or until patties are lightly browned, or broil 4 to 6 inches from heat source for 4 to 5 minutes on each side.

3. Transfer croquettes to individual plates, garnish with parsley and lemon wedges, and serve.

SERVES 4

Twice-Baked Potatoes with Salmon-Basil Stuffing

DUFFIELD FARMS, PIKE PLACE MARKET

The Duff family, Judy and Dave and their daughter Deanna, come to the Market with a bounty of organic baby lettuces, vegetables, herbs, edible flowers, and potatoes, including Yukon gold and yellow Finn. Yellow Finns are among the most well known of the specialty potatoes that are sweeping the country as consumers demand an option to the ubiquitous russet. Yellow Finns have a slightly rough, thin, pale gold skin. The flesh is yellow, with a traditional potato flavor, and is best when baked. Yukon Golds also take well to baking. They are round, with yellow-tan skin, rich yellow flesh, and a sweet, buttery flavor. Washington is the second largest producer of potatoes in the United States, trailing Idaho.

4 MEDIUM TO LARGE OR 8 SMALL YUKON
    GOLD OR YELLOW FINN POTATOES,
    SCRUBBED AND DRIED
1/2 POUND SALMON FILLETS, RINSED,
    DRAINED, AND PATTED DRY
2 TABLESPOONS CANOLA OR VEGETABLE OIL
2 TABLESPOONS ALL-PURPOSE FLOUR
1 CUP NONFAT OR LOWFAT MILK
2 TABLESPOONS STORE-BOUGHT PESTO
    SAUCE
SALT AND FRESHLY GROUND PEPPER
    TO TASTE
2 TABLESPOONS FRESHLY GRATED
    PARMESAN CHEESE
BASIL LEAVES, FOR GARNISH

1. Preheat oven to 350°.

2. Prick potatoes, in a baking dish, and cook for 1 hour, or until tender. During last 15 minutes of baking, lightly coat a second baking dish with oil or nonstick cooking spray, and place salmon fillets skin side down in dish. Bake 7 to 10 minutes, or until salmon is opaque throughout. Remove from oven and set aside until salmon is cool enough to handle, then remove salmon skin and bones and discard. Crumble salmon and reserve.

3. When potatoes are done, remove from oven and cut in half lengthwise. Gently scoop out cooked potato with a spoon, being careful not to tear potato skin. Mash potato flesh with a potato masher, ricer, or fork until smooth, then set aside mashed potato flesh and potato skin shells.

4. Heat oil in a skillet over medium heat and add flour. Cook 1 to 2 minutes, stirring continuously, until mixture is smooth. Add milk slowly, stirring after each addition to prevent lumps. Stir continuously until mixture thickens. Remove from heat, add pesto, and stir to mix thoroughly.

5. Add mashed potatoes to pesto cream sauce and stir well to mix. Add salmon and stir gently to mix. Season to taste with salt and pepper. Divide potato-salmon stuffing among reserved potato skins. Place potato skins on baking sheet and cook 10 minutes, or until stuffing is heated through.

6. To serve, divide stuffed potatoes among warmed individual plates. Sprinkle with Parmesan cheese, garnish with basil leaves, and serve immediately.

SERVES 4

Steamed Salmon Cantonese Style

———— ⊰✦⊱ ————

WILD GINGER,
SEATTLE, WASHINGTON

Wild Ginger, a very popular local restaurant near Pike Place Market, is one of my favorite places to go for a leisurely dinner, Saturday lunch, or late-night bite to eat. When salmon is steamed with fresh ginger, fish sauce, and premium rice wine, it takes on a creamy texture that cannot be achieved with any other cooking method. As a final step, hot, garlic-fla-vored oil is poured over the salmon to sear in the juices. The recipe is versatile; try substituting fresh basil, gin-gerroot, or cilantro for the garlic, or different kinds of fish, such as rockfish or steelhead. And although I give instructions for steaming in a wok to keep the recipe authentic, the basic instructions for steaming on a rack (see page 31) could be substituted.

3 CUPS WATER

1/2 POUND SALMON FILLETS, BONES
    REMOVED, RINSED, DRAINED, PATTED
    DRY, AND CUT INTO 2 (4-OUNCE) PIECES

1/2-INCH LENGTH GINGERROOT, VERY THINLY
    SLICED

2 TABLESPOONS SHAO HSING CHINESE
    RICE WINE OR MIRIN

2 TABLESPOONS THAI FISH SAUCE
    (*NAM PLA*)

2 TO 3 TABLESPOONS PEANUT OIL

1 CLOVE GARLIC

2 GREEN ONIONS, TOP 2 INCHES REMOVED,
    REMAINING PORTION JULIENNED

2 SPRIGS CILANTRO, FOR GARNISH

1. To steam in a wok, cross two chopsticks in an "X," then cut a groove in the lower chopstick so that the top one fits snugly. Set the chopsticks in the wok and add water to 1 inch below the level of the chopsticks. Place lid on wok and turn heat to high.

2. Place salmon skin side down on a glass pie plate or rimmed glass plate slightly smaller than the diameter of the wok. Place salmon on plate and cover with ginger slices. Pour rice wine and fish sauce over fish.

3. When the water is boiling, remove lid from wok and position plate containing salmon and seasonings on top of chopsticks. Replace lid and cook 7 to 8 minutes, or until salmon just turns opaque and begins to flake.

4. Two to three minutes before salmon is done steaming, heat peanut oil in a small skillet over high heat. When oil is very hot, add garlic clove and cook until browned. Discard garlic, but do not turn off heat until you use the oil; it must be very hot to sear the fish properly.

5. When salmon is cooked, transfer to a warm plate. Place green onion strips on top of fish and immediately pour hot oil over fish and onions. Garnish with cilantro and serve immediately.

SERVES 2 AS AN ENTRÉE, OR 4 AS AN APPETIZER

Sephardic Salmon

———— ⊰≬⊱ ————

Sephardic Jews from the Mediterranean came to the Market during its early days and were some of the first fishmongers to work the stalls and own the businesses. Today, relatives of many of the original families still sell fish in the Market. This salmon dish, with its sweet-and-sour sauce, is my rendition of a traditional fish course served by Sephardic Jews for a Passover Seder dinner. And while I have taken the liberty of substituting several typically Northwestern ingredients such as dried cherries and hazelnuts for some of the classic ingredients, I think the recipe still captures the joy of this holiday. This dish can be served either hot or at room temperature and therefore makes a good potluck dish or addition to the buffet table.

1/2 CUP WHITE WINE VINEGAR

1/2 CUP BALSAMIC VINEGAR

1 CUP WATER

2 TABLESPOONS SUGAR

1 TABLESPOON SOY SAUCE

1 TABLESPOON TOMATO PASTE

2 CLOVES GARLIC, PEELED AND SMASHED
    WITH THE FLAT PART OF A KNIFE BLADE

2 QUARTER-SIZE ROUNDS OF SLICED
    GINGERROOT, SMASHED WITH THE FLAT
    PART OF A KNIFE BLADE

SALT AND FRESHLY GROUND BLACK PEPPER
    TO TASTE

1 TABLESPOON VEGETABLE OIL

2 ONIONS, SLICED 1/8 INCH THICK

1/4 CUP DRIED CHERRIES OR DRIED
    CRANBERRIES

1/4 CUP CHOPPED HAZELNUTS

1 1/2 POUND SALMON STEAKS, 3/4 INCH
    THICK, RINSED, DRAINED, AND PATTED
    DRY

1. Add white wine vinegar, balsamic vinegar, water, sugar, soy sauce, tomato paste, garlic, and gingerroot to a saucepan and bring to a boil. Stir well, reduce heat to medium, and cook 15 minutes, or until sauce thickens to a light syrupy consistency and about 3/4 cup remains. Stir occasionally. Season to taste with salt and pepper and stir well to mix. Strain out solids and discard. Place vinegar mixture in a bowl and set aside.

2. Heat vegetable oil in a large skillet over medium-high heat. Add onion slices and cook 2 minutes, stirring often. Turn down heat to medium and cook 8 minutes, stirring occasionally, or until onions are soft and lightly browned. Do not allow onions to burn.

3. Pour reserved reduced vinegar mixture over onions and stir well. Add dried cherries and hazelnuts, stir well, and remove from heat. Set aside.

4. Preheat oven to 350°. Lightly coat a baking sheet with oil or nonstick cooking spray. Lightly sprinkle salmon with salt and pepper, then place on baking sheet. Cook 3 to 4 minutes, turn fish, then cook 3 to 4 minutes more, or just until fish turns opaque. (For well-done fish, as prescribed by Jewish dietary law, see page 101)

5. To serve, place salmon steaks on a large warmed platter and spoon onions and sauce over fish.

SERVES 4

Note: Leftover sweet-and-sour sauce, which is similar to a chutney or compote, is delicious served with other types of fish and chicken, or even with cream cheese and bagels.

Cold-Smoked Salmon with Corn Bread Pudding, Shiitake Relish, and Fried Basil

——✦——

ETTA'S SEAFOOD, SEATTLE, WASHINGTON

This is one of the best renditions of salmon in town. It's chef/owner Tom Douglas's signature dish from Etta's Seafood, located just north of the Pike Place Market. The cold-smoked salmon harks back to Northwest native cooking techniques, while the corn pudding is pure down-home goodness, and the shiitake relish gives a final Pacific Rim twist. This recipe requires advance preparation.

¼ CUP SUGAR

1 TABLESPOON KOSHER SALT

1 TEASPOON MINCED FRESH THYME

2 TABLESPOONS SWEET PAPRIKA

2¼ TEASPOONS COARSELY GROUND BLACK
  PEPPER

1½ POUNDS SALMON FILLETS, SKIN AND
  BONES REMOVED, RINSED, DRAINED, PAT-
  TED DRY, AND CUT INTO 4 (6-OUNCE)
  PIECES

2 TEASPOONS BUTTER

1 TABLESPOON OLIVE OIL

30 FRESH BASIL LEAVES

CORN BREAD PUDDING (RECIPE FOLLOWS)

SHIITAKE RELISH (RECIPE FOLLOWS)

½ LEMON, CUT INTO 4 WEDGES, FOR
  GARNISH

1. In a small bowl, combine sugar, salt, thyme, paprika, and black pepper. Pat spice mixture over both sides of salmon fillets. Wrap fillets in plastic wrap and refrigerate 3 to 6 hours.

2. Rinse fillets under cold running water, then pat dry with paper towels. Put fillets on a plate, do not cover, and place in refrigerator overnight to dry.

3. Prepare an electric smoker according to manufacturer's instructions and cold-smoke the salmon fillets at 80° to 100° for 1 hour. Remove from smoker and refrigerate until ready to use.

4. Ten minutes before cooking, preheat oven to 450°. Lightly coat a baking sheet with oil or nonstick cooking spray, and set aside.

5. Heat a large skillet over medium-high heat. Add butter and, when melted, add salmon fillets, flesh side down. Cook 2 minutes, or until lightly browned. Turn and cook 2 minutes more, or until skin is lightly browned. Place salmon on baking sheet skin side down and bake in oven for 4 to 5 minutes, or until salmon is just opaque.

6. Meanwhile, heat olive oil in a small skillet over medium-high heat. When pan is very hot, add basil leaves and cook 30 seconds to 1 minute, or until basil turns bright green. Drain basil leaves on several layers of paper towels and reserve.

7. To serve, spoon warm Corn Bread Pudding into center of warmed individual plates. Top with salmon, placing it slightly to one side. Spoon Shiitake Relish over salmon fillets and sprinkle with fried basil leaves. Garnish with lemon slices and serve immediately.

SERVES 4

Corn Bread Pudding

5 CUPS CUBED CORN BREAD (1-INCH
    CUBES) (RECIPE FOLLOWS)

1 TABLESPOON BUTTER PLUS EXTRA

1 ONION, CUT INTO $1/8$-INCH-THICK SLICES

3 CUPS HEAVY WHIPPING CREAM

6 EGGS

1 $1/2$ CUPS GRATED DRY MONTEREY JACK
    CHEESE

1 $1/2$ TABLESPOONS MIXED CHOPPED FRESH
    PARSLEY, CHIVES, AND THYME OR OTHER
    HERBS

2 TEASPOONS SALT

1 TEASPOON FRESHLY GROUND BLACK
    PEPPER

1. Preheat oven to 375°. Grease a deep 12 x 9-inch baking pan or a 13 x 9-inch baking pan with butter.

2. Fill baking pan with corn bread cubes. Heat 1 tablespoon butter in a large skillet over medium-low to medium heat and cook onions 20 minutes, or until very soft and golden brown. Recipe may be prepared up to this point, 1 day in advance.

3. One hour before serving, whisk whipping cream and eggs until well blended. Stir in cooked onion, Monterey jack cheese, herbs, salt, and pepper. Pour cream mixture over corn bread in pan. Bake 45 minutes, or until pudding is set, the top is golden, and a knife blade inserted in the center comes out clean.

Corn Bread

1 CUP ALL-PURPOSE FLOUR

2 TEASPOONS BAKING POWDER

1 TEASPOON SALT

$3/4$ CUP CORNMEAL

$1/2$ CUP GRATED PEPPER JACK CHEESE

2 EGGS

1 CUP MILK

1 TABLESPOON HONEY

4 TABLESPOONS BUTTER, MELTED

1. Preheat oven to 425°. Generously grease a 9 x 9-inch baking pan.

2. Sift flour, baking powder, and salt together into a large mixing bowl. Add cornmeal and cheese and mix well.

3. In a small mixing bowl, whisk together eggs, milk, and honey. Make a well in center of dry ingredients and add wet ingredients, stirring just to combine. Stir in melted butter. Pour batter into baking pan and bake 20 to 25 minutes, or until top is golden brown and a toothpick inserted in the center comes out clean. The corn bread may be made up to 3 days in advance, and allowed to dry slightly before making the pudding.

Shiitake Relish

$3/4$ POUND FRESH SHIITAKE MUSHROOMS

2 TO 3 TABLESPOONS OLIVE OIL

SALT AND FRESHLY GROUND BLACK PEPPER
    TO TASTE

2 TABLESPOONS MINCED SHALLOTS

2 TEASPOONS MINCED GARLIC

2 TABLESPOONS MIXED CHOPPED FRESH
    THYME, ROSEMARY, SAGE, OREGANO, AND
    PARSLEY OR OTHER HERBS

1 TABLESPOON BALSAMIC VINEGAR

1 $1/2$ TEASPOONS FRESHLY SQUEEZED
    LEMON JUICE

2 TABLESPOONS EXTRA VIRGIN OLIVE OIL

1. Preheat grill.

2. Remove stems from mushrooms and discard. Wipe mushroom caps with damp paper towels to remove surface dirt. Brush caps lightly with 1 to 2 tablespoons of the olive oil and place on grill. Grill on both sides until browned and cooked through, about 2 to 3 minutes on each side. Cut mushrooms into very thin strips, place in a bowl, season lightly with salt and pepper, and reserve.

3. Heat remaining 1 tablespoon olive oil in skillet over low heat. Add shallots and garlic and sweat 3 to 4 minutes, or until soft, stirring occasionally. Do not allow to brown. Allow to cool slightly, then add shallots to mushrooms. Stir in fresh herbs.

4. In a small mixing bowl, whisk together balsamic vinegar, lemon juice, and extra virgin olive oil. Pour over mushroom mixture and toss gently. Season to taste with salt and pepper. Shiitake Relish is best served the same day it is made.

MAKES 1 ½ CUPS

Note: Cold-smoking can be a tricky technique. At Etta's, they use a commercial smoker; many home smokers simply are not capable of duplicating the results. As an alternative, the salmon may be taken to a local smokehouse, such as Portlock or Jensen's in Seattle, and cold-smoked there. A simpler alternative is to pat the salmon fillets with the spice rub (Step 1), wrap and refrigerate the fillets several hours or overnight, rinse and pat dry, then proceed with the recipe as written, continuing with Step 4. The result will be different because there will be no smoky flavor, but it will still be delicious.

HANDY SALMON TIP

Here's the late James Beard's favorite method for broiling salmon: Generously brush salmon steaks or fillets with oil and squirt with a little lemon juice. For variations in flavor, rub in a little of his favorite salmon herbs—rosemary, dill, or tarragon—before broiling the fish.

FUN FACTS

• The U.S. salmon industry got its start in the early 1850s, when 100-pound Chinook salmon were netted from California's Sacramento River to feed the gold miners. When canning was introduced in the 1860s, salmon pioneers quickly headed north to the Columbia River between Oregon and Washington, where there were so many Chinooks the fishermen needed horses to haul in the catch.

• According to Northwest Native Americans, salmon were spirit people living in a magic village under the sea who were sent upriver to feed the human race. Indeed, in several native languages, the word for fish is the same as the word for salmon. Each year, the people prayed for the salmon to return. The arrival of the salmon was anticipated with eagerness, because it meant that the dried fish of winter could be replaced with succulent fresh salmon. Only after the bones of the first salmon were returned to the river, ensuring their annual return, could the harvest begin. Today, as in ancient times, the arrival of the first spring Chinook creates excitement among Native Americans in the Northwest.

Alaskan Salmon with Warm Blackberry and Shallot Compote

―――⊰≫⊱―――

McCORMICK & SCHMICK'S, SEATTLE, WASHINGTON

At FishExpo Seattle, a three-day trade show for commercial fishers, I attended a class entitled "Cooking with Great Seafood Chefs" and watched Greg Soukup, former executive chef at Seattle's McCormick & Schmick's seafood restaurant, prepare this dish for an appreciative crowd. I was impressed with his use of seasonal ingredients in a simple, yet tasty way. This would be the perfect dish to make at the height of summer, when blackberries are in their prime and Alaskan sockeye salmon are running strong.

3 TO 4 SHALLOTS, PEELED

2 TABLESPOONS OLIVE OIL

1/4 CUP SUGAR

2 CUPS FRESH BLACKBERRIES, GENTLY
    RINSED, DRAINED, AND PATTED DRY

1/4 CUP RASPBERRY VINEGAR

1/4 CUP ALL-PURPOSE FLOUR

1 TABLESPOON MINCED FRESH CHERVIL

1 TABLESPOON MINCED FRESH PARSLEY

PINCH OF SALT

PINCH OF FRESHLY GROUND BLACK PEPPER

1 1/2 POUNDS SALMON FILLETS, SKIN AND
    BONES REMOVED, RINSED, DRAINED, AND
    PATTED DRY, AND CUT INTO 4 (6-OUNCE)
    PIECES

1. Preheat oven to 400°.

2. In a mixing bowl, toss shallots, 1 tablespoon of the olive oil, and the sugar. Spread in a baking pan and cook 10 to 15 minutes, or until shallots are lightly browned and soft. Remove from oven and spoon shallots and syrup into a nonreactive mixing bowl with a lid. Add blackberries and raspberry vinegar and toss gently to mix ingredients, being careful not to break up berries. Cover bowl and set aside.

3. Place a nonstick skillet large enough to hold salmon fillets without crowding over medium heat. When pan is hot, add the remaining 1 tablespoon olive oil. While oil is heating, mix together flour, chervil, parsley, salt, and pepper on a plate or a piece of waxed paper. Pat both sides of salmon fillets in flour mixture, then shake off excess.

4. When oil is hot, add salmon fillets and cook 3 to 5 minutes. Turn and cook 3 to 5 minutes more, or until fish just turns opaque.

5. To serve, remove salmon fillets to individual plates and spoon compote over tops of fillets.

SERVES 4

Seared Salmon with Thai Curry Peanut Sauce

⚬⟋⟍⚬

PONTI SEAFOOD GRILL, SEATTLE, WASHINGTON

Perched on the ship canal under the Fremont Bridge, Ponti Seafood Grill is one of the premier seafood houses in Seattle. When fusion cuisine first became popular, executive chef Alvin Binuya gained national attention for his deft handling of this new way of cooking. His dishes combine the best features of Asian, Southwest, Northwest, and European (primarily Italian) classics. Chef Binuya has this advice: Anything goes for preparation, but don't mask the characteristics of the seafood by burying it in ingredients.

1/2 CUP ROASTED, UNSALTED PEANUTS

2 TABLESPOONS OLIVE OIL

1/2 CUP DICED ONION

2 TEASPOONS CHOPPED GINGERROOT

1 TABLESPOON THAI YELLOW CURRY PASTE

2 TABLESPOONS THAI FISH SAUCE
   (NAM PLA)

1 (14-OUNCE) CAN COCONUT MILK

1 TABLESPOON SMOOTH PEANUT BUTTER

2 TEASPOONS FRESHLY SQUEEZED LIME
   JUICE

1/2 CUP CHOPPED PAPAYA, APPLE, OR
   BANANA

1/2 CUP ALL-PURPOSE FLOUR

1/4 TEASPOON SALT

1/8 TEASPOON FRESHLY GROUND BLACK
   PEPPER

1 1/2 POUNDS SALMON FILLETS, SKIN AND
   BONES REMOVED, RINSED, DRAINED,

PATTED DRY, AND CUT INTO 4 (6-OUNCE)
   PIECES

AROMATIC BASMATI RICE (RECIPE
   FOLLOWS)

THAI RED CABBAGE SLAW (RECIPE
   FOLLOWS)

SNIPPED FRESH CHIVES, FOR GARNISH

1. Place peanuts in a resealable plastic bag, seal, and pound with the flat side of a mallet until peanuts are finely ground.

2. To make peanut sauce, in a medium saucepan or skillet, heat 1 tablespoon of the olive oil over medium-high heat. Add onion and gingerroot and cook 5 to 7 minutes, or until onion is soft, stirring occasionally. Add ground peanuts, yellow curry paste, fish sauce, coconut milk, peanut butter, lime juice, and papaya. Stir well, decrease heat to low, and simmer 30 minutes, stirring often, or until sauce thickens and darkens in color.

3. About 10 minutes before serving, heat the remaining 1 tablespoon olive oil over medium-high heat. Mix flour, salt, and black pepper on a plate or a piece of waxed paper and dredge salmon fillets in seasoned flour, patting off excess.

4. When oil is very hot, add salmon fillets and cook 3 to 5 minutes. Turn and cook 3 to 5 minutes more, or until salmon is just opaque, about 10 minutes per inch of thickness.

5. To serve, cover individual plates with a thin layer of peanut sauce and place a mound of basmati rice in the center of the sauce. Flatten rice slightly and place a salmon fillet on top. Divide Red Cabbage Slaw over tops of fillets, and garnish with chives.

SERVES 4

Thai Red Cabbage Slaw

1 TABLESPOON FRESHLY SQUEEZED LIME
   JUICE
2 TEASPOONS Thai FISH SAUCE (*NAM PLA*)
2 TABLESPOONS OLIVE OIL
1/4 HEAD RED CABBAGE, CUT INTO VERY
   THIN SLIVERS

In a medium mixing bowl, whisk together lime juice, fish sauce, and olive oil. Add cabbage, toss to mix thoroughly, cover, and refrigerate until ready to serve.

MAKES 1 CUP

Aromatic Basmati Rice

1 TABLESPOON UNSALTED BUTTER
1 TABLESPOON CHOPPED ONION
1 CUP UNCOOKED BASMATI RICE
1 1/2 CUPS WATER
1/2 TEASPOON SALT
1 TEASPOON CURRY POWDER

In a saucepan, heat butter over medium-high heat. When butter has melted, add onion and cook 3 minutes, or until onion is soft, stirring occasionally. Add rice and stir continuously, until rice grains are evenly coated with butter. Add water, salt, and curry powder and stir to mix well. Bring to a boil, turn down heat to low, cover pan, and cook 20 minutes, or until rice is tender and water has evaporated.

MAKES 3 1/2 CUPS

BRUCE GORE SALMON

AMONG FROZEN FISH, those produced by Bruce Gore set the standard. Bruce, who has fished southeastern Alaskan waters for over twenty-five years, and the other fishermen he has trained to use his method, handle the wild Alaska salmon they catch with the utmost care and respect.

Bruce explains that fish is caught by hook and line and killed in the water, so there is no bruising. They are handled one at a time and dressed immediately so their hearts stop beating. Then they are force-bled, cleaned, and placed into the hold within 15 to 90 minutes of catching. The fish are frozen pre-rigor mortis so no enzymatic degeneration occurs. When the fish are thawed, they look like they just jumped out of the water. Biochemically, the fish are two hours old.

Each fish is tagged after it is caught so it can be tracked for consistency. When restaurants or upscale grocery stores around the country thaw a Bruce Gore salmon weeks or months later, biologically the fish is fresher than some "fresh runs" that spend more time in transit. Even in a seafood town such as Seattle, some of the finest white-tablecloth restaurants serve Bruce Gore salmon when wild fresh fish isn't available, proudly touting the fact on their menus.

Salmon Cakes with Yellow Corn Relish

———— ✦ ————

RAY'S BOATHOUSE, SEATTLE, WASHINGTON

Wayne Ludvigsen is the dining room manager and former longtime chef at Ray's Boathouse and a self-described Market lover. You can find Wayne in the Market at the height of the summer growing season without too much trouble. As he says, "I'm the guy with a mouthful of Rainier cherries and raspberries, chasing it with basil." Wayne suggests using end pieces and scraps of salmon in this recipes as a budget-stretching measure. The patties can be cooked, then frozen for up to 3 months.

3/4 POUND SALMON, SKIN AND BONES REMOVED, RINSED, DRAINED, PATTED DRY, AND COARSELY CHOPPED

2 TABLESPOONS STEMMED, SEEDED, AND DICED RED BELL PEPPER

2 TABLESPOONS STEMMED, SEEDED, AND DICED RED ONION

1 TABLESPOON MINCED FRESH TARRAGON

2 TABLESPOONS CAPERS, DRAINED AND MINCED

1/2 CUP MAYONNAISE

1 1/2 TEASPOONS DIJON MUSTARD

1 TABLESPOON OLD BAY SEASONING

2 TABLESPOONS MINCED GREEN ONIONS

1/2 TEASPOON GROUND CAYENNE PEPPER

1/2 TEASPOON FRESHLY GROUND BLACK PEPPER

1/2 TEASPOON SAMBAL OELEK CHILI PASTE

1 TABLESPOON FRESHLY SQUEEZED LEMON JUICE

2 1/2 CUPS PANKO BREAD CRUMBS OR UN-SEASONED SOFT BREAD CRUMBS (SEE PAGE 9)

2 TABLESPOONS OLIVE OIL

CORN RELISH (RECIPE FOLLOWS)

1. Preheat oven to 200°.

2. Place salmon in a food processor and pulse until finely chopped but not puréed. Transfer to a large mixing bowl and add red bell pepper, onion, tarragon, capers, mayonnaise, mustard, Old Bay seasoning, green onions, cayenne, black pepper, Sambal Oelek, lemon juice, and 1/2 cup of the panko bread crumbs. Gently toss until ingredients are thoroughly combined.

3. Form salmon mixture into 8 patties by rolling into equal-sized balls, rolling in remaining 2 cups panko bread crumbs, then flattening into patties.

4. Heat olive oil in a large skillet over medium-high heat. Add salmon patties without crowding, cooking in two batches if necessary. Cook 2 to 3 minutes, turn, and cook 2 to 3 minutes more, or until patties are golden brown on the surface and just opaque inside. Place patties on baking sheet and keep warm in oven.

5. To serve, divide Corn Relish among individual plates. Place 2 salmon cakes on each plate in the center of each mound of relish.

SERVES 4

Note: Sambal Oelek is a multipurpose condiment made of chiles, brown sugar, and salt. It is available in Indonesian and some Chinese markets.

Yellow Corn Relish

4 EARS YELLOW CORN, HUSKS REMOVED

1 TABLESPOON STEMMED, SEEDED, AND
　　DICED RED BELL PEPPER

1 TABLESPOON STEMMED, SEEDED, AND
　　DICED RED ONION

$1/2$ TEASPOON MINCED GARLIC

2 TABLESPOONS MINCED CILANTRO

$1/4$ TEASPOON GROUND CUMIN

$1/4$ TEASPOON GROUND CURRY POWDER

$1/4$ TEASPOON SAMBAL OELEK CHILI PASTE

$1/2$ TEASPOON BUTTER

2 TABLESPOONS WHITE WINE

1. Preheat grill and oil rack lightly or spray with nonstick cooking spray.

2. Place ears of corn on grill and cook 3 to 5 minutes per side, turning often, or until corn is tender and has golden brown grill marks. Let cool, then cut off kernels and place in mixing bowl. Add remaining ingredients and mix well.

3. Warm a small skillet over medium heat, add relish, and cook 3 minutes, or until warmed through, stirring occasionally. Keep warm over low heat until ready to serve.

MAKES $3^1/2$ CUPS

HANDY SALMON TIP

Jon Rowley, well-known in Seattle as the "seafood guru," likes to cook salmon fillets or steaks on a grill, then cover the grill and roast the salmon. Indoor cooks can sear the salmon on both sides in an oven-proof pan, then transfer the pan to a hot oven. The fish should emerge medium-rare in the center with a firm, crusty surface that has an almost caramel taste.

FUN FACTS

- The salmon was the first fish specifically mentioned in American history. Eric the Red reported that the Vikings had encountered larger salmon here than they had ever seen before.

- In earlier times, there were so many salmon throughout the waters of the world that salmon was a cheap fish eaten by everyone from slaves to monks. In Paris in the Middle Ages, salmon were taken from the Seine River, and the Rhine River in Germany ran with salmon until 25 years ago.

- Although man first attempted hatching salmon eggs over 200 years ago, it wasn't until scientists in Norway and Scotland tried again in the 1960s that the modern era of salmon farming started. Atlantic salmon are the easiest species to farm, and account for more than three-quarters of the world's pen-raised salmon production. Atlantics grow to a weight of 3 to 10 pounds in 12 to 18 months.

Spicy Smoked Salmon with Wasabi Dipping Sauce

———❧———

By curing a side of salmon overnight in a marinade brimming with freshly ground spices and a touch of liquid smoke, then cooking the fish in a low oven, the pink flesh becomes meltingly tender and flavorful, with a taste similar to smoked salmon. You can serve Spicy Smoked Salmon straight from the oven, at room temperature, or refrigerate it and serve later. It's a perfect dish for buffets. Just be sure to pass the Wasabi Dipping Sauce, which is very hot and spicy—a little bit goes a long way.

1 TABLESPOON SALMON SPICE MIX (RECIPE
    FOLLOWS)
1 TABLESPOON SOY SAUCE
1 TABLESPOON MIRIN
1 TABLESPOON SAKE
1 TABLESPOON UNSEASONED RICE VINEGAR
1 TABLESPOON CANOLA OR SESAME OIL
1 TABLESPOON MAPLE SYRUP
1 TABLESPOON LIQUID SMOKE
PINCH OF SALT
PINCH OF FRESHLY GROUND BLACK PEPPER
PINCH OF CRUSHED RED PEPPER FLAKES
1 SIDE OF SALMON, FILLETED AND BONED,
    WITH SKIN (ABOUT 2 1/2 POUNDS)
FRESHLY GROUND SZECHWAN
    PEPPERCORNS, TOASTED (PAGE 10),
    OPTIONAL
WASABI DIPPING SAUCE (RECIPE FOLLOWS)

1. Place Salmon Spice Mix, soy sauce, mirin, sake, rice vinegar, canola oil, maple syrup, liquid smoke, salt, black pepper, and red pepper flakes in a small nonreactive bowl with a lid and mix until well blended.

2. Place a piece of plastic wrap lengthwise on a baking sheet, allowing 8 inches of extra wrap at each end to cover salmon. Place salmon on plastic wrap skin side down. Spoon half the marinade over salmon and rub it into the flesh. Turn salmon over and cover completely with plastic wrap. Place salmon and leftover marinade in refrigerator overnight.

3. One hour before cooking, remove salmon and the remaining marinade from refrigerator and let sit at room temperature. Ten minutes before cooking, preheat oven to 275°. Place a rack large enough to hold fish on a baking sheet and spray the rack with nonstick cooking spray.

4. When oven is hot, place salmon on rack skin side down. Pour half of remaining marinade onto salmon, patting it gently.

5. Place baking sheet on top rack of oven and roast salmon for 15 minutes. Remove salmon from oven and cover with remaining marinade. Return salmon to oven for 30 to 45 minutes more, or until opaque throughout and golden brown in color.

6. To serve, remove skin (if desired), and place fish on a serving platter. Sprinkle with Szechwan peppercorns and pass the Wasabi Dipping Sauce at the table.

SERVES 12 AS AN APPETIZER; 6 TO 8 AS
    AN ENTRÉE

Salmon Spice Mix

1 WHOLE STAR ANISE

1 TABLESPOON WHOLE CORIANDER SEED

4 WHOLE ALLSPICE

1 (3-INCH) STICK CINNAMON, BROKEN INTO
   SEVERAL PIECES

Place all of the ingredients in a spice mill or small electric coffee grinder and process until very finely ground. Pour spices into a small non-reactive bowl or jar with a lid, cover, and set aside.

Wasabi Dipping Sauce

1 TABLESPOON WASABI POWDER

1 TABLESPOON SOY SAUCE

1 TABLESPOON WATER

2 TABLESPOONS HONEY MUSTARD

Stir together all of the ingredients in a small nonreactive bowl. Allow to sit at room temperature at least 10 minutes to allow flavors to blend, or cover and refrigerate until ready to use.

MAKES ABOUT ¼ CUP

FUN FACTS

• In 1941 salmon fishing was Puget Sound's newest boom industry. By the end of the war years, more than 100 boathouses like Ray's, Baronof's, and Lloyd's dotted the shores of the Sound. The boathouses offered bait, fishing gear, and rental boats for a successful day of angling. Salmon derbies had become so popular by the 1940s that fishing competitions proliferated, with almost every town along the Sound, and businesses and organizations, sponsoring one. Boats, motors, and even cars were awarded as prizes for 62-pound kings or 16-pound silvers.

• Northwest natives often left their salmon in the smokehouse for two weeks, which resulted in a dark brown, very smoky salmon. They also took smoked salmon, dried and seasoned it, and cut it into thin strips to make "squaw candy," something similar to beef jerky that was eaten between meals as a snack. "Squaw candy" is a popular food for modern-day hikers and campers.

The Odd Skillet of Finfish

THIS CHAPTER HIGHLIGHTS a collection of finfish that are unusual in various ways. Both the flesh and roe of the shad are eaten. With over 365 bones, the shad is a true test of a fishmonger's expertise. Skate, a member of the ray family, has long been a European favorite but has only recently gained acceptance on American tables thanks to its sweet, scalloplike flavor and melting texture. Smelt are small, bony fish related to salmon and trout. They are most often fried in butter and eaten whole. The sturgeon has a fierce, prehistoric appearance due in part to the rows of bony plates, or scutes, along its sides. While the fish once faced extinction, it has seen a resurgence thanks to aquaculture.

Shad

The American shad (*Alosa sapidissima*) is a member of the herring family Clupeidae. Reaching lengths of 2 1/2 feet to 3 feet, the American shad is the largest member of the 190-member family, which includes sardines, shads, alewives, menhaden, and herrings. The American shad, also known as the common shad or white shad, is found along the West Coast from Baja California to Alaska; however, it is most common from central California to British Columbia.

Like the salmon, the shad is an anadromous fish that hatches in fresh water, swims to the ocean to grow for three to five years into adulthood, then most likely returns to spawn in the river in which it was born, although this has not been definitively proven. Almost all fish die after spawning, but a few survive to spawn again the following year.

Shad is originally an East Coast fish, found in rivers that spill into the Atlantic from the Gulf of St. Lawrence down to Florida. It was transplanted to California's Sacramento River in California in 1871, with additional plants made in the Oregon's Columbia, Snake, and Willamette rivers in 1885 and 1886. The plants were spectacularly successful, and the fish quickly spread along the coast into Puget Sound and the Fraser River of British Columbia.

Today, most of the shad found in the Market come from the Columbia River in late June and early July. However, the shad is overshadowed by the Northwest's salmon fishery. In fact, much of the commercially caught shad is taken for the roe only, and the carcasses are used for animal food or crab bait.

The shad is an attractive fish, with a blue back, bright silver sides, and a single row of dark spots on the back. It has large scales, a small head, and row of keeled scales on the belly. The rounded, compressed body weighs 3 to 6 pounds. From a culinary standpoint, the female shad is more desirable than the buck because it contains roe and it is a bigger, fatter fish with larger fillets.

But whether male or female, the shad carries a reputation for the rows of Y-shaped pin bones in each fillet that are very tricky to remove. It is best to ask an experienced fishmonger to bone the fillets; don't try boning a shad at home. As an option to boning the fish, some cooks braise a whole shad for several hours to soften the bones. The fishmongers at Pure Food Fish report that Indian and Pakistani customers sometimes ask for the whole fish,

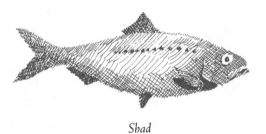

Shad

which they then cook slowly in curry sauce. Other shad aficionados cook it whole for less time and simply eat around the bones.

Whatever way you prepare your shad, you will find the white, sweet, tender, fatty meat a distinct treat. This oily fish is best suited to baking, braising, grilling, smoking, or sautéing. If you ask for a whole shad to be filleted, keep in mind that each fillet has three sets of pin bones that, when removed, result in three pockets of flesh. While some people might see this as a detriment, the pockets make great receptacles for stuffings of all sorts.

SHAD ROE

The two deep red egg sacs that come out of the bellies of spawning female shad are called shad roe. Considered a delicacy by gourmets, they have a hearty, slightly earthy flavor. The egg sacs are in skeins, or sets, joined by a thin membrane. They weigh 2 to 10 ounces per pair and must be handled with great care at all times. Like the shad fish, shad roe is available on the West Coast in late June and early July.

Roe is tastiest when the eggs are small and the sacs are a dark rosy red hue. Roe is sold in a set ready to cook. One set, or pair, of roe should be a sufficient entrée-sized portion.

Be sure to rinse the roe gently under cool running water before cooking, and do not cut apart the egg sacs until after they are cooked. Cook gently until firm all the way through, 8 to 10 minutes at most; overcooking dries out the roe and causes the membrane surrounding the eggs to split. Shad roe is often dredged in flour and fried, poached and added to scrambled eggs or sauces, or grilled. Because of its hearty taste, shad roe are often paired with bacon or capers.

FUN FACTS

- Because shad is such a bony fish, Native American legend says that the shad was a discontented porcupine that asked the gods to be changed. The gods complied and turned it inside out.

- George Washington was very fond of shad, and members of the U.S. Congress often sailed down the Potomac for the sole purpose of eating shad and enjoying a few drinks.

Skate

The skate is a member of the ray family, Rajidae, which contains slightly more than 100 known living species found in oceans worldwide. It is a flat-bodied, kite-shaped creature with mottled gray or brown skin and a long, spiny, pointed tail. Its unique skeleton is composed of cartilage rather than bone and its pectoral fins are winglike structures that protrude on each side of its body. The wings propel the skate through the water in an undulating motion and have a striated, fanlike configuration and corrugated texture, like corduroy. The wings are the only edible portion of the skate and consist of two meaty layers of flesh separated by a layer of cartilage. The cartilage layer can be filleted away before or after

Skate

cooking, or diners can eat their way around it.

Even though plentiful and excellent to eat, skates are seldom fished. The world's largest skate, *Raja binoculata*, or the **big skate**, is the species most commonly found in West Coast seafood markets, although the **longnose skate** (*Raja rhina*) is also sometimes available. Unfortunately, no matter what the species, most of the skate in local markets is caught unintentionally when fishers are hunting other fish (this is known as "by-catch"), so supplies are limited and inconsistent. Fishers often discard the skates they catch at sea along with other unsellable or low-priced creatures.

The East Coast skate fishery is more developed and boasts a more regular supply than the Pacific skate fishery. This is due, in great part, to the late Gilbert LeCoze, a Frenchman who crossed the Atlantic to open Le Bernardin in New York City in the 1980s. As soon as the godfather of today's upscale seafood restaurants put skate on his menu, the fish became fashionable.

Although skate is less appreciated on the West Coast, upscale restaurants are beginning to feature it on their menus, and it is sometimes available at the fish stalls in the Pike Place Market. Perhaps as skate becomes more familiar and prices paid for it rise so that it is worth the effort to harvest it, supplies in our seafood shops will increase.

The flesh of the skate is ridged or striated and should be firm, pearly white, and translucent, with hues of light pink running through it. The lean meat turns white when cooked and tastes sweet and delicate, with a flavor some describe as similar to halibut or scallops, although the texture is more like that of crabmeat because of its long fibers or strands. The fish gains its delicious shellfishlike sweetness from its diet of clams, mussels, and other mollusks. Less-than-scrupulous restaurateurs sometimes cut skate into circular shapes and sell it as scallops because it costs so much less than the real shellfish.

Skate skin is thick and inedible; it is generally removed before the skate comes to market. If the skin has not been removed, ask the fishmonger to clean the fish for you. If this is not possible, simply bring the skate wing home and put it in a pot of rapidly boiling water. Lower the heat and simmer for 1 to 2 minutes. Remove the fish, place it on a cutting board,

HANDY SKATE TIP

Skate has always been popular in France, where it is known as *raie*. According to James Beard in *James Beard's New Fish Cookery*, "*Raie beurre noir* is the best-known fashion of serving skate. Simply prepare a court bouillon of vinegar, salt, and water and poach skate wings ten minutes per inch of thickness. Drain thoroughly and place them in a serving dish. Melt and brown butter, add a little wine vinegar, and plenty of capers. Pour the *beurre noir* (brown butter) over the skate."

and scrape away the skin with a sharp knife. Repeat on the second side. Once skinned, the meat can easily be filleted off the center cartilage, then cooked as desired. And don't discard the liver; some gourmets swear it is delicious when pan-fried, although I haven't had the nerve to try it (yet).

Like shark, skate carry a natural metabolic product in their flesh called urea. If skate wings are not removed from the fish and iced immediately after landing, the harmless urea will impart a strong ammonia odor. If a slight ammonia smell exists, it can be removed by soaking the skate in water mixed with lemon for 30 minutes. A solution of 2 tablespoons white vinegar per quart of water also works well. Refrigerate the fish in this solution for 2 to 3 hours.

Unlike most other fish, skate actually gets better with age; letting it sit in the refrigerator 2 to 3 days before cooking firms the texture and improves the flavor. It will last for up to a week if stored over ice and properly handled.

Skate is available both fresh and frozen, most commonly in the form of whole, skinless wings and sections of wings. Whole wings weigh from $1/3$ to 3 pounds and yield about 65 percent of their weight in meat. Each skate wing forms two thin fillets; therefore, one small wing or half of a large wing is plenty for each person.

Skate can be poached (the classic method), baked, braised, sautéed, broiled, steamed (in a steamer, wrapped in foil and baked, or cooked *en papillote*), grilled, or cut into pieces and used in soups or stews. It can be eaten hot or cold. Because of its unique taste and texture, simple preparations are preferred. Skate readily accepts strong flavors. Capers, lemon, fresh herbs, and brown butter are classic pairings, while toasted nuts and ginger are contemporary matches.

The skate is more widely available and prices are lowest in the winter.

FUN FACTS

- The Northwest's biggest skate measured 8 feet and weighed 200 pounds.

- Some West Coast skates propel themselves on wings that weigh up to 5 pounds each Skates sometimes catch their prey by enveloping it in their wings.

- Skates are said to be sensitive to music.

Smelt

Smelt are members of the Osmeridae family ("odorous family" in Greek), of which there are only twelve known living species, including smelt, capelin, and eulachon. Smelt are found on the East and West Coasts and in the Great Lakes. They are related to and resemble tiny salmon, with flashing silver sides and olive green undertones. Also like the salmon, some species can adapt to both fresh and salt water. Smelt measure 4 to 6 inches long and weigh 2 to 6 ounces apiece.

There are two major commercially marketed species of smelt in the Northwest—the surf smelt and the eulachon (*Thaleichthys pacificus*). The latter is also known by the names Columbia River smelt, candlefish, or hooligan

Eulachon

smelt, among others, and ranges from central California to Alaska, but is most abundant from Oregon northward. They are small, slim fish, bluish or blue-silver with silvery bellies, tiny black dots on their backs and sometimes on their caudal fins. Once this smelt enters its spawning rivers, it is gillnetted by the moderately-sized commercial fishery along much of its range and sold in local markets.

The surf smelt (*Hypomesus pretiosus pretiosus*) is also known as the silver smelt, smelt, or day smelt because it spawns during the daytime. They range from southern California to Alaska. This small, slender fish is blue-green

on its back and silvery on its sides and belly, with a silvery band along its sides. Commercial fishers take the abundant surf smelt with gill nets or purse seine nets set from sandy

Surf Smelt

beaches and market it fresh. A smaller, leaner fish than the eulachon, surf smelt are considered better in quality because of their firmer meat and sweeter taste.

Smelt are usually sold whole with the head, tail, and innards intact, although larger smelt can be sold dressed, with the head and intestines removed. It's not necessary to fillet smelt, for there simply would not be much left. Ten to 12 smelt make a pound; allow $^3/_4$ pound per person.

Smelt are very high in oil content, and their meat is white and rich yet still delicate and mild. Their aroma is likened to that of cucumber or violets. Smelt are soft-boned and are most often cooked whole, with bones, viscera, and skin intact. Smelt bones are soft enough that you can eat them from head to tail, particularly if smelt are crisp-fried. The bones of larger smelt can be lifted out in one piece after cooking; however, many of those who enjoy smelt eat the bones, skin, and all.

While pan-frying or deep-frying are the classic cooking techniques for smelt, they can also be sautéed, baked, pickled, or grilled. Smelt deteriorate quickly and should be eaten as soon as possible after purchase. However, smelt can be frozen for up to 3 months by simply placing the fish head down in an airtight container, filling the container to the top with water, and freezing.

Fresh eulachon smelt are available from January to May. Surf smelt spawn throughout the year but are most plentiful from July to September. Fresh-frozen smelt are available year-round.

FUN FACTS

- The maximum recorded size for a eulachon is 10 inches; 12 inches for a surf smelt.

- Native Americans living along large rivers have trapped, raked, or netted the highly prized eulachon for centuries. Eulachon, and particularly their vitamin D-rich oil, was a staple food for many Northwest coastal tribes, which used the fish in some way with every meal. These fish were vital to the aboriginal economy not only because they represented food and fat, but also because eulachon oil and meat were carried to the interior along "grease trails"—well-beaten, well-known paths—where they were bartered with inland tribes.

Sturgeon

Twenty-five species of sturgeon make up the rather primitive family Acipenseridae. The sturgeon is a sharklike, prehistoric-looking fish whose slim body is covered with rows of knifelike, diamond-shaped bony plates, or scales, called "scutes." Barbels (whiskery appendages) hang from the bottom of its long snout in front of its mouth. The barbels are equipped with taste buds that help the fish locate food in the dark, murky waters along the bottoms of the silty rivers and lakes where they are most often found.

The three species of sturgeon in the United States include **Atlantic sturgeon** (*Acipenser oxyrhynchus*), **green sturgeon** (*Acipenser medirostris*), and **white sturgeon** (*Acipenser transmontanus*). For years sturgeon flourished on both the East and West coasts; by the late nineteenth century, pollution and overfishing were responsible for the fish almost disappearing. In recent years, thanks to rigid fishing restrictions, there has been a slow recovery of the sturgeon population and the fresh fish is once again available.

The sturgeon has always been popular because of its many uses. The flesh is in high demand for cooking fresh or smoking, although this rare delicacy, which compares to smoked breast of turkey both in taste and texture, carries a high price tag. Sturgeon eggs, or roe, are made into highly regarded caviar. In fact, earlier this century, California's caviar production was second only to Russian and Iranian enterprises in the Caspian and Black seas. Today, with the former Soviet Union's caviar industry in chaos, the demand for Columbia River sturgeon caviar far exceeds supplies.

Columbia River caviar, or any salted American sturgeon eggs, can be sold as caviar only as long as it is marketed as American caviar to distinguish it from imported sturgeon caviars. Roe from other fish, such as whitefish and lumpfish, can also be sold as caviar as long as the name of the fish from which the roe was taken is included in the name, e.g., American paddlefish caviar.

Only green and white sturgeon are available in the Northwest, found in bays, rivers, and lakes from Alaska to Baja California. White sturgeon farm-grown in California is also available and is helping to renew the dwindling supply of sturgeon. In only two years the farmed fish can reach weights between 8 and 10 pounds.

The white sturgeon is also sometimes known as the Pacific sturgeon, Oregon sturgeon, Sacramento sturgeon, or Columbia sturgeon. The Columbia River boasts the largest commercial harvest of white sturgeon, which is sold for both the flesh and the roe. Because of past overharvesting, the white sturgeon is protected so that egg-bearing females cannot be taken before they spawn. Adults do not spawn every year; four to eleven years pass between episodes.

Sturgeon

The white sturgeon is grayish white, with 38 to 48 scutes arranged in 5 rows along its body. It is by far the largest freshwater fish in the western part of North America, reaching 13 feet and 1,300 pounds and averaging 82 years, although pre-1900 reports claim white sturgeon reached as large as 20 feet and 1,800 pounds. The meat of the white sturgeon is revered for its distinctive flavor and firm texture, which some people compare to veal.

The green sturgeon is usually olive green, though sometimes gray, with white lateral stripes, 23 to 30 scutes along its flanks, and 1 or 2 scutes behind the dorsal fin. Smaller than

the white sturgeon, it grows 3 to 5 feet long and weighs 50 to 100 pounds. Green sturgeon is fattier than its white relative and is generally considered inferior. Because its flesh is more earthy tasting and retains a reddish color after cooking, it is most often smoked.

Sturgeon meat keeps well and actually tastes better after it is stored in the refrigerator for 2 to 3 days. Sturgeon is available as fillets and steaks, with 6 to 8 ounces in either form sufficient as an entrée-sized serving.

No matter which species, all sturgeon meat is very firm and fatty. Preferred cooking methods include baking, braising, broiling, poaching, microwaving, grilling, sautéing, and smoking. Sturgeon is commonly used in chowders, stews, or kebabs. Although its dense texture holds up well to grilling, sturgeon toughens if grilled over high heat, so lower heat is better.

Fresh wild white sturgeon is available from March to July, while farm-raised white sturgeon is available on and off year-round.

FUN FACTS

- Isinglass, a liquid once used to make glue, jelly, and to clarify beer, was prepared from sturgeon swim bladders.

- Sturgeon love to eat herring eggs, but one sturgeon was even more ambitious—when its stomach was opened, it contained the remains of a domestic cat.

Sautéed Shad Roe with Sorrel Sauce

———— 🪢 ————

Shad roe sautéed and served with sorrel sauce show-cases of the best Northwest fish and herbs of the season.

SALT AND FRESHLY GROUND PEPPER

4 PAIRS SHAD ROE, 8 TO 10 OUNCES EACH

ALL-PURPOSE FLOUR FOR DREDGING

4 TABLESPOONS BUTTER

4 TABLESPOONS DRY WHITE WINE

4 TABLESPOONS MINCED FRESH SORREL

2 TABLESPOONS MINCED FRESH PARSLEY

2 TABLESPOONS FRESHLY SQUEEZED
   LEMON JUICE

1/2 LEMON, CUT INTO 4 WEDGES

1. Lightly sprinkle salt and pepper on both sides of room temperature roe. Dredge roe in flour, then gently pat off excess flour.

2. In a large skillet that will hold the roe without crowding, heat butter over medium-high heat. When butter stops foaming and just begins to color, add roe and sauté 5 to 7 minutes per side, or until golden brown on both sides and springy when pressed. Transfer to a plate and cover to keep warm. If skillet is not large enough, cook roe in two batches, and keep first batch warm in a 200° oven.

3. Return skillet to medium-high heat and add wine. Cook until reduced slightly, then add sorrel, parsley, and lemon juice. Swirl pan to mix herbs, then pour sauce over roe.

4. Divide roe among individual plates and place a lemon wedge on each plate.

SERVES 4

Broiled Northwest Shad

———— 🪢 ————

Shad is a very oily fish with a distinct flavor, which is why I like to cook it as simply as possible. You can substitute other fresh or dried herbs for the dill.

1 1/2 POUNDS SHAD FILLET, BONES
   REMOVED, RINSED, DRAINED, AND PATTED
   DRY

4 TABLESPOONS BUTTER, MELTED

1 TABLESPOON FRESH SNIPPED DILL, OR 1
   TEASPOON DRIED DILL, CRUMBLED

1 LEMON, CUT INTO 8 WEDGES

1. Preheat broiler. Generously coat a baking sheet with oil or nonstick cooking spray.

2. Place fish fillets on baking sheet skin side down and brush with some of the melted butter. Place fish 3 to 4 inches under broiler. Broil 2 minutes, then remove from oven and brush with some of the melted butter. Broil 2 minutes more, then brush with remaining butter and sprinkle with half the fresh dill. Cook 2 to 5 minutes more, or just until fish flakes. Remove fish from broiler and sprinkle with remaining dill.

3. To serve, divide fish and lemon wedges among individual plates.

SERVES 4

Sautéed Skate with Georgian Walnut Sauce

———⎯⟨⎯⟩⎯———

PIROSMANI, SEATTLE, WASHINGTON

Laura Dewell, chef and co-owner of Pirosmani, uses the Pike Place Market as a resource and inspiration for the Georgian/Mediterranean cuisine she serves at her restaurant. Chef Dewell explains that this rich, mustard-colored sauce comes from the Republic of Georgia in the former Soviet Union, where it is called baje *and is normally used for poultry or game birds. She has modified the recipe, redolent with saffron and cumin, to be light enough so as not to overpower the mild flavor of sautéed skate wing or catfish. The sauce could also pair with firm-fleshed, lean fish such as grilled tuna, swordfish, or sturgeon.*

1 TABLESPOON OLIVE OIL
SALT AND FRESHLY GROUND BLACK PEPPER
2 POUNDS SKATE WING, SKIN REMOVED,
    RINSED, DRAINED, PATTED DRY, AND CUT
    INTO 4 (8-OUNCE) PIECES
GEORGIAN WALNUT SAUCE (RECIPE
    FOLLOWS)

1. Heat a nonstick pan large enough to hold skate wings without crowding over medium heat. When pan is hot, add olive oil. Lightly sprinkle skate wings on both sides with salt and pepper. When oil is hot, place skate in pan and cook 3 to 4 minutes. Turn fish and cook 3 to 4 minutes more, or just until fish turns opaque.

2. To serve, divide skate among individual plates and drizzle with Georgian Walnut Sauce.

SERVES 4

Georgian Walnut Sauce

1 3/4 CUPS WATER
1/2 TEASPOON SAFFRON THREADS
1/2 POUND (ABOUT 2 CUPS) WALNUTS
2 CLOVES GARLIC, PEELED AND HALVED
1 JALAPEÑO PEPPER, STEM REMOVED AND
    COARSELY CHOPPED
1 1/2 TEASPOONS GROUND CORIANDER
1 1/2 TEASPOONS GROUND FENUGREEK
1 1/2 TABLESPOONS WHITE WINE VINEGAR
1 1/2 TEASPOONS SALT

1. In a small saucepan, combine 1 cup of the water and the saffron and bring to a boil. Stir to dissolve saffron, remove pan from heat, and allow liquid to cool.

2. Place walnuts, garlic, jalapeño, coriander, and fenugreek in a food processor or blender and pulse until a paste forms, scraping down the sides of the container as needed to redistribute mixture. Add vinegar and process briefly. With machine running, pour in saffron mixture and 1 teaspoon of the salt. Taste and add remaining salt, if desired. The sauce should be thick; if necessary, add the additional 3/4 cup water 1 tablespoon at a time until desired texture is achieved.

3. Use immediately, or pour sauce into a bowl, cover, and refrigerate until ready to use.

MAKES ABOUT 2 CUPS

Note: Be sure to use kosher or sea salt in this recipe, or the sauce will be too strong in taste otherwise.

Pan-Fried Smelt with Lemon Butter

———⟨⟩———

Pan-frying the freshest smelt is an ideal way to cook these small-in-size but big-in-flavor fish.

1/4 CUP ALL-PURPOSE FLOUR

1/4 CUP CORNMEAL

1/4 TEASPOON SALT

1/8 TEASPOON FRESHLY GROUND BLACK PEPPER

2 POUNDS SMELT, RINSED AND PATTED DRY

4 TABLESPOONS CANOLA OIL

1 LEMON, CUT INTO 8 WEDGES

2 TABLESPOONS BUTTER

1. Preheat oven to 200°.

2. In a large plastic bag, mix flour, cornmeal, salt, and pepper. Add half the smelt, close bag securely, and shake well to coat fish with flour mixture.

3. Heat 2 tablespoons of the oil in a large skillet over medium-high heat. Add the smelt, without crowding, and fry 3 to 4 minutes, turning once, until fish are golden brown and opaque throughout (cut into one to check for doneness). Place smelt on a baking sheet and keep warm in oven.

4. Repeat procedure with remaining flour mixture and the remaining 2 tablespoons canola oil. When all smelt are cooked, decrease heat to medium, squeeze 4 of the lemon wedges into oil remaining in pan, and scrape up any cooked bits of fish or batter left in skillet. Add butter and cook until melted, stirring well.

5. Divide smelt among individual plates and drizzle lemon butter over fish. Serve immediately, garnished with remaining lemon wedges.

SERVES 4

FUN FACTS

- During cold winter months, Northwest natives mixed summer-cut grass with eulachon fat to form fishcakes. They also dried eulachons, inserted a wick, and used them as a light source; hence, one of their nicknames—candlefish.

- Native Americans, such as the Quillehutes on the outer coast of the Olympic Peninsula, dried white-fleshed surf smelt on cedar bark and based much of their tribal lore on these easy-to-gather schooling fish. To this day, the Quillehutes welcome the seasonal appearance of the surf smelt.

- Some sources suggest that smelt got their name because the word "smelt" in Old English (*smoelt*) translates as "smooth and shining." Others believe the smelt is a contraction of the words "smell" and "it," because the aroma of fresh smelt is like fresh-cut cucumbers, or violets.

Applewood-Smoked Sturgeon with Corn Salsa, Tomatillo Syrup, and Anaheim Chile Oil

———⊁———

THE PAINTED TABLE, SEATTLE, WASHINGTON

Tim Kelley, executive chef at the Alexis Hotel's The Painted Table restaurant, came to his present post after stints with the acclaimed French chef David Bouley of Bouley restaurant and Jean-Georges Vongerichten of Vong, New York's premier Thai restaurant. Because of his training, and as an American of Thai descent, Tim skillfully fuses Asian, American, and French influences throughout his cooking. He is also committed to using produce from farmers' markets and Asian markets and collects greens the way some people hoard used books or fine wines. By using vegetables as the soul of a dish rather than just an accompaniment, he maintains a heavy emphasis on local and regional herbs and vegetables, and there is a decided seafood presence on his menu. This dish requires advance preparation.

¼ CUP KOSHER SALT

¼ CUP SUGAR

2 TABLESPOONS CELERY SEED

1 POUND STURGEON FILLETS, RINSED, DRAINED, AND PATTED DRY

APPLEWOOD CHIPS, FOR SMOKING

CORN SALSA (RECIPE FOLLOWS)

TOMATILLO SYRUP (RECIPE FOLLOWS)

ANAHEIM CHILE OIL (RECIPE FOLLOWS)

1 LIME, SLICED INTO THIN ROUNDS, FOR GARNISH

SEVERAL SPRIGS OF CILANTRO, FOR GARNISH

1. To prepare the sturgeon, mix salt, sugar, and celery seed in a small mixing bowl. Gently press the curing mixture into all sides of the sturgeon. Cover and refrigerate overnight.

2. Prepare a stovetop smoker according to manufacturer's instructions, using the applewood chips. When the smoker is hot, place the sturgeon on the smoking rack and smoke for 10 to 12 minutes, or until fish flakes. Remove fish from the smoker, place it on a cutting board, and remove any skin or bones. Cool sturgeon, wrap well, and refrigerate several hours or overnight to allow flavors to intensify.

3. To serve, place a mound of Corn Salsa in the center of individual plates. Thinly slice the sturgeon and place several slices over the salsa. Drizzle Tomatillo Syrup and Anaheim Chile Oil around the edge of the plate and garnish with lime and cilantro.

SERVES 4

Corn Salsa

3 EARS FRESH CORN

1 RED ONION, DICED

1 TOMATO, DICED

2 TABLESPOONS CHOPPED CILANTRO

JUICE OF 1 LIME

2 TABLESPOONS OLIVE OIL

SALT AND FRESHLY GROUND BLACK PEPPER

Cook corn in boiling water for 3 minutes and immediately place in ice water to stop the cooking process. When cool enough to handle, pat corn dry, cut kernels from cobs, and place kernels in a mixing bowl. Add onion, tomato, cilantro, lime juice, and olive oil and stir to mix well. Season to taste with salt and pepper, cover, and refrigerate several hours or overnight to allow flavors to blend.

MAKES 1 CUP

Tomatillo Syrup

5 TOMATILLOS, CORED, SEEDED AND
   CHOPPED
2 TOMATOES, CORED, SEEDED AND CHOPPED

Place tomatillos and tomatoes in a blender and pulse until smooth. Strain through a fine-meshed sieve into a medium saucepan, using the back of a wooden spoon to press liquid through. Discard solids and place saucepan over medium-high heat. Cook 15 to 20 minutes, or until liquid reduces enough to coat the back of a spoon. Pour into a nonreactive bowl, cover, and refrigerate until ready to use.

MAKES ³/₄ CUP

Anaheim Chile Oil

2 ANAHEIM PEPPERS, STEMMED, SEEDED,
   DERIBBED, AND CHOPPED
¹/₄ CUP GRAPESEED, VEGETABLE, OR
   OLIVE OIL
SALT AND FRESHLY GROUND BLACK PEPPER

Place peppers and oil in a food processor or blender and blend until smooth. Season to taste with salt and pepper.

MAKES ²/₃ CUP

Note: The sturgeon can be sautéed instead of smoked. To sauté, rinse, drain, and pat dry sturgeon. Remove any skin and bones. Cut sturgeon into 4 (6-ounce) pieces and lightly sprinkle with salt and freshly ground black pepper. Dust fish fillets with flour and pat off any excess. Heat 2 tablespoons clarified butter (see page 303) over medium-high heat in a skillet large enough to hold fish fillets without crowding. When pan is hot, add fillets and decrease heat to medium. Cook 3 to 5 minutes, or until sturgeon is lightly browned, then turn fish and add the juice of 1 lemon wedge. Cook 3 to 5 minutes more, or until sturgeon just flakes. Divide Corn Salsa among individual plates, then top with sturgeon fillets. Drizzle with Tomatillo Syrup and Anaheim Chile Oil and garnish with lime and cilantro.

Note: Grapeseed oil is pressed from grapeseeds after the production of wine. Its delicate flavor and body make it perfect for sautéing, baking, or even deep-frying because of its high flashpoint (the point at which the oil begins to smoke). It is available in the Pike Place Market at DeLaurenti Specialty Foods (see page 326) and at many gourmet markets and retailers.

Poached Sturgeon with Sorrel and Wild Mushroom Sauce

―――⚓―――

LE GOURMAND,
SEATTLE, WASHINGTON

Bruce Naftaly, chef/owner of Le Gourmand, is a chef with an eye for detail. He makes his own tomato paste and irons the tablecloths and napkins for his charming restaurant in Ballard, a neighborhood just north of Seattle. He knows the name of the cow (Brenda) that supplies the milk for the butter he uses. For years he has worked closely with individual farmers who supply him with untreated produce, meat, and seafood. When a detail-minded individual such as he describes his sorrel and wild mushroom sauce as an easily accessible version of a complicated French sauce, home cooks rejoice.

1 1/2 POUNDS STURGEON FILLETS, SKIN
    AND BONES REMOVED, RINSED, DRAINED,
    PATTED DRY, AND CUT INTO 4 (6-OUNCE)
    FILLETS
1 LEEK, ROOT AND TOP 1 INCH REMOVED,
    CLEANED, AND COARSELY CHOPPED
1 CUP DRY WHITE WINE
3 SPRIGS OF FRESH THYME
3 SPRIGS OF FRESH PARSLEY
COLD WATER
SORREL AND WILD MUSHROOM SAUCE
    (RECIPE FOLLOWS)

1. To poach sturgeon, place fillets in a skillet large enough to hold fish without crowding. Add all of the ingredients except sauce and enough water to cover fillets. Bring to a boil, then decrease heat to low and cook 10 minutes, or until fish just flakes. Place fish on several layers of paper towels to drain or use a clean kitchen towel to blot.

2. To serve, place fish fillets on warmed individual plates and spoon Sorrel and Wild Mushroom Sauce over fillets.

SERVES 4

Sorrel and Wild Mushroom Sauce

1/2 CUP REDUCED WHITE WINE FISH STOCK
    (RECIPE FOLLOWS)
2 CUPS HEAVY WHIPPING CREAM, OR 1 CUP
    HEAVY WHIPPING CREAM AND 1 CUP
    CRÈME FRAÎCHE
1/4 CUP DRY MADEIRA
3/4 POUND CHANTERELLE, MOREL, SHIITAKE,
    OR OYSTER MUSHROOMS, CHOPPED
1 CUP FRESH SORREL CHIFFONADE
SALT AND FRESHLY GROUND WHITE PEPPER

Place a nonreactive saucepan over medium-high heat and add stock, whipping cream, Madeira, and mushrooms. Cook 10 to 15 minutes, or until mixture is reduced by half, stirring occasionally. Add sorrel and cook 5 to 7 minutes, or until reduced to a sauce consistency. Season to taste with salt and pepper. Keep warm over very low heat or in a double boiler while preparing fish.

MAKES 1 1/2 TO 2 CUPS

Reduced White Wine Fish Stock

2 CUPS DRY WHITE WINE

1 LARGE LEEK, ROOT AND TOP 1 INCH
REMOVED, CLEANED, AND COARSELY
CHOPPED

1 SMALL ONION, COARSELY CHOPPED

1 POUND FRESH OR FROZEN HALIBUT
BONES, COARSELY CHOPPED INTO
FIST-SIZED PIECES AND RINSED

COLD WATER

1. In a large stockpot or Dutch oven, place 1 cup of the wine, the leek, and onion over medium-high heat and bring to a boil. Reduce heat to a simmer and cook 10 minutes, or until vegetables are tender. Add the remaining 1 cup of wine and the fish bones, and cook until fish on bones is partially cooked. Cover with water and bring to a boil. Skim and discard any foam or substance that rises to the surface of the stock. Lower heat and simmer for 30 minutes, continuing to skim surface of stock as needed.

2. Strain stock through a wide-meshed sieve to remove solids, then strain stock through a fine-meshed sieve. Return stock to pot, increase heat to medium-high, and cook 15 to 20 minutes, or until liquid is reduced by half. Cool, strain, and use immediately, or refrigerate or freeze until needed.

MAKES 1 CUP

HANDY STURGEON TIP

Be sure to skin sturgeon steaks before cooking or the skin will shrink and make the steaks misshapen. Sturgeon works well in swordfish and tuna recipes, and either fish can substitute for sturgeon in a pinch, although they are leaner and cook more quickly.

FUN FACTS

- There are stories of 1,500-pound sturgeon being hauled out of California waters by mule teams at the turn of the twentieth century.

- The world's largest freshwater fish is a member of the Acipenseridae family. The beluga of northern Asia may attain a length of 28 feet and a weight of 3,000 pounds. Now that's a big fish!

- King Edward II of England declared sturgeon a royal fish and decreed that every sturgeon caught had to be offered to the court.

Swordfish

SWORDFISH, ALSO KNOWN as the broadbill or broadbill swordfish, is the only member of the family Xiphiidae. So even though the color of the flesh may vary depending on the fish's diet, the swordfish you find in Rome is the same species you get on your plate in Seattle.

Swordfish are found in temperate and tropical seas throughout the world, and on both the Atlantic and Pacific coasts of the United States. On the Pacific side, they range from British Columbia south to Baja California, and further south to Chile. Worldwide, swordfish are a major commercial species. No matter where they are found or caught, they are one of the most popular fish in the sea, and they always command a high price.

The swordfish gets its name from its long, flattened bill, which extends from the upper part of the jaw. The fish uses this "sword" to swat, stun, slash, and impale its prey—and sometimes passing ships! The fish is torpedo-shaped, tapering off narrowly at the tail end. It is black or brownish-black, has no pelvic fins, and its sword is beaklike and flat. This sets the swordfish apart from other billfishes (such as various marlins and the sailfish), who have rounded bills and pelvic fins.

The swordfish is one of the heaviest round-fish in the sea, averaging 50 to 200 pounds in the commercial catch, with occasional specimens reaching up to 1,200 pounds. It is also a long fish, reaching a maximum length of 15 feet (including the sword). Documented reports show it lives at least up to nine years, but probably longer. In spite of their great size and readily available defense mechanism, swordfish often laze on the surface of the water and can be harpooned, but are most often caught by long lines or gill nets.

Atlantic swordfish is pink in color, while California swordfish is creamy white. All swordfish meat has a distinct blood-red line down the center, which is muscle meat. You can remove this dark meat before cooking, but it isn't really necessary; the dark meat lightens to gray when cooked and is perfectly edible.

Swordfish has a distinctive, full, rich flavor and is moderately oily. Its flesh is firm, dense, and short-grained, with an almost meatlike texture. For this reason, it is often referred to as the beefsteak of finfish, and many meat-eaters find it an appealing change of pace. Tuna, marlin, and mako shark are the only other fish comparable in texture and quality to swordfish.

In fact, because demand often exceeds supply, the less expensive mako shark is sometimes substituted for swordfish by unscrupulous fishmongers. Luckily, it is easy to tell the difference between the two. While the swordfish is scaleless and has smooth skin, the shark has rough skin similar in texture to coarse sandpaper. Mako also has a more circular pattern in its meat and is darker in color than true swordfish.

When buying swordfish, look for slightly translucent flesh with a bright sheen and a bright red bloodline. Older swordfish meat is easy to spot because it turns grayish and the red muscle meat becomes brown. Also keep in mind that domestic swordfish, which is most often sold fresh, is usually higher quality than imported varieties because it is better handled and brought to shore more quickly. Imported swordfish is often frozen, then thawed, before being sold. While less expensive, it can be inconsistent in quality. Among imported swordfish, Japanese products are the highest quality and, if properly handled at sea, frozen Japanese swordfish can be superior to fresh domestic. As with all finfish that has been frozen, swordfish that has been thawed should never be refrozen.

Swordfish is sold as boneless steaks, fresh or frozen, skin on. Occasionally, fishmongers

Swordfish

sell swordfish cubes, the trimmed pieces leftover after cutting whole swordfish into steaks. They are usually less expensive and are great for kebabs or for use in soups, salads, or stews. Buy swordfish steaks at least 1-inch thick; the thickness helps keep the steaks moist as you cook them. Buy swordfish cubes in at least 1-inch squares.

Steaks range from 6 ounces to about 1 pound, with 4 to 6 ounces considered an entrée-sized serving.

Swordfish is traditionally broiled, grilled, baked, or sautéed. However, it also lends itself to smoking, poaching, frying, or microwaving. Swordfish cubes are great in chowders, stews, brochettes, and stir-fries. They can also be poached or baked, then chilled and used cold in salads, where they work particularly well because they don't flake or become mushy.

Swordfish is best cooked quickly over, or under, very high heat. Swordfish does not separate into flakes when tested with a skewer; when it is properly done, the flesh will be opaque. To test for doneness, cut into the thickest part with the tip of a small, sharp knife. Remove the fish from the heat shortly before it is fully cooked, as the heat within the exterior layer of the firm-textured fish will continue to cook it, retaining more of the moisture. As a further measure to prevent swordfish from drying out, cover with a light topping or sauce, or marinate before cooking and baste several times during the cooking process. Swordfish skin is thick and smooth and can either be removed before or after cooking.

Fresh swordfish is available year-round, with the best buys in late spring and early fall, although swordfish is never cheap.

Swordfish Teriyaki

———⊷———

I cut my teeth on James McNair's simple yet flavorful recipe for teriyaki marinade when we first moved to Seattle and I immersed myself in Asian cuisines. Since that time, I have added my own touches to his original recipe, such as substituting low-sodium soy sauce, using brown sugar instead of granulated, and adding a whisper of toasted sesame oil. Still a fairly traditional teriyaki sauce, my version works well on all kinds of finfish and shellfish. To tweak the sauce even more, try adding a bit of citrus juice and zest (use lemon, lime, orange, or even tangerine) to suit your taste. Teriyaki dishes are traditionally served with steamed rice, stir-fried or steamed vegetables, and green tea, sake, or Japanese beer.

1 1/4 CUPS LOW-SODIUM SOY SAUCE

1/3 CUP MIRIN

3 TABLESPOONS FIRMLY PACKED BROWN
    SUGAR

3 CLOVES GARLIC, MINCED

1 TABLESPOON MINCED OR GRATED
    GINGERROOT

1/2 TEASPOON TOASTED SESAME OIL

1 1/2 POUNDS SWORDFISH STEAKS, RINSED,
    DRAINED, AND PATTED DRY

1 GREEN ONION, CUT ON THE DIAGONAL
    INTO 1/8-INCH PIECES

2 TABLESPOONS TOASTED SESAME SEEDS
    (SEE PAGE 10)

1. Combine soy sauce, mirin, brown sugar, garlic, gingerroot, and toasted sesame oil in a nonreactive baking dish large enough to hold fish fillets without crowding. Stir well to dissolve sugar.

2. Add swordfish and turn to coat both sides of fish with marinade. Cover and marinate in refrigerator 20 minutes to 2 hours (the longer the better), turning occasionally.

3. Ten minutes before cooking, preheat broiler. Lightly coat a baking sheet with oil or nonstick cooking spray.

4. Arrange swordfish steaks on baking sheet without crowding and place 3 to 4 inches under broiler. Broil 2 minutes, then remove from oven and brush lightly with teriyaki marinade. Repeat this process two more times, for a total of 6 minutes of cooking time, then cook 3 to 4 minutes more, depending on thickness of fillets, which should just turn opaque.

5. While fish finishes broiling, place remaining marinade in a small saucepan and bring to a boil over medium heat. Allow to boil at least 2 minutes, watching carefully and stirring occasionally so that marinade does not boil over, then decrease heat and keep warm until serving.

6. Remove fish from broiler, cut into serving-sized portions, and divide among individual plates. Sprinkle with green onions and sesame seeds. Serve warm marinade at the table as a dipping sauce.

SERVES 4

Grilled Swordfish
Spinach Salad

———⊶⊷———

Because swordfish is such a meaty, firm-fleshed fish (much like tuna or marlin, which would also work well in this recipe), it can stand up to a hearty brown marinade that includes lots of garlic, Worcestershire sauce, and Tabasco sauce. Just be sure not to over-marinate, or the fish will begin to "cook." Try this recipe on meat-eaters who think they don't like fish— it's so rich they will almost believe they're eating steak! Good crusty bread and a bottle of sweet riesling or gewürztraminer are the only accompaniments you will need for this main-dish salad.

2 TABLESPOONS MINCED GARLIC

6 TABLESPOONS WORCESTERSHIRE SAUCE

1/2 TEASPOON TABASCO SAUCE

6 TABLESPOONS EXTRA VIRGIN OLIVE OIL

1 1/2 POUNDS SWORDFISH STEAKS, RINSED, DRAINED, PATTED DRY, AND CUT INTO 4 (6-OUNCE) FILLETS

2 CUPS FRESH MUSHROOMS, CUT IN HALF (OR QUARTERS IF EXTRA-LARGE)

1 BUNCH SPINACH LEAVES, RINSED, DRAINED, TOUGH STEMS REMOVED, AND WELL DRIED

2 CARROTS, CUT INTO 1/8-INCH-WIDE SLICES

1/2 RED ONION, CUT INTO 1/8-INCH-WIDE SLICES

1. Place garlic, Worcestershire sauce, Tabasco, and olive oil in a nonreactive mixing bowl large enough to hold fish without crowding, and stir or whisk to blend. Divide marinade in half. To half of marinade, add fish fillets, turning well to coat. To marinade remaining in the other bowl, add mushrooms, and stir well to coat. Cover both bowls and refrigerate 20 minutes to 2 hours, turning occasionally.

2. Ten minutes before cooking, heat grill, then lightly coat rack with oil or nonstick cooking spray. Remove fish fillets from marinade, pat dry, and place on grill. Cook 3 to 5 minutes, then turn and cook another 3 to 5 minutes, about 10 minutes per inch of thickness, or just until fish turns opaque. Discard fish marinade.

3. To serve, divide spinach leaves among individual plates. Place a fish fillet in center of leaves, then divide carrot and onion slices among plates, sprinkling the slices over fish fillets and spinach leaves. Spoon marinated mushrooms and any remaining marinade over and around fish and vegetables.

SERVES 4

FUN FACTS

- The world's record swordfish weighed in at 1,182 pounds.

- The swordfish's strong fins propel it through the water with great speed. The swordfish may be the fastest fish in the sea, reaching 60 miles per hour.

- The swordfish's sword makes up one-third the length of its body. With this fierce weapon, swordfish have been known to ram ships, plunging deep into oak planking, and have even attacked submersible research vessels.

Trout

TROUT, SALMON, AND CHARS are members of the family Salmonidae, which includes more than sixty known living species. But when it comes to trout, only one species is of culinary importance—the **rainbow trout** (*Oncorhynchus mykiss*), the most widely farmed fish in the world, both for the purpose of angling and for sale to consumers and to the restaurant trade. A native of western North America, the rainbow has been introduced all over the world and is found on every continent except Antarctica.

Farm-Raised Trout

The farming of trout is nothing new—trout have been cultured since the fourteenth century, when a French monk discovered that their eggs could be artificially impregnated. Trout farming began in the United States in 1864 in New York, but it wasn't until advances in transportation and packaging in the late 1960s that trout farming really took off in this country.

All rainbow trout in the marketplace are farm-raised. In the United States, rainbows are farmed in all fifty states, but 75 percent come from Idaho, where they are grown in ponds fed by spring water.

The fish get their name from the luminescent rainbow streak that runs down their sides from gills to tail. Their bodies are olive green on top and silver below, with dark spots. Farm-raised fish are often duller in color than wild fish. The fish weigh from 1 to 5 pounds, although farm-raised specimens are a consistent $3/4$ to 1 pound apiece.

Another type of farm-raised fish you may occasionally see for sale is the **golden trout**, a color-mutated strain of the rainbow. The meat is red because the fish are given salmon feed containing pigments that turn the flesh from white to red. In addition to the color difference, goldens have a longer shelf life, slightly firmer meat, a stronger bone structure, and richer flavor than rainbows. Several million pounds of golden rainbows are produced each year by four farms in Idaho.

Steelhead

The **steelhead**, which some people refer to as the salmon-trout, coastal rainbow trout, half-pounder, or steelhead trout, is simply an anadromous rainbow trout. Much like the salmon, the steelhead hatches in fresh water, migrates to the ocean, then returns to fresh water to spawn. With a range from Baja California to Alaska, the steelhead gets its name because of its coloration at sea. With a bluish back, silvery belly, and small black spots on its back, dorsal, and caudal fins, the fish appears grayish, or the color of steel.

Recent studies have shown a slight genetic difference between oceangoing rainbows (steelheads) and rainbows that do not go to sea. Steelhead also differ from their close relative the salmon since some steelhead, particularly females, may spawn up to four times during their lifetimes. Also unlike the salmon, steelhead continue to eat while spawning, munching on salmon eggs, insects, and plants.

Sport fishers probably don't care about this magnificent fish's eating habits as long as they have the chance to catch a "steelie," for no other Northwest fish matches the steelhead's fighting spirit. The fish of anglers' dreams also grows larger than inland rainbow trout. Indeed, the largest steelhead measured 45 inches and weighed 43 pounds—imagine cooking that over the campfire!

There is an ongoing tension between the sport fishers, who want to keep the steelhead all to themselves, and commercial harvesters. In California, it is illegal to fish commercially for steelhead, while from Oregon northward, there is a fairly large catch by gill net and trollers.

The flesh of the steelhead is at its peak of flavor just after it has started up the river to spawn. It is bright orange at this time, similar to the flesh of king salmon. Once it starts upriver, the bright color gradually fades to pale white. The fish has a more muscular, "wild" flavor than rainbow trout. With a medium oil content, the steelhead lends itself to the same types of preparation as trout or salmon.

A recent innovation, farmed steelhead, will increase supplies of steelhead to the public. The farmed fish are marketed at $^1/_2$ to $^3/_4$ pound sizes, and others are grown to weights of 4 to 7 pounds, similar to farm-raised Atlantic salmon.

Farm-raised rainbow trout have a somewhat milder flavor than their wild counterparts. They are also consistent from fish to fish and season to season, whereas wild trout vary in flavor intensity. The flesh of farmed rainbows is creamy white and firm, with a mild, nutty flavor. The tender, flaky meat holds together well during cooking, especially when the skin is left on. The thin skin is not only edible, but a tasty contrast to the flesh. But even if serving the trout skinless, it is best to cook it

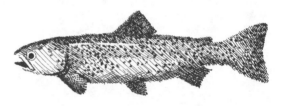

Rainbow Trout

with the skin intact, removing it when cool. Also avoid scaling trout, as this damages the fish's ability to take a coating, which is recommended in many forms of preparation, such as the classic trout meunière.

The rules for buying farmed trout are similar to buying any fish. Select fresh fillets that are translucent and moist. Whole trout are fresh when they have shiny skin and rounded, clear eyes. The flesh should be firm and spring back when pressed lightly. If your finger leaves an indentation, choose another fish. The gills should be bright and clear; if dark or slimy, reject the fish. Most important, open the belly cavity and sniff. A good trout will have a fresh, clean smell.

When you get the trout home, rinse the

fish, pat it dry with paper towels inside and out, wrap in plastic, and seal it in an airtight plastic bag. Place the fish in the refrigerator and use within 1 to 2 days. Store frozen trout properly wrapped at 0° or below and use within 1 month. Thaw frozen trout in the refrigerator overnight and use within 1 day. Use cooked trout within 2 days. It is better to use cooked trout cold than to reheat it.

Farm-raised trout weigh ³/₄ to 1 pound apiece, a perfect single-serving size. Farmed trout are most commonly sold dressed (gills and viscera removed) with the head, tail, and bones still intact. You will also sometimes find

Steelhead (female)

them boned, boned with the head removed, filleted, or butterflied (split down the back, opened out, and boned). Alternately, a good fishmonger will be glad to butterfly or fillet a whole fish for you. Boneless butterflied fillets weigh 5 to 8 ounces, plenty for a single entrée-sized portion, while fillets weigh 3 to 5 ounces each, another ample single portion.

Steelhead should be portioned as most other finfish. Allow 6 ounces of fillet per entrée-sized portion and 8 ounces of steaks.

Preferred cooking methods for trout include baking, poaching, steaming, braising, grilling, broiling, frying, smoking, sautéing, and microwaving. They also take well to stuffing and are good in soups and chowders. Stir-

frying is one method that isn't good for trout since quick stirring over high heat can break up the delicate flesh. Butterflied trout are especially tasty when broiled, grilled, or planked.

Trout are often simply pan-fried in butter or oil (or a combination of the two) with a bit of lemon juice, some capers, or a handful of toasted nuts thrown in to finish the dish. Fresh dill and ginger are other assertive ingredients frequently paired with trout. A slice of pimiento-stuffed olive or red radish is perfect for covering the eye of a whole, dressed fish.

Trout have a simple skeleton that can be lifted out of a cooked fish quite easily if you prefer serving the fish boneless. If you are served a whole trout, simply eat the top fillet of the fish down to the backbone, then lift off the whole backbone with ribs, tail, and head (if still attached), and discard. One whole fillet will remain, ready for easy eating.

Farm-raised trout (both rainbow and golden) are available year-round. Wild steelhead runs in the early summer and early winter; farmed steelhead is available on and off, year-round.

For people who prefer to catch their own trout, species available in the Northwest include the brook trout, brown trout, cutthroat trout, Dolly Varden (which is actually a char), lake trout, and of course, the rainbow and steelhead.

FUN FACTS

- Ancestors of present-day trout and salmon lived at least 40 million years ago during the lower Eocene epoch. The smelt (see page 124), which shares certain structural similarities with the salmonids, is a close relative of the salmon and trout.

Salt-Baked Trout

~~~⊱~~~

In her cookbook Short Cuts to Great Cuisine, *Carol Foster shows home cooks how to produce elegant dishes in record time. She recommends cooking small whole fish encased in salt and baked in the hottest possible oven, so that the fish retain all their juices and inherent flavor without interference from extraneous ingredients. If you can't find trout that weigh 8 ounces and substitute 12- to 16-ounce fish, increase the baking time by 2 to 3 minutes. For a dramatic presentation, Carol suggests removing the skin between the head and the tail of each trout after baking.*

5 POUNDS COARSE KOSHER SALT
4 WHOLE, DRESSED TROUT, ½ POUND
    EACH, RINSED, DRAINED, AND PATTED
    DRY
¼ CUP OLIVE OIL
1 LEMON, CUT INTO WEDGES (OPTIONAL)
FRESHLY GROUND BLACK PEPPER
    (OPTIONAL)

1. Preheat oven to 500°.

2. Pour about two-thirds of the salt into a large shallow baking pan that will hold fish without crowding. Spread the salt fairly evenly and place in the oven for 5 minutes.

3. Carefully remove pan from oven and arrange trout on salt with space between. Cover fish with remaining salt and bake, uncovered, 15 minutes.

4. With two metal spatulas, crack off the salt from the trout. Brush off all remaining salt and drizzle with olive oil.

5. Serve trout immediately with a wedge of lemon and a grating of pepper, if desired.

SERVES 4

Note: To remove skin from a cooked fish, cut the skin neatly at the head and the tail. With the point of a knife or the tines of a fork, lift the skin off carefully. It should come off in one piece per side of fish. If you like, scrape off any dark oily flesh before serving.

FUN FACTS

- Idaho's Snake River Plain boasts the perfect conditions for growing trout—crystal clear, well-oxygenated waters at a near-constant 58°. The region's potential for aquaculture was first recognized in 1928, when several small trout farms were built. More farms followed in the years after World War II. Today, there are three major producers and over seventy-five small contract growers in Idaho who together harvest over 40 million pounds of rainbow trout each year. The world's largest trout farm, Clear Springs Foods, accounts for one-third of that total.

- Nobody is quite sure where the golden rainbow trout came from. One story has it spontaneously mutating from regular rainbow trout in a lake in Pennsylvania; another says they come from a stream in California. In no way are they related to the magnificent wild species *Salmo aguabonita*, renowned for its striking beauty. Once found only in California's Sierra Nevada Mountains, today golden trout are also found at elevations above 8,000 feet in Wyoming and Idaho, where they are caught by sport fishers.

Wild Rice-Stuffed Trout

——✤——

A hearty stuffing studded with walnuts, dried cherries, and green onions goes great with the mild flavor of farm-raised trout and would be a particularly desirable meal during the depths of winter served with steamed or sautéed ruby chard or curly kale. Served à deux in front of a crackling fire, this could make for a very cozy and memorable dining experience.

2 TABLESPOONS OLIVE OIL

1 TABLESPOON UNSALTED BUTTER

1 ONION, DICED

2 CLOVES GARLIC, MINCED

1/2 RED PEPPER, DICED

1/2 CUP WILD RICE, RINSED AND WELL
    DRAINED

3/4 CUP WATER

3/4 CUP CHICKEN STOCK

1/4 TEASPOON THYME

1/4 TEASPOON SALT

1/8 TEASPOON FRESHLY GROUND BLACK
    PEPPER

PINCH OF GROUND ALLSPICE

1/4 CUP TOASTED WALNUTS, FINELY
    CHOPPED (SEE PAGE 10)

1/4 CUP DRIED CHERRIES OR DRIED
    CRANBERRIES, DICED

2 GREEN ONIONS, FINELY CHOPPED

4 WHOLE, DRESSED TROUT, 3/4 POUND
    EACH, RINSED, DRAINED, AND PATTED
    DRY

SALT AND FRESHLY GROUND BLACK PEPPER

1. Melt 1 tablespoon of the olive oil and butter in a medium saucepan over medium-high heat and add onion, garlic, and red pepper. Cook 10 minutes, or until vegetables are tender, stirring occasionally. Do not allow vegetables to brown. Add wild rice and cook 2 minutes, stirring often to coat individual rice grains with oil. Add water, chicken stock, thyme, salt, pepper, and allspice and bring to a boil. Turn down heat to medium-low and simmer 45 minutes, or until rice kernels blossom and rice is tender. Remove rice from heat, drain off any excess water, and stir in walnuts, dried cherries, and green onions.

2. Ten minutes before cooking, preheat oven to 350°. Lightly coat a baking sheet large enough to hold trout without crowding with oil or non-stick cooking spray.

3. Sprinkle inside cavities of fish lightly with salt and pepper. Spoon one-quarter of the stuffing into the cavity of each fish and place on baking sheet. Brush outside of trout with remaining olive oil and cook 18 to 20 minutes, or until trout are opaque through the thickest part (just behind the head).

4. Divide trout among individual plates and serve immediately.

SERVES 4

FUN FACT

- The rainbow trout is America's most popular sport fish. There are 9 million trout fishers in the United States. Half are fly fishers, who use hand-tied flies designed to imitate the insects trout eat; in 1995 they spent $227 million on the sport.

Steelhead Fillets in Basil Rice Paper

Rice paper is an edible, transparent paper made from the pith of the rice-paper plant and water. This Vietnamese staple, often used as spring roll wrappers, has the texture of plastic until soaked briefly in warm water, when it becomes pliable. When plump steelhead fillets embedded with fresh basil leaves are wrapped in softened rice paper, then cooked in a hot pan, the rice paper fuses to the surface of the fish and the basil leaves show through, almost like autumn leaves pressed between sheets of waxed paper. Fragrant jasmine rice and a stir-fry of mixed Chinese vegetables make appealing side dishes here.

16 TO 24 FRESH BASIL LEAVES, RINSED, DRAINED, AND PATTED DRY

1 1/2 POUNDS STEELHEAD FILLETS, SKIN AND BONES REMOVED, RINSED, DRAINED, AND PATTED DRY

4 PIECES RICE PAPER

1 TABLESPOON SESAME OIL

VIETNAMESE DIPPING SAUCE (SEE PAGE 85)

1. Place 2 or 3 basil leaves (depending on size) on top and bottom of each of the 4 fish fillets, pressing in leaves to adhere to surface of fish. The leaves should not cover the steelhead fillets completely; there should still be fish flesh showing in between and around outer edges of leaves.

2. Pour 1/4 inch warm water onto a plate. Place one piece of rice paper in the water and allow to soak for 30 seconds to 1 minute, or until pliable. Do not allow to soak too long or rice paper will tear. Transfer rice paper to a dry plate.

3. Place a fish fillet in the center of the rice paper, fold the ends of the rice paper to the center of the fillet until they overlap, then repeat with the opposing ends. Turn fillet over and place on another dry plate. Repeat procedure with remaining fillets.

4. Over medium heat, place a nonstick skillet large enough to hold fillets without crowding. When pan is hot, add oil. When oil is hot, add fillets, decrease heat to medium-low, and cook 3 to 5 minutes, depending on thickness of fish. Turn fish, being careful not to tear rice paper, and finish cooking another 3 to 5 minutes. You will see the steelhead change from translucent to opaque as it cooks. If unsure about doneness, check by carefully cutting into the middle of one of the packets with the tip of a small, sharp knife.

5. To serve, divide steelhead packets among warmed individual plates and drizzle with Vietnamese Dipping Sauce.

SERVES 4

FUN FACT

- Steelhead are highly migratory fish; one tagged steelhead traveled from Washington to the Aleutian Islands in Alaska, a distance of 2,275 miles. Wonder if it ever came up for air?

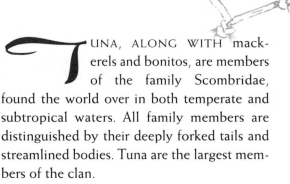

Tuna

UNA, ALONG WITH mackerels and bonitos, are members of the family Scombridae, found the world over in both temperate and subtropical waters. All family members are distinguished by their deeply forked tails and streamlined bodies. Tuna are the largest members of the clan.

Tuna migrate great distances from their spawning grounds in search of food. Their smooth, barrel-like bodies, which taper off toward the head and tail, are built for speed and endurance. Even the fins retract so they can become more aerodynamic and swim faster.

Tuna are known as the "sirloin of the sea" for their steaklike heartiness. All tuna meat is firm and compact, fine grained and dense. The skin of tuna is tough and leathery and is often removed before being offered for sale, although it peels off quite easily after cooking.

There are many species of tuna, but only two species reach the fresh market on the West Coast: Albacore and yellowfin. Only albacore tuna are caught in Northwest waters.

The **albacore** (*Thunnus alalunga*), also known as longfin tuna or white tuna, ranges from southeastern Alaska to Mexico on the West Coast, and is the only tuna found locally. The fish is primarily taken by long lines, trolling, and pole and line.

The albacore is one of the smaller members of the tuna family, weighing between 10 and 25 pounds with a maximum length of 4 $\frac{1}{2}$ feet. The fish is a streamlined wonder, from its pointed nose to its muscular bullet shape, and has a dark blue to steel-gray back and a silver belly. The fish is distinguished by its 12- to 20-inch pectoral (side) fins, which can be tucked into a groove along the fish's side for less water resistance. Because of these extremely long pectoral fins, the Japanese call albacore *tomboshibi*, or "dragonfly," tuna.

The albacore has the lightest flesh of the mackerel family. The pinkish to light red flesh

Albacore Tuna

turns white during cooking, and is small-flaked, firm, and drier than most tuna. It is milder and more delicate in flavor but has the same circular flake as other species of tuna. Albacore is best baked, braised, sautéed, broiled, or marinated and grilled. Traditionally used for canning, only albacore tuna can legally be labeled white meat tuna. Because of its premium quality, albacore carries a higher price tag than light meat tuna. Albacore tuna is available whole and dressed, or as fillets or steaks. Allow 8 ounces of steaks per person; 4 to 6 ounces of fillets are an entrée-sized portions.

Yellowfin tuna (*Thunnus albacares*) is also known as ahi, yellowfin ahi, or ahi tuna, its Hawaiian name. It is readily available fresh in U.S. fish markets but is perhaps best known as light meat tuna, the most commonly canned tuna in the United States. It is the most abundant of the tuna species and ranges from central California to Peru on the West Coast. Worldwide, purse seine, gill net, long line (for the fresh and fresh-frozen market), and pole fishers take lots of yellowfin.

The weight range in the commercial catch is from 20 to 120 pounds, although the fish can weigh up to 300 pounds and reach over 6 feet in length. Yellowfin are colorful, with bluish backs, silvery bellies, and light yellow fins edged in black.

Yellowfin has a slightly stronger, heartier flavor than albacore tuna, a large circular flake, and a meaty appearance. Freshly cut yellowfin should be translucent red in color, although the color may vary depending on how it is stored. For example, yellowfin tuna for the Japanese market is held at temperatures below 55° and remains a bright pink color.

Yellowfin tuna for the United States market is often held at higher temperatures, which causes the flesh to turn brown. "Chocolate" tuna, as it is known, is excellent in recipes calling for cooked tuna, although it is not suitable for recipes that call for raw fish. Unless the browning is well advanced, there is little difference in flavor or appearance between the two colors of tuna; what differs is the price.

Fresh tuna should be a deep translucent pink (albacore) or red (yellowfin) and glistening on the surface. Tuna can lose its bright color quickly when exposed to oxygen, so keep it refrigerated, well covered in plastic wrap or in a tightly sealed plastic bag with all of the air pressed out, and out of direct contact with air or ice.

Market forms of yellowfin tuna include loins, fillets, boneless steaks, cubes, and thin medallions. Steaks of $1/2$ to 1 inch thick are best. Allow about 4 to 6 ounces per entrée serving.

Yellowfin tuna can be broiled, baked, braised, sautéed, blackened or bronzed, eaten

Yellowfin Tuna

raw in sushi or sashimi, poached and served hot (or cold in salads), grilled, poached, stir-fried, microwaved, smoked, or cut into chunks for use in chowders. The meat turns light tan to light gray and forms large flakes after cooking. When grilling or broiling, either marinate or brush lightly with olive oil on both sides before cooking.

Yellowfin is available year-round. Fresh albacore tuna runs during the months of July, August, and September; canned albacore is available year-round.

FUN FACTS

• Over 1 billion cans of tuna are purchased each year. But fresh tuna is finding a wide and appreciative audience due to the popularity of sashimi, as well as health-conscious Americans who enjoy tuna's similarity to filet mignon when cooked rare to medium-rare.

Braised Tuna with Pike Place Fish Secret Sauce

PIKE PLACE FISH,
PIKE PLACE MARKET

Pike Place Fish sells an all-natural, preservative- and sugar-free bottled spice blend called Northwest Seafood Seasoning. From reading the ingredients list, I thought it might be a rather ordinary herb and spice mixture of garlic, lemon, salt, and dill. However, the first time I used it, my husband said it was one of the best dishes I had ever made! Ruddy red in color, the sauce is reminiscent of a hearty steak sauce and goes particularly well with the "filet mignon of the sea"—fresh tuna.

1 TABLESPOON NORTHWEST SEAFOOD
    SEASONING (SEE NOTE)
1 CUP DRY WHITE WINE
2 TABLESPOONS UNSALTED BUTTER
1 1/2 POUNDS TUNA LOIN OR STEAKS,
    RINSED, DRAINED, PATTED DRY, AND CUT
    INTO 4 (6-OUNCE) PIECES

1. In a small bowl, stir together Northwest Seafood Seasoning and 2 tablespoons of the white wine and reserve.

2. Heat butter in a large skillet over medium-high heat. When butter foams, add tuna pieces and cook 1 to 2 minutes, or until the outside surface turns white. Turn fillets and cook another 1 to 2 minutes, or until the second side turns white. Remove tuna fillets to a plate and reserve.

3. Add reserved wine mixture to pan and stir, scraping up any browned bits of fish that have accumulated on the bottom of pan. Add remaining white wine and stir well. Add tuna fillets and spoon sauce over fillets. Decrease heat to medium-low, cover pan, and cook until tuna is pale pink in the middle, about 3 to 6 minutes depending on thickness of fish.

4. Remove fillets from pan and reserve. Increase heat to medium-high and reduce sauce until thickened slightly, stirring often.

5. To serve, divide tuna and sauce among individual plates.

SERVES 4

Note: Northwest Seafood Seasoning can be used in numerous ways. Add it to melted butter and lemon juice and spread on fish fillets before grilling or broiling. Sprinkle a bit in seafood soups or stews, or sprinkle some directly on fish before sautéing, baking, or poaching. Add it to flour and dredge fish before pan-frying or deep-frying. It is available at the Pike Place Fish's stall under the famous Market clock or by mail (see page 329).

HANDY TUNA TIP

Tuna is so lusty that a brush of olive oil and a simple sprinkling of seasoning will suffice, although it holds up well to strongly flavored accents such as garlic, pepper, mustard, soy sauce, and ginger. Unlike more delicate fish, tuna can be marinated for several hours without "cooking" the flesh.

Bronzed Tuna

My good friend, fellow cookbook author, boating and gardening expert Carol Foster, of Anacortes, Washington, graciously allowed me to reprint this recipe from her book, Short Cuts to Great Cuisine. *She explains that bronzing, as opposed to the blackening cooking method, requires a cast-iron skillet to reach only 350° versus 500°, which allows the home cook to enjoy juicy, tender, spice-encrusted fish without an accompanying smoke alarm. Carol's original recipe called for red snapper, but she suggests substituting any firm-fleshed fish, such as salmon or tuna, which I have chosen for this rendition.*

2 TEASPOONS SWEET PAPRIKA

1 1/2 TEASPOONS DRIED THYME, CRUMBLED

1 1/2 TEASPOONS DRIED OREGANO,
    CRUMBLED

1 TEASPOON SALT

1/2 TEASPOON FRESHLY GROUND BLACK
    PEPPER

1/4 TEASPOON GROUND CAYENNE PEPPER

3/4 CUP UNSALTED BUTTER

1 1/2 POUNDS TUNA LOIN OR STEAKS,
    3/4 INCH THICK, RINSED, DRAINED,
    PATTED DRY, CUT INTO 4 (6-OUNCE)
    PIECES, AT ROOM TEMPERATURE

1. In a small bowl, blend the paprika, thyme, oregano, salt, black pepper, and cayenne. Melt the butter in a small skillet and keep over low heat.

2. Place a large cast-iron skillet over medium-high heat. When the skillet is very hot, dip the tuna pieces in the butter and sprinkle both sides evenly with the spice mixture. Place in skillet immediately (do not place on another surface or the spices will be lost) and cook about 3 minutes. Turn and cook another 2 minutes, depending upon thickness and degree of doneness desired. Transfer fish to a warmed serving plate.

3. Pour the remaining warm butter into the cast-iron skillet, scraping up any browned bits and spices that may have accumulated on the bottom. Pour over the fish and serve immediately.

SERVES 4

FUN FACTS

• The very dark lateral strip of meat that is found in tuna and some other types of fish (such as mackerel and swordfish) is known as red muscle and is crucial to the fish for long-range swimming. Nutritionally, it offers a high level of iron and copper, as well as higher levels of protein than the flesh that surrounds it. Its intense flavor is often described as bitter, and some people like it more than others (the Japanese often eat it for its health benefits). This part of the flesh also spoils more quickly than the surrounding meat, but if the fish is fresh and you enjoy the taste and don't mind the color, there is no reason to remove it before cooking.

• Bluefin tuna, another member of the mackerel family found in North Atlantic waters, can weigh as much as 2,000 pounds and grow up to 12 feet long. They are often compared to baby elephants and are prized by the Japanese, who pay top dollar for the fish for use in sashimi. In spite of fishing quotas, the National Audubon Society has proposed that the bluefin be listed as an endangered species.

Tuna Escabèche

———※———

Virazon,
Seattle, Washington

Judy Schocken is co-owner with chef Astolfo Rueda of Virazon, a fine French restaurant along First Avenue just south of the Market. At home, she enjoys cooking simple country-style dishes, such as escabèche. *A popular dish in Provence, Spain, and Latin America,* escabèche *is composed of poached or fried fish flavored with vinegar. In olden times, this method of marinating fish in a pickling liquid was used as a form of preservation. It was introduced to Europe by the Moors in the fourteenth century, then transported to Latin America. The beauty of an* escabèche *is its flexibility, because any type of fish fillet and vegetables can be used and it can be served warm out of the pan or at room temperature.*

3 TABLESPOONS OLIVE OIL

1 1/2 POUNDS TUNA LOIN OR STEAKS,
    RINSED, DRAINED, PATTED DRY, AND CUT
    INTO 4 (6-OUNCE) PIECES

1 ONION, CUT IN HALF, THEN INTO 1/8-INCH-
    THICK SLICES

1 RED PEPPER, CUT IN HALF, STEMMED,
    SEEDED, DERIBBED, AND CUT INTO
    1/8-INCH-THICK SLICES

1 YELLOW PEPPER, CUT IN HALF, STEMMED,
    SEEDED, DERIBBED, AND CUT INTO
    1/8-INCH-THICK SLICES

1/2 CUP 1/8-INCH-THICK SLICES ZUCCHINI

1 TEASPOON CHOPPED GARLIC

4 TABLESPOONS RED WINE VINEGAR

SALT AND PEPPER

1. Place olive oil in a large skillet over medium-high heat. When oil is hot, add tuna fillets, without crowding. Cook 2 minutes per side, turn, and cook 2 to 3 minutes more, or until tuna is opaque on the outside but still pink in the middle (medium-rare). It is better to undercook than to overcook this recipe. Remove tuna and reserve.

2. Return skillet to heat and add onion, red pepper, yellow pepper, zucchini, and garlic. Cook 7 to 10 minutes, stirring occasionally, until vegetables are tender. Add extra oil or a few tablespoons of water if needed to prevent sticking. Do not allow vegetables to brown. Remove pan from heat, add vinegar, and stir well to blend. Season to taste with salt and pepper.

3. To serve, arrange tuna fillets on a large serving platter, surround with vegetables, and serve family style. Alternatively, allow tuna and vegetables to cool, then cover and refrigerate. About 30 minutes before serving, remove from refrigerator and let come to room temperature.

SERVES 4

HANDY TUNA TIP

Tuna can easily dry out if overcooked and is best undercooked, served rare to medium-rare. For rare to medium-rare tuna, simply cook the outside surfaces of the tuna quickly to seal in the juices, much like you would cook rare steak, leaving it red to pink in the middle. For well-done tuna, cook the fish until it is white or ivory in color all the way through. Cooked fresh tuna can be used like canned tuna but is much more flavorful.

Yin and Yang Tuna

This dish has a playful combination of flavors, textures, and colors, as opposite as yin and yang.

1/2 CUP LOW-SODIUM SOY SAUCE

4 TABLESPOONS MIRIN

1 TABLESPOON SEASONED RICE VINEGAR

1 TABLESPOON PLUS 1/8 TEASPOON TOASTED
   SESAME OIL

1/2 TEASPOON CHILE OIL, PLUS A FEW EXTRA
   DROPS

1 1/2 POUNDS TUNA FILLETS, 3/4 TO 1 INCH
   THICK, SKIN REMOVED, RINSED, DRAINED,
   PATTED DRY, CUT INTO FOUR (6-OUNCE
   PIECES), THEN CUT IN HALF HORIZON-
   TALLY TO FORM 8 THIN PIECES

1/4 CUP SZECHWAN PEPPERCORNS, TOASTED
   (SEE PAGE 10)

1/4 CUP WHITE SESAME SEEDS, TOASTED
   (SEE PAGE 10)

1 TABLESPOON SESAME OIL

1. Place soy sauce, mirin, rice vinegar, 1 tablespoon of the toasted sesame oil, and 1/2 teaspoon of the chile oil in a nonreactive baking dish large enough to hold tuna fillets without crowding and stir well. Add tuna fillets, turning several times to coat with marinade. Cover baking dish, place in refrigerator, and marinate 1 to 2 hours, turning occasionally.

2. While fish fillets are marinating, place cooled Szechwan peppercorns in a spice mill or electric coffee grinder and process until they become a very fine powder. Put powder in a fine-meshed sieve and tap or push through to extract all of the pepper. Reserve pepper only.

3. When fish fillets have marinated for 1 to 2 hours, remove from refrigerator and pat dry. Reserve marinade and place in a small saucepan. Bring to a boil and cook for 2 to 3 minutes, then cover pan, remove from heat, and reserve.

4. Spread reserved Szechwan pepper on a plate. Pat pepper into one side of each of four of the tuna fillets. Place fillets on a sheet of waxed paper until ready to cook. Discard any remaining pepper, rinse off plate, and dry completely. Spread sesame seeds on plate and pat seeds onto one side of remaining four tuna fillets.

5. Mix sesame oil, the remaining 1/8 teaspoon toasted sesame oil, and remaining couple of drops of chili oil in a small bowl. Heat a nonstick skillet large enough to hold four of the tuna fillets without crowding over medium heat. When pan is hot, add half the oil mixture. When oil is hot, place the four sesame seed-coated tuna fillets in the pan coated side down and cook for 30 seconds to 1 minute. Turn fillets and cook another 30 seconds to 1 minute. Tuna should still be red (raw) in the middle, with thin layers of white tuna on the outside. Transfer fillets to a warm plate and reserve.

6. Add the remaining oil to skillet and repeat procedure with Szechwan-coated fillets, cooking the pepper-coated side first.

7. To serve, place one pepper-coated fillet and one sesame seed-coated fillet on a plate, slightly overlapping the two. Be sure the sides of the fillets embedded with the peppers and sesame seeds face up. Drizzle with warm marinade. For a more formal presentation, mound cooked soba noodles in center of plate and top with broccoli florets. Cut fillets in half and evenly space tuna pieces around edge of plate.

SERVES 4

Part 3

SHELLFISH

Clams

CLAMS ARE BIVALVE mollusks. Most clams have a "foot" at one end of their body and a "neck" at the other, which are actually siphons that perform the clam's respiratory and digestive functions. There are two siphons, one through which the clam sucks in water to bring oxygen to the gills and food to the stomach, and the exhaust siphon, which carries off wastes. There are many different varieties of clams. Northwest varieties of commercial importance include native littleneck, Manila, butter, razor, and geoduck clams.

The native littleneck clam (*Protothaca staminea*) and naturalized Manila clam (*Venerupis philippinerum*) are so similar in appearance that for years they were sold interchangeably. It takes a trained eye to tell the difference between the sometimes lighter, more rounded littleneck and the usually darker, more mottled and more oblong Manila clam. Today, most markets sell Manilas and littlenecks separately because of their marked cooking differences.

Littlenecks are less desirable of the two species because of their erratic cooking time, shorter shelf life, tougher texture, and milder flavor. Found from California to Alaska, littlenecks are gradually being displaced by the more commercially desirable Manila. They are unrelated, except in size, to the East Coast littleneck, which is a small quahog (pronounced "KO-hog"). Littleneck meat is lean and lends itself to steaming and sautéing. To encourage littlenecks to open more consistently, many Asian cooks freeze the clams in their shells before cooking.

Manila clams (also sometimes called Japanese littleneck) arrived in the Northwest mixed in with oyster "seed" purchased from aquacul-

Native Littleneck Clam

turists in Japan and Asia in the 1920s. Found from California to British Columbia, the immigrant Manila clam is the predominant commercial clam on the West Coast. Most Manila clams these days are cultivated. Small clams from hatcheries and nurseries are seeded, or planted, on intertidal beaches where they are harvested after 2 or 3 years by hand rakes. Less than 1 percent are dredged.

While most markets separate Manilas and littlenecks, some do not. Consumers should request Manilas for uniform and quick opening, longer shelf life, sweeter flavor, and more tender texture. Some markets sell these clams in mixed sizes; others classify them as small (20 to 25 per pound), medium (12 to 20 per pound), and large (fewer than 12 per pound).

Manilas are the primary West Coast steamer clam, but can also be sautéed, stir-fried, baked, or opened in a stew. They are not typically eaten raw on the half shell. Quite versatile in the kitchen, Manilas are especially well utilized in Chinese and Italian cooking.

Manila clams will keep 7 days (depending on how old they are when you buy them), but are best eaten as soon as possible after purchase. The clams spawn from May to August, depending on the growing area. Fall, winter, and spring are the prime seasons for eating clams, since spawning clams have a bitter taste and very short shelf life.

Butter clams (*Saxidomus giganteus*) are large, hard-shell clams whose heavy, grayish white shells are relatively smooth with fine-etched concentric lines. Found from California to Alaska, butter clams range in size from 2 to 6 inches. Their pinkish meat is tender and lean and lends itself to being served raw on the half shell when the clams are small, or steamed, sautéed, stuffed, baked, or fried for larger sizes.

Razor clams (*Siliqua patula*) are found on sandy ocean beaches from California to Alaska. The clams have powerful diggers and smooth, lacquered shells that allow them to burrow at a rate of up to 9 inches a minute in sand. They become exposed to the surf at extremely low, or minus, tides.

Inexperienced clam diggers quickly learn to reach after the thin, razor-sharp, 6-inch-long, yellow-brown shells with caution. Sport and commercial fishers hunt their popular quarry with clam "guns," short-handled shovels with long, narrow blades, or clam tubes, aluminum or hard plastic tubes, about 3 1/2 feet long, with a thumb-sized hole and a handle on top. However, digging has become more and more restricted in recent years.

Razor clams are an exceptionally meaty shellfish with ivory-colored meat that can be

Razor Clam

fork-tender or shoe-leather tough depending on the skill of the cook. Razor clams are usually cooked quickly in a skillet, a method in which precise timing is essential, or used in chowders or to make clam fritters, which are popular with coastal residents. And although many cookbooks recommend pounding the clams to relax the meat, if prepared by an experienced razor clam cook, this step can be omitted.

Live razors can be purchased whole or cleaned, but have a very short shelf life. If purchased whole, they should be removed from their shells and eviscerated as soon as you get them home, then consumed within 1 to 2 days.

The geoduck clam (*Panopea abrupta*) (pronounced "GOOEY-duck") is the largest burrowing clam in the world, and lives on the West Coast of North America from Baja California to Alaska. Its average weight is 3 to 7 pounds, but giants of 14 and 20 pounds have been recorded. Geoducks can live to be more than 100 years old; the oldest geoduck on record was 146.

The almost rectangular, chalky white shell of the clam measures up to 9 inches, with a syphon measuring 18 inches in repose and up to 39 inches fully extended. The syphon resembles an elephant's trunk that retracts and extends at the animal's whim. Once situated, the geoduck never moves; instead, it works its neck to the surface of the sand to gather food.

Geoducks are now being farmed for the

Geoduck

first time. Most geoducks are exported to Asia, although live geoducks are available year-round at the Pike Place Market and in Asian markets.

When buying geoducks, look for short, fat siphons that flinch when you touch them. Although the beige to deep brown color is not an indication of freshness, the lighter color is preferred for sashimi and brings a higher price. Geoduck has a rich, sweet flavor. Leftover geoduck meat also freezes well. The meat-to-shell ratio on geoducks is 20 percent; breasts, 15 percent. Use the neck for sashimi, and the breast for everything from fritters to chowders to fried clams.

Clams are sold live in the shell, fresh or frozen shucked, and canned. By law, all mollusks must carry a shipping certificate with the harvest location, harvest date, and shipping date on the shipping container. Consumers can and should request to see this tag before making their purchase.

Native littleneck and Manila clams should either be tightly closed or stay shut when you press their shells together, which shows that the clams are alive. Sniff butter, razor, and geoduck clams before purchasing; if they have any off odor, don't buy them. Also touch the neck of the geoduck; if it moves, the geoduck is alive.

When you get your clams home, immediately remove them from their plastic bag or they could suffocate. Place clams in a shallow tray or platter so that they fit in one layer and do not sit on top of each other, then cover loosely with a damp paper towel. Place the tray in the refrigerator at temperatures between 35° and 40°. Temperatures colder than this may overstress live clams and cause unnecessary death. As with any seafood, clams should be consumed as soon as possible after purchase.

Shucked clams should be plump and their liquid (liquor) clear. Store shucked clams in a tightly sealed container embedded in a bowl of ice and use as soon as possible within no more than 4 days. Razor clams, butter clams, and geoducks should be removed from their shells and eviscerated before freezing. Otherwise, enzymes will continue to work away at their flesh during freezer storage.

Manila clams and littlenecks can be frozen in the shell for up to 3 months. Simply scrub them, place them in plastic freezer bags, and seal tightly. Just before cooking, remove clams from the freezer and rinse in cold water. Cook as desired, but do not eat raw on the half shell because clams become soft during freezing.

Allow 1 pound of live native littleneck or Manila clams in the shell per person as an entrée, 1 dozen small to medium clams per person as an appetizer. One pound of live Manilas or littlenecks typically yields about $1/4$ pound of meat. Allow $1/4$ pound of razor clam, butter clam, or geoduck clam meat per serving. Allow 4 to 10 small clams per person as an appetizer, 12 to 20 small clams as an entrée. Per person, 2 to 8 medium or large clams are sufficient as an appetizer; 9 to 16 medium or large clams are good as an entrée.

If using clams on the half shell that must be shucked, after purging them, it helps to freeze the clams for 30 minutes right before you plan to shuck them to relax the muscles. To open a clam, use a clam knife, oyster knife, or a dull paring knife. Wear a thick mitt, rubber glove, or use several thicknesses of kitchen towels to hold the clam securely and to protect your hand. Work over a bowl so you can catch any clam juices that might escape.

Cup the clam in one hand with the hinge pointing toward your wrist, then squeeze the blade of the knife (not the tip) sharply inward between the lips of the shell opposite the hinge. Work the knife around the clam shell, twisting the blade to force the halves open. Slide the blade along the inside of the top shell to sever the top of the clam. Twist off the freed half shell, then slide the knife blade under the meat of the lower shell and sever the bottom of the clam meat.

Native littlenecks, Manila clams, butter clams, and geoducks are available year-round, but are best in the fall, winter, and spring. Razor clams are mostly available fresh from April to October.

Young, lean white wines such as sémillon, sémillon-chardonnay, chardonnay (lean,

acidic styles that are not heavily oaked or buttery), sauvignon blanc, chenin blanc, fumé blanc, sauvignon blanc-sémillon blends, pinot gris, melon, riesling, and dry rieslings all pair well with the unique taste and texture of clams. Of course, much depends on the sauce served with the bivalves. If serving clams in a spicy tomato-based sauce, some light red wines, such as beaujolais or pinot noirs that have been slightly chilled, make good matches. When cooking clams with Asian-style treatments, sake or Asian beer may make a better partner.

FUN FACTS

- The Nisqually tribe of Washington State were the earliest settlers of southern Puget Sound and the original hunters of the geoduck clam, which they called *gweduc*, meaning "dig deep." The Nisqually and other Northwest coastal tribes gathered geoducks using a 4-foot-long digging stick made of maple or cherry wood. Although some clams were eaten fresh, most geoduck necks were smoked and stored for future consumption. The smoked geoducks were used in clam chowders in winter months and some were accumulated to trade with other tribes.

Basic Steamed Clams

———⚬———

A big bowl of steamed clams accompanied by a cup of warm clam nectar, a ramekin of melted butter for dipping, and lots of crusty bread for sopping up all the flavorful broth, helps chase away Northwest winter blues better than anything I know. This easy-to-make recipe is also the foundation for several other recipes in this chapter.

4 POUNDS LIVE PURGED MANILA OR NATIVE
  LITTLENECK CLAMS, SHELLS SCRUBBED
1 CUP WATER, FISH STOCK, DRY WHITE
  WINE, OR BEER
MELTED BUTTER (OPTIONAL)

1. In a large stockpot or Dutch oven, combine the clams and water. Cover and bring to a boil. Decrease heat to a simmer and steam for 6 to 10 minutes, or until clams open. Throughout the cooking process, shake the pot occasionally, as though you were making popcorn, to redistribute the clams.

2. Remove clams that have opened to a serving bowl. Cover pot again and cook any clams that have not opened an additional 2 minutes. Discard any that still do not open. Strain the cooking liquid into a large bowl through a fine-meshed sieve lined with several thicknesses of cheesecloth or a paper coffee filter.

3. To serve, divide clams among 4 bowls or transfer to a large serving bowl. Divide clam nectar among 4 cups. Serve with melted butter, if desired.

SERVES 4 AS AN ENTRÉE, 8 AS AN APPETIZER

FUN FACTS

- In his informative and entertaining book, *Field Guide to the Geoduck,* David George Gordon explains that during spring and summer months, Native American women devoted much of their time to digging and processing shellfish. To lighten their workloads, they developed an ingenious method for cleaning their catch. Clams were put in open, birdcage-weave baskets made from the roots and bark of cedar and spruce trees. The baskets were then suspended in seawater, so the clams could be purged of sand and mud by incoming and outgoing tides.

Daisy Sage's Clam Chowder

Du jour is a sunny, bright spot along First Avenue with great views of Elliott Bay and a Continental feeling to the atmosphere and the food. Chef Aaron Hinchy explains that his recipe for clam chowder is in constant evolution. Through the years, it has contained spinach, jalapeño peppers, smoked salmon, and sweet potatoes (although, mercifully, not all at the same time!). This version, however, is as close as he has come to the way his great-grandmother, Daisy Sage, used to make it. Aaron has a taste for freshly ground black pepper and recommends using 3/4 tablespoon; you might try adding less pepper to start, and increase the amount depending on your taste.

1 TABLESPOON BUTTER

1 LARGE YELLOW ONION, DICED

3 CLOVES GARLIC, MINCED

1 CUP CHOPPED CELERY STALKS AND
   LEAVES

1 1/2 CUPS DICED NEW POTATOES, UNPEELED
   AND SCRUBBED

2 (6.5-OUNCE) CANS CHOPPED CLAMS WITH
   JUICE

2 CUPS CLAM JUICE

8 CUPS WHOLE MILK

2 BAY LEAVES

1 1/2 TEASPOONS DRIED MARJORAM,
   CRUMBLED

SALT AND FRESHLY GROUND BLACK PEPPER

1. In a large stockpot or Dutch oven, heat butter over medium-high heat. Add onion, garlic, celery, and potatoes. Cook 5 to 7 minutes, or until onions are transparent, stirring occasionally. Do not allow vegetables to brown. If vegetables begin to stick or brown too quickly, add 1 to 2 tablespoons water and stir well.

2. Add clams and their juice plus the additional clam juice. Bring to a simmer, then decrease heat to medium or medium-low. Cook for 15 minutes, stirring occasionally.

3. Add milk, bay leaves, and marjoram, stir well, and cook, uncovered, for 1 hour over medium-low to medium heat, stirring occasionally. Do not allow mixture to come to a boil. Taste and adjust seasoning with salt and pepper.

4. To serve, divide among soup bowls.

SERVES 4 TO 6 AS AN ENTRÉE, 8 TO 10 AS AN APPETIZER

Note: This chowder, while very flavorful, is lighter in texture and calories than traditional clam chowders, which often include heavy whipping cream and cornstarch to thicken. If you want a thicker, richer chowder, you can whisk in a bit of white roux 15 to 20 minutes before the end of cooking time. To make the roux, melt 1/4 cup butter in a heavy-bottomed skillet over medium heat. Whisk in 1/4 cup flour and cook 10 to 15 minutes, whisking frequently, until roux just begins to turn beige. Add roux to chowder bit by bit, whisking well to prevent lumps from forming, until the chowder reaches the consistency you want.

Northwest
Clambake in the Oven

———⦿———

Even though the idea of a real clambake on the beach appeals to my senses, I'm neither patient nor adventurous enough to dig a hole, build a bonfire, and wait 6 hours to eat. This clambake can be done in your own kitchen with no big mess to clean up, but yields results as tasty as if it had been cooked in the great outdoors. The quantities given will generously feed one hungry diner or two light eaters; double or quadruple as needed. Melted butter or margarine for the corn, lemon wedges for the fish, a loaf of crusty bread, and a good Washington State sémillon-chardonnay are the only other accompaniments you'll need.

2 LARGE SOFT LETTUCE LEAVES, SUCH AS
   BIBB, GREEN LEAF, OR ICEBERG

1 LINGCOD OR HALIBUT FILLET, ABOUT 3
   OUNCES, SKINNED AND BONED

6 CLAMS, PURGED AND SHELLS SCRUBBED

6 MUSSELS, SCRUBBED AND DEBEARDED
   JUST BEFORE READY TO COOK

3 ALASKAN SPOT PRAWNS, CUT DOWN THE
   BACK WITH SCISSORS AND VEIN
   EXTRACTED

2 TO 3 SMALL NEW POTATOES, ABOUT 1 1/2
   INCHES IN DIAMETER, CUT IN HALF

1 EAR CORN, HUSK REMOVED AND BROKEN
   OR CUT INTO THIRDS

6 SNOW PEAS, STRINGS REMOVED

1 SMALL YELLOW SQUASH OR ZUCCHINI
   SQUASH, ENDS REMOVED AND CUT INTO
   1/2-INCH ROUNDS

1 CLOVE GARLIC, MINCED

FRESH ROSEMARY, THYME, OR TARRAGON
   SPRIGS

1/4 CUP CLAM JUICE, FISH STOCK, OR
   CHICKEN STOCK

1. Preheat oven to 350°.

2. Cut two 24-inch lengths of aluminum foil and place on a flat surface in a cross-shaped pattern. Place lettuce leaves in center of foil and top with lingcod fillets, then place clams, mussels, and spot prawns on top. Place potatoes, corn, snow peas, and yellow squash around lingcod, then pull up sides of foil around vegetables to form a bowl shape. Sprinkle garlic over seafood and vegetables, place herb sprigs on top of seafood, then drizzle clam juice over all.

3. Bring long sides of foil up until they meet in the middle and secure tightly. Fold remaining ends to seal tightly. Place packet on a baking sheet and bake 1 hour.

4. To serve, place packet on individual plate and unfold or cut open aluminum at the table for an informal presentation. Alternately, unfold aluminum foil in the kitchen, transfer contents of packet to a plate, and discard foil.

SERVES 1

Boston-Style Clam Chowder

The Athenian Inn's creamy clam chowder, an original recipe served for the past twenty years, may be the most popular rendition of this dish in the Market, judging by the vast quantities ordered by loyal customers. Owners Louise and Bob Cromwell report that they serve 225 bowls a day.

¹⁄₂ CUP DICED BACON

¹⁄₂ CUP DICED ONION

¹⁄₂ CUP DICED CELERY

1 CUP DICED, COOKED BOILING POTATOES

DASH OF SALT

DASH OF FRESHLY GROUND PEPPER

1 BAY LEAF

PINCH OF DRIED THYME, CRUMBLED

PINCH OF DRIED MARJORAM, CRUMBLED

PINCH OF DRIED OREGANO, CRUMBLED

3 CUPS CLAM JUICE

¹⁄₄ CUP BUTTER

¹⁄₂ CUP ALL-PURPOSE FLOUR

1 CUP MILK

2 (6.5-OUNCE) CANS CHOPPED CLAMS,
   DRAINED

1. In a medium skillet over medium heat, cook bacon 3 to 5 minutes, or until light brown, stirring occasionally. Add onions and celery and cook 5 to 7 minutes, or until vegetables are tender, stirring occasionally. Add potatoes, salt, pepper, herbs, and 1 cup of the clam juice and stir well. Bring to a boil, then remove from heat and set aside.

2. In a large saucepan, melt butter over medium heat. Add flour, whisking continuously until smooth. Add the remaining 2 cups clam juice and the milk a little at a time, whisking after each addition to prevent lumps from forming. Bring to a boil. Add clams and reserved vegetable mixture and stir well.

3. To serve, divide soup among soup bowls.

SERVES 4 AS AN APPETIZER

FUN FACTS

- Female razor clams produce 6 to 10 million or more eggs annually.

- Clams' hearts beat 2 to 20 beats per minute, compared with the squid's 40 to 80 beats.

Stir-Fried Clams

⟨knot ornament⟩

Most people wouldn't think of putting clams in a stir-fry, but the mollusks taste great among the vegetables in this salty-sweet, glossy brown sauce, teeming with the hot bite of fresh ginger. Serve over the traditional white or brown rice or, less conventionally, over rice spaghetti, a clear, rather mild noodle that picks up the flavors of the sauce beautifully.

4 POUNDS MANILA OR NATIVE LITTLENECK
   CLAMS, PURGED AND SHELLS SCRUBBED

1/2 CUP SAKE OR MIRIN

1 TABLESPOON MAPLE SYRUP

1/4 CUP LOW-SODIUM SOY SAUCE

PINCH OF CRUSHED RED PEPPER FLAKES

1 TABLESPOON CORNSTARCH

1 TABLESPOON PEANUT OIL

6 GREEN ONIONS, TOP 2 INCHES REMOVED,
   REMAINING PORTION CUT INTO 1/4-INCH
   ROUNDS

2 CLOVES GARLIC, MINCED

1 TEASPOON GRATED GINGERROOT

1/2 RED BELL PEPPER, STEMMED, SEEDED,
   AND JULIENNED

6 CUPS COOKED WHITE OR BROWN RICE

1. Cook clams as described on page 156. Remove clams from shells and save the best 16 shells for garnishing. Discard remaining shells. Strain cooking liquid through a fine-meshed sieve lined with several thicknesses of cheesecloth or a paper coffee filter and reserve for later use.

2. In a small nonreactive bowl, combine sake, maple syrup, soy sauce, red pepper flakes, and cornstarch, mixing until cornstarch is dissolved. Set aside.

3. Heat peanut oil in a large wok or skillet over medium-high heat. Add green onions, garlic, and gingerroot and stir-fry 2 minutes. Add red bell pepper and stir-fry 1 minute. Remove pan from heat, add reserved sauce, and stir-fry 1 minute, or until vegetables are tender-crisp. Add a tablespoon or two of reserved clam juice if sauce thickens too rapidly.

4. Return pan to heat, add clams, and stir well to coat evenly with sauce. Cook 1 to 2 minutes, or until clams are warmed through.

5. To serve, divide rice and stir-fry among individual plates, and arrange reserved clam shells around the edges of the plates.

SERVES 4

FUN FACT

- Evergreen College in Olympia, Washington, adopted the geoduck as its mascot, dubbing its football team the Fighting Geoducks.

Smoky Clam Chowder

JACK'S FISH SPOT, PIKE PLACE MARKET

Jack's Fish Spot started out as a one-man operation in the Madison Park section of Seattle. A dry-cleaning business named Spot Cleaners was the previous occupant of the space Jack Mathers leased when he started his fish stall. Casting around for a name, Jack noticed the Spot Cleaners sign, and thus Jack's Fish Spot was born. Jack moved to the Market in December 1982, where his business stands apart as the only fish stand with fresh seafood tanks and a small seafood bar. The bar serves this delicious chowder, along with oysters on the half shell, cracked crab, and fried seafood (the scallops win rave reviews). The addition of hard-cooked smoked salmon, also known as salmon jerky and sometimes sold under the name "squaw candy," gives this rendition of clam chowder a hearty flavor and a real Northwest flair. To make informal croutons, lightly butter saltine crackers, place them on the bottom of the soup bowls, and pour the chowder over.

2 TABLESPOONS BUTTER

1 1/2 CUPS 1/2-INCH CUBED BOILING
   POTATOES

1/2 CUP CHOPPED CELERY

1/2 CUP CHOPPED ONION

1 (8-OUNCE) BOTTLE CLAM JUICE

2 CUPS MILK

PINCH OF DRIED THYME, CRUMBLED

PINCH OF CRUSHED RED PEPPER FLAKES

2 (6.5-OUNCE) CANS CHOPPED CLAMS,
   WITH JUICE

1 CUP HEAVY WHIPPING CREAM

2 TO 3 TABLESPOONS DICED HARD-SMOKED
   SALMON

SALT AND FRESHLY GROUND BLACK PEPPER

1. Melt butter in a large saucepan over medium heat and add potatoes, celery, and onion. Cook 5 minutes, stirring occasionally, or until vegetables are tender-crisp.

2. Add clam juice, milk, thyme, and red pepper flakes. Stir well and bring to a simmer. Simmer gently 10 minutes, stirring occasionally, until potatoes are tender. Add clams, whipping cream, and smoked salmon, and stir well. Cook several minutes more, or until mixture is warmed through. Season to taste with salt and pepper.

3. Ladle clam chowder into soup bowls and serve right away.

SERVES 4

Manhattan Clam Chowder

———◆———

Chowder owes its name to the French chaudière, *a three-legged heavy iron cooking pot. Fishermen returning to their villages would throw a portion of their catch into the pot as the villagers gathered to welcome the men home and share the meal. In the 1600s, the tradition crossed the Atlantic as French colonists settled what is now eastern Canada. Through the years, there evolved two main types of chowder. In northern New England, chowder is made with milk or cream. In Rhode Island and the New York area, chowder is made with tomatoes and broth. Manhattan-style chowder is generally healthier and more vegetable-based, as in this version. If served with a green salad and crusty whole-grain bread, this makes a one-saucepan dinner for four.*

2 CUPS WATER

4 POUNDS MANILA OR NATIVE LITTLENECK
   CLAMS, PURGED AND SHELLS SCRUBBED

2 TABLESPOONS OLIVE OIL

1/2 ONION, DICED

2 CLOVES GARLIC, MINCED

1 STALK CELERY, DICED

1/2 GREEN BELL PEPPER, STEMMED,
SEEDED, AND DICED

1/2 RED BELL PEPPER, STEMMED, SEEDED,
   AND DICED

1 CARROT, PEELED AND DICED

6 SMALL NEW POTATOES, SCRUBBED AND
   QUARTERED, OR 1 BAKING POTATO, DICED

1 (28-OUNCE) CAN WHOLE TOMATOES,
   COARSELY CHOPPED, JUICE RESERVED

1/8 TEASPOON TABASCO SAUCE

1 TABLESPOON WORCESTERSHIRE SAUCE

1/2 TEASPOON DRIED OREGANO, CRUMBLED

1 BAY LEAF

1 TEASPOON SUGAR

1/2 TEASPOON SALT

1/8 TEASPOON FRESHLY GROUND BLACK PEP-
   PER

1 TABLESPOON CORNSTARCH

2 TABLESPOONS WATER

1. In a large stockpot or Dutch oven, combine the water and clams. Cover and bring to a boil over high heat. Decrease heat to medium-low, cover, and steam for 6 to 10 minutes, or until clams open. Shake pot occasionally to redistribute clams.

2. Remove clams to a bowl and reserve the cooking liquid. Discard any clams that have not opened. Strain cooking liquid through a fine-meshed sieve lined with several thicknesses of dampened cheesecloth. Allow clams to cool, then shuck meat from shells and discard shells. Cover and place clam meat in refrigerator for later use. Measure 2 cups of cooking liquid and discard the rest or save for another use. Cover and refrigerate for later use. Rinse and dry stockpot or Dutch oven.

3. Place olive oil in stockpot over medium-high heat. Add onion and garlic and cook 3 to 5 minutes, or until onion is tender-crisp, stirring often. Add celery, green and red bell pepper, carrot, and potato. Cover and cook 8 to 10 minutes, or until vegetables are tender-crisp, stirring occasionally. If vegetables begin to stick or brown too quickly, add 1 to 2 tablespoons water and stir well.

4. Add tomatoes and their juice, reserved clam cooking liquid, Tabasco sauce, Worcestershire

sauce, oregano, bay leaf, sugar, salt, and pepper and stir well. Bring to a boil, decrease heat and simmer 15 to 20 minutes, covered, or until potatoes and carrots are tender. Stir occasionally.

5. Taste broth and add additional salt and pepper, if necessary. In a small bowl, mix cornstarch with water until well blended. Remove pot from heat and add cornstarch mixture. Stir well to blend completely, then return pan to heat. Cook 1 to 2 minutes more, stirring occasionally, or until soup thickens. For an even thicker, creamier

consistency, place $^1/_2$ of the vegetable mixture (about $3^1/_2$ cups) in a food processor or blender and process until smooth. Add back to pot and stir well. Add clams, stir well, and cook until clams are warmed through. Do not overcook, or clams will be tough.

6. Remove bay leaf and divide chowder among soup bowls.

SERVES 4 AS AN ENTRÉE, 8 AS AN APPETIZER

"TO PURGE OR NOT TO PURGE"

THERE SEEMS TO BE much debate on purging clams of sand, including the question of whether it is necessary at all. Many cookbooks suggest using cornmeal (the tried and true standby), flour (less common), black pepper (which gives the clam a "hot foot" so it spits out its grit along with the pepper), and even vinegar in either salt water or fresh water. Some sources advise to purge for no more than 15 minutes; others advise several hours and with several changes of water.

According to Seattle's resident seafood expert, Jon Rowley, "All clams are harvested from sandy or muddy bottoms so they need to be purged before going to market. This is something that should be done on the shipping end with circulating seawater. Consumers should request purged clams (not all

are). If purging your own clams, scrub and rinse them as well as possible after digging at the seashore. Here you could put clams in seawater and change the water frequently. Make certain the area and the water are approved for shellfish harvest."

If you buy clams at a fish market and insist on purged clams, you will need only to scrub the shells with a stiff brush or nylon pad before cooking, but it's always a good idea to ask your fishmonger for advice on handling the clams. If you dig your own and seawater is not available, scrub the shells well, put clams in a large bowl without crowding, and cover with a solution of 1 cup of salt dissolved in 3 quarts of cold water. Place the clams in the refrigerator for several hours or overnight, then scrub the shells before using.

Baked Razor Clams with an Asian Accent

———✦———

Razor clams have a distinct, sweet-nutty taste and firm texture. Many recipes suggest breading them and sautéing in several tablespoons of oil and butter, but that can lead to a heavy outcome. This is a much lighter version that gets its Asian twist from the use of panko, Japanese bread crumbs that have a very light crumb with a coarser texture and more crunch that regular bread crumbs. For extra flavor, the panko is mixed with five-spice powder, a potent blend of ground cinnamon, cloves, fennel seed, star anise, and Szechwan peppercorns, used extensively in Chinese cooking. A drizzle of seasoned rice vinegar finishes the dish, much as malt vinegar often pairs with deep-fried fish fillets. All of these ingredients are readily available in the Asian section of most grocery stores or at all Asian markets.

16 MEDIUM RAZOR CLAMS, OR 1 TO 1¼
    POUNDS CLEANED RAZOR CLAM MEAT
1 EGG OR 2 EGG WHITES
3 TABLESPOONS MILK
DASH OF TABASCO SAUCE
1½ CUPS PANKO BREAD CRUMBS
1½ TEASPOONS FIVE-SPICE POWDER
FLOUR FOR DUSTING
SALT AND FRESHLY GROUND BLACK PEPPER
SEASONED RICE VINEGAR

1. Preheat oven to 400°. Lightly coat a baking sheet with oil or nonstick cooking spray. Set aside.

2. To clean razor clams, place them in a colander and rinse with hot tap water just until shells open. (Do not rinse longer or razor clams will begin to cook.) Immediately plunge clams into cold water. Next, cut shells away from meat and discard shells. Cut each clam on one side lengthwise to expose entrails; remove and discard. Skin the siphons (diggers, or necks), place clams in a colander, and allow to drain. Reserve for later use. If using shucked razor clams, rinse meat well and drain, then cut away any remaining intestinal veins before using.

3. In a small mixing bowl, beat eggs, milk, and Tabasco sauce. In another small bowl, mix the panko bread crumbs and the five-spice powder.

4. Dry the clams with a paper towel. Remove to a cutting board and tenderize with a meat mallet, if desired. Pay extra attention to the tough siphon, the narrow part of the clam. Do not hit it too hard or the clam meat may break. Spread flour on a piece of waxed paper and dip clams in the flour, then shake well to remove excess. Dip clams in egg mixture and drain off any excess. Dip clams in the crumbs to coat completely. Lay breaded razor clams on the prepared baking sheet and allow to rest for 15 minutes at room temperature.

5. Place clams in oven and cook for 5 to 7 minutes, or until breading looks dry, but clams are still tender (you may want to cut one in half and taste to determine texture). Do not overcook, or clams will be tough. Sprinkle with salt and pepper.

6. To serve, divide clams among individual plates and allow everyone to drizzle with seasoned rice vinegar at the table.

SERVES 4

HOW TO CLEAN A GEODUCK

ALL PARTS OF THE geoduck—the largest burrowing clam in the world—are usable or edible, except for the outer skin. Even the shells make great serving dishes. The fishmongers at Pure Food Fish have the following tips for cleaning and preparing "the duck":

1. Plunge the geoduck, shell and all, into boiling water for 30 to 45 seconds (no longer, or the geoduck will cook). Immediately plunge the geoduck into cold water.

2. Drain, then run a knife between the body and shells to separate them.

3. Pull off the dark outer skin covering the neck (siphon) and body (mantle or breast) of the clam. It will peel off easily, like slipping off a rubber glove.

4. Remove the sack containing the stomach and set aside. This part may be used in chowder.

5. Split the neck by inserting a knife or scissors into the lower siphon hole, at the end where the stomach was removed, and cutting lengthwise. Wash siphon, removing all traces of sand and grit.

6. The large piece of meat remaining, which consists of the neck and the body, can be cut into two or more steaks, or it may be chopped or ground. The body meat is more tender than the neck meat, so many people use the body meat for steaks, and chop or grind the neck meat for chowder or fritters.

7. If using geoduck steaks, be sure to pound or score them before cooking to tenderize. Pound with the flat side of a mallet, the bottom of a skillet, or a rolling pin. After cleaning the geoduck, allow it to rest for 1 hour before cooking. As with all seafood, do not overcook geoduck, as it will become tough and rubbery.

Geoduck Fritters

—∞—

PURE FOOD FISH, PIKE PLACE MARKET

Washingtonians are known as independent thinkers, which may explain why they tried to make the geoduck the official state animal. Or perhaps they wanted to honor the creature after sampling these light, melt-in-your-mouth fritters, full of the unmistakable flavor of the geoduck clam.

1 CUP ALL-PURPOSE FLOUR

1 TEASPOON BAKING POWDER

1/2 TEASPOON SALT

1/8 TEASPOON FRESHLY GROUND BLACK PEPPER

DASH OF GROUND NUTMEG

1/3 CUP CLAM JUICE

2 EGGS, BEATEN

1/3 CUP MILK

2 TEASPOONS BUTTER, MELTED

1 GEODUCK, CLEANED AND DICED (SEE PAGE 165)

VEGETABLE OIL, FOR FRYING

LEMON WEDGES, FOR GARNISH

1. Preheat oven to 200°. Line a baking sheet with paper towels and set aside.

2. Sift flour, baking powder, salt, pepper, and nutmeg into a mixing bowl. Add clam juice, eggs, and milk and beat thoroughly with a wire whisk. Fold in butter and geoduck.

3. Fill a large saucepan or wok halfway with vegetable oil and heat to 375°. Very carefully, drop large spoonfuls of batter into the hot oil and cook 3 to 4 minutes, turning once, or until fritters are golden on both sides. Drain on paper towels, then transfer fritters to prepared baking sheet and place in oven to keep warm. Repeat procedure with remaining batter.

4. To serve, divide fritters among individual plates and serve immediately.

SERVES 4

FUN FACTS

- "The Nisqually and other coast-dwelling tribes prepared clam chowders in winter months, using dried, powdered clams for a base. In one traditional recipe, clams were pulverized, then simmered in bentwood boxes or baskets filled with hot water. Wild onions and dried seaweed helped season the chowder; only with the arrival of European settlers and their crops did Native Americans add potatoes, celery, carrots, salt, pepper, and a particular favorite—bacon fat—to their geoduck chowders and stews."—*Field Guide to the Geoduck*

- Geoducks make up the largest mass of any marine animal in Washington's Puget Sound, which is inhabited by an estimated 130 million of the creatures.

Crab

THE CRAB IS A CRUSTACEAN whose wide, flat body is protected by a hard shell or carapace. Crabs have four or five pairs of legs that vary in size according to the species. The first pair, or pincers, are generally much larger and equipped with strong claws.

There are 4,000 different species of crab worldwide. North America has more different types of crabs and is the greatest provider of edible crabs in the world. Local crabs are available in many parts of the United States—the blue crab along the East Coast, the stone crab in Florida, and the Dungeness crab on the West Coast. Local crabs are shipped across the country, and many of them are available all year long.

Crabs feed on a variety of marine animals including clams, fish, and other crabs, which produces white, fine-textured meat with a delicate flavor. Crab is the second most popular shellfish in the United States, after shrimp.

Dungeness crab (*Cancer magister*) is the prize catch of the oldest shellfish fishery in the North Pacific. It provides one of the best traditional foods of the region—fresh cracked crab. The Dungeness, or "big crab," is a rock crab. It is found in coastal waters from Alaska to Baja California. The crab is named after Dungeness, a small fishing village on the Strait of Juan de Fuca in Washington State, where it was first commercially caught.

Dungeness crab landings start in California in the winter and end in Alaska in summer and fall. Thus, the season for Dungeness runs nearly the entire year, with greater availability and lowest prices during the winter months (December through February), when the crabs are at their prime. Both commercial fishing and sport collecting of Dungeness are regulated and the harvest is limited. The largest Dungeness crabs are fished in Alaskan waters, with smaller crabs fished in Oregon and Washington.

By law, only adult males at least $6^{1}/_{4}$ inches across the carapace and weighing $1^{1}/_{2}$ to 4 pounds can be harvested. It takes about 4 years for male crabs to reach legal size. After capturing the crabs in pots, fishers put them in live tanks and deliver them to shoreside processing plants where they are cooked immediately or shipped live.

Dungeness crabs (or "Dungies") have a brownish red to dark violet top shell and beige underbelly. Once cooked, Dungeness crab turn bright red on top and cream colored below. They are sold live, whole cooked, whole cooked and frozen, as crab clusters (the walking legs and claws from one side of the body), as single legs, and as crabmeat extracted from the shell.

The meat is sweet, delicate, and buttery rich. Creamy white, large of flake, and firm-textured, it is more akin to lobster than other types of crabs. The mild flavor of Dungeness crab takes well to a wide range of seasonings and other ingredients.

The crab is most commonly steamed and eaten whole with butter or a sauce. Dungeness crab in the shell is good in seafood stews or soups, sautés, salads, and appetizers. Meat removed from the shell can be used in soups, sautés, creamed dishes, casseroles, and salad. Precooked Dungeness crab can be warmed through, steamed, or served chilled.

On rare occasions, Dungeness crab carry domoic acid, a toxin that can be harmful to

Dungeness Crab

humans. Domoic acid accumulates only in the crab's viscera, often called the crab "butter." For peace of mind, or for those with compromised immune systems, eat only the meat of the crab. If you just can't give up the crab butter, be aware of domoic acid warnings and buy crab only from reputable fishmongers.

King crabs are not true crabs, such as the Dungeness crab, but are related to hermit crabs. The **red king crab** (*Paralithodes camtschaticus*) is the largest and the preferred species, with blue and brown/golden following. King crabs can live 10 years or more and weigh up to 25 pounds, although 10 pounds is average. Unlike most crabs, king crabs have only 8 ap-

pendages (6 legs and 2 claws) rather than 10.

King crabs are found nearly ½ mile deep in the chilly waters of the North Pacific and the Bering Sea. The former Soviet Union is the largest producer of king crab, while Alaska is the sole producer of king crab in the United States.

Peak season occurs midwinter off the coast of Alaska in subfreezing, rough seas. The crabs are captured in large baited pots fished from sturdy steel-hulled vessels of 100 feet or more in length. When the crab are landed, they are kept alive in a tank aboard the boat. Alaska king (and snow) crab are transported to processing plants on shore. Only live crab are accepted for processing and are cleaned, cooked, and frozen almost immediately.

King crab features large pieces of white meat brilliantly edged in red. It is prized for its delicate, sweet flavor and tender texture, which is almost scalloplike in quality and richness. Frozen king crab legs previously cooked in the shell are the principal market item, although precooked clusters, legs, claws, or picked king crabmeat are available. Sometimes you'll find precooked split legs and claws, and the back meat is often canned.

Since it is already cooked, king crab can simply be warmed, steamed for a short time, or served chilled. The legs hold more meat than the claws, so when buying king crab, ask for all legs, or a fair proportion, such as three legs to one claw.

Snow crab (*Chionoecetes opilio, C. tanneri, C. bairdi*) is a market name for the various spider crabs, among them the Atlantic snow crab (on the East Coast), the queen crab (in eastern Canada), and the tanner crab (in Alaska).

Resembling king crabs, but only about half the size, snow crabs weigh up to 5 pounds and measure 3 feet from leg tip to leg tip. Their bodies are covered with dense hairs.

The crab derives its name from its snow-white meat and delicate flavor. The *opilio* is the most important species of snow crab weighing in at 2 pounds, while the *bairdi* measures about 5 pounds. The *opilio* is more numerous and less expensive than *bairdi*, as well as the only species caught in both the Atlantic and Pacific oceans. It has supported major fisheries in both the Canadian Maritimes and Alaska since the mid-1960s, with the largest fishery now in eastern Canada.

Virtually all snow crab is shipped frozen and is available year-round in single-cut legs or leg and shoulder clusters, meat, and cocktail claws. Scored legs, where the shell has already been cut, are particularly convenient, allowing a simple snap to remove the meat.

Buying and Handling Live Crab

Once placed in saltwater holding tanks, live crabs do not feed and lose body weight rapidly. Therefore, it is imperative to ask your fishmonger when the crab was harvested and delivered. Live crab should be purchased and cooked within 1 week of harvest.

The best live crab will be cold to the touch and sluggish, but show some leg movement. The more lively the crab, the better. The legs and shell should be intact, with clean, brightly colored shells without cracks. The crab should feel heavy in the shell; if you can't tell, ask

your fishmonger for advice. Smell the crab, being very careful not to get your nose pinched! Fresh or cooked crab will smell sweet

King Crab

and clean, like the ocean. Older crabs will smell like ammonia.

Store live crabs in your refrigerator for up to 24 hours. Do not keep the crab in a plastic bag, an airtight container, in water, or on ice. If your fishmonger wraps the live crab in a newspaper (no plastic bags) and you plan to cook the crab within 6 to 8 hours of purchase, keep the crab in its original wrapping in the refrigerator. For longer storage, remove crabs from their packaging and refrigerate in a shallow tray covered with a damp towel. Cook live crabs the same day you buy them. If any crabs die before you have a chance to cook them, throw them away.

Buying and Handling Cooked Crab

Crab that isn't alive should be precooked. This is no problem, because almost all the crab harvested are cooked while still alive, often within hours after capture so they retain their just-caught flavor. The quality of the cooked meat can be very high, and you're spared the trouble of handling live animals. Nonetheless, when buying cooked crab, be selective; ask how and when the crab was cooked. A crab that dies before being cooked—even for just a few hours—will not only suffer loss of quality, but the meat will be difficult to extract from the shell.

At the fish market, cooked whole crab should be stored on ice or in a refrigerated case. The crab should feel cold to the touch. Feel the back of the crab to make sure it is very cold; otherwise, there's a chance bacteria may have started to grow. The shells should be bright red-orange without cracks. The crab should feel heavy for its size. Tap the shell; the crab should sound firm and solid. Gently shake the cab; there should be no sloshing sound of water within the shell. Ask to sample a leg—the meat should taste sweet and clean and not be overly salty.

Cooked crabs should be eaten within 3 days of being cooked—another reason it is imperative to ask your fishmonger exactly when the crab was boiled. At home, store whole cooked crab in the coldest part of your refrigerator (usually the back of the bottom shelf) packed in ice and covered with a damp towel. Pour off the water and replenish the ice as it melts and use the crab within 1 day. Cooked crabmeat in an airtight container should also be stored in ice. When buying packaged crabmeat, sniff to check for freshness a few seconds after opening the container; there should be no hint of ammonia.

Buying and Handling Frozen Crab

When buying frozen crab, the shell should have a smooth glaze of ice without areas of frost on the crab or the packaging. A brownish coloring of the meat, caused by oxidation, shows poor handling or crab beyond its prime. If properly wrapped, crab can be frozen up to 3 months. Allow frozen crab to thaw overnight in the refrigerator, then use within 24 hours.

Dungeness crab gives a typical yield of 25 percent meat. At an average weight of 2 pounds, a Dungeness will provide 8 to 10 ounces of crabmeat, or about $1^{1}/_{2}$ to 2 cups. King and snow crab legs yield 50 percent meat, so 1 pound of legs offers an 8-ounce portion of meat. Allow $^{3}/_{4}$ to 1 pound of king or snow crab claws, clusters, or legs per serving; $^{1}/_{4}$ pound of king or snow crabmeat per person. For a whole-crab feed, plan on 8 ounces of meat per person, or about 1 Dungeness crab each (and always cook a few more—there's never too much crab at a crab feed).

Boil whole live crabs 5 to 8 minutes per pound; steam whole live crabs 10 minutes per pound. The crab is done when the shell changes to bright red or orange. Pieces of raw crab still in the shell can be stir-fried or sautéed for 8 to 10 minutes over medium-high heat. In soups and stews, simmer raw crab pieces for 10 to 15 minutes. Crabmeat can be made into sautéed or oven-fried crab cakes, added to curries, quiches, croquettes, mousses, chowders, soufflés, and soups.

Basic Cooked Crab

———◦∞◦———

The fishmongers at the Pike Place Market sell Dunge-
ness crabs that are already cooked and need nothing
more than to be cleaned, which they will do for free or
which you can do yourself at home. You can eat the
crab chilled, or steam or boil it if you prefer crab with
a bit more flavor (read about "Crab Feeds," page
175). Jack's Fish Spot in the Market has live crabs in
saltwater holding tanks, which allows you to choose
your own crab and cook it yourself.

You can cook live crab by steaming or boiling it.
There are advantages to each method: Steaming pro-
duces a white, very crabby-tasting flesh, but some of
the body meat is lost when the crab is cut in half. Boil-
ing keeps all the meat in the shell, but many people
claim that the crab's body juices tinge the crabmeat
yellow and make the flesh a bit less sweet. In my opin-
ion, no matter how you choose to cook it, Dungeness
crab is tops served with melted butter, homemade may-
onnaise, or a good-quality cocktail sauce.

1 LIVE DUNGENESS CRAB

FRESH SEAWATER, OR A MIXTURE OF
    KOSHER SALT AND FRESH WATER
    (APPROXIMATELY 3 TABLESPOONS SALT
    PER GALLON OF WATER)

Steamed Crab

1. Be sure crab has been refrigerated several
hours or put it in the freezer 10 minutes before
cooking to make it more docile. Prepare a steaming rack large enough to hold the crab in one
layer. Bring 2 inches of seawater to a boil no
higher than 1 inch below rack. While water is
heating, take out a large mixing bowl and fill
with ice cubes and cold water.

2. If the shell will not be used in presentation, remove the crab from the refrigerator or freezer,
lay it on its back, and cut it in half from top to
bottom, cutting entirely through the shell using
a large, heavy knife or cleaver. Hold half of the
crab with one hand from underneath and, with
the other hand, pull off the top shell. If the shell
is used in presentation, approach crab from the
rear and grasp the legs and claws on both sides of
the body so you are holding the crab with two
hands. Crack the underside of the crab on the
counter edge or the edge of a heavy cutting
board to stun the crab. Pull off the shell, rinse
under cool running water, pat dry, and reserve.
Cut the crab in half down the center from top to
bottom.

3. To clean out the crab, scoop out and save the
cream-colored "crab butter," if desired. Run your
thumb along the sides of the body cavity to
scrape away feathery gills. Rinse under cool water to remove any remaining viscera. Repeat with
remaining crab half. Prepared to this point, crab
may be used in any recipe calling for fresh, uncooked crab (such as stir-fried or sautéed crab),
or it can be steamed.

4. Place crab halves on steamer rack for 6 minutes per pound, then immediately plunge crab
halves in ice water. Drain well, allow to cool, and
refrigerate until ready to use. Proceed with step
4 of directions for boiled crab (see below).

SERVES 1 AS AN ENTRÉE, 2 AS AN APPETIZER

Boiled Crab

1. Bring 2 to 3 gallons of seawater or salt water
mixture to a boil in a large stockpot or Dutch
oven. Take out a large mixing bowl and fill with
ice cubes and cold water.

2. Add crab to pot back side (shell side) down so that the legs fold over the belly. Cook for 5 to 8 minutes per pound, or until crab turns reddish orange and floats.

3. Immediately immerse crab in ice water. When thoroughly chilled, hold the crab with one hand from underneath and, with the other hand, pry off the large top shell. Scoop out and save the cream-colored "crab butter," if desired. Run your thumb along the sides of the body cavity to scrape away feathery gills. Rinse under cool water to remove any remaining viscera.

4. Grasp crab in both hands and break body in half lengthwise, forming two sections with the legs attached. Remove legs by breaking off at joints closest to the body. Separate claw portion from the leg at the first joint. Bend back and remove the smaller claw pincer, along with attached claw cartilage. Crack the claw with an aluminum crab cracker, the back of a knife, or a mallet, being careful not to crush the meat. Repeat with second claw.

5. With kitchen shears, cut along each side of the leg shells, or simply crack carefully to open. With the palm of your hand, press the top of the crab body until you feel the interior shells give slightly. Do not press so hard that you smash the top and bottom shells together.

6. You are now ready to eat your crab. Remove the meat from the legs, claws, and body of the crab using your fingers, a crab pick, a seafood fork, or a crab "toe" (the tip of a crab claw)—anything is legal when eating Dungeness crab.

SERVES 1 AS AN ENTRÉE, 2 AS AN APPETIZER

WINES

Wines that pair well with the delicate, yet distinctive flavor of crab include Johannisberg riesling, chenin blanc, sémillon blanc, fumé blanc, sauvignon blanc, and muscat canelli. Dry fino sherries are less well known, yet entirely appropriate matches for crab.

FUN FACTS

- Thousands of years ago, Native Americans harvested Dungeness crabs in baited pots.

- The female Dungeness crab carries her eggs on the underside of her abdomen, which is wider and flatter than that of the male, and forms an apronlike structure that circulates water over the eggs. Two weeks after fertilization, the eggs hatch, releasing free-swimming larvae. Following several molts, the larvae settle to the bottom of the sea, where they metamorphose into adult crabs. One virile male crab can fertilize as many as 200 females at a time.

Chandler's Crab Cakes

CHANDLER'S CRABHOUSE AND FRESH FISH MARKET, SEATTLE, WASHINGTON

Chef Brian Poor is crazy for crab at his restaurant on the south shore of Lake Union, just north of downtown Seattle. During the restaurant's annual Crabfest, he not only prepares Caesar salad with fried crab legs, red king crab tagliatelle, and snow crab cannelloni, but he also features crab ice cream on the menu. Made with crab-shell stock, bourbon, sherry, honey, and vanilla, the rich dessert is surprisingly tasty, with just a hint of crab essence and a pale tawny color. The chef's recipe for crab cakes is a good, basic version—a rich, spicy, and colorful mix of crab chunks and minced bell peppers simply bound by mayonnaise and beaten eggs. A citrus beurre blanc (see page 305) or a good homemade or bottled salsa, cole slaw or three-bean salad, and freshly baked corn bread make perfect accompaniments.

3 TABLESPOONS OLIVE OIL

1/4 CUP MINCED WHITE ONION

1/4 CUP MINCED CELERY

2 TABLESPOONS MINCED RED BELL PEPPER

2 TABLESPOONS MINCED GREEN BELL PEPPER

2 TABLESPOONS MINCED ORANGE BELL PEPPER

1 TABLESPOON MINCED GARLIC

2 LARGE EGGS

2 1/2 TABLESPOONS GOOD-QUALITY MAYONNAISE

2 1/2 TABLESPOONS WORCESTERSHIRE SAUCE

2 1/2 TABLESPOONS MINCED FRESH PARSLEY

2 1/2 TEASPOONS OLD BAY SEASONING

2 1/2 POUNDS (4 1/2 CUPS) FRESH DUNGENESS CRABMEAT, PICKED OVER FOR SHELLS AND CARTILAGE

2 TABLESPOONS BUTTER

2 CUPS FRESH UNSEASONED BREAD CRUMBS

1. In a medium skillet, heat 1 tablespoon of the olive oil over medium-high heat. Add onion, celery, the peppers, and garlic, and sauté for 3 to 5 minutes, or until vegetables are tender-crisp, stirring occasionally. Allow vegetables to cool, then transfer to a small bowl, cover, and refrigerate until chilled.

2. About 10 minutes before you are ready to cook, preheat oven to 200°. Beat eggs and mayonnaise in a large mixing bowl until well blended. Add Worcestershire sauce, parsley, and Old Bay seasoning. Add vegetables and stir well to blend ingredients. Drain any excess juice from crab, add crab, and mix gently. Divide crab mixture into 12 portions, then shape into patties.

3. Heat butter and remaining oil in a large skillet over medium-high heat. Place bread crumbs on a large dinner plate or piece of waxed paper and lightly coat patties with crumbs. Place crab cakes in skillet without crowding, cooking in batches and adding more butter and oil if necessary. Cook the patties 5 to 7 minutes per side, or until golden brown, turning once. Place cooked crab cakes on a plate lined with several layers of paper towels to drain, then transfer to a baking sheet and place in oven to keep warm.

4. To serve, divide crab cakes among individual plates.

SERVES 4 AS AN ENTRÉE, 8 AS AN APPETIZER

Cold Crab Cakes with Fresh Chive Aïoli

ROVER'S,
SEATTLE, WASHINGTON

Necessity is often the mother of invention, as Thierry Rautureau, chef/owner of Rover's in Seattle's Madison Park district, found out one hot sunny September morning. Knowing he had to prepare several hundred crab cakes for a fundraiser that afternoon, the chef opened his larder to see what was on hand. Taking into account the weather and his deadline, chef Rautureau was inspired to make a cold crab salad. He molded the salad in metal rings and voilà! He created these cold crab cakes.

1/2 POUND SNOW PEAS, STRINGS REMOVED

1 RED BELL PEPPER, STEMMED, SEEDED, AND DICED

1 YELLOW BELL PEPPER, STEMMED, SEEDED, AND DICED

3 TABLESPOONS OCEAN SALAD (OPTIONAL, SEE NOTE)

2 TABLESPOONS MINCED SHALLOTS

10 OUNCES (2 CUPS) FRESH DUNGENESS CRABMEAT, PICKED OVER FOR SHELLS AND CARTILAGE

2 EGG YOLKS

2 CLOVES GARLIC, MINCED

1 1/2 TEASPOONS DIJON MUSTARD

1 1/2 TEASPOONS PREPARED HORSERADISH

6 TABLESPOONS EXTRA VIRGIN OLIVE OIL

1 TABLESPOON RED WINE VINEGAR

1 TABLESPOON MINCED FRESH CHIVES

SALT AND FRESHLY GROUND WHITE PEPPER

MESCLUN SALAD MIX, FRISÉE, OR MIXED BABY SALAD GREENS OF YOUR CHOICE, FOR GARNISH

1. In a medium saucepan, bring enough water to cover snow peas to a boil, add snow peas, and cook 1 to 2 minutes. Drain and rinse with cold water to stop the cooking process. Drain again, pat dry, and cut vertically into 1/8-inch slices. Place in a large mixing bowl along with red bell pepper, yellow bell pepper, ocean salad, shallots, and crabmeat. Cover bowl and refrigerate.

2. To make aïoli, whisk egg yolks, garlic, mustard, and horseradish until thoroughly blended. Add olive oil in a thin stream, whisking continuously until mixture emulsifies. Add vinegar and chives, and season to taste with salt and pepper.

3. Take out crab mixture, add aïoli, and toss thoroughly but gently.

4. To serve, place a 2- or 3-inch aluminum ring on a plate and spoon crabmeat mixture into ring, packing loosely and leveling off top. Prepare 1 crab cake per plate if serving as an appetizer, 2 cakes if serving as an entrée. Carefully remove ring and repeat with remaining crabmeat. Garnish plate with a handful of mesclun.

SERVES 4 AS AN ENTRÉE, 8 AS AN APPETIZER

Note: Recent concerns about salmonella poisoning have called into question the use of raw eggs in food preparation. I would encourage the use of the freshest eggs available and a thorough washing and drying of the eggs before use. Individuals with chronic or autoimmune diseases should be informed of the uncooked eggs before eating this dish.

Crab Veneto

ELLIOTT'S OYSTER HOUSE & SEAFOOD RESTAURANT, SEATTLE, WASHINGTON

At Elliott's on Pier 56, chef Andy Juhl not only teaches "crab school" for local food professionals and interested laypeople but offers what many consider the definitive Dungeness crab service in town. Elliott's serves the crustaceans cooked to order, cracked, and ready to eat in five different ways: Steamed and served with melted butter, chilled with Dijon mayonnaise, heaped into bowls of brilliant red cioppino, heated in black bean sauce, or chilled and tossed with olive oil and a few vital ingredients, as in this recipe. An extra-large crab bib, a cocktail fork, a shell bowl, a hot towel and plenty of paper towels, a finger bowl brimming with hot tea and lemon water, and a crushed-cracker handwash (saltine crackers pulverized to a fine dust) make the messy job of eating Dungeness crab even more enjoyable.

1 CLOVE GARLIC, MINCED

2 TABLESPOONS FRESHLY SQUEEZED LEMON JUICE

2 DASHES OF WORCESTERSHIRE SAUCE

1/2 TEASPOON MINCED PARSLEY

1/2 CUP PLUS 2 TABLESPOONS PURE OLIVE OIL

1 PRECOOKED 2- TO 2 1/2-POUND DUNGE-NESS CRAB IN THE SHELL, CHILLED AND CRACKED INTO PIECES SUITABLE FOR PICKING (SEE PAGE 171)

1. In a large, deep bowl, mix together garlic, lemon juice, Worcestershire sauce, parsley, and olive oil.

2. Add crab pieces and toss gently. Let stand 3 minutes before serving.

SERVES 2 AS AN APPETIZER, 1 AS AN ENTRÉE

CRAB FEEDS

The crab feed is a Northwest tradition that can take place on the beach, in the backyard, or in the privacy of one's home. Crab feeds are informal affairs where newspapers are thrown on the picnic table instead of tablecloths and lots of paper napkins stand in for cloth ones. Dungeness crab, the star of the show, can be served chilled or, as I prefer, warmed in a spicy or herb-infused crab boil. Popular side dishes include sourdough bread and tossed green salad, cole slaw, baked beans, potato salad, and garlic bread. Live music and dancing along with lots of cold beer and crisp white Northwest wines are popular additions to any crab feed.

Crab-Stuffed Peppers

———〜♦〜———

FLOWER REFLECTIONS, PIKE PLACE MARKET

For over twenty years, Joe and Geri Lamanno have combined their passions for gardening and art into a successful business, Flower Reflections. They grow colorful flowers and buds, gather and dry them, then press the delicate buds and leaves between pieces of clear and stained glass to form inspired window hangings that they sell on the day tables in the Market. This is a family recipe often prepared by Joe's mother, Nicolena, on Fridays, when the family was discouraged from eating meat due to religious dietary laws. The peppers were served with heaping bowls of pasta topped with what Joe fondly calls "dirty sauce," a fresh tomato sauce made of nothing more than ripe tomatoes, fresh basil, good-quality olive oil, and salt and freshly ground black pepper to taste. Shrimp can be substituted or used in combination with the crab.

4 LARGE YELLOW, ORANGE, OR RED BELL
    PEPPERS

1 1/2 CUPS FINELY GROUND DRY, UNSEA-
    SONED BREAD CRUMBS, OR ITALIAN-
    STYLE BREAD CRUMBS

1/3 CUP FRESHLY GRATED PARMESAN OR
    ROMANO CHEESE

3 CLOVES GARLIC, MINCED

3 TABLESPOONS MINCED FRESH BASIL, OR
    1 TABLESPOON DRIED BASIL

1 TABLESPOON MINCED FRESH PARSLEY

3 TABLESPOONS OLIVE OIL

5 OUNCES (1 CUP) FRESH DUNGENESS
    CRABMEAT, PICKED OVER FOR SHELLS
    AND CARTILAGE

FRESHLY GROUND BLACK PEPPER

1. Prepare a steaming rack large enough to hold peppers without crowding, or preheat the oven to 350°. Lightly coat a baking dish that will hold peppers without crowding with oil or nonstick cooking spray.

2. Rinse peppers and pat dry. Cut off top 1/2 inch and remove cores, ribs, and seeds, being careful not to tear through peppers. Set aside.

3. In a mixing bowl, combine bread crumbs, Parmesan cheese, garlic, basil, and parsley. Heat a skillet over medium-high heat and add olive oil. When olive oil is hot, add bread crumb mixture and cook 3 to 5 minutes, or until crumbs turn golden, stirring often. Decrease heat if crumbs brown too quickly. Remove pan from heat and add crabmeat. Season to taste with pepper. Spoon filling into peppers and place upright in steamer or baking dish.

4. Steam for 20 minutes or bake for 25 minutes, or until peppers are tender and stuffing is heated through.

SERVES 4

Hood Canal Crab Cakes with Honey-Yogurt Salsa

———⊷———

This recipe comes from good friends Doug and Sue Ethridge, who catch fresh crabs just outside the back patio of their getaway cabin on Hood Canal when the tide rolls in. We spent part of an evening picking crabmeat, drinking wine, and exchanging fish tales before they whipped up these extraordinary crab cakes. For the calorie-conscious, remember that while the crab cakes themselves are rich, they are baked in the oven, not pan-fried, which cuts down on the amount of fat used. The accompanying nonfat salsa is bursting with flavor. Serve these spicy cakes family style at the table, along with the Honey-Yogurt Salsa, and all you'll need is a big salad for accompaniment.

1/2 CUP CHUNKY HOT SALSA

1/2 CUP NONFAT YOGURT OR NONFAT SOUR CREAM

1 1/2 TEASPOONS HONEY

1 1/2 POUNDS (4 1/2 CUPS) FRESH DUNGE-NESS CRABMEAT, PICKED OVER FOR SHELLS AND CARTILAGE

1/2 CUP STEMMED, SEEDED, AND DICED RED BELL PEPPER

1/2 CUP DICED YELLOW ONION

1/2 CUP CREAM CHEESE

1/2 CUP MAYONNAISE

1/2 TEASPOON MINCED JALAPEÑO PEPPER, OR 1 TABLESPOON DICED CANNED GREEN CHILES, WELL DRAINED

1 TEASPOON WHITE OR DARK WORCESTER-SHIRE SAUCE

1 TABLESPOON MINCED GARLIC CHIVES, OR 1 CLOVE GARLIC, MINCED

1 TABLESPOON MINCED CILANTRO

1 TO 2 CUPS ITALIAN-STYLE BREAD CRUMBS

1. Preheat oven to 350°. Lightly coat a large baking sheet with oil or nonstick cooking spray.

2. In a small mixing bowl, stir together salsa, yogurt, and honey. Taste to be sure that honey has mellowed the heat of the salsa. If not, add a bit more honey to taste. Set aside at room temperature while preparing crab cakes.

3. Drain any excess juice from crab, then lightly toss crab, red pepper, and onion together in a large mixing bowl. In a small mixing bowl, combine cream cheese, mayonnaise, jalapeño, Worcestershire sauce, garlic chives, and cilantro. Add mixture to crabmeat and fold in gently.

4. Add bread crumbs a little bit at a time, stirring until crab cakes reach patty consistency. The amount of bread crumbs you add will depend on the amount of water in the crabmeat.

5. Place leftover bread crumbs on a plate or piece of waxed paper. Form crabmeat mixture into 12 patties of equal size. Lightly coat each crab cake with bread crumbs on both sides before placing on the prepared baking sheet. When all patties are coated, place crab cakes in oven and bake for 15 to 20 minutes, or until golden brown and a bit crusty on the edges.

6. To serve, place crab cakes on a large serving platter and pass crab cakes and salsa at the table.

SERVES 4

Herb Crepes with Dungeness Crab, Sweet Peppers, and Crème Fraîche

———✦———

CAFÉ SOPHIE, PIKE PLACE MARKET

Café Sophie serves European-style cuisine featuring Market-fresh ingredients in one of the most memorable locations in all of Seattle. The building, which originally housed a funeral parlor, opened in 1908, and is reportedly where the term "mortuary" was coined. Chef/proprietors Sue and Scott Craig have owned the place since 1993. The café serves these crepes as an appetizer, but they work equally well for a romantic dinner or Sunday brunch. Making crepes may seem like a lot of trouble, but you can cook them up to one day ahead and store them in the refrigerator until ready to use. They can also be frozen for up to 2 months (see Note). The Mornay Sauce should, however, be made just before the crepes are filled so it doesn't set up.

DUNGENESS CRAB FILLING (RECIPE FOLLOWS)

12 CREPES (RECIPE FOLLOWS)

1 CUP CRÈME FRAÎCHE, FOR GARNISH

BASIL LEAVES, FOR GARNISH

1. Preheat oven to 450°. Lightly coat a baking sheet with oil or nonstick cooking spray.

2. Place 2 heaping tablespoons of the Dungeness Crab Filling in center of a prepared crepe and roll lengthwise. Place crepe seam side down on the prepared baking sheet. Repeat with remaining crepes. Cover baking sheet with aluminum foil and bake for 10 minutes, or until heated through.

3. Place 3 crepes on individual plates and cut each crepe into thirds. Top with a dollop of crème fraîche and a basil leaf. Or mince basil and mix with crème fraîche and freshly squeezed citrus juice to taste, then top crepes with flavored crème fraîche.

SERVES 4 AS AN ENTRÉE, 6 AS AN APPETIZER

Dungeness Crab Filling

1 POUND (3 CUPS) FRESH DUNGENESS CRABMEAT, PICKED OVER FOR SHELLS AND CARTILAGE

JUICE OF ½ ORANGE

JUICE OF ½ LEMON

1 TABLESPOON MINCED FRESH BASIL

½ RED BELL PEPPER, STEMMED, SEEDED, AND DICED

¼ GREEN BELL PEPPER, STEMMED, SEEDED, AND DICED

¼ YELLOW BELL PEPPER, STEMMED. SEEDED, AND DICED

MORNAY SAUCE (RECIPE FOLLOWS)

TABASCO SAUCE

SALT AND FRESHLY GROUND PEPPER

In a mixing bowl, combine crabmeat, orange juice, lemon juice, basil, and red, green, and yellow bell peppers. Add just enough Mornay Sauce so that mixture holds together, but is neither pasty (too dry) nor gooey (too wet). Season to taste with Tabasco, salt, and pepper. Cover and refrigerate until ready to fill crepes.

Mornay Sauce

3 TABLESPOONS UNSALTED BUTTER

6 TABLESPOONS ALL-PURPOSE FLOUR

2 CUPS MILK

½ CUP FRESHLY GRATED GRUYÈRE CHEESE

¼ CUP FRESHLY GRATED PARMESAN
   CHEESE
PINCH OF GRATED NUTMEG
SALT AND FRESHLY GROUND WHITE PEPPER

In a nonreactive saucepan, melt butter over medium heat. Add flour and whisk 1 minute, stirring continuously. Add milk slowly, stirring after each addition to prevent lumps from forming. When sauce is smooth, add Gruyère cheese, Parmesan cheese, and nutmeg and stir until cheese is melted. Season to taste with salt and pepper.

Crepes

1 CUP ALL-PURPOSE FLOUR
¼ TEASPOON SALT
1 TABLESPOON MINCED FRESH HERBS,
   SUCH AS THYME, BASIL, AND PARSLEY
1 CUP MILK
3 EGGS
¼ CUP PLUS 1 TEASPOON OLIVE OIL

1. In a food processor, combine flour, salt, and minced herbs. Pulse to thoroughly mix, then add milk slowly to prevent lumps from forming. Add eggs and ¼ cup olive oil, process until smooth, and set aside.

2. Heat a 6- or 7-inch nonstick skillet over medium-high heat. When pan is hot, add the remaining 1 teaspoon olive oil. Swirl oil around pan, then discard excess. Immediately pour in 1 to 1½ tablespoons crepe batter and swirl around pan to coat bottom and sides. Return pan to heat and cook 1 minute, or until crepe is lightly browned on the bottom and the top looks cooked but not dry. Turn crepe and cook 30 seconds on second side. Place crepe on a plate and reserve. Repeat with remaining batter, adding

additional olive oil as necessary and stacking finished crepes on plate.

MAKES ABOUT 18 CREPES

Note: To store the 6 leftover crepes, allow them to cool, then stack on a plate with a piece of waxed paper between each crepe. Place the stack in a heavy-duty resealable plastic bag and store in refrigerator for up to 1 day or in freezer for longer storage (up to 2 months). Thaw the crepes for 1 to 2 hours at room temperature, or overnight in the refrigerator, before filling.

FUN FACTS

- Dungeness crabs shed their shells and produce new ones, a process called molting, up to twenty times in the four years it takes to reach maturity.

- Most female crabs have to shed their shells (molt) before mating. To help her, the male clasps her by the claw and around the sea floor they go, until he literally dances her out of her shell. It often takes hours for the female to emerge from her old shell.

Crab Soufflé Cakes with Sweet Pepper and Corn Relish

※

Kathy Casey is a talented Northwest chef, cookbook author, newspaper food columnist, television personality, and restaurant consultant. Here she lightens the traditional crab cake by adding a purée of corn kernels, buttermilk, and gently beaten egg whites. The accompanying salsa is low in calories, full of flavor, and a perfect complement. These are upscale crab "pancakes" for grown-ups.

1/3 CUP BUTTERMILK

1/2 CUP FRESH OR FROZEN CORN

2 LARGE EGGS

1 TEASPOON FRESHLY SQUEEZED LIME
    JUICE

1/4 TEASPOON TABASCO SAUCE

1/2 TEASPOON SALT

1/2 TEASPOON BAKING POWDER

1/3 CUP YELLOW CORNMEAL

1/4 CUP ALL-PURPOSE FLOUR

1/2 POUND (1 1/2 CUPS) FRESH DUNGENESS
    CRABMEAT, PICKED OVER FOR SHELLS
    AND CARTILAGE

2 GREEN ONIONS, FINELY MINCED

1 TABLESPOON OLIVE OIL

SWEET PEPPER AND CORN RELISH
    (RECIPE FOLLOWS)

1/4 CUP SOUR CREAM, FOR GARNISH

4 SPRIGS CILANTRO, FOR GARNISH

1/2 LIME, CUT INTO 4 WEDGES, FOR GARNISH

1. Preheat oven to 200°.

2. Place buttermilk and corn in a blender and process on high speed for 30 seconds, or until mixture is smooth.

3. Separate eggs, reserving whites. Place yolks in a bowl and add corn mixture, lime juice, Tabasco, and salt, stirring to mix well.

4. Sift together baking powder, cornmeal, and flour into a medium bowl. Add to corn mixture and mix well.

5. Drain any excess juice from crab and add crabmeat to batter. Add green onions and stir gently.

6. Just before cooking, beat egg whites until soft but not dry peaks form. Gently fold into batter.

7. Heat a large nonstick skillet over medium heat until hot (until a drop of water evaporates immediately). Add olive oil and swirl to coat pan. Spoon a heaping tablespoonful of batter into skillet, cooking 3 or 4 cakes at a time to avoid crowding. Cook cakes about 1 1/2 minutes, or until golden, then turn and continue cooking until second side is golden and cakes puff slightly. Continue cooking cakes in batches, adding more oil if necessary. Place cooked cakes in oven to keep warm.

8. To serve cakes, spoon 1/4 cup Sweet Pepper and Corn Relish onto center of a warmed plate and place 3 crab cakes around relish. Top each crab cake with a small dollop of sour cream. Garnish plate with a sprig of cilantro and a lime wedge.

SERVES 4

Sweet Pepper and Corn Relish

1 STRIP RAW BACON, MINCED (OR OMIT AND
    INCREASE OLIVE OIL TO 1 TABLESPOON)

2 TEASPOONS OLIVE OIL

1/2 CUP 1/4-INCH DICED RED BELL PEPPER

1/2 CUP 1/4-INCH DICED RED ONION

1 TEASPOON MINCED GARLIC

3/4 CUP FRESH OR FROZEN CORN

2 TABLESPOONS FRESHLY SQUEEZED LIME
    JUICE

1 1/2 TABLESPOONS FIRMLY PACKED BROWN
    SUGAR

1/8 TEASPOON GROUND CAYENNE PEPPER

PINCH OF CRUSHED RED PEPPER FLAKES

1/4 TO 1/2 TEASPOON SALT

1 GREEN ONION, MINCED

2 TABLESPOONS CHOPPED CILANTRO

1. Cook bacon in a medium nonstick skillet over medium-high heat about 2 minutes, or until crisp. Add olive oil, red pepper, red onion, and garlic and cook for 2 minutes, or until the mixture just begins to soften, stirring occasionally. Add corn and cook another 1 to 2 minutes, stirring occasionally.

2. Add lime juice, brown sugar, cayenne, red pepper flakes, and salt and remove pan from heat. Let cool to room temperature, then stir in green onions and cilantro. Place relish in a small bowl or a covered jar and refrigerate until ready to serve.

MAKES 1 CUP

CRAB PICKERS VS. CRAB PILERS

"CRACKED CRAB" means the shell has been split so eaters have only to gently twist and break the shell. Dungeness crab connoisseurs agree the bigger the crab, the better, simply because bigger crabs have more meat. Since the crab is large, the meat is relatively easy to extract anyway.

Some cracked crab eaters pick and eat as they go, while others refrain from tasting even a single morsel until they have a good-sized pile. The Pickers and the Pilers are fascinated with each other since neither understands the other at all. A methodical Piler couldn't begin to comprehend devouring each chunk of crab as soon as it's out of the shell, while a hedonis-

tic Picker could never imagine waiting to dive in until every bit of crabmeat is painstakingly gathered. For the record, I am an avowed and devoted Picker, for I feel there is no time like the present.

The body meat, contained in the brittle shell segments adjoining the legs, is choice but often neglected by those novices who don't know how to get it out. The trick is to press the palm of the hand gently but firmly on top of the body-meat section until you feel the interior shell sections give way. If a piece of crabmeat breaks while you are removing it from the shell, use a slender, curved crab "toe" (the tip of a crab claw) to extract the pieces— much more efficient than a cocktail fork.

SURIMI SEAFOOD

AVAILABLE throughout the year, surimi seafood is a ready-to-eat shellfish substitute that requires no shelling, cooking, or shucking. This economical, easy-to-prepare, nutritious fish product can be used in almost any recipe that calls for shellfish.

The benefits of surimi are catching on. Surimi seafood is one of the food products whose popularity is growing most quickly in the United States, with nearly 150 million pounds consumed each year. Americans now eat more surimi "crab" than real crab. But American statistics are nothing compared to the Japanese, the inventors of surimi, who consume 2 billion pounds each year.

The origin of surimi dates back to around 1100 A.D., when Japanese fishermen began preserving their leftover catch by turning it into a fish paste called *chikuwa*. The fishermen found that by mixing fish meat, salt, sugar, water, and a starch binder, they could double the shelf life of their freshly caught fish.

Today, surimi is most often made from Alaska pollock (a white-fleshed fish similar in taste and texture to cod), although hoki from New Zealand (another member of the cod family) and Pacific whiting from the Pacific Northwest are also used. The fish is deboned, minced, rinsed, and turned into an odorless white paste.

The surimi is then frozen and shipped to processing plants. At the processor, the paste is thawed and flavored with concentrates from cooked shellfish and other sources. A small portion of unprocessed shellfish may also be added. The surimi is then formed, cooked, cut into appropriate shapes, and colored.

In Japanese, the word *surimi* means "minced fish." "Surimi" refers to the raw material from which all surimi seafood is produced. "Surimi seafood" refers to the product that is formed when surimi (the raw material) is blended with other ingredients and processed.

Surimi seafood stays fresh for 3 months; be sure to look at the expiration date printed on the package and use the product before that time. After opening, surimi seafood keeps in the refrigerator up to 4 days. While freezing poses no health risk, makers of surimi seafood don't recommend it because the texture can become rubbery. If you must freeze, use the product within 3 months.

Surimi seafood is sold at seafood counters and in the refrigerator case of many supermarkets, breaded or unbreaded, in many different shapes or forms. Surimi crab, lobster, scallop, and shrimp meat are commonly available. Whole legs resembling Alaskan crab legs are good for dipping. Mini cuts, or bite-sized portions, can be added to salads, stir-fries, or other cooked dishes. Salad or flake-style surimi seafood is cut into chunks that look and taste like fresh crabmeat. These are good in seafood salads, sandwiches, and pasta salads. Shredded surimi seafood can be added to salads, stuffings, and hot or cold sandwiches and spreads.

The quality of surimi seafood products varies from manufacturer to manufacturer. Premium surimi seafood products contain about 50 percent fish, and will list fish, not water, at the top of the ingredients list. The fillers and starches on the list affect taste and texture, too. Fillers and starches high on the list mean more filler, less fish. Check the species of fish used, too. Alaska pollock is considered the best quality, and the better products add a bit of natural shellfish for a fuller flavor. Products with "whitefish" on the label commonly combine two or more species of fish and may be of lesser quality.

Fully cooked surimi seafood does not need any preparation before combining with other ingredients. Its mild, slightly sweet flavor blends well with many other foods, a fine substitute in almost any of your favorite shellfish dishes.

If serving surimi seafood cold, simply add flakes or chunks to the finished dish. If serving hot, add during the final minutes of cooking just to heat it through. Be careful not to overcook surimi; like real shellfish, it will toughen if cooked too long or at too high a temperature. When broiling or baking surimi seafoods, it is best to lightly brush them first with butter, oil, or marinade to prevent surface drying. Cook just until heated through, generally 2 to 4 minutes.

Whether served hot or cold, surimi seafood is good in salads, tacos, pasta dishes, fajitas, sandwiches, soups, stews, stir-fries, quiches, omelets, dips, appetizers, spreads, and casseroles. It also makes a good pizza topping.

Surimi seafood is 100 percent edible protein, and since it is precooked, there is no waste. Therefore, you can use as little as 3 ounces per serving, although 4 to 6 ounces is a more generous serving per person.

Surimi seafood can be used as a supplement to pricier shellfish. Mix surimi crab with real shellfish to make stuffings for flounder or sole, or combine surimi seafood with the real thing in seafood stews.

Spicy Crab Boil

Although the sweet, distinctive meat of the Dungeness crab is a joy to eat plain and unadulterated, sometimes it's fun to spice it up a bit, as in this piquant version of the traditional crab boil.

3 CUPS WATER

1 TEASPOON YELLOW MUSTARD SEED

1/2 TEASPOON CRUSHED RED PEPPER
   FLAKES

1 BAY LEAF

1 PRECOOKED 2- TO 2 1/2-POUND DUNGE-
   NESS CRAB IN THE SHELL

In a large stockpot or Dutch oven, bring water, mustard seed, red pepper flakes, and bay leaf to a boil and add crab. Turn down heat to a simmer and cook 3 to 5 minutes, turning crab once. Drain crab and serve immediately.

SERVES 1 AS AN ENTRÉE, 2 AS AN APPETIZER

Tarragon Crab Boil

This elegant poaching liquid, infused with the essence of anise-flavored tarragon, takes the already superlative Dungeness crab to new heights. It can also be used to boil shell-on shrimp or as a poaching liquid for a variety of fish fillets.

2 CUPS WATER

1 CUP DRY WHITE WINE

1 TABLESPOON DRIED TARRAGON, CRUM-
   BLED

1 PRECOOKED 2- TO 2 1/2-POUND DUNGE-
   NESS CRAB IN THE SHELL

In a large stockpot or Dutch oven, bring water, white wine, and tarragon to a boil and add crab. Turn down heat to a simmer and cook 3 to 5 minutes, turning crab once. Drain crab and serve immediately.

SERVES 1 AS AN ENTRÉE, 2 AS AN APPETIZER

FUN FACT

- The Alaska crab fishery is one of the wildest and most dangerous. In the mid-1970s, the heyday of king crabbing, young crewmembers raked in shares of more than $100,000 in a few weeks of intense fishing. The resource crashed in 1981 and has never recovered to previous levels, although Alaska king crab is still widely available today.

Hot Crab and Artichoke Dip

―――⚭―――

CUTTERS BAYHOUSE, SEATTLE, WASHINGTON

From its waterfront location just north of the Pike Place Market, Cutters Bayhouse, or "Cutters" as it's affectionately referred to by locals, serves up Market-fresh seafood and produce while diners enjoy views of Elliott Bay and the Olympic Mountains. This appetizer has been a mainstay on the menu for years and with good reason—nothing beats a rich blend of Dungeness crab, rich mayonnaise, artichoke hearts, sliced sweet onions, and Parmesan cheese.

1 CUP GOOD-QUALITY MAYONNAISE

1 CUP ARTICHOKE HEARTS PACKED IN WATER, DRAINED AND CHOPPED INTO $1/2$- TO 1-INCH PIECES

$1/4$ POUND ($3/4$ CUP) DUNGENESS CRABMEAT, PICKED OVER FOR SHELLS AND CARTILAGE

$1/2$ CUP FRESHLY GRATED PARMESAN CHEESE

$1/2$ YELLOW ONION, PEELED, QUARTERED, AND SLICED PAPER-THIN

1 FRENCH OR ITALIAN BAGUETTE, CUT INTO THIN SLICES

1. In a small mixing bowl, combine mayonnaise, artichoke hearts, crabmeat, Parmesan cheese, and onion. Place crab mixture in an ovenproof baking dish no more than 1 inch thick. Cook immediately, or cover and refrigerate.

2. About 10 minutes before cooking, preheat oven to 350°. Bake crab mixture 15 to 20 minutes, or until dip is hot and lightly browned on top. Do not overbake or mixture will separate and become oily.

3. Remove baking dish from oven and place in the center of a heatproof plate. Arrange baguette slices in a circle around the dip, or place bread in a small basket and serve with the warm dip.

SERVES 2 TO 4 AS AN APPETIZER

Note: To achieve the correct consistency for the dip, it is important to use a good-quality mayonnaise and freshly grated Parmesan cheese.

FUN FACT

• The largest king crab on record was caught off Alaska's Kodiak Island, weighed 25 pounds, and measured 6 feet from claw to claw.

Crab and Cheese Canapés

~~~
≈⊗≈
~~~

QUALITY CHEESE, PIKE PLACE MARKET

Quality Cheese takes pride in offering one of Seattle's most varied and unusual cheese selections, with over 130 choices imported from all over the world. Standouts include Appenzeller (the granddaddy of Swiss cheeses), Parmigiano-Reggiano, and fresh mozzarella balls flown in from New York City. Northwest cheeses include Tillamook cheeses from Oregon, Sally Jackson's handcrafted cheeses from eastern Washington, and The Farm on Vashon's goat's milk cheeses (chèvre), produced on nearby Vashon Island, just a ferryboat ride from downtown Seattle. This recipe combines farm-fresh cheeses with Market-fresh produce and seafood for a winning appetizer that looks spectacular on the buffet table.

6 OUNCES PLAIN CHÈVRE

1/3 CUP SKIM, PART-SKIM, OR WHOLE-MILK RICOTTA CHEESE

1/4 CUP MINCED FRESH PARSLEY

1 TEASPOON MILK

1/4 TEASPOON SALT

1/8 TEASPOON FRESHLY GROUND WHITE PEPPER

4 HEADS BELGIAN ENDIVE, LEAVES SEPA-RATED, RINSED, DRAINED, AND PATTED DRY

24 BASIL LEAVES, RINSED, DRAINED, AND PATTED DRY

3 OUNCES (1/2 CUP) FRESH DUNGENESS CRABMEAT, PICKED OVER FOR SHELLS AND CARTILAGE

1 SMALL RED ONION, THINLY SLICED

1. In a small mixing bowl, combine chèvre, ricotta cheese, parsley, milk, salt, and white pepper until well mixed.

2. Place an endive leaf on a flat surface. Line the wide end of the endive leaf with a basil leaf. Place 1 teaspoon of the cheese mixture over the basil leaf and top with a pinch of crabmeat. Place a couple of onion slices over cheese and crabmeat and put finished canapé on a large platter. Repeat with remaining ingredients.

MAKES 24 APPETIZERS

FUN FACT

• A king crab walks diagonally across the ocean floor. Smaller king crabs sometimes travel in domes, with as many as a thousand crabs stacked as high as 40 feet and as wide as 60. Crabs scamper down the front and up the back in a vortex, like a walking house of crab, in what biologists claim is a crab defense mechanism.

Mussels

USSELS ARE BIVALVE mollusks with oblong, blue-black or brown shells. The foot of the mussel is located just inside the narrow end of the shell and is attached to the animal's stomach. The bundle of dark, slender fibers that look like sea grass near the hinge of the mussel are the byssus threads, also called the beard. The byssus threads, which are composed of protein, are secreted by the mussel and harden upon contact with seawater. The beard allows the mussel to attach itself to a firm surface, such as other mussels, rocks, or ropes. Once firmly attached, the mussel feeds itself by filtering 10 to 15 gallons of water a day. Because it consumes virtually everything that passes through its body, the mussel is particularly susceptible to pollution.

Nicknamed the "the poor man's oyster," mussels taste like a cross between an oyster and a clam, and are plentiful, inexpensive, versatile, and easy to cook. Mussels, which belong to the marine family Mytilidae, are found the world over. By far the most common edible species is the blue mussel (although it is really black in color), which occurs in Europe, eastern North America, and the Pacific Coast. California mussels and large horse mussels also grow on the West Coast, although they are inferior to the common blue and are not harvested commercially.

Mussels found in the wild are smaller and more leathery than those that have been farmed. Their shells are usually uneven in size, ridged, thick, and covered with barnacles. Natural mussels may contain as little as 15 percent meat, compared to a minimum of 25 percent in cultivated mussels.

Today, most mussels on the market are cultivated. Commercial mussel farming provides shellfish of uniform size with smooth, thin, practically barnacle-free shells. Cultivated mussels have a good flavor and are consistently safe. They come to market washed and sorted according to size and are usually free of grit and barnacles. They need simply to be scrubbed and debearded before cooking. The recipes in this chapter are for cultivated mussels. If you want to gather mussels yourself, consult your state fish and wildlife department or health department for up-to-date harvest information and to determine what permits or licenses are needed to legally harvest the shellfish.

Mussels are grown in one of two ways: by suspension between the surface and the sea floor on ropes or poles (off-bottom culture) or on the sea floor in prepared beds (bottom culture). Bottom-cultured mussels are more akin to wild mussels, with thicker, ridged shells sometimes dotted with barnacles. The bottom-culture method is used more often in New England and Europe (particularly the Netherlands) than on the West Coast.

Off-bottom mussels are shiny black and sometimes brown, with smooth, delicate shells. They are higher quality than bottom-raised mussels because they put their energy into plumping up their meat rather than into growing a thick, protective shell. They reach harvestable size in about a year.

Off-bottom mussel farming began in North America in 1975 when Peter Jefferds

Blue Mussel

started a mussel farm in Penn Cove in Whidbey Island in Washington. Jefferds suspended his mussels on ropes attached to log booms, which kept them submerged so they grew plump. Because they never faced rough surf or exposure to the sun or freezing temperatures, Penn Cove mussels were uncommonly tender and quickly caught the eye, and palate, of local restaurateurs and seafood markets. In 1986 Pete's sons, Ian and Rawle, bought the mussel farm, which has since grown into the largest off-bottom mussel farm in the United States.

The blue mussel (*Mytilus edulis*) is found from California north to the Arctic, as well as on the Atlantic coasts of Canada, the United States, and Europe. Blue mussels are plentiful in bays and inlets along the low-tide line and are also easy to cultivate. The blue mussel is recognized by its smooth, dark blue shell, which is covered by a black, brown, or blue outer skin, and ranges from 1 to 3 inches long. The inside of the shell is pearly and margined

in violet. The flesh can range in color from ivory to bright orange.

The flavor of the blue mussel is sweet, sometimes a tad smoky, and has a refined taste. It is the prime species for cooking and the type you will usually find at fishmongers' stalls and restaurants. The shells of the blue mussel are easy to clean and the byssus, or beard, is pulled off with relative ease. They are best steamed, sautéed, fried, or smoked.

Blue mussels spawn in late spring and early summer (mid-May through early June), becoming lean and watery, although they are still edible. They are at their peak for eating during the fall, winter, and early spring, with prime harvest months from October to May.

Mediterranean mussels (*Mytilus galloprovincialis*) are distinguished by their large size, for they can grow as large as 7 inches long and 5 inches wide, with a meat-to-shell ratio averaging 40 percent. They grow naturally in Mediterranean waters, with huge quantities farmed in Spain and Italy. In North America, they grow naturally and on aquaculture farms in California and Washington.

How Mediterranean mussels came to the United States from Europe is a matter of much speculation. One theory contends that the mussels hitched a ride on U.S. Navy vessels stationed at Bremerton Naval shipyard near Seattle, then spread to nearby Dyes Inlet. Jon Rowley, a local seafood expert, hypothesizes that Mediterranean mussels arrived on United States shores hundreds of years ago on the hulls of Spanish galleons. They established colonies in West Coast waters but were not identified in California and Washington until the mid-1980s.

Mediterranean mussels have a mild taste and soft texture. Cleaning these mussels is easy because they emerge from the water shiny and clean, requiring no more than a quick rinse. Debearding is easy, too—one swift tug and the beard is gone. They come in three sizes: Regular (16 and over per pound), large (10 to 15 per pound), and jumbo (4 to 9 per pound).

A key difference between Mediterranean and other mussels is their behavior when cooked, for this variety often pops open quickly and sometimes prematurely. This popping action does not signal that the mussels are totally cooked, however, and they often require a few minutes more cooking time. Because their wide, shiny black shells are so big, they are perfect for broiling on the half shell or stuffing.

Mediterranean mussels differ from blue mussels in their spawning period, which is generally late January and into February. This means they are at their peak during July, August, and September, when native mussels are spawning and not in prime market condition. Mediterranean mussels are also more resistant to disease, making them easier to farm than the native blues.

Occasionally **greenshell or greenlipped mussels** (*Perna canaliculus*), a farmed mussel from New Zealand, are available at the Market and in other specialty seafood markets across the nation. They are an impressive looking specimen, running 3 to 4 inches long, with brown shells edged in forest green. The meat is a large knob of ivory flesh, with a slightly more pronounced taste than native mussels. They are best steamed, sautéed, fried, pickled, or smoked. Greenshells spawn in September and October, so it is best to avoid buying them then, if they are even available, because they are not in prime market condition.

Importation of the New Zealand greenshell mussel and the introduction of the Mediterranean mussel means that mussels are now available year-round.

Make sure mussels are alive when you buy them. Cultivated mussels generally have a 7- to 10-day shelf life from the day they are harvested. Don't be shy about asking your fishmonger when the mussels were delivered and, if in doubt, ask to see the shipping tag. If your fishmonger will let you, handpick your mussels to be sure each one is alive.

Many of us have learned never to cook a mussel whose shells are open. However, because of the different nature of farmed mussels, this axiom must be modified to say, "Don't use a mussel if it does not close." Mussels that are farmed have thinner shells and need to breathe more once they are harvested, so their shells may gape a bit.

To check their freshness, squeeze the mussel's shells together with your thumb and forefinger to activate its closure muscle. If it is alive, it will stay closed. If the shells don't stay closed, are cracked or broken, slide from side to side, or smell bad, the animals are old or dead and should be discarded.

The fishmonger will usually pack your mussels in a plastic bag. Remove them from the plastic bag as soon as possible and spread the shellfish in a single layer on a shallow dish or platter. Cover the mussels with damp paper towels or a damp cloth and refrigerate between 38° and 40° until ready to cook.

Under the right conditions, live mussels will keep 7 to 10 days, but it's best to cook them within 1 or 2 days or purchase. After cooking, mussels may be kept in the refrigerator for 2 days. Cover cooked mussels in their own broth so they don't dry out or shrivel. If you don't have enough liquid, make a homemade brine of 1 teaspoon salt to 1 cup water.

If you need to use raw, shucked mussels in a recipe and don't want to shuck them, steam them just until the shells give way enough to insert a knife tip, then open the shells and shuck the meats. Don't steam too long, or the meat will begin to cook. Shucked mussel meat keeps for 7 to 10 days, but it is preferable to eat them within 1 to 2 days.

Farmed mussels are available frozen, and will keep up to 3 months if properly wrapped.

If serving steamed mussels as an appetizer, allow $^1/_2$ to $^3/_4$ pound of mussels in the shell per serving; as a main course, allow 1 to $1^1/_2$ pounds per serving. Six medium to large mussels form an adequate appetizer-sized portion when broiled on the half shell or used in soup. Expect a minimum of 25 percent meat-to-shell weight. This means 2 pounds of mussels in the shell should yield at least $^1/_2$ pound of mussel meat.

The beard of a mussel is edible, but the texture is chewy and rough and best avoided. Do not debeard mussels until just before you are ready to cook them, because when the beard is pinched off, the mussel goes into shock and can die within a few hours.

To debeard, first rinse and scrub the mussel shells with a stiff vegetable brush under cold running water. For a better presentation, scrape off any barnacles (although there should be few, if any, on farmed mussels) with your fingernail, the tip of a knife, or an old toothbrush. Next, grasp the beard firmly between your thumb and forefinger and pull downward toward the hinge with a sharp jerking motion. If this doesn't work, pull up and straight out and the beard should come out with a bit of encouragement. If not, simply snip the beard or cut it off with the tip of a sharp knife, but remember that the remaining portion of the beard should be removed before eating.

When steaming mussels they should be cooked 5 to 7 minutes or until they open, then 30 seconds more. If you overcook mussels a bit, don't worry; mussels don't get tough and rubbery as easily as clams do, so there is a greater margin for error. Mussels cook faster than clams, however, so if you want to combine the two in a recipe, put the clams in first.

Mussels may be steamed, microwaved, sautéed, fried, broiled, roasted, or smoked. They may also be stuffed or used in salads, soups, pasta dishes, omelets, and pâtés. You will also find mussels dried, smoked, pickled, canned, and frozen.

Wines that pair well with mussels include chenin blanc, sémillon blanc, sémillon, sauvignon blanc/sémillon blends, sparkling wines (such as blanc de noirs), and pinot gris. Lean, acidic chardonnays with lemon-citrus undertones may also work, although strong, oaky, buttery chardonnays are best avoided. Chilled light reds such as gamay beaujolais and pinot noir match mussels, particularly when the shellfish is cooked in a tomato-based sauce or broth.

Cinchy Steamed Mussels

———✦———

The basic recipe for steamed mussels is a joy to make because of its sheer simplicity. Once cooked, you can serve the mussels as is, hot or cold, or with a variety of sauces (see Seafood Sidekicks, pages 300-322).

4 1/2 POUNDS MUSSELS, SCRUBBED AND
   DEBEARDED JUST BEFORE COOKING
1/2 CUP WATER, DRY WHITE WINE, BEER,
   CLAM BROTH, OR FISH STOCK
2 BAY LEAVES

1. In a large stockpot, Dutch oven, or saucepan, combine mussels, water, and bay leaves. Bring to a boil over medium-high heat, cover, and cook 5 to 7 minutes, or until mussels open. Shake pan occasionally during cooking to redistribute mussels.

2. With a slotted spoon, remove mussels that have opened and continue cooking remaining mussels 1 to 2 minutes longer. Remove open mussels and discard any that have not opened.

3. If serving mussels right away, divide mussels and mussel liquid among serving bowls or serve in one large communal bowl. Alternatively, save mussel liquid for another use, first straining it through several layers of dampened cheesecloth. The liquid can be covered and refrigerated for a few days or frozen for up to 3 months.

4. When mussels are cool enough to handle, remove meat from shells. Discard shells or save for stuffing, depending on recipe.

SERVES 4 AS AN ENTRÉE, 8 AS AN APPETIZER

Roasted Mussels

———✦———

Cookbook author Sharon Kramis studied with the late James Beard, who taught her that simple preparations of the freshest foods are best.

4 1/2 POUNDS MUSSELS, SCRUBBED AND
   DEBEARDED JUST BEFORE COOKING
2 TABLESPOONS BUTTER
2 CLOVES GARLIC, MINCED
1/4 CUP MINCED FRESH PARSLEY

1. Preheat oven to 400°. Place mussels on two 15 x 10-inch rimmed baking sheets in a single layer. Place baking sheets on center oven rack and cook 5 to 7 minutes, or until mussels open. With a slotted spoon, remove mussels that have opened to a large bowl and continue cooking remaining mussels 1 to 2 minutes longer. Remove open mussels and discard the rest. Cover bowl with aluminum foil and set aside. Reserve baking sheets.

2. While mussels are cooking, melt butter in a small skillet over medium-high heat, add garlic, and sauté 2 to 3 minutes, stirring often, until garlic is softened. Add parsley and cook 30 seconds more, or until parsley turns bright green, stirring continuously. Remove from heat.

3. Drizzle butter sauce over reserved mussels and toss gently. Place mussels in a single layer on baking sheets and return to oven 1 to 2 minutes more, or until mussels are just warmed through.

4. Divide mussels among individual bowls or transfer to a large serving bowl and serve immediately.

SERVES 4 AS AN ENTRÉE, 8 AS AN APPETIZER

Gingery Mussels

Consulting chef and cookbook author Sharon Kramis has been described by local food critic John Hinterberger as a hidden local genius because of her behind-the-scenes creations over the years, many of which have gone on to become classics on area menus. Whenever I call my multitalented friend and colleague, I am regaled with the latest recipe from her repertoire. This mussel recipe is one of my all-time favorites, for it contains no added fats, but the broth (a flavorful combination of sake or mirin, garlic, and ginger) is the perfect complement to rich mussels. Depending on which liquid you use to steam the mussels, you will get a savory (sake) or sweet (mirin) broth. If you want to add a bit of cream, butter, toasted sesame oil, or hot chile oil before serving, go ahead, but the dish really doesn't need anything except a loaf of good, crusty bread to sop up all the juices.

4½ POUNDS MUSSELS, SCRUBBED AND
    DEBEARDED JUST BEFORE COOKING

1 CUP RICE WINE (SAKE OR MIRIN)

10 CLOVES GARLIC, PEELED AND SMASHED
    WITH THE FLAT BLADE OF A KNIFE

10 QUARTER-SIZED ROUNDS SLICED
    GINGERROOT, SMASHED WITH THE FLAT
    BLADE OF A KNIFE

4 TABLESPOONS CHOPPED CILANTRO
    (OPTIONAL)

1. In a large stockpot, Dutch oven, or saucepan, combine mussels, rice wine, garlic, and gingerroot. Bring to a boil over medium-high heat, cover, and cook 5 to 7 minutes, or until mussels open. Shake pan occasionally during cooking to redistribute mussels.

2. With a slotted spoon, remove mussels that have opened and continue cooking remaining mussels 1 to 2 minutes longer. Remove open mussels and discard the rest.

3. Divide mussels and mussel liquid among individual bowls, or transfer to one large serving bowl. If desired, sprinkle with cilantro.

SERVES 4 AS AN ENTRÉE, 8 AS AN APPETIZER

HANDY MUSSEL TIP

Bruce Naftaly, chef/owner of Le Gourmand, a French restaurant in the Ballard neighborhood of Seattle, suggests steaming mussels in dry riesling, along with garlic cloves, shallots, and flat-leaf parsley leaves that have been puréed together in a food processor or blender. Add unsalted butter for extra richness, if desired. Serve hot, with plenty of bread for dipping.

Moules à la Marinière

François Kissel, chef/owner of Maximilien's, offers his guests the consummate version of this classic French dish—mussels steamed in a rich broth redolent with butter, shallots, white wine, whipping cream, and parsley. With typical Gallic understatement, he describes this dish as similar to American steamed clams but more elaborate. And although mussels are served as an appetizer in his restaurant, François explains that in France, where mussels are highly regarded and widely available, the dish is often served as a main course with a fruity dry or semidry white wine for sipping and lots of good French bread for soaking up all the delicious juices. The main course is followed by a lightly dressed green salad and rounded out with a great dessert. Ah, the French really do know how to live, don't they?

4 TABLESPOONS UNSALTED BUTTER

6 SHALLOTS, PEELED AND CHOPPED

4 1/2 POUNDS MUSSELS, SCRUBBED AND
   DEBEARDED JUST BEFORE COOKING

2 CUPS WHITE WINE

1 CUP HEAVY WHIPPING CREAM

1/4 CUP CHOPPED FRESH PARSLEY

1. In a large skillet, saucepan, or Dutch oven, melt 2 tablespoons of the butter over medium-high heat. Add shallots and cook 5 minutes, or until light brown in color, stirring occasionally.

2. Add mussels, wine, whipping cream, and the remaining 2 tablespoons butter and bring to a boil over medium-high heat. Cover pan and cook 5 to 7 minutes, or until mussels open. Shake pan occasionally during cooking to redistribute mussels.

3. With a slotted spoon, remove mussels that have opened to a large communal bowl and continue cooking remaining mussels 1 to 2 minutes longer. Remove open mussels and discard the rest. Add parsley to remaining liquid and stir well.

4. To serve, pour broth over mussels and serve immediately.

SERVES 4 AS AN ENTRÉE, 8 AS AN APPETIZER

FUN FACT

- Ancient Romans cooked mussels in white wine and herbs, much like the French recipe, *Moules à la Mariniere*, is prepared.

Mussel, Potato, and Tomato Salad

—⚓—

You'll enjoy the combination of textures and flavors in this salad, which is best made with the smaller blue mussel (as opposed to the greenlipped or Mediterranean) in the spring, when both blue mussels and new potatoes are in season.

4½ POUNDS MUSSELS, SCRUBBED AND
    DEBEARDED JUST BEFORE COOKING

2 POUNDS SMALL (1- TO 1½-INCH) NEW
    POTATOES, SCRUBBED

4 GREEN ONIONS, TOP 2 INCHES REMOVED,
    REMAINING PORTION CUT INTO ¼-INCH
    SLICES

2 TABLESPOONS SNIPPED FRESH DILL

2 TEASPOONS DIJON MUSTARD

2 TABLESPOONS WHITE DRY VERMOUTH OR
    DEFATTED CHICKEN STOCK

2 TABLESPOONS WHITE WINE VINEGAR

2 TABLESPOONS RESERVED MUSSEL LIQUID

2 TABLESPOONS EXTRA VIRGIN OLIVE OIL

SALT AND FRESHLY GROUND BLACK PEPPER
    TO TASTE

1 PINT CHERRY TOMATOES, RINSED

1 POUND SPINACH LEAVES, RINSED,
    DRAINED, AND SPUN DRY

1. Cook mussels using the recipe for Cinchy Steamed Mussels, page 191. Strain mussel liquid through several layers of dampened cheesecloth and reserve 2 tablespoons of the liquid. When mussels are cool enough to handle, remove meat from shells and reserve. Discard shells.

2. Place potatoes in a large saucepan and cover with water. Bring to a boil, cover, decrease heat to simmer, and cook 15 to 20 minutes, or until potatoes are tender but not mushy.

3. While potatoes are cooking, make salad dressing by whisking together green onions, dill, mustard, vermouth, white wine vinegar, reserved mussel liquid, and extra virgin olive oil in a small bowl. Season to taste with salt and pepper and reserve.

4. When potatoes are done, drain them, cool slightly, and cut in half. Place potatoes in a large nonreactive bowl. While they are still warm, pour on half the reserved dressing and toss gently to coat.

5. In another nonreactive bowl, place cherry tomatoes, mussels, and remaining dressing and toss gently to coat.

6. To serve, divide spinach leaves among individual plates and spoon one-quarter of the mussel-tomato mixture in the center of each plate. Spoon one-quarter of the potatoes around the mussel-tomato mixture.

SERVES 4

Mussels and Millet in Curried Yogurt Sauce

My friend Emily Bader, an accomplished cooking teacher who specializes in healthy cuisine, created this recipe for a class on combining grains with seafood. Emily suggests serving these mussels with a fresh green salad and chapati bread. Millet is a small, round, golden grain that is a major food source for over one-third of the world's population, particularly those living in Asia, North Africa, and India. It is mildly flavored, with a hint of cashew and corn, and can be found in health food stores and in some supermarkets.

1 TABLESPOON CANOLA OR SAFFLOWER OIL

1/2 TEASPOON BLACK MUSTARD SEEDS

2 ONIONS, CUT IN HALF, THEN INTO
   1/4-INCH-THICK SLICES

1 CUP PLAIN LOWFAT YOGURT

2 TOMATOES, CHOPPED, OR 3 CANNED
   TOMATOES, DRAINED AND CHOPPED

1 TEASPOON GRATED GINGERROOT, OR
   1/2 TEASPOON GROUND GINGER

1/2 TEASPOON GROUND CORIANDER

1/2 TEASPOON GROUND CUMIN

1/2 TEASPOON GROUND CAYENNE PEPPER

1/4 TEASPOON GROUND TURMERIC

2 POUNDS MUSSELS, SCRUBBED AND
   DEBEARDED JUST BEFORE COOKING

2 CUPS COOKED MILLET (RECIPE FOLLOWS)

CHOPPED CILANTRO, FOR GARNISH

1. Heat canola oil in a large saucepan over medium-high heat and add black mustard seeds. Cook 3 minutes, or until seeds begin to pop and release their aroma. Turn down heat to medium, add onions, and cook until onions are wilted but not browned, about 5 minutes, stirring occasionally.

2. Add yogurt, tomatoes, gingerroot, coriander, cumin, cayenne, and turmeric. Stir well, cover, and bring to a simmer.

3. Add mussels, cover, and cook 5 to 7 minutes, or until mussels open. (Discard any mussels that have not opened.) Add millet and toss well to combine.

4. To serve, divide mussels and millet among individuals plates and sprinkle with cilantro.

SERVES 4

Millet

2 1/2 CUPS WATER

1 CUP UNCOOKED MILLET, RINSED AND
   DRAINED

In a medium saucepan, bring water to a boil. Add millet, stir once, cover, and reduce heat. Bring millet to a simmer, then cook until tender, about 25 to 30 minutes. Measure 2 cups millet for recipe. Use any leftover millet as you would rice or couscous.

MAKES ABOUT 3 CUPS

Mussels Provençal

ETTA'S SEAFOOD,
SEATTLE, WASHINGTON

This steamed mussel dish is one of the most unique you'll ever eat because of the addition of shiitake mushrooms and kalamata olives to a tomato wine broth. It is served at Etta's Seafood, one of the new breed of Seattle seafood restaurants, where you can have everything from salt cod and russet potato spread to a sashimi tuna salad with green onion pancakes. The brainchild of chef Tom Douglas, the wildly popular Etta's is located just past the north boundary of the Market.

¼ CUP OLIVE OIL

1 CUP SHIITAKE MUSHROOMS, STEMS RE-
  MOVED AND DISCARDED, THINLY SLICED

4 CLOVES GARLIC, CHOPPED

1 CUP PEELED, SEEDED, AND CHOPPED
  TOMATOES

24 OIL-CURED OLIVES, SUCH AS KALAMATA
  OR NIÇOISE, PITTED

4 TEASPOONS CHOPPED MIXED FRESH
  HERBS, SUCH AS ROSEMARY, SAGE,
  THYME, AND/OR PARSLEY

2½ POUNDS MUSSELS, SCRUBBED AND
  DEBEARDED JUST BEFORE COOKING

¼ LEMON, CUT INTO 2 WEDGES

1 CUP DRY WHITE WINE

2 TABLESPOONS BUTTER, AT ROOM
  TEMPERATURE

SPRIGS OF FRESH ROSEMARY AND FRESH
  THYME

SALT AND FRESHLY GROUND BLACK
  PEPPER TO TASTE

1. Heat olive oil in a large skillet or Dutch oven over medium-high heat until small bubbles form. Add shiitake mushrooms and cook 1 to 2 minutes, stirring often. Add garlic, tomatoes, olives, herbs, and mussels. Squeeze lemon wedges over contents of pan and toss wedges in pan. Add white wine, butter, and rosemary and thyme sprigs. Shake pan or stir to mix well.

2. Cover and cook 5 to 7 minutes, or until mussels open. Shake pan occasionally during cooking to redistribute mussels. With a slotted spoon, remove mussels that have opened and continue cooking remaining mussels 1 to 2 minutes longer. Remove open mussels and discard the rest. Taste the broth and season with salt and pepper, if desired. (I find olives provide enough salt and the garlic and lemon enough flavor that pepper isn't necessary.)

3. To serve, divide mussels, mushrooms, olives, and broth among individual bowls, or transfer to a large serving bowl. Be sure to provide seafood forks, a shell dish, and extra napkins for handy cleanup.

SERVES 2 AS A LIGHT ENTRÉE, 4 AS AN
APPETIZER

Mussels in Pinot Noir Butter

Chef John Doerper, a world-renowned expert on Pacific Coast food and wine, is the author of countless recipes, articles, and books on the art of cooking and eating Northwest foods, particularly shellfish. Although many people believe that red wines and seafood don't mix, in this recipe John proves otherwise with delicious results. Cornichons, tiny French pickles, are available in the Pike Place Market at Quality Cheese and DeLaurenti Specialty Foods and in gourmet food stores and supermarkets.

³/₄ cup Oregon pinot noir

2 dozen large mussels (about 1 ¹/₂ pounds), scrubbed and debearded just before cooking

2 tablespoons finely minced shallots

2 tablespoons freshly squeezed lemon juice

¹/₂ cup unsalted butter, cut into pieces

6 tiny cornichons, cut lengthwise into quarters

1. Bring ¹/₂ cup of the pinot noir to a boil in a large nonreactive saucepan or Dutch oven. Reduce heat to medium-high, add mussels, cover, and steam until mussels open, about 5 to 7 minutes, shaking pan occasionally to redistribute mussels. With a slotted spoon, remove mussels that have opened and continue cooking remaining mussels 1 to 2 minutes longer. Remove open mussels and discard the rest. Reserve mussels and cooking juices in separate containers for later use.

2. While mussels cool, place the remaining ¹/₄ cup pinot noir, the shallots, and lemon juice in a medium, nonreactive skillet and reduce over low heat, about 5 to 7 minutes, or until liquid is almost gone. Stir in reserved mussel cooking juices and reduce over medium heat until liquid thickens slightly and is to reduced to about 3 tablespoons. In the final stages, the liquid thickens rapidly, so watch it carefully and do not allow liquid to burn.

3. Remove pan from heat and add 1 or 2 small cubes of butter. Add remaining butter a cube at a time. Whisk steadily until blended. The butter sauce should have the consistency of homemade mayonnaise, neither too solid nor too liquid. (The warm skillet should retain sufficient heat to do this smoothly; if the temperature drops too much, return the skillet to low heat. If butter separates or curdles, whisk rapidly to emulsify.)

4. Remove mussels from shells and discard upper shells. Place a cornichon quarter in lower shells, place a mussel on each cornichon, and cover with sauce.

5. To serve, divide mussels on individual plates or on a large serving platter and serve immediately.

Serves 4 as an appetizer

Five-Spice Rice with Mussels

I'm sure I'm breaking all the rules in this example of fusion cuisine gone berserk, but the unusual blending of Asian flavors in rice pilaf, a traditional recipe from the Near East, works so well with plump, buttery mussels, it is irresistible.

1 TABLESPOON PEANUT OIL

$1/4$ TEASPOON TOASTED SESAME OIL

3 CLOVES GARLIC, MINCED

1 TABLESPOON MINCED GINGERROOT, OR
   1 TEASPOON GROUND GINGER

1 TEASPOON FIVE-SPICE POWDER

1 CUP WHITE LONG-GRAIN RICE

2 CUPS FISH STOCK, CLAM JUICE, DEFATTED
   CHICKEN STOCK, OR WATER

$1/8$ TEASPOON SALT

ZEST OF $1/2$ ORANGE

$1/4$ CUP WATER

$2 1/2$ POUNDS MUSSELS, SCRUBBED AND
   DEBEARDED JUST BEFORE COOKING

CHOPPED CILANTRO, FOR GARNISH

1. In a medium saucepan, heat peanut oil and toasted sesame oil over medium-high heat. Add garlic and gingerroot and cook for 30 seconds, stirring continuously. Add five-spice powder and rice and cook, stirring continuously, until rice is evenly coated with oil and five-spice powder is evenly distributed.

2. Add fish stock, salt, and orange zest and bring to a boil. Decrease heat to a simmer, cover, and cook until the liquid is absorbed, about 15 to 20 minutes.

3. About 10 minutes before rice is done, bring water to a boil in a large saucepan. Decrease heat to medium-high, add mussels, cover, and cook 5 to 7 minutes, or until mussels open. Shake pan occasionally to redistribute mussels. With a slotted spoon, remove mussels that have opened and continue cooking remaining mussels 1 to 2 minutes longer. Remove open mussels and discard the rest.

4. To serve, place a mound of rice in center of individual plates and arrange mussels in a circular pattern around rice. Garnish with chopped cilantro.

SERVES 4

FUN FACTS

- "In ancient Greece, the threads of the mussel were collected and woven into byssus gloves for the hands of fishers. These gloves had to be kept wet or they would lose their durability. They were stored in buckets of seawater and lasted so long they were handed down from generation to generation. They were truly indestructible, more so than any man-made fiber."—A. J. McClane, *The Encyclopedia of Fish Cookery*

- In a kitchen midden found on Catalina Island in California and dated at 4000 to 3500 B.C., two kinds of shellfish dominated—the abalone and the mussel.

Saffron Mussel Bisque

It's always a joyous occasion when Julia Child comes to town. Her love of Northwest seafood (especially Dungeness crab) is legendary, and she makes a point to walk through the Market whenever she visits. In February 1995, the Pacific Northwest chapter of the American Institute of Wine and Food (AIWF), a food-lover's group that she helped found, threw a luncheon in her honor at the Sorrento Hotel. The menu, prepared by executive chef Eric Lenard, featured this mussel bisque, which serves 4 as an entrée along with a hearty salad and crusty bread. One-half-cup servings of the rich, pale-gold soup form 8 appetizer portions.

3 TABLESPOONS UNSALTED BUTTER

3 TABLESPOONS ALL-PURPOSE FLOUR

2 CUPS WHITE WINE

1/4 CUP CHOPPED SHALLOTS

1/4 TEASPOON SAFFRON THREADS

1 BAY LEAF

2 SPRIGS FRESH THYME

2 POUNDS MUSSELS, SCRUBBED AND
    DEBEARDED JUST BEFORE COOKING

4 CUPS CLAM JUICE OR FISH STOCK

2 CUPS HEAVY WHIPPING CREAM

SALT AND FRESHLY GROUND WHITE
    PEPPER TO TASTE

FRESHLY SQUEEZED LEMON JUICE TO TASTE

1. Melt butter in a small skillet over medium heat. When butter begins to foam, whisk in flour. Continue whisking until mixture turns a light golden brown and smells like toasted nuts. Remove from heat and allow to cool.

2. Combine wine, shallots, saffron, bay leaf, and thyme in a large saucepan over high heat and bring to a boil. Reduce heat to medium-high, add mussels, cover, and cook 3 to 5 minutes, or until mussels just open, shaking pan occasionally to redistribute mussels. With a slotted spoon, remove open mussels and continue remaining mussels 1 to 2 minutes longer. Remove open mussels and discard the rest. When mussels are cool enough to handle, remove meats from shells and discard shells. Cover mussel meats and refrigerate. Remove bay leaf and thyme sprigs.

3. Return saucepan to high heat. Reduce cooking liquid by one-third, add clam juice, and reduce cooking liquid by 1 cup. Strain liquid through a fine-meshed sieve and return to pan. Add whipping cream and bring mixture to a boil.

4. Whisk the cooled flour mixture (roux) into the soup a few teaspoons at a time, allowing the soup to return to a simmer for 2 to 3 minutes after each addition. If necessary, decrease heat to keep soup from cooking too fast. The soup is the desired consistency when it coats the back of a spoon. Be patient—this step could take up to 20 minutes.

5. Season to taste with salt, pepper, and lemon juice. Remove mussel meats from refrigerator, add meats to soup, stir well, and cook 1 to 2 minutes more, or until mussels are warmed through.

6. Divide soup and mussels among soup bowls and serve immediately.

SERVES 4 AS AN ENTRÉE, 8 AS AN APPETIZER

The Odd Kettle of Shellfish

THIS CHAPTER IS A compendium of shellfish with unique characteristics. Abalone are becoming increasingly scarce and mind-bogglingly expensive. Lobsters are not found in Northwest waters but remain an all-American favorite. Neither octopus nor crawfish are commonly prepared by home cooks, although both deserve a wider audience and greater appreciation. In short, no comprehensive seafood cookbook would be complete without this odd kettle of shellfish.

Abalone

The abalone is a univalve, a mollusk with a single shell. The shell protects the animal's body, while allowing its tough, muscular "foot" to crawl over and cling to rocks. Its shell is dotted with holes through which it breathes while it feeds on seaweed. Although the outside is often encrusted with barnacles, the inside of the shell boasts iridescent shades of pink, blue, and green and is often used to make mother-of-pearl trinkets and decorations.

The flesh of the abalone is ivory- or gray-colored and resembles a human ear in shape and size. Many gourmets claim abalone has a delicious clamlike flavor, although its flavor and firm yet melty texture are truly unique.

Various species of abalone are found in many parts of the world. Here, in the Pacific Northwest, abalone grows from the central coastline of California to British Columbia and Alaska, with red or California abalone (*Haliotis rufescens*) the largest species in size. From earliest times, wherever abalone occurs it has been exploited as much for making jewelry and crafts from its opalescent inner shells as for food.

The future of these slow-growing, slow-moving animals does not look bright. As easy prey for both humans and certain sea creatures (particularly sea otters), populations of abalone are dwindling. According to *Simply Seafood* magazine, the annual commercial

Abalone

abalone catch has dropped from 4 million pounds in the late 1960s to just 500,000 pounds.

Aquafarming of abalone seemed a viable alternative to harvesting of wild abalone, but the process is slow and expensive since it takes an abalone 3 to 5 years to grow to marketable size. What little is farmed is usually sold to

Asian countries, whose customers are willing to pay top dollar for the product.

In Seattle, abalone is quite scarce and expensive. The fishmongers at the Pike Place Market supply it only once every couple of years, and then only for a few days. Uwajimaya, the area's largest Asian grocery and specialty food store, stopped selling it because customers wouldn't pay its high price. Seattle's famed Mutual Fish carries it on a regular basis but at prices ranging from $50 to $60 per pound for fresh, fresh-frozen, and even canned abalone, which pales in comparison to the fresh or fresh-frozen product.

Abalone is definitely a splurge term. Much of it goes to high-end restaurants, where it is invariably the most expensive item on the menu. A clone called "scalone," which is a mixture of scallops and abalone formed into patties, may allow abalone lovers to indulge in their passion more frequently and at reasonable prices.

Nonetheless, if you are ever fortunate enough to find abalone and are able to pay for the privilege of cooking and eating it, there are several time-honored ways to prepare it, depending on its form. Fresh or fresh-frozen abalone can be eaten raw (a traditional Japanese dish), cut into steaks and sautéed, or cut into strips for stir-fries or soups (normally in Asian-style preparations). Canned abalone is not suitable for eating raw, but works well in soups and stir-fries. As with all seafoods, but especially with abalone, never overcook abalone or it will be tough. Cooking 20 to 30 seconds per side is sufficient for abalone steaks; 1 minute per side if stir-fried.

Crawfish

The crawfish is a small (3 to 4 inches long) lobsterlike crustacean that inhabits fresh water on all continents except Africa. The Pacific Coast harvest consists of the species *Pacifastacus leniusculus* and most of it comes from Washington, Oregon, and California, although many crawfish available today are farm-raised.

In his writings, the late James Beard lovingly recalls his boyhood crawfish-hunting

Crawfish

excursions along the Necanicum River in Oregon, where he used a piece of liver on a string to entice the creatures out of their hiding places. As an adult, he enjoyed great plates of them, along with many glasses of beer, at Jake's Crawfish Parlor in Portland. Jake's has been serving crawfish since 1892.

Crawfish are usually harvested when they are about 4 inches long. They are available live, cooked in-shell, cooked in-shell and frozen, or as fresh or frozen cooked and peeled meats. While the peeled meats are easy to work with, crawfish connoisseurs always opt for the live animals, which are considered the most flavorful as well as the most economical.

Purchase live crawfish the day you plan to cook them and place them in a shallow pan in the refrigerator, loosely covered with damp

THE BEST WAY TO EAT A WHOLE BOILED CRAWFISH

PICK UP THE CRAWFISH with one hand on the tail section and the other on the body section. Bend crawfish sideways to break apart the sections. If desired (this is not for the faint of heart!), suck the flavorful "fat" out of the body cavity, or reserve it to enrich a spicy Creole sauce.

Pinch the slender tail end between your thumb and index finger as you would pinch together a drinking straw; this should force the tail meat out through the open end. If not, just peel away the shell like you would a shrimp. Consider yourself victorious as you eat your small, hard-earned, well-deserved morsel of crawfish meat.

paper towels. Do not store in fresh water for they will quickly use up the oxygen in the water and die.

The crawfish body is large compared to its tail, where the largest proportion of the meat is found. In fact, 1 pound of whole crawfish yields only about $2^1/_2$ ounces of meat, or 7 pounds of crawfish for 1 pound of meat. It is best to plan on 2 pounds of crawfish per person for a crawfish boil, which many people consider the best way to eat the animal.

Raw crawfish must be alive when cooked because otherwise the meat spoils very quickly. You'll have no trouble distinguishing live crawfish; at the Pike Place Market, I've watched them climb out of their holding crates, plop onto the tiles below (unharmed), and skittle away in a last mad dash for survival! Before cooking, throw away any critters that are limp or inactive, then cook the lively ones for about 5 to 8 minutes, or until their shells turn bright red. Cooked crawfish can also be tightly wrapped and frozen for up to 2 months.

Lobster

The American, or northern lobster (*Homarus americanus*) is caught in the western North Atlantic from Newfoundland to New Jersey and is by far the most important species of lobsters with claws. They are usually sold live but are also cooked whole and sold fresh and frozen. Consumers generally find lobsters ranging in size from $1^1/_4$ to 2 pounds. The smaller lobsters are considered 1 serving and yield from 4 to 6 ounces of meat. Larger lobsters are often split lengthwise after cooking and shared by two people.

Do not buy a lobster until the day you want to cook it. To choose a good one, look in the lobster tank and find an active specimen with no dark blemishes. Bypass any that are limp or immobile. Ask the fishmonger to remove the lobster you have chosen. Make sure it feels heavy for its size. Watch the animal's response to being out of water; the lobster should arch its back, raise its claws, and wave its antennae. If the claws or tail droop, ask for another lobster. To test a store-bought pre-cooked lobster for freshness, pull its tail out straight. When released, it will snap back into its curled position if the lobster was cooked while still alive.

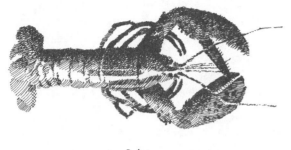

Lobster

Some people claim female lobsters contain more meat and have sweeter flesh than the males, but I've never put much stock in that. When using the lobster coral, or roe (the unripened eggs often found in female lobsters), in a sauce, you will need to purchase a female lobster. You can tell a female by turning it over on its back and looking for two small swimmerets, or fins, on its underside near where the tail joins the body. Soft, feathery swimmerets signal a female; hard ones, a male. The female's body is also broader and more splayed than the male's, which is almost round.

The tomalley, which functions as the lobster's liver and pancreas, is a pea-green substance found in all lobsters. Many people consider it a delicacy, but recent health warnings about high PCB content have deterred some gourmets. Coral has been determined to be safe from carcinogenic residues, although both the roe and the tomalley are high in cholesterol.

To store a live lobster once it has been removed from the water, keep it cold and damp by placing it in a paper bag moistened with water and pierced with several holes so the lobster can breathe. Close the bag loosely around the lobster so it is lying flat on its stomach and place it in the refrigerator.

When buying lobster, an appetizer portion is $1^1/_2$ to 3 ounces of lobster meat; an entrée portion 4 to 6 ounces. A 3- to 5-ounce tail constitutes an appetizer portion, while a 6- to 8-ounce tail forms an entrée portion. For one person, $^1/_2$ to $^3/_4$ pound of whole lobster is the proper appetizer size; a $1^1/_4$ pound whole lobster forms an entrée-sized portion.

FUN FACT

- Lobster Newburg got its start in Delmonico's restaurant in New York City. A man named Wenberg brought the recipe up from the Caribbean and it became a successful menu item called Lobster Wenberg. One night Wenberg got drunk, tore up the main dining room, and was strongly encouraged never to return. The dish was given a "new" name—Lobster Newburg.

Octopus

The octopus is a cephalopod, or shell-less mollusk related to the squid. It is found in tropical and temperate oceans worldwide, with United States species found on both the Atlantic (*Octopus vulgaris*) and Pacific (*Octopus dofleini*) coasts. The Puget Sound octopus, the Great Pacific, is found in local waters and may be the world's largest species. It regularly reaches an arm spread of more than 10 feet

COURT BOUILLON FOR OCTOPUS

OR A MORE FLAVORFUL cooking liquid for octopus, follow the cooking instructions on page 210 and add the following ingredients to the salted water.

2 CUPS DRY WHITE WINE

1 YELLOW ONION, PEELED AND CUT IN
  QUARTERS

1 CARROT, PEELED AND CUT IN HALF

1 CLOVE GARLIC, PEELED

1 STALK CELERY AND LEAVES, CHOPPED

1 BAY LEAF

4 WHOLE PEPPERCORNS

2 WHOLE CLOVES

Once your octopus is boiled, there are many different ways to prepare it. One of my favorites is a composed Asian salad. To make the salad, cut boiled octopus on the diagonal into thin slices. Steam or boil snow or sugar snap peas until they are tender-crisp. Peel and thinly slice fresh water chestnuts, or substitute the canned variety. Thinly slice green onions, carrots, celery, and red bell peppers. To serve, line individual plates with soft lettuce leaves, such as Bibb, green or red leaf, or iceberg. Arrange sliced octopus in the center of the lettuce. Place vegetables in a pleasing pattern around the octopus slices. Drizzle with Black Bean Vinaigrette (see page 302).

Mediterranean preparations for boiled octopus are classics and the one I like is surprisingly easy to make. Just heat 2 to 3 cups of Marinara Sauce (see page 319), then add bite-sized boiled octopus pieces and cook until the octopus is just warmed through. If homemade tomato sauce is not available, substitute 2 or 3 cups of good-quality bottled spaghetti sauce mixed with 1/4 cup red wine. Cook sauce until it thickens to desired consistency and add octopus pieces. Serve over cooked pasta or rice.

and a weight of 100 pounds, although 400-pound specimens have been found.

The octopus is nicknamed "devilfish," probably because of its big head, bulging eyes, and eight tentacles, which are crowded with suction cups. However, the nickname is a misnomer, for the creature is really very shy. Highly intelligent, it eats only the most delectable crabs, lobsters, clams, and scallops, which it catches by stalking and sneak attacks.

If frightened, the octopus squirts an octopus-sized cloud of ink that serves as a phantom to fool its attacker.

The octopus feeds mostly on shellfish, which results in a firm, chewy flesh with a sweet, mild taste. The meat is milky white when raw and bright white when cooked.

If buying a whole octopus, select one 1 1/2 pounds in weight; smaller specimens yield more tender meat than larger ones. Ask your fishmonger to cut away the eyes and tough beak and separate the tentacles and head. Precook the pieces in simmering salted water for 1 hour, then let cool in the cooking liquid. Scrape or rub off the purplish skin, then cut it into smaller pieces for frying, braising, baking, sautéing, grilling, marinating, or use in sushi, cold salads, or stews. The ink can be used in sauces and to color homemade pasta.

Octopus also comes fresh-frozen pre-cleaned and precooked. A breeze to prepare, you just defrost it overnight in the refrigera-tor, then slice it and warm it in your favorite octopus recipe.

The Japanese, Chinese, Greeks, and people of other Mediterranean countries have been eating and enjoying octopus for centuries, so cookbooks focusing on those cuisines are great sources for octopus recipes.

FUN FACT

• The skin between an octopus's arms is called webbing. An octopus can carry a dozen or so crabs back to its den in that webbing.

WHAT TO DRINK WITH YOUR ODD KETTLE

ALTHOUGH THERE ARE no hard and fast rules with these unique seafoods, some wines and beers are better matches than others. Lobster pairs well with Johannisberg riesling, chenin blanc, sémillon blanc, fumé blanc, sauvignon blanc, muscat canelli, and sparkling wines or Champagne. Abalone, whose taste is often likened to that of clams, may go best with wines usually associated with clams and mussels, such as chenin blanc, sémillon blanc, and sémillon. Crawfish is often served in infor-mal settings (such as at a crawfish boil) and is frequently paired with beer, although the lob-ster wines will also work. Octopus is often cooked in Asian or Italian preparations. A spicy zinfandel or merlot would be good with octopus dishes cooked in Italian-inspired tomato-based sauces or stocks, while spicy, sweet wines such as Johannisberg riesling, gewürztraminer, or white zinfandel would partner well with the Asian-inspired dishes. Even a slightly chilled merlot or a light-bodied chardonnay can pair well with Asian-inspired octopus dishes.

Golden Abalone

⟨knot illustration⟩

The last time I ate abalone was in 1994 at Scoma's waterfront restaurant in San Francisco. It was quite an extravagant evening, but how can you put a price on the meal of a lifetime? This is my rendition of that fabulous entrée.

1 TO 1 ½ POUNDS FRESH OR FRESH-FROZEN (AND DEFROSTED) ABALONE IN THE SHELL (SEE NOTE)

1 CUP ALL-PURPOSE FLOUR

¼ TEASPOON SALT

¼ TEASPOON FRESHLY GROUND WHITE OR BLACK PEPPER

DASH OF GROUND CAYENNE PEPPER

2 EGGS

4 TABLESPOONS UNSALTED BUTTER

2 TABLESPOONS OLIVE OIL

2 TABLESPOONS FRESHLY SQUEEZED LEMON JUICE

1 TABLESPOON CHOPPED FRESH PARSLEY

1. Shuck the abalone by running a thin, sharp knife between the shell and the foot of the abalone. Sever the connector muscle as if shucking a clam, then cut around the interior of the shell to remove as much of the foot as possible. Rinse under cold running water to remove the viscera. Scrub the foot to remove any remaining viscera, and pat dry. Scrub or trim off any dark portions around the edges, then cut thin steaks by slicing the foot horizontally across the muscle, about ⅛ inch thick.

2. Mix flour, salt, white pepper, and cayenne and pour onto a large plate or piece of waxed paper.

Beat eggs in a shallow bowl until frothy and place next to seasoned flour.

3. In a large skillet, heat 2 tablespoons of the butter and the olive oil over medium-high heat. When oil is very hot, coat the abalone steaks lightly on both sides with seasoned flour, pat to remove excess, then dip into eggs. Slide abalone into pan and cook 30 seconds, then turn abalone and cook another 30 seconds. Do not overcook or abalone will be tough. Transfer abalone to a plate and cover. Repeat with remaining abalone.

4. Return skillet to heat and add remaining 2 tablespoons butter, the lemon juice, and parsley. Cook, swirling, just until butter melts.

5. To serve, divide abalone among individual plates and drizzle with sauce.

SERVES 4

Note: If using fresh abalone for another recipe, such as a stir-fry or soup, after scrubbing and trimming foot, cut into strips by slicing vertically with the grain. Pound meat with a mallet for a few seconds until tender but not shredded.

Although there is no substitute for abalone, geoduck steaks or calamari steaks can be used in place of abalone steaks. Lightly steamed and shucked native littleneck or Manila clams can be used in place of abalone in stir-fries and soups.

Crawfish Boil

———&———

I must admit that I wasn't much of a fan of crawfish during the sixteen years I lived in Dallas. Perhaps their nickname "mudbug" was offputting to me, or it seemed like so much work for such a small amount of edible meat, or maybe it was just their overexposure in the general area. But once I moved to the Northwest and tried the local crawfish, I was pleasantly surprised. As a general rule, crawfish raised in Northwest waters are larger and less muddy tasting than craw-fish raised in the South. Their greater body size means less work for more meat. Their mild-flavored flesh is reminiscent of earthy-tasting lobster, especially when boiled with spices and aromatics, as in the following recipe, which imparts a sea-salty, back-of-the-throat peppery taste to both the shellfish and vegetables.

6 QUARTS WATER

2 1/2 CUPS WHITE WINE

4 ONIONS, PEELED AND CUT IN QUARTERS

8 CLOVES GARLIC, PEELED

18 WHOLE CLOVES

4 STALKS CELERY, INCLUDING LEAVES,
   COARSELY CHOPPED

1 LEMON, CUT IN HALF

2 BAY LEAVES

10 SPRIGS FRESH PARSLEY

2 1/2 TABLESPOONS SALT

1 TABLESPOON BLACK PEPPERCORNS

2 TEASPOONS GROUND CAYENNE PEPPER

1/2 CUP CRAB OR SHRIMP BOIL SEASONING
   MIX

2 POUNDS NEW POTATOES, SCRUBBED

2 EARS CORN, CUT IN HALF

8 POUNDS LIVE CRAWFISH, RINSED

1. In a large (14- to 16-quart) stockpot, combine water, wine, onions, garlic, cloves, celery, lemon, bay leaves, parsley, salt, peppercorns, cayenne, and seasoning mix. Bring to a boil, cover, and simmer 15 minutes. Add potatoes, bring water back to a boil, cover, and cook 5 minutes. Add corn, cover, and cook 5 minutes more.

2. Drop crawfish into the pot one by one to keep the water boiling continuously (tongs work well for this task). When the water comes back to a full boil, cover pot and cook crawfish 5 to 8 minutes, or until shells turn red and tails curl. Place pot in a sink or basin half-filled with cold water and allow crawfish to sit 5 to 10 minutes to absorb seasonings. If you want an even spicier taste, let them sit up to 20 minutes more.

3. To serve, cover dining room or picnic table with newspaper. Drain crawfish, corn, and potatoes, place on large serving platters, and let everyone serve themselves. Have plenty of napkins or paper towels on hand and extra dishes for shells.

SERVES 4

Cooking a Live Lobster

———✦———

When I was growing up in suburban Philadelphia, my parents delighted in searching out the best lobster restaurants in the area. On weekends, we would trek to northeast Philadelphia, Delaware, or even New Jersey on our quest. Eyebrows lifted if a restaurant served only boiled lobsters; to my parents' well-tuned palates, steamed lobsters were the only way to go. These days I have also come to realize the value of a good steamed lobster. The following recipe is easy and it produces lobster meat that is firm and flavorful.

SEAWATER OR TAP WATER

LIVE LOBSTERS

1. Put 1 inch of seawater in a pot large enough to comfortably contain the number of lobsters you want to cook. Be sure the pot has a tight-fitting lid. Alternately, use a smaller pot and cook only 1 or 2 lobsters at a time.

2. Cover pot and bring water to a full, rolling boil, with a huge head of steam escaping from underneath the lid. Rinse lobsters briefly under cold running water and remove the elastic bands from their claws (the rubber can taint the taste and smell of the cooking liquid).

3. Grab lobster(s) firmly in the middle of the back and put in pot head first, tail tucked under. Cover pot and cook 5 to 7 minutes for the first pound, 3 minutes for each pound thereafter, starting cooking time the moment the water returns to a boil. A 1 1/4-pound lobster takes about 7 minutes to cook; 2-pound lobsters take about 10 minutes. If you stack more than 3 or 4 layers of lobsters in the pot, cook for 10 to 12 minutes. To check for doneness, take hold of an antenna and give it a slight tug. If it separates easily, the lobster is cooked. If it is difficult to pull out, continue cooking a few minutes longer.

4. Lift lobster(s) from pot with tongs and place in a colander or on a kitchen towel to drain. Allow lobster to cool 5 to 10 minutes before eating.

Note: If putting a live animal into a steaming pot disturbs you, you can kill the lobster right before cooking it. Place the lobster on a sturdy cutting board stomach side down. Place the point of a long, sharp chef's knife 1 inch behind and in between the lobster's eyes and cut straight down and through the top and bottom shells until the head is split in two. The lobster will die relatively quickly and painlessly.

HOW TO REMOVE MEAT FROM A LOBSTER

After the lobster is cooked, drained, and cooled, twist off the claws and crack lobster shell with a lobster cracker or nutcracker, a small mallet, or the back side of a blade of a heavy knife, working gently to keep from crushing the meat. Place lobster on its back on a kitchen towel (preferably in the sink to catch any spurting water), and split the body and tail with a heavy knife, cutting from the center of the head down to the tail flippers. Pull out the intestinal vein and the stomach sac, a small gritty pouch behind the eyes, and discard. The green tomalley and reddish roe are edible, but avoid the gray, spongy gills. If desired, break off the small legs and suck out the meat and juice.

Lobster Medallions and Couscous Salad with Ginger Vinaigrette

———⟨⟩———

This recipe was inspired by a meal at Campagne, the country-French restaurant located across the courtyard from the Inn at the Market. When I sampled this dish, chef Tamara Murphy draped pieces of succulent lobster meat over a bed of saffron-scented couscous, then drizzled the whole with a light and refreshing ginger vinaigrette. For home cooks, if the cost of real lobster is prohibitive, the salad would work almost as well with surimi lobster.

$^1/_2$ CUP UNSWEETENED RICE VINEGAR

$^1/_2$ TEASPOON SALT

2 TABLESPOONS HONEY

1 TEASPOON GRATED GINGERROOT

$^1/_4$ CUP FRESHLY SQUEEZED LIME JUICE

$^1/_8$ TEASPOON FRESHLY GROUND WHITE
   PEPPER

2 TABLESPOONS ALMOND, SESAME, OR
   CANOLA OIL

3 CUPS SAFFRON COUSCOUS (RECIPE
   FOLLOWS)

4 COOKED LIVE LOBSTERS OR 4 PRECOOKED
   FRESH OR FROZEN THAWED LOBSTERS

4 LARGE, WHOLE BIBB LETTUCE LEAVES OR
   OTHER SOFT LETTUCE LEAVES

CHOPPED FRESH MINT, FOR GARNISH

CHOPPED CILANTRO, FOR GARNISH

1. Place rice vinegar, salt, honey, gingerroot, lime juice, and white pepper in a nonreactive mixing bowl and whisk until honey dissolves. Add almond oil in a thin stream, whisking continuously, until vinaigrette emulsifies (becomes thick and smooth).

2. Prepare couscous and allow to cool. Prepare lobster and allow to cool, then remove meat from body and claws (see page 208), keeping pieces as large as possible.

3. Place a lettuce leaf on an individual plate and mound one-quarter of the couscous in the center. Arrange lobster meat from one lobster over couscous. Drizzle with vinaigrette and sprinkle with mint and cilantro. Repeat with remaining ingredients.

SERVES 4

Saffron Couscous

1 $^1/_4$ CUPS WATER

1 TABLESPOON UNSALTED BUTTER

$^1/_2$ TEASPOON SALT

$^1/_4$ TEASPOON CRUSHED SAFFRON THREADS

$^1/_8$ TEASPOON FRESHLY GROUND WHITE
   PEPPER

1 CUP UNCOOKED COUSCOUS

Bring water, butter, salt, saffron, and white pepper to a boil in a small saucepan. Add couscous and stir. Cover pan, remove from heat, and let stand 5 minutes, or until couscous is tender and liquid is absorbed. Break up couscous with a fork, then allow to cool completely. Refrigerate until ready to use.

MAKES 3 CUPS

Boiled Octopus

———⚭———

I cooked my first octopus on a cold afternoon in Feb-ruary, when a storm was blowing in from the coast. The sheets of rain clattering down the windows and the plaintive wails of the ferry whistles outside seemed somehow fitting as I wrestled with this strange crea-ture. As limp as a rag doll out of water, the minute the octopus hit hot water it plumped up and turned a vivid red. As it continued to cook in the roiling water, the octopus shrank, its skin turned purple-black, and the cooking water leached Easter-egg purple. Just when I thought the creature would never become tender, the meat relaxed and was easily pierced with the tip of a sharp knife—I had conquered the octopus. After cool-ing the animal and scraping away the skin and suck-ers, the white, mild-flavored meat was ready to use.

4 QUARTS WATER

1 1/2 TEASPOONS KOSHER SALT

1 (1 1/2-POUND) RAW OCTOPUS, DEFROSTED
    IF FROZEN, OR 1 1/2 POUNDS RAW SMALL
    OCTOPI (8 TO 10 OUNCES EACH),
    DEFROSTED IF FROZEN

1. Bring water and salt to a boil in a large nonre-active pot. Rinse octopus and cut away the eyes and tough beak if your fishmonger has not al-ready done this. If the octopus is large (1 1/2 pounds), separate the tentacles and head; for smaller octopi, cook whole.

2. Add octopus to pot. When the liquid returns to a boil, decrease heat, cover pot, and simmer for 45 minutes to 1 hour (begin testing after 45 minutes), or until octopus is tender but slightly resistant when poked with the tip of a sharp knife.

3. Allow octopus to cool in the cooking liquid about 40 minutes, then drain cooking liquid and discard. (If you are in a hurry, you can skip this step, but the octopus will be a bit less tender and somewhat more difficult to skin.) Rub and scrape off the loose purple skin with the tip of a small, sharp knife, and cut off suckers, if desired. Rinse well, then cut octopus as needed for your recipe.

FUN FACT

• Because it has no bones in its body (only a spiny beak), a 3-foot octopus can squeeze through a dime-sized hole.

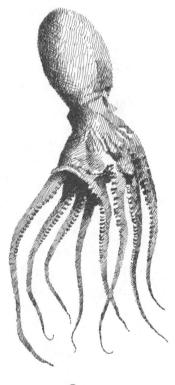

Octopus

Oysters

THE OYSTER IS A BIVALVE, a mollusk with two hinged shells or valves. The shells are rough, craggy, and paisley-shaped. Different from its close relatives the mussel and the clam, the oyster's upper and lower shells are dissimilar. The top shell is flat, while the lower shell is rounded and bowl-shaped, to contain the oyster and its juice. The two shells fit together to form a watertight seal. Near one end of the shell is the powerful adductor muscle, which controls the opening and closing of the shell. The adductor muscle makes shucking oysters difficult, because it must be severed before the oyster body and its delicate liquor are free.

Oysters grow in brackish water and spend their entire adult lives firmly attached to rocks, old shells, or other firm objects in shallow or tidal waters. Oysters are vegetarians, feeding mostly on one-celled plants called diatoms. The diatoms are nourished by various minerals including copper, iron, and iodine, which contribute to the distinct flavor and color of oysters. Feeding on tiny plankton it filters through the water, a single oyster might siphon 20 to 40 gallons of water a day. An oyster's shape, size, color, texture, plumpness, and flavor are defined by the quality of its habitat, which is why the animal is so vulnerable to pollution.

The shape of the oyster depends on the species and how it was grown—whether farmed in suspended trays, sacks, or racks, or left to grow wild in uncultivated clumps. The flavor and texture of the oyster are determined not only by the growing method but by the salinity, nutrients, and minerals present in the water. The taste of oyster varies from one season to the next, sometimes even day to day, depending upon such factors as rainfall and spawning cycles. There are even differences between oysters grown on one end of an inlet to the other.

Whatever the species of oyster, the first note to hit the tongue is sweetness, a taste that comes from glycogen, the starchy white matter in an oyster. After the initial sweetness, oysters can taste salty or briny, or like kelp, iodine, or flinty minerals. Cucumbers, mushrooms, tapioca, watermelon, roses, and toasted nuts are other adjectives used to describe the nearly indescribable taste of oysters. An aftertaste (some say sensation) lingers in the mouth after swallowing oysters. The final impression of an oyster may be strong, bland, metallic, crisp, and clean, or have one or more of these qualities.

The Pacific Northwest is the nation's leading oyster-producing region, edging out the Gulf Coast and Chesapeake Bay areas. And Washington State, where more than 90 percent of all West Coast oysters are grown, produces 9 million pounds of oysters per year. Raking in 40 million dollars annually for its efforts, Washington is the nation's largest oyster-producing state, beating out Louisiana and Maryland. The Northwest harvests 4 of 6 recognizable species of oyster—Kumamoto, European flat, Olympia, and Pacific—nowhere else in the world can claim that many.

Meaty Pacific oysters, which range from California to Alaska and throughout the world, dominate. The native Olympia oyster, a much smaller and less hearty species, can be found in some parts of Washington and British Columbia but is not nearly as common as the Pacific oyster. European flat oysters, also known as Belons or Westcott Bay Euro-Flats, are farmed on both the East and West coasts of the United States. True to their name, the shells of European flat oysters are usually round and fairly flat. The Kumamoto is a small Pacific oyster with a deep-cupped shell to hold the delicate liquor. In addition to these broad species of oysters, dozens of varieties named after their growing area beckon the oyster lover.

More than half of Washington State's production comes from Willapa Bay, a shallow bay on the southwestern Washington coast. Here the cold waters of the Pacific meet the waters of the wild coastal rivers. Much like the bays of France, which are renowned for oyster production, Willapa Bay boasts profuse algae food sources and the cleanest bay of water in all of Puget Sound, the perfect location for growing oysters.

Willapa Bay and other farm-raised oysters are grown using various techniques. The traditional method of cultivating oysters is to grow them behind dikes in the shallow pools of tideland areas. Oysters grown directly on the beach are exposed to the elements of tide, air (at low tide), and the motion of the water. They are generally full flavored and hearty.

In the French table, or rack-and-bag method, oysterlings are placed in large bags of plastic netting that sit on metal racks a foot or more above tidal flats. Because they are not exposed to any of the same elements as beach-grown oysters, their shells are softer and the meat more sweetly flavored.

In the Japanese lantern-net method, oysters are suspended in deep water in long, tubular nylon nets attached to floats which rise and sink with the tide. This allows the oysters to devote their entire energy to rapid growth of firm, fatty meat.

The Pacific oyster (*Crassostrea gigas*), also called the West Coast or Japanese oyster, has a deeply cupped grayish white to dark gray shell with ruffled edges measuring 2 to 10 inches long. The oyster can grow up to 12 inches, live for 20 years or more in the wild, and reach a weight of several pounds, but is best eaten when it is between 2 and 3 inches long. The meat is silver-gray to tan to silver-green. It is mild, sweet-tasting, and rich, with a cucumber aftertaste. Those from California have a slightly more pronounced flavor.

The Pacific oyster was first introduced in Washington State after it was imported from Japan in the early 1900s in an effort to revitalize the West Coast oyster industry. Pacific oysters are sold under many names, including Westcott Bays, Quilcenes, and Willapa Bays. They take three to six years to reach harvestable size.

About 85 percent of Pacifics are sold as shucked meats; the remainder are sold live. Ten years ago, only 5 percent were sold live in the shell; the number has increased due to demand from consumers in Asia and from upscale restaurants in this country. Pacifics are best eaten uncooked on the half shell, or

Pacific Oyster

steamed, grilled, baked, poached, smoked, or fried. Older, larger Pacific oysters are best used in oyster stews and pies.

The Northwest's native Olympia oyster (*Ostrea lurida*) once produced huge harvests, but almost died out due to pollution and overharvesting. Overharvesting took place during the Gold Rush era, when schooners from San Francisco arrived in Seattle, filled their holds with Olympia oysters (sometimes tons at a time), and used them as ballast for the trip south. Many of these oysters were never consumed and simply dumped overboard once ships reached home port. By the early 1900s, the Northwest's native oyster was nearly extinct.

Overharvesting slowed, but emissions from the area's pulp mills became the next threat to the delicate Olympia, and it took 25 years for the crop to recover. Killer frosts, the oyster's own finicky nature, and natural predators have conspired to keep harvests low. Even today the Olympia oyster is considered a rare delicacy, with prices to match.

The Olympia is a much smaller and more delicate mollusk than the large Pacific oysters introduced to the West Coast. Especially popular with first-time oyster eaters, its superb taste more than makes up for its drab exterior—a tiny, round, flat, dark brown to dark green shell, about the size of a quarter. The meat ranges from silver-gray to green and has a robust flavor with a mild coppery aftertaste. It is grown on dikes in Totten Inlet in south Puget Sound. Because of its small size and delicate nature, this oyster must be harvested by hand with the aid of a long-tined fork.

Unlike Pacific oysters, tiny Olympias are rarely cooked and almost always served on the half shell. Because of their size, 13 to 15 oysters are considered "a dozen" and nearly 250 meats are required to fill a single pint. Olympians are available in fall and winter.

The European flat (*Ostrea edulis*) is a flat, round oyster with a dark brownish to greenish craggy shell. It is a close, though larger, relative of the Olympia. This oyster is also sometimes referred to as the Belon oyster, although this is a misnomer, for only oysters actually harvested in the Belon Bay of France's Brittany region are rightfully entitled to use the name. Thankfully, although the European Flat is dwindling in its homeland, it is thriving in Northwest waters.

The meat of the European flat is silvery gray to green, firm and crisp, and must be eaten raw on the half shell. With a mild, sweet, metallic, truly memorable taste, this oyster is well worth the steep price it commands. The European flat oyster is available in fall and winter.

The Kumamoto (*Crassostrea sikamea*) is a relative of the Pacific oyster, although it is smaller in size, has a more complex and delicate flavor, and a more deeply cupped, ridged shell. Although native to Japan, the Kumamoto is now thought to be extinct in its homeland. Introduced to Washington State in the 1940s, the oyster is flourishing both here and in California. Its plump, ivory-colored meat is milder than most Pacific oysters and has a smooth buttery texture, slightly fruity flavor, and sweet, mild aftertaste. Some people also claim the Kumamoto tastes of hazelnuts. It is best eaten fresh on the half shell.

Oysters should be consumed only in months with the letter "r" in them, particularly in December through March. The "r" rule came about because oysters spawn during the summer months of May, June, July, and August. When oysters are spawning, half the oyster's body weight is devoted to reproduction, and the animals consume their glycogen reserves (an animal starch) to produce both sperm and eggs. The by-product of this glycogen consumption is lactic acid (the same acid found in milk), which gives the oysters a milky appearance, makes them mushy, and causes a less assertive flavor. Although spawning oysters are safe to eat, their quality suffers, which is the reason many people prefer to eat oysters only in cooler months.

Generally, East Coast oysters remain in better condition than Pacific oysters during the summer months, so you might try seeking out Chincoteagues or Blue Points instead. Oysters imported from southern hemisphere countries, such as Chile, are also increasingly available during the summer.

When buying fresh oysters, make sure they are still alive. At the fish market, oysters should never be buried in ice, but displayed cup side down on a bed of ice. Ask for the harvest date of the oysters, records of which stores are required to keep. If the oysters have been out of the water more than 10 days, don't buy them. They may not be spoiled, but quality deteriorates over time. Also tap together the shells of two oysters. They should sound solid and compact, like two rocks. If there is a hollow, dull sound, the oyster is dead.

If the shell is damaged around its edges, cracked, or even the slightest bit opened, don't buy the oyster. Any of these characteristics is a sign of moisture loss, lack of quality and freshness, and poor handling. The shells should either be closed tightly or should close readily after being tapped. When selecting oysters, the size of the cup is the best indication for the size of the meat.

Before opening oysters, rinse and scrub the shells under cool running water. Once they are opened, look for lots of clear liquid inside the shell and plump, bright meat. Oyster meats are usually tan or gray, but the color can vary, depending on the animal's diet or certain environmental conditions. Green or reddish pigmentations are harmless and the colors disappear during cooking. However, a pink color and an off odor indicate the presence of yeast; these oysters should be discarded.

If you open an oyster and the meat is dried out, discard the oyster. The meats should have a fresh, mild, saltwater odor. Oysters that have turned bad have a sulfurous smell; if there's any off odor, discard them. Do not wash oysters once they are opened, for their liquid, or "liquor," helps keep them moist and succulent. Once opened, oysters should be eaten within an hour if they are to be served raw.

Oysters are sold live in the shell or as shucked fresh meats. Only live oysters should be consumed raw. Fresh shucked oyster meats should be plump and creamy and packed in their own juices, which should be clear, never cloudy.

Shucked oysters may be frozen for up to 3 months if properly wrapped. Once thawed, the texture of the meat becomes softer and the oysters are not suitable for raw consumption. However, frozen oysters are quite acceptable when they are cooked. Oysters should be frozen immersed in their liquor or water and excess air should be expelled from the containers to provide protection from freezer burn. Frozen oysters on the half shell and oyster meats should always be thawed slowly under refrigeration, normally for 24 hours. Never refreeze thawed oysters.

Unlike Gulf Coast oysters, those from the cooler water of the Pacific Northwest do not carry the toxic organisms known as *Vibrio vulnificus*, which has been responsible for outbreaks of illness. The organism occurs mostly in Gulf of Mexico oysters, and few of those are imported into the Northwest. Anyone concerned about the safety of an oyster should ask to see a purveyor's shellfish shipping certificate, which lists the date of the harvest and origin and verifies safe waters.

The organism *Vibrio parahaemolyticus* has been found occasionally in oysters from Hood Canal and causes flu-like intestinal symptoms, but cooking oysters kills this organism. "Red tide," another harmful organism, occurs in local shellfish periodically and is not killed by cooking. This is more of a problem with shellfish gathered by sport fishers than commercially harvested shellfish. Before harvesting oysters, call the Washington State red tide hotline, (800) 562-5632, to find out if there is an alert.

Live oysters need to breathe. Never store them in airtight bags or containers. Keep live oysters away from fresh water, which will kill them, and out of sunlight. Store live oysters cup side down (flat side up) in a single layer in a shallow pan to keep them bathed in their own natural juices. Cover them loosely with damp paper towels or kitchen towels before

OYSTERS ON THE HALF SHELL

TO OYSTER CONNOISSEURS, the only acceptable way to eat a freshly shucked oyster is by sipping the ice-cold mollusk directly from the shell, liquid, and all. The following instructions explain several different ways to shuck oysters, from traditional to innovative.

TRADITIONAL METHODS (STABBING METHOD, HINGE METHOD)

1. Protect your hand with an oyster mitt, heavy cotton glove, or several layers of kitchen towels. To use the stabbing method, place an oyster in your protected hand with the rounder end down and the oyster hinge facing the lower joint of your thumb. Hold the oyster knife with your other hand and poke the knife tip between the two shells wherever you see an opening (you may need to try several locations). Push the knife into the oyster about ¼ inch and twist gently to pry open the oyster part way. Continue with Step 3.

2. To employ the hinge method, hold the wide or front end of the oyster in the protected hand, rounder end down. Insert oyster knife near the hinge, and apply pressure to slide the knife through the hinge. The shells should pop open slightly.

3. Detach the oyster from its top shell by pointing the tip of the knife upwards and cutting the muscle that holds it in place. Cut carefully or you will slice into the oyster meat.

4. Pry open the oyster completely, then separate the oyster from the bottom shell by cutting around the oyster, again being careful not to cut into the oyster. Work over a bowl to catch any of the oyster liquor that escapes. Carefully twist off the top shell if serving on the half shell, or discard both shells if using in other recipes. If serving on the half shell, before serving, be sure to inspect the oysters carefully and remove any pieces of shell that may have fallen into the oysters.

MICROWAVE METHOD

A short period of microwaving makes oysters open partially before shucking, so this method works well if you're in a hurry or aren't strong enough to shuck oysters conventionally.

1. Place oysters in a microwave-safe glass dish and place in microwave for 5 minutes on WARM.

2. Remove oysters from microwave and shuck immediately as described in Step 3. The oysters will remain uncooked; however, if you wish to cook the oysters completely, microwave them for 3 minutes on HIGH, then pry open and shuck as described in Step 3.

OVEN-AND-ICE METHOD

This method is a viable alternative if you don't have a microwave.

1. Preheat oven to 400°. Prepare a dishpan or sink full of ice water. Adjust oven rack so it is in the center of the oven.

2. Arrange oysters on a baking sheet and place in oven for 5 minutes. Immediately remove oysters and place in the chilled water. Pat dry oysters, then pry open and shuck as described in Step 3.

refrigerating. They will be at their best and most flavorful if shucked within 1 to 2 days but will keep for up to 1 week unshucked.

It is important to closely adhere to the recommended expiration date on containers of shucked oysters. Shucked oysters should be stored in their original container embedded in ice. Stored properly, shucked oysters will stay in good condition for up to 2 weeks, but always try to use them as soon as possible. Raw and cooked oysters should be handled separately to avoid possible cross-contamination.

A dozen oysters on the half shell used to be considered an appetizer-sized serving, but with oysters so expensive nowadays, they are usually sold by the half dozen. When paired with a rich sauce, 3 to 6 oysters are sufficient for an appetizer serving. For 1 person, 8 to 12 oysters is considered a main-course serving when paired with a rich sauce, served in an oyster stew, or combined with a starch such as noodles or rice. A pint of oysters extended with other ingredients will serve 4.

Oysters in the shell can be steamed, baked, roasted, or grilled. Raw oysters on the half shell are best when slurped from the shell just after opening, but they can also be baked or broiled. Shucked oysters can be stewed, poached, battered and fried, sautéed, or skewered and grilled. Large oysters or oysters out of the shell for a few hours are good in stews, chowders, or pies. Very large oysters can be cut into smaller pieces before cooking.

When cooking oysters, do not heat them too quickly or for too long. Oysters lose their color definition when cooked, becoming a dull silver-gray. Pay close attention, for as soon as the mantle around the oyster starts to curl, the oyster is done, regardless of cooking method. Once cooked, serve immediately.

Health guidelines from the Food and Drug Administration recommend the following cooking times for oysters: Cook live oysters (those still in the shell) in boiling water 3 to 5 minutes, or until the shells pop open. Steam live oysters 4 to 9 minutes in a ready steamer. Use small pots to boil or steam oysters. Do not crowd oysters in the pot because the ones in the middle may not get fully cooked. Discard any oysters that do not open during the cooking process.

Shucked oysters should be boiled or simmered for at least 3 minutes, or until the edges curl. Fry shucked oysters in oil for at least 3 minutes at 375°. Broil shucked oysters 3 to 4 inches from the broiler for 3 minutes. Bake shucked oysters for 10 minutes at 450°.

Oysters on the half shell should be shucked and consumed within 5 minutes of opening because they start to fade the moment the muscle is sliced. They are best presented on platters of shaved ice, arranged in a symmetrical circle with their rounded ends pointed outward. Kosher or coarse salt is an alternative to ice if oysters on the half shell are already cold and will be served immediately. If they must be shucked in advance, place ice on a plate or tray, cover it with a doubled kitchen towel, then place the oysters on it so they are not in direct contact with the ice. Cover oysters with aluminum foil or plastic wrap and don't let them sit longer than 1 hour in the refrigerator. Take a moment to "taste the oyster with your fingertips," advises Jon Rowley, Northwest seafood expert, "and feel the chill and roughness of the shell in your hand, then bring the oyster to your nose and sniff." An oyster should always be smelled before it is eaten, for oysters have complex bouquets, just like wines, and unless you savor this harmony of scents, you lose much of the pleasure of eating a fresh oyster.

An oyster should not be swallowed in one gulp, a much too precipitous method of ingestion. Instead, slurp the oyster into your mouth, and carefully chew. The meat and juices should go down together. A bit of bread to neutralize the palate between oysters and a wine that is dry and clean are the only other accompaniments you need.

Pairing the proper wines with oysters has become a passion among Northwest wine connoisseurs because it is such a delicious challenge. All agree that when it comes to wine and oyster pairing, both must be the same temperature—ice cold. Young, lean white wines with crisp acids that slice through the briny, metallic sea flavors of the oysters and refresh the palate routinely win wine and oyster pairing contests. Wines that let the oyster be an oyster are favorites. These include sémillon, sémillon-chardonnay, chardonnay, sauvignon blanc, chenin blanc, fumé blanc, sauvignon blanc-sémillon blends, pinot gris, melon, riesling, and dry riesling. Big, buttery, oaky chardonnays don't do as well.

Some oyster connoisseurs prefer beer with their oysters, particularly stout, porter (the traditional "oyster ale"), and wheat ales.

Some people enjoy light red wines with oysters, especially California beaujolais and California or Oregon pinot noirs. This may make more sense on reflection than it does at first blush, when you consider that *mignonette*, a sauce made of red wine vinegar (see page 222), is a classic with oysters. Cooked oysters are easier to match with drink than raw oysters, because the seasonings that influence a recipe's flavor help determine the beverage choice.

FUN FACTS

- As legend has it, at the height of Gold Rush fever in San Francisco, prospectors who had made their millions in gold paid for a plate of Olympia oysters with 20-dollar gold pieces.

- On the West Coast, Native Americans came from as far north as Alaska to raid the oyster beds in Puget Sound, feasting for days after cooking the oysters over hot coals. On both the Pacific and Atlantic coasts, pre-Columbian Native Americans seem never to have eaten oysters raw, which is one of the reasons they are often credited with inventing American oyster stew.

- The female Pacific oyster may spawn up to 200 million eggs in a season.

- Oysters take anywhere from two years in warm waters to six years in cold waters to grow to marketable sizes. The Pacific oyster takes about two years to reach maturity; the smaller Olympia, four years.

- Legend has it that "Hangtown Fry" was made with Olympia oysters. The concoction of oysters and eggs was invented by a condemned man in a burg called Hangtown (now Placerville), California, when the convict asked for the two most expensive items in town for his final meal.

- Washington territorial politicians were so impressed with the region's native oyster that they dubbed it the "Olympia oyster" in 1889. Not wanting to leave the source of this tasty morsel, and to ensure their personal supply of oysters, they selected Olympia as the capital city of Washington, where it remains to this day.

- Oysters like to change their sex, usually starting out as males, changing to females after a year or two, then switching back to males later in life.

- You can tell an oyster's age by counting the ridges, or shoots, on its shell. Each circle represents a season of growth.

WHERE TO EAT FRESH OYSTERS ON THE HALF SHELL IN SEATTLE

Anthony's Homeport, 6135 Seaview Ave. N.W. (Shilshole Marina) (206) 783-0780, and other locations throughout the Puget Sound area

The Brooklyn Seafood, Steak & Oyster House, 1212 Second Ave. (Downtown) (206) 224-7000

Chandler's Crabhouse and Fresh Fish Market, 901 Fairview Ave. N. (Lake Union) (206) 223-2722

Chinook's at Salmon Bay, 1900 W. Nickerson St. (Fisherman's Terminal) (206) 283-4665

Cutters Bayhouse, 2001 Western Ave. (Downtown) (206) 448-4884

Elliott's Oyster House & Seafood Restaurant, Pier 56, Alaskan Way (Downtown) (206) 623-4340

Emmett Watson's Oyster Bar, 1916 Pike Place, #16 (Pike Place Market) (206) 448-7721

Etta's Seafood, 2020 Western Ave. (Downtown) (206) 443-6000

Flying Fish, 2234 First Ave. (Downtown) (206) 728-8595

F. X. McRory's, 419 Occidental Ave. S. (Downtown, Pioneer Square) (206) 623-4800

Ivar's Acres of Clams, Pier 54, Alaskan Way (Downtown) (206) 624-6852

Jack's Fish Spot, 1514 Pike Place (Pike Place Market) (206) 467-0514

Maximilien-in-the-Market, 81A Pike St. (Pike Place Market) (206) 682-7270

McCormick & Schmick's, 1103 First Ave. (Downtown) (206) 623-5500

McCormick's Fish House and Bar, 722 Fourth Ave. (Downtown) (206) 682-3900

Place Pigalle, 81 Pike St. (Pike Place Market) (206) 624-1756

Ray's Boathouse, 6049 Seaview Ave. N.W. (Shilshole Marina) (206) 789-3770

Salty's on Alki, 1936 Harbor Ave. S.W. (West Seattle) (206) 937-1600

Shuckers, 411 University Ave., Four Seasons Olympic Hotel (Downtown) (206) 621-1984

Baked Oysters

Oysters are one of nature's perfect foods because they come in their own self-contained, self-marinating packages to be cooked right on the grill, in the barbecue, or in the oven. They are great as is or served with a bit of melted butter mixed with Tabasco, Old Bay seasoning, or shichimi togarashi, *a flavorful Japanese spice blend.*

FRESH OYSTERS, SHELLS RINSED AND
   SCRUBBED
ROCK SALT (OPTIONAL)

1. Preheat oven to 400°. Place a cooling rack on a baking sheet. Alternately, sprinkle a jelly roll pan or long, shallow pan with ¹/₂ inch of rock salt, which will help steady the oysters. Place oysters rounded side down (flat side up) evenly spaced over the long, thin crossbars of the rack or the bed of rock salt.

2. Place baking sheet on center rack of oven. Cook 7 to 15 minutes, depending on the size of the oysters, until the shells open slightly, or until steam or bubbles escape around the fluted edges. Do not turn oysters during cooking.

3. Using an oyster knife, prepare oysters as described on page 216. Oysters will open easily when fully cooked. If an oyster is not done to your liking, just return it to the oven and cook and extra minute or two.

ELLIOTT'S ANNUAL OYSTER NEW YEAR'S

ACH YEAR IN LATE October when Northwest skies turn oyster-shell gray, a 6,000-square-foot tent is erected along downtown Seattle's waterfront. For one glorious evening, oyster lovers gather at Pier 56 under the "oyster top" to celebrate the return of West Coast oysters. While moonlight shimmers on the waters of Elliott Bay just outside, the crowds inside get festive at Oyster New Year's, sponsored by Elliott's Oyster House & Seafood Restaurant and benefiting the Pacific Coast Oyster Growers Association.

For 50 dollars, oyster aficionados can eat to their heart's content, choosing from over 30 kinds of freshly shucked oysters on the half shell, and washing them down with specially selected oyster wines, microbrews, and imported beers. Oysters gathered from Northern California, Oregon, Alaska, British Columbia and, of course, Washington, with lyrical names such as Lasquetti Golden, Snow Creek, Pearl Point, and Canoe Lagoon, are the stars of the show.

For the faint of heart, cooked oyster and seafood dishes such as oysters Rockefeller, steamed clams and mussels, shrimp-in-the-shell, and Elliott's signature crab cakes join the groaning board. A live band adds to the lively spirit of the evening as the crowds stroll and eat, thankful to be in the largest oyster-producing region in the United States.

Oyster and Corn Casserole

⸻❦⸻

This traditional recipe comes from A Cook's Tour of the Market, *a self-published cookbook written in the 1970s by Elizabeth Tanner and reissued in 1996 as part of the "Keeping the Market" festivities. The festivities commemorated the twenty-fifth anniversary of the efforts of the Friends of the Market, a citizens group that helped prevent the market's demolition in 1971. By raising public awareness, the Friends brought out 76,000 Seattle voters who passed an initiative that saved the Market from the wrecking ball and established the only historic district in the United States created by citizen vote. The initiative also specified the Market's purpose—as a farmers' market, an incubator for small businesses, and a provider of services and housing for low-income people. Elizabeth suggests serving Oyster and Corn Casserole with a whole baked salmon or a Thanksgiving turkey. It also serves as a simple, filling, and comforting dinner for two when accompanied by steamed kale or Swiss chard and a loaf of crusty bread.*

1 (10-OUNCE) JAR FRESH, SHUCKED EXTRA-
    SMALL OR YEARLING OYSTERS (OR SHUCK
    YOUR OWN OYSTERS OVER A BOWL AND
    SAVE ANY LIQUID THAT ESCAPES)

3/4 CUP WHOLE MILK

4 TABLESPOONS BUTTER

1 TABLESPOON ALL-PURPOSE FLOUR

1/2 CUP DRY UNSEASONED BREAD CRUMBS,
    FINELY GROUND

1 (15 1/2-OUNCE) CAN CORN, DRAINED

SALT AND FRESHLY GROUND BLACK PEPPER

1. Preheat oven to 400°. Generously coat a 1-quart baking dish with butter or nonstick cooking spray.

2. Place a fine-meshed sieve over a measuring cup and drain oysters. Reserve oysters, then add enough whole milk to oyster liquor to make 1 cup liquid. Set aside.

3. In a small skillet or saucepan, melt 2 tablespoons of the butter over low heat and stir in flour until it forms a paste. Gradually add the oyster liquid, stirring continuously to avoid lumps from forming. Cook and stir until smooth and thick, about 5 minutes, and reserve.

4. Place bread crumbs in a medium bowl. Melt the remaining 2 tablespoons butter and add to bread crumbs. Pat half the crumb mixture in the bottom of prepared baking dish. Layer corn, reserved oysters, and reserved cream sauce over crumbs. Add salt and black pepper to taste. Sprinkle remaining crumbs on top and bake until lightly browned, about 20 to 25 minutes.

SERVES 4 AS AN APPETIZER OR SIDE DISH, 2 AS
AN ENTRÉE

Oysters on the Half Shell with Mignonette Ice

CAMPAGNE,
PIKE PLACE MARKET

Campagne chef Tamara Murphy, winner of the James Beard Foundation's Best American Chef, Pacific Northwest Region award for 1995, uses the bounty of the Market to create exquisite Provençal cuisine with Mediterranean influences that she serves to guests in this country-French restaurant overlooking the hustle and bustle of Pike Place. Here, keeping in mind that oysters on the half shell should be served very, very cold, she takes the traditional mignonette sauce, adds pinot noir, and freezes the mixture to create a bracing twist on the French classic.

1 CUP GOOD-QUALITY RED WINE VINEGAR

1/2 CUP PINOT NOIR

1 TABLESPOON FINELY DICED SHALLOT

1 TEASPOON SALT

FRESHLY GROUND BLACK PEPPER

ROCK SALT

24 YEARLING OYSTERS IN THE SHELL,
SHUCKED IMMEDIATELY BEFORE SERVING
(SEE PAGE 216)

1. Stir together red wine vinegar, pinot noir, shallot, salt, and pepper in a small nonreactive mixing bowl until salt is dissolved. Place mixture in a shallow pan and freeze, uncovered, for 2 to 3 hours, scraping with a fork every 1/2 hour to break up ice crystals. After undergoing this procedure, the ice should be flaky.

2. Immediately before serving, divide oysters on the half shell among plates lined with a bed of rock salt, then put a small ramekin of ice in the center of each plate.

SERVES 4 AS AN APPETIZER

BARBECUED OYSTERS

TO BARBECUE OYSTERS, prepare barbecue or grill. Place oysters on ungreased barbecue or grill 4 inches from hot coals or heat element. Be sure oysters are rounded side down so they cook in their own juices. If using a barbecue with a hood, lower hood. If using a grill, loosely cover oysters with a tent of aluminum foil. Cook 7 to 15 minutes, depending on the size of the oysters. Do not turn oysters during cooking. Shells may open slightly when oysters are done, but not always. Look for steam or bubbles around the fluted edges as a signal that they are ready.

Margaret's Oyster Stew

———✦———

This recipe comes from Margaret Wherrette, a co-author of The Market Notebook, *a Pike Place Market cookbook published in 1980. As she says in her recipe introduction, "After work on a cold night, this is an excellent choice for dinner—it takes only 10 minutes from start to finish. Be sure to serve with Trenton Oyster Crackers (available at DeLaurenti Specialty Foods in the Market); these are the real oyster crackers, hard all the way through, not hollow, saltine-like crackers."*

1/4 CUP BUTTER

1 TEASPOON SWEET PAPRIKA

4 TEASPOONS WORCESTERSHIRE SAUCE

GENEROUS PINCH OF GROUND CAYENNE
     PEPPER OR TO TASTE

2 (10-OUNCE) JARS FRESH, SHUCKED
     EXTRA-SMALL OR YEARLING OYSTERS,
     DRAINED

4 CUPS WHOLE MILK OR HALF-AND-HALF

SALT TO TASTE

1. In a medium saucepan, heat butter, paprika, Worcestershire sauce, and cayenne over medium heat until butter melts. Add oysters and cook 2 to 3 minutes, or until oysters plump and edges curl.

2. Add milk and heat until tiny bubbles form around the edges of saucepan. Do not allow milk to boil or oysters will toughen. Season to taste with salt and additional cayenne pepper, if desired.

SERVES 4

Variation: One dreary evening when I didn't have any fresh oysters in the house but wanted a seafood stew, I prepared Margaret's recipe using the following substitutions, with delicious results. Substitute 4 cups evaporated skim milk for the whole milk or half-and-half, with 1 cup clam juice added. Substitute 1 cup fresh chopped salmon fillet (skin and bones removed) for the oysters. Prepare soup as directed, adding chopped fresh salmon and cook 5 minutes instead of 2 or 3 minutes. Add the evaporated milk mixture and bring to just below a boil. Add 1/4 cup diced hot-smoked (kippered) salmon (skin and bones removed) and cook 1 minute more, or until smoked salmon is warmed through. Remove from heat and serve immediately.

SERVES 4

Fried Oyster Caesar Salad

—⚓—

Fried oysters are inherently rich, but I assuage the guilt by serving the crispy bites with lots of greens and a lightened Caesar-style dressing for an unusual main dish salad. The greens are served whole instead of torn. For a fun, informal meal, encourage friends and family to pick up the leaves and dip them in the dressing before munching away.

24 FRESH OYSTERS IN THE SHELL, OR 1
   (10-OUNCE) JAR FRESH, SHUCKED OYS-
   TERS, JUICED DRAINED THROUGH A FINE
   SIEVE AND RESERVED
1 CUP ALL-PURPOSE FLOUR OR CORNMEAL
1 TEASPOON SWEET PAPRIKA
1/4 TEASPOON SALT
1/4 TEASPOON FRESHLY GROUND WHITE
   PEPPER OR BLACK PEPPER
PEANUT OIL FOR FRYING
1 HEAD ROMAINE LETTUCE, RINSED,
   DRAINED, SPUN DRY, AND SEPARATED
   INTO INDIVIDUAL LEAVES
1 HEAD RED LEAF LETTUCE, RINSED,
   DRAINED, SPUN DRY, AND SEPARATED
   INTO INDIVIDUAL LEAVES
LIGHTENED CAESAR DRESSING (RECIPE
   FOLLOWS)

1. Shuck oysters (see page 216) over a bowl to catch as much of the oyster liquor as possible. Discard top and bottom shells, and reserve oysters and their liquor.

2. On a piece of waxed paper, mix together flour, sweet paprika, salt, and white pepper. Dredge oysters in seasoned flour, then shake well to remove excess.

3. Pour 1/8 inch oil into a large skillet or wok. Heat over medium-high heat until almost smoking. Add oysters and cook 1 to 2 minutes per side, or until oysters are golden in color. Do not overcook or oysters will become tough. As oysters finish cooking, transfer to a plate lined with several layers of paper towels to drain excess oil.

4. Place several whole romaine and red leaf lettuce leaves on individual plates. Position 6 oysters around the perimeter of each plate, and a ramekin of Caesar dressing on the side for dunking oysters and lettuce leaves.

SERVES 4

Lightened Caesar Dressing

1/4 CUP DEFATTED CHICKEN STOCK
1/4 CUP RESERVED OYSTER LIQUOR (ADD
   ADDITIONAL CHICKEN STOCK OR CLAM
   JUICE TO MAKE 1/4 CUP, IF NECESSARY)
1/4 CUP FRESHLY SQUEEZED LEMON JUICE
2 TABLESPOONS CAPERS, MINCED
2 CLOVES GARLIC, MINCED
1/4 TEASPOON SALT
1/2 TEASPOON FRESHLY GROUND BLACK
   PEPPER
1/2 TEASPOON WHITE OR DARK WORCESTER-
   SHIRE SAUCE
1/4 CUP FRESHLY GRATED PARMESAN OR
   PARMIGIANO-REGGIANO CHEESE
2 TABLESPOONS EXTRA VIRGIN OLIVE OIL

In a small mixing bowl or a small jar with a lid, add chicken stock, oyster liquor, lemon juice, capers, garlic, salt, pepper, Worcestershire sauce, and Parmesan cheese. Stir or shake well. Whisk in olive oil or shake until well blended.

MAKES 1 CUP

Oysters Chez Shea

CHEZ SHEA,
PIKE PLACE MARKET

Chez Shea is a romantic hideaway perched above the Market in the historic Corner Market Building, constructed in 1912. Through towering arched windows, diners have a bird's-eye view of the famous Market clock (reputed to be the oldest neon sign in Seattle) and the ferryboats and tankers that ply Elliott Bay. The restaurant's French-inspired four-course, prix fixe menu reflects the bounty of the season, with ingredients fresh from the Market stalls below, where you'll often find chef Peter Morrison. He reports that the crowds part quickly when he's carrying a 17-pound salmon, because people don't want to get "slimed." This recipe is best made in the winter months when oysters are in top form and plentiful. Chef Morrison suggests serving them with Champagne or sparkling wine.

ROCK SALT OR DRIED BEANS

12 FRESH YEARLING OYSTERS IN THE
    SHELL, SHELLS SCRUBBED

1/2 TEASPOON VEGETABLE OIL

1 1/2 TEASPOONS MINCED GINGERROOT

1 TABLESPOON FRESHLY SQUEEZED LIME
    JUICE

1 CUP COCONUT MILK

1 TABLESPOON MAPLE SYRUP

1/4 TEASPOON CRUSHED RED PEPPER
    FLAKES, PLUS ADDITIONAL FOR GARNISH

SALT AND FRESHLY GROUND BLACK PEPPER
    TO TASTE

2 TABLESPOONS MINCED CILANTRO, PLUS
    ADDITIONAL SPRIGS, FOR GARNISH

LIME WEDGES

1. Cover a rimmed baking sheet with 1/2 inch of rock salt or dried beans. Shuck oysters (see page 216) over a bowl to catch as much of the oyster liquor as possible. Place oysters in a separate bowl and refrigerate oysters and juice until ready to use. Reserve bottom oyster shells. Heat a small pot of water to boiling, then boil reserved oyster shells 2 minutes to disinfect. Drain well, dry shells, place on prepared baking sheet, and set aside for later use.

2. Heat vegetable oil in a small saucepan over medium-high heat. Add gingerroot and cook for 1 minute, stirring often. Add lime juice and swirl pan to mix. Add coconut milk, maple syrup, red pepper flakes, and reserved oyster juice. Bring sauce to a boil, decrease heat to simmer, and cook 3 to 5 minutes, or until sauce coats the back of a spoon. Season to taste with salt and black pepper.

3. Add oysters to sauce and cook 2 to 3 minutes, or until oysters plump and edges curl. Remove from heat and spoon oysters into reserved shells. Spoon additional sauce over oysters and sprinkle with cilantro and red pepper flakes, for garnish.

4. To serve, divide oysters and lime wedges among individual plates.

SERVES 4 AS AN APPETIZER

Oyster Fritters
Shelton Style

———⚓———

I sampled these oyster fritters in person at the Shelton OysterFest—they were hot, plump, and delicious as prepared by the Shelton Rotary.

1 POUND FRESHLY SHUCKED OYSTERS OR
    2 (10-OUNCE) JARS FRESH, SHUCKED
    OYSTERS

3 1/2 CUPS ALL-PURPOSE FLOUR

2 TEASPOONS OLD BAY SEASONING

1 TEASPOON REGULAR-GRIND BLACK
    PEPPER PLUS 1 TEASPOON COARSELY
    GROUND BLACK PEPPER

1 TEASPOON SALT

2 TEASPOONS GARLIC POWDER

1 TEASPOON ACCENT OR MONOSODIUM
    GLUTAMATE (OPTIONAL)

1/2 TEASPOON BAKING POWDER

3 GREEN ONIONS, OR 4 SHALLOTS, MINCED

2 CLOVES GARLIC, MINCED

2 TABLESPOONS CHOPPED FRESH PARSLEY

2 TO 2 1/2 CUPS BEER

PEANUT OR VEGETABLE OIL, FOR DEEP-
    FRYING

1. Drain oysters and pat dry. Mix together 1 cup of the flour, the seafood seasoning, the 1 teaspoon regular-grind black pepper, and salt, and place on a plate or piece of waxed paper. Dredge oysters in mixture, setting aside on a plate or baking sheet as they are dusted with flour.

2. Mix the remaining 2 1/2 cups flour with the garlic powder, the 1 teaspoon coarsely ground black pepper, the Accent, and baking powder and stir well. Add green onions, garlic, and parsley, and toss to mix.

3. Add 1 cup of the beer and stir well. Continue adding beer 1/2 cup at a time, stirring after each addition, until batter becomes smooth and reaches the consistency of pancake batter. You may not need to use the final 1/2 cup beer, depending on moisture of flour and humidity of air.

4. In a large, deep saucepan or a wok, heat several inches of peanut oil to 375°. One by one, dredge oysters in batter, shaking off excess, and place in hot oil. Cook 2 minutes, or until golden brown and crisp on both sides, turning once. Remove with a slotted spoon and place on several layers of paper towels to drain. Serve immediately.

SERVES 4

SHELTON OYSTERFEST

SINCE 1982 the Skookum Rotary Club has hosted the annual Washington State Seafood Festival and West Coast Oyster Shucking Championships. Affectionately referred to by locals as "OysterFest," the biggest festival of its kind on the West Coast takes place at the Mason County Fairgrounds, just north of Shelton, Washington, and about 85 miles southwest of Seattle, on the first full weekend in October. The friendly faces behind the seafood stands are members of non-profit groups such as the Lions and Rotary clubs that serve Mason County residents.

About 25,000 visitors celebrate the bounty produced by the local aquaculture industry as they eat their way through the OysterFest each year. Oysters are presented in many guises—on the half shell, wrapped in bacon, raw as "shooters" with cocktail sauce, in Cajun oyster sandwiches, in oyster stew, grilled and barbecued, in oyster fritters, and scalded.

The scalded oysters, prepared by the Hood Canal Lions Club, were my favorite among the dozens of oysters I sampled one chilly, sunny day. Fresh, well-scrubbed oysters in the shell were dropped into a huge cauldron of boiling water spiked with oyster boil. When I asked for the recipe, a quick conference among the Lions determined that vinegar, rock salt, and chopped celery (or celery seeds, depending on which Lion I talked to) figured in the mix. When I pressed the Lions for exact proportions, the chief Lion told me that nobody knew

for sure exactly what or how much was in the oyster boil. If you try this recipe at home, taste the cooking liquid before you add the oysters. If it's salty, acidic, and bracing, you've probably got it just about right.

Oysters are not the only seafood to shine in the spotlight at the festival. Other seafood favorites such as clam chowder, steamed clams, assorted seafood hors d'oeuvres, barbecued salmon, smoked trout, clam linguine, shrimp gumbo, and fish-and-chips are also available for sampling.

Exhibits at OysterFest include geoduck and seaweed aquaculture, clam harvesting, shellfish-opening demonstrations, habitat protection, and seafood cookery. A touch-tank aquarium arranged by tidal zones beckons both the young and young-at-heart to get up close and personal with a starfish, oyster, sea cucumber, or hermit crab.

The OysterFest Cook-Off is another integral part of the festival, with a panel of distinguished professional chefs judging amateur and professional recipes, which become part of the official *OysterFest Cookbook*. The oyster shucking contest attracts professional and amateur shuckers from up and down the West Coast. Novices can also try their hands at oyster shucking and are awarded certificates proving their prowess.

With so many fun-filled events in store, the Shelton Oysterfest is a family-oriented, all-American affair that showcases the best of the Northwest seafood bounty.

Scallops

THE SCALLOP IS unique among mollusks, for unlike its bivalve relatives—clams, mussels, and oysters—nearly all adult scallops can swim freely through the water. The scallop moves about by opening its shell and clapping it shut again, thus expelling jets of water than propel it up and off the sea floor. This constant action results in the development of the adductor muscle, or "eye," the fleshy, drum-shaped disk that we think of as the scallop. The adductor opens and closes the thin, winglike shells of the scallop and is the key to the animal's rather awkward flight.

Of the nearly 400 species of scallops found worldwide, only about a dozen are harvested commercially. Europeans and Asians eat the entire contents of the scallop and find it exceptionally tasty. Scallops are frequently sold live in their shells in these parts of the world. In the United States, only the adductor muscle is eaten, not only due to American sensibility, but for practical reasons.

Scallops cannot completely close their shells, and, once out of water, quickly lose moisture and die. Scallops survive for only 4 or 5 days when left in the shell. Shucking the scallop after harvest maintains the body moisture and the freshness of the catch for up to 2 weeks.

Pink (singing) scallops (*Chlamys rubida*) are small bivalves with a pale pink and white ribbed shell that measures up to 3 inches across. They are common in the inland waters of the Northwest but must be harvested by divers from depths of 30 to 180 feet, so they appear rather sporadically and are sometimes of suspect quality when they do. They were first called "steamer scallops," an allusion to steamer clams. When that name didn't catch on, they were renamed singing scallops because their shells, which open and close as they jet through the water, cause them to look like mouths singing in the silence of the ocean.

Singing scallops are a Northwest phenomenon, a novel, fun item to try. They are good to eat (bright orange roe and all, if you're brave!) after being steamed in the shell in a light broth or shucked and used in any type of scallop recipe.

Make sure singing scallops are alive when you buy them. They are best when served 3 to 4 days once they are out of the water. The shells will gape slightly but should close slowly when you touch them. About 22 singing scallops make a pound, enough for a hearty appetizer for two, or an entrée for one.

The Pacific sea scallop (*Patinopecten caurinus*), also known as the Alaska or weathervane scallop, is about the same size at the Atlantic sea scallop and of similar flavor and sweetness. It is found from Alaska to Oregon, harvested commercially in deep water offshore.

Available primarily in the Northwest at

specialty seafood stores and upscale supermarkets, it is a very high-quality product, frozen at sea within hours of harvesting, which can result in a superior product to fresh scallops. Because it is large in size, rich in taste, and chemical-free (never having been soaked in phosphates), the Pacific sea scallop commands prices comparable to Atlantic sea scallops. From 10 to 30 scallops comprise a pound. They are available on and off during the year, particularly July through December.

Bay scallops (*Argopecten irradians*) are found on the East Coast, although because of their dwindling numbers, most of the bay scallops available in the United States come frozen from China, where they are farm-raised.

The shell of the bay scallop measures 2 to 3 inches in diameter and yields meats up to $1/2$ inch across. They are ivory in color, with a slight golden tone. From 60 to 120 meats make up a pound.

Bay scallops have a delicate, sweet flavor and cook in 30 seconds to 4 minutes. Portioned by nature into bite-sized pieces, they are perfect for stir-frying and are also good in salads, casseroles, soups, and stews. Steaming, poaching, sautéing, and baking are other preferred methods of cooking bay scallops.

Sea scallops (*Placopecten magellanicus*) are found on the East and West coasts of the United States, as well as in Alaska and Canada. The Atlantic sea scallop is the best known and most widely available sea scallop in the United States. Shells measure up to 9 inches in diameter, with meats 1 to $1 1/2$ inches across and about as thick. From 5 to as many as 35 scallops can make up a pound.

Sea scallops have a fuller flavor than bay scallops and a rich ivory color. Because of their large size, sea scallops are well suited to pan-frying, grilling, or broiling or recipes where high heat or longer cooking is involved. Other favorite techniques for cooking sea scallops include steaming, sautéing, poaching, baking, oven-frying, deep-frying, skewering as kebabs, or adding to soups and stews. Sea scallops cook in 4 to 6 minutes.

When buying scallops, look for firm meats that hold their shape, are slightly sticky, and are free of excess liquid. Scallops range in color from creamy white to light tan, sometimes with a pinkish hue. A pinkish orange mottling will sometimes occur when the meat is stained by the roe. This is harmless and does not affect quality.

Scallops should be translucent; if they look "too" white, they may have been soaked in chemicals during processing to reduce water loss and improve shelf life. Soaked (as opposed to "dry") scallops will excrete a milky

Sea Scallop

white liquid and feel slimy. They should be avoided, not only because of the added chemicals to which some people may be sensitive, but because they expel excess liquid when cooked and end up steaming, rather than sautéing. Fresh scallops will be shiny; a dull exterior indicates age.

Fresh scallops have a sweet, briny aroma. First-time buyers are sometimes surprised by the distinctive odor of scallops, but a strong odor doesn't mean poor quality; rather, a sour, iodine-like, or sulfur smell is a sign of trouble. A hearty smell is to be expected and is desired.

Live scallops in the shell appreciate a cold, damp environment and should be stored in the refrigerator in an open container. Place a damp towel on the bottom of the container to collect any juice that the scallops discharge, and lay another damp towel loosely over the top of the container. Live scallops will survive out of water for only 4 to 5 days at most; therefore, it's best to eat them the same day you purchase them.

Shucked scallops may be frozen up to 3 months if properly wrapped. They should be thawed in the refrigerator, then used like fresh ones. Refrigerate fresh or defrosted scallops sealed in a plastic bag placed over ice in a pan. Pour off water and replenish ice as it melts, and keep no more than 2 days after purchase, preferably only 1 day.

One appetizer serving is $1^{1}/_{2}$ to 3 ounces of shelled scallops; 4 to 6 ounces are an entrée portion. One pound of scallops will serve 3 to 4 people, particularly if combined in pasta or rice dishes, although 6 ounces per person is a more generous serving. Try choosing scallops of uniform size so they cook evenly, or cut them to similar size. To make large scallops cook more quickly, thin them by slicing crosswise into $^{1}/_{4}$- to $^{1}/_{2}$-inch disks, also called scallop coins. For live scallops, $^{1}/_{2}$ pound is an appetizer serving; 1 pound makes a hearty entrée.

When properly cooked, scallops have a juicy, rich texture that's succulent and velvety. When overcooked, they're like little rubber balls. Scallops cook extremely quickly (especially the small bay scallops), so the trick is to take them off the heat just as they lose their translucence, or when the outer surface of the meats turns opaque.

Don't worry if the scallops seem underdone in the middle—that preserves their texture and flavor. If you're unsure, cut a scallop in half to test for doneness. And don't forget: Because scallop meats are perfectly safe to eat raw, undercooking is preferable to overcooking.

Before sautéing or stir-frying, pat scallops dry to avoid spatters. Make sure the pan and oil you cook in are both very hot before you add the scallops. Scallops should sizzle and brown quickly, otherwise the meats will lose their natural juices. Small bay scallops take only 1 to 2 minutes to sauté; sea scallops require no more than 4 to 5 minutes. Add a minute when poaching, and subtract a minute when broiling or grilling. And unless a recipe requires it, do not cook scallops in advance or hold them on the heat after cooking; they will exude their juices and become dry.

FUN FACT

- The Chinese bay scallop industry began with 26 scallops that survived the arduous trip from Massachusetts to China. Today, Chinese farms produce over 400,000 tons per year.

Scallops St. Jacques

PURE FOOD FISH, PIKE PLACE MARKET

This recipe combines the best aspects of the elegant French Coquille St. Jacques and the homey English shepherd's pie. Devised by a local chef and John Russell, one of my favorite fishmongers at Pure Food Fish in the Market, this comfort food for seafood lovers is a good way to use up leftovers, particularly leftover bacon and mashed potatoes. Guaranteed to chase away the chill of our Northwest winters, the scallops are best served with a green salad and crusty bread.

3 SLICES MEATY BACON (OPTIONAL)

1 CUP HEAVY WHIPPING CREAM

2 TABLESPOONS UNSALTED BUTTER

3 CLOVES GARLIC, MINCED

$\frac{1}{3}$ CUP DRY WHITE WINE

$\frac{1}{4}$ TEASPOON SALT

$\frac{1}{8}$ TEASPOON FRESHLY GROUND WHITE PEPPER

1 POUND BAY SCALLOPS, RINSED, DRAINED, AND PATTED DRY

1 CUP SHUCKED FRESH PEAS OR THAWED FROZEN PEAS

2 CUPS COOKED MASHED POTATOES, SEASONED TO TASTE WITH SALT AND PEPPER

1. Preheat oven to 350°. Grease a casserole dish that will hold scallops in a single layer lightly with butter or spray with nonstick cooking spray. Set aside. If using bacon, cook in a small skillet over medium-high heat until well browned. Crumble and set aside.

2. Place whipping cream, butter, garlic, and wine in a medium saucepan and bring to a boil over medium-high heat. Reduce mixture by half, stirring frequently so cream does not boil over, then remove pan from heat and stir in salt and pepper. Add bacon (if using), scallops, and peas, making sure to completely coat ingredients with cream sauce.

3. Pour scallops into prepared casserole dish and cover completely with mashed potatoes. Bake 15 minutes, or until mashed potatoes begin to look dry. Switch oven to broil and broil potatoes 3 to 4 inches from heat source until they turn golden brown around the edges, about 5 minutes.

4. Bring casserole to the table and serve family style.

SERVES 4

FUN FACT

- The scallop's body is a bit of an enigma. Like other bivalves, scallops have no head. But they can have up to 100 eyes, which are arranged like tiny strands of beads along the outer edge of the scallop's mantle. Scallop eyes have a cornea, lens, retina, and an optic nerve, yet they cannot distinguish form, only light and movement. Divers searching for scallops often look for shiny rows of beady little eyes that peer out from under the edges of the half-opened scallop shells. Besides numerous eyes, the scallop's body is made up of gills, an intestinal tract, roe, and testes (the scallop is a hermaphrodite) wrapped around the adductor muscle.

Sea Scallops and Snow Pea Bisque

—⚓—

FOUR SEASONS OLYMPIC HOTEL, SEATTLE, WASHINGTON

Brooke Vosika, executive sous chef at the Four Seasons Olympic, taught me almost as much about working with scallops as he did about soups. Use the freshest scallops you can find for this recipe, since their essence is so important to the final taste of the bisque. Oysters or shrimp could also substitute for the scallops. Make this elegant bisque in the spring or summer when snow peas are tender.

1 POUND SEA SCALLOPS, RINSED, DRAINED, AND PATTED DRY

1 TABLESPOON PLUS 1/4 TEASPOON OLIVE OIL

1 SMALL ONION, DICED

2 RIBS CELERY, CHOPPED

2 SHALLOTS, CHOPPED

2 CLOVES GARLIC, CRUSHED

1 SPRIG OF FRESH ROSEMARY, ABOUT 3 TO 4 INCHES IN LENGTH

1 CUP WHITE DRY VERMOUTH

3 CUPS HOMEMADE OR STORE-BOUGHT VEGETABLE STOCK

1 CUP HEAVY WHIPPING CREAM, HALF-AND-HALF, OR WHOLE MILK

1/2 POUND SNOW PEAS, RINSED, DRAINED, PATTED DRY, AND STRINGS REMOVED

1/2 CUP LOOSELY PACKED SPINACH LEAVES, RINSED, DRAINED, AND PATTED DRY

SALT AND FRESHLY GROUND BLACK PEPPER TO TASTE

PADDLEFISH CAVIAR, FOR GARNISH

1. Reserve the 4 most attractive scallops for garnish. Place in a small bowl, cover, and refrigerate for later use.

2. Heat 1 tablespoon of the olive oil in a large saucepan or Dutch oven over medium-high heat. Add onions, celery, shallots, garlic, and rosemary and cook 5 to 7 minutes, or until onions are translucent, stirring often. Add scallops and cook 5 to 7 minutes more, or until scallops shrink and crack around the edges, stirring occasionally.

3. Add vermouth and vegetable stock, stir well, and bring mixture to a boil. Cook about 20 minutes, or until reduced by half. Add cream, decrease heat, and simmer 20 minutes.

4. Remove scallops and rosemary sprig and discard. Add snow peas and spinach, stir, and simmer 1 to 2 minutes, or until snow peas are tender. If snow peas are tough, cook a bit longer.

5. Using a large ladle, add soup to a food processor or blender and process in batches until smooth. When all soup is puréed, return to pot and season to taste with salt and pepper. Cover pot and keep warm over very low heat.

6. Heat a small nonstick skillet over medium heat. When pan is hot, add remaining 1/4 teaspoon olive oil and heat until smoking. Add the four reserved scallops and cook 2 minutes. Turn and cook 1 to 2 minutes more, or until scallops are white on the outside, but still raw in the middle. Remove immediately from pan and keep warm.

7. To serve, ladle soup into individual bowls. Garnish each bowl with a sea scallop topped with a dollop of paddlefish caviar.

SERVES 4 AS AN APPETIZER

Singing Scallops Steamed with Fresh Fennel

FRIDAY HARBOR HOUSE, FRIDAY HARBOR, WASHINGTON

Greg Atkinson lives in Friday Harbor in Washington's San Juan Islands, where he established dinner programs at the Mariella Inn and at Friday Harbor House. He currently serves as consulting chef at the venerable Canlis restaurant in Seattle, where his dishes reflect a passion for Northwest ingredients and an appreciation for classic techniques. In this simple presentation, singing scallops are showcased in a light, aromatic steaming liquid.

2 POUNDS LIVE SINGING SCALLOPS, RINSED
   AND SHELLS SCRUBBED

1 CUP WHITE WINE

1 CUP THINLY SLICED FRESH FENNEL BULB,
   OR 2 TEASPOONS FENNEL SEED

2 CLOVES GARLIC, CHOPPED

FRESHLY GROUND BLACK PEPPER TO TASTE

SPRAYS OF FRESH FENNEL LEAVES FOR
   GARNISH (OPTIONAL)

1. Place scallops, white wine, fennel, garlic, and pepper in a large saucepan and bring to a boil over high heat. Cover and cook 5 to 6 minutes, or until shells open. Discard any scallops that do not open.

2. Transfer scallops and steaming liquid to a large communal bowl, or divide among 4 individual bowls. If desired, garnish with sprays of fresh fennel leaves.

SERVES 4 AS AN APPETIZER, 2 AS AN ENTRÉE

SHUCKERS' SCALLOP AND SPINACH SALAD

THIS CASUAL seafood restaurant in the Four Seasons Olympic Hotel in downtown Seattle serves one of my favorite seafood salads. A bed of baby spinach leaves perfectly washed and dried is sprinkled with chunks of Gorgonzola cheese (Oregon Blue would substitute nicely) and chopped tomatoes, then pan-seared scallops are placed atop the spinach leaves. A light tomato-basil vinaigrette completes the dish.

To pan-sear the scallops, heat a nonstick skillet over medium heat. When pan is hot, add $1/2$ to 1 teaspoon olive oil and heat until smoking. Add the sea scallops and cook 2 minutes. Turn and cook 1 to 2 minutes more, or until scallops are white on the outside, but still raw in the middle. Remove immediately from pan and arrange atop salad.

Thai Curry Scallops

FLYING FISH,
SEATTLE, WASHINGTON

Ever since chef/owner Christine Keff opened Flying Fish in the artsy Belltown section of downtown Seattle in the summer of 1995, this seafood lover's paradise has received acclaim not only locally from the readers of Seattle Weekly, but nationally, from Bon Appetit, Gourmet, and the Television Food Network. Many of the menu items are Asian because chef Keff feels that Asian flavors are cleaner and simpler, less likely to obscure the taste of seafood.

Fresh green curry paste is a staple in Thai cooking. This recipe calls for such unusual ingredients as galanga root and fresh turmeric. Although not widely available, fresh or fresh-frozen turmeric can sometimes be found in Asian markets or at Asian wholesale food distributors; if unavailable, the recipe is easily altered as shown.

2 TABLESPOONS PEANUT OIL

20 LARGE SEA SCALLOPS, RINSED,
   DRAINED, AND PATTED DRY

3 TABLESPOONS CURRY PASTE (RECIPE
   FOLLOWS)

2/3 CUP CHICKEN STOCK

1/2 CUP COCONUT MILK

SALT TO TASTE

1. Heat a large nonstick skillet over medium heat. When pan is hot, add oil. When oil begins to smoke, remove pan from heat and quickly add scallops one at a time. Return pan to heat and cook 2 minutes. Turn scallops and cook 2 minutes, or until opaque on the outside, but still slightly translucent in the middle.

2. Remove scallops to a warm plate and cover to keep warm. Discard extra oil from skillet, add curry paste, and cook 1 minute over medium heat, stirring continuously. Do not allow curry paste to brown. Add chicken stock, bring to a boil, and reduce by half. Add coconut milk, stir, and continue to reduce until sauce thickens enough to coat the back of a spoon. Season to taste with salt.

3. To serve, divide scallops among individual plates and pour sauce over scallops.

SERVES 4

Curry Paste

2 OUNCES PEELED FRESH GALANGA ROOT,
   CUT INTO CHUNKS

2 OUNCES PEELED GINGERROOT, CUT INTO
   CHUNKS

2 OUNCES PEELED FRESH OR FROZEN
   TURMERIC ROOT, CUT INTO CHUNKS, OR
   AN EXTRA 1 OUNCE EACH FRESH
   GALANGA ROOT AND FRESH GINGERROOT
   PLUS 1/2 TEASPOON GROUND TURMERIC
   FOR COLOR

2 OUNCES PEELED SHALLOTS

1/2 HEAD GARLIC, CLOVES PEELED

1 CUP LOOSELY PACKED COARSELY CHOPPED
   CILANTRO (1/2 BUNCH), STEMS INCLUDED

2 THAI CHILE PEPPERS, RINSED AND PAT-
   TED DRY, STEMS REMOVED, SEEDS AND
   MEMBRANE LEFT INTACT

JUICE OF ONE LIME

PEANUT OIL

Place galanga root, gingerroot, turmeric root, shallots, garlic, cilantro, peppers, and lime juice in a food processor and pulse to break up vegetables into very small pieces. Drizzle in just enough peanut oil to make a paste and continue to process until paste is fairly smooth. Leftover curry paste keeps for 2 to 3 weeks in the refrigerator and is great added to other recipes, such as stirred into the water used to cook rice, in soups, or in other curry dishes.

MAKES 1 ½ CUPS

Note: Turmeric is the root of a tropical plant related to ginger. It is cultivated in India and the Caribbean, although it originated in Asia. Galanga root or galangal is a rhizome (underground stem) with cream-colored flesh and is often used as a substitute for gingerroot. Thai chiles, also known as birds-eye chiles, are tiny green, yellow, or red peppers most often found packaged in small plastic bags in the produce section of Asian specialty stores or well-stocked grocery stores. They can be refrigerated for about 1 month or frozen for up to 6 months.

FUN FACT

- The farm-raised bay scallop's life cycle begins when ocean-grown brood stock are placed in spawning tanks. When larvae develop, they are situated first in mesh bags, then in nets suspended from ropes in open water. The scallops receive no feed once they are returned to open water. Relying on the same natural foods as their wild counterparts, aquacultured bay scallops reach marketable size in 8 months.

Blue Sea Scallops

CANTER-BERRY FARMS, PIKE PLACE MARKET

Canter-Berry Farms produces a broad array of blueberry-based products which they sell in the North Arcade of the Market or by mail (see page 326). In this quick and easy dish, fresh sea scallops are sautéed in butter and blueberry vinegar, then the mixture is thickened with sour cream. Surprisingly, the sauce and scallops turn a beautiful pale pink color and taste great served over freshly cooked fettucine, linguine, fragrant basmati rice, or jasmine rice.

2 TABLESPOONS BUTTER

⅓ CUP BLUEBERRY VINEGAR

1 ½ POUNDS SEA SCALLOPS, RINSED, DRAINED, AND PATTED DRY

3 TABLESPOONS SOUR CREAM

4 TO 6 CUPS COOKED PASTA OR COOKED RICE

1. Heat butter and blueberry vinegar in a large skillet over medium heat. When liquid sizzles, add scallops and cook 3 to 4 minutes, turning once, or until scallops just turn opaque. Remove skillet from heat and stir in sour cream, mixing until sour cream is complete incorporated.

2. To serve, divide cooked pasta or rice among individual plates and spoon scallops and sauce over top.

SERVES 4

Note: For a variation, sauté 1 cup fresh mushroom slices and ¼ cup minced shallots in the butter for 3 to 4 minutes before adding the blueberry vinegar, then proceed with the recipe.

Coconut Soup with Sea Scallop Medallions

⎯⎯❧⎯⎯

Thai and Indian soups and curries cooked with coconut milk have become a popular item on many menus and in many homes, but coconut milk is notorious for its high level of saturated fat, the type we are encouraged to avoid whenever possible. In this recipe, I have devised a fat-free coconut milk that will allow you to enjoy a favorite taste with nary a heart flutter. Thai chile peppers and kaffir lime leaves are available at El Mercado Latino in the Pike Place Market or in Latin and Asian specialty stores and some supermarkets.

2 CUPS EVAPORATED SKIM MILK

2 TABLESPOONS MAPLE SYRUP

1 1/2 TEASPOONS COCONUT EXTRACT

4 THAI CHILE PEPPERS, OR 1 JALAPEÑO
    PEPPER

1 TEASPOON PEANUT OR SESAME OIL

1/2 TEASPOON CURRY POWDER

1 TABLESPOON FRESHLY SQUEEZED LIME
    JUICE

2 CUPS DEFATTED CHICKEN STOCK

2 KAFFIR LIME LEAVES, OR 1 TEASPOON
    FRESHLY MINCED LIME ZEST

1 1/2 POUNDS SEA SCALLOPS, RINSED,
    DRAINED, PATTED DRY, AND CUT IN HALF
    HORIZONTALLY TO FORM SCALLOP COINS

1/4 TEASPOON SALT

2 CUPS COOKED JASMINE OR BASMATI RICE

4 GREEN ONIONS, TOP 2 INCHES REMOVED,
    REMAINING PART SLICED 1/8 INCH THICK

8 SPRIGS CILANTRO, LEAVES ONLY, MINCED

2 TABLESPOONS UNSALTED PEANUTS,
    MINCED

CRUSHED RED PEPPER FLAKES (OPTIONAL)

1. To make coconut milk, stir together evaporated skim milk, maple syrup, and coconut extract in a small mixing bowl or measuring cup and set aside.

2. Cut 2 slits in each Thai chile pepper from just below the stem end to just above the bottom of the peppers so that the soup stock can flow through the chiles and pick up flavor. Use the same technique if using a jalapeño pepper. Set peppers aside.

3. Heat a large nonstick saucepan over medium heat. When pan is hot, add peanut oil. When oil is hot, add curry powder and cook for 30 seconds, stirring continuously. Add Thai chile peppers and lime juice and stir continuously for 30 seconds. Add chicken stock, coconut milk, and kaffir lime leaves, stir well, and heat to just below the boiling point. Cook 5 minutes, then add scallops and cook 3 to 5 minutes, or until scallops are opaque on the outside and translucent in the center. Remove pan from heat and add salt, stirring well to mix. Taste and add more salt if needed.

4. Place rice in the bottom of a large communal soup tureen or divide among individual bowls. Ladle soup over rice and sprinkle with green onions, cilantro, and peanuts. If desired, sprinkle with crushed red pepper flakes.

SERVES 4

Note: Bay scallops can be substituted for sea scallops, if desired. Decrease cooking time to 2 to 3 minutes.

Shrimp and Prawns

SHRIMP ARE THE MOST common crustaceans in the world and America's favorite shellfish. There are more than 300 species of shrimp worldwide but only two important commercial groups—warm-water, or tropical, shrimp (Penaeidae family), and cold-water, or northern, shrimp (Pandalidae family).

Warm-water shrimp are caught in the Gulf of Mexico, Australia, Asia, and off the coasts of South and Central America and make up by far the larger catch. They include Gulf of Mexico, China, or West Coast white; Gulf of Mexico pink or brown; blue shrimp; black tiger shrimp; and rock shrimp.

Cold-water species are smaller in size but considered by many to be sweeter, firmer, and more delicate in taste. Northern shrimp come from New England, Norway, Canada, the West Coast of the United States, and Alaska. There are two species of pink cold-water shrimp sold in the U.S.—northern pink shrimp and giant spot.

When shrimp are harvested, they are graded by size or the amount it takes to make a pound, then sold by count, or the number of shrimp per pound. Shrimp are usually flash-frozen at sea, then thawed before being sold.

The United States is the biggest consumer of shrimp in the world. You may be lucky enough to find fresh local shrimp at your fishmonger's stall if you live along the coast of Louisiana, Texas, Georgia, or the Northwestern states. However, 70 percent of the U.S. catch is imported, and much of it is farmed. Almost all of it arrives on our shores frozen and with the heads removed. Worldwide, shrimp farmers now account for almost one-third of the total shrimp production, and the percentage is growing.

Most of the farming takes place in the tropics of Asia and Latin America, with China, Thailand, Indonesia, and Ecuador leading the way. China now farms more than 350 million pounds of China white shrimp a year, making China the world's leading shrimp supplier. Popular types of farmed shrimp you may encounter include Ecuadorean or Mexican white shrimp, Gulf pink, Gulf white, Chinese white, and black tiger shrimp.

There is much confusion about shrimp and prawns, but there really shouldn't be. In common usage, shrimp and prawns refer to the same species, although in some culinary circles (particularly among restaurants and retailers) the word "shrimp" indicates small shrimp, while "prawn" indicates larger specimens. The United Nations has ruled that the term "shrimp" should be used when referring to species harvested from salt water, while the term "prawn" should refer to species harvested from fresh water; however, in common usage the terms have become virtually interchangeable. A shrimp is a shrimp is a prawn is a scampi; you'll never go wrong calling a shrimp a shrimp.

Most shrimp marketed in the United States as "fresh, raw shrimp" has been previously frozen. Retailers buy shrimp in frozen block form, thaw it, then sell it to you. This works out well for everyone, for shrimp freezes well and the difference between fresh and frozen shrimp is minimal. A good brand of shrimp, if frozen quickly after harvesting and properly handled at the retail market, should be indistinguishable from the fresh product, so do not hesitate to buy frozen.

Regardless of species or color, most shrimp available in the market are sold in the green headless form, which means raw, heads removed, shells on. Rarely, if ever, will you see raw shrimp with the head left on, not only for esoteric reasons, but because the head portion contains most of the internal organs, which spoil quickly. Since virtually all of the edible portion is in the tail anyway, with the heads removed, shrimp stay fresher longer. However, if you ever do purchase whole shrimp, the heads make a rich stock (see pages 244 and 318).

Other forms of shrimp you may find in the market include thawed or frozen raw, peeled shrimp (either with or without the final section of their tail shells removed); thawed or frozen raw, peeled, and deveined (either with or without the final section of their tail shells removed); thawed or frozen shrimp cooked in their shells; and thawed or frozen shrimp that have been peeled, deveined, and cooked. Canned shrimp, shrimp paste, and dried shrimp are also available.

The sidestripe, coonstripe, brokenback, pink shrimp, and giant spot are Northwest cold-water shrimp. The giant spot shrimp (*Pandalus platyceros*), often called the Alaskan spot prawn because of its large size, is generally the only species of shrimp available fresh. Named for the four bright white spots on its pinkish red body, it commonly ranges in size from 3 to 6 inches, although specimens of up to 9 inches (seven to the pound) are prize catches. Harvested in waters from Alaska to

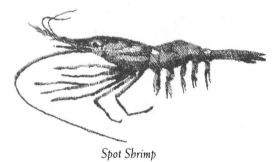

Spot Shrimp

San Diego, local "spots" usually come from Alaska or Hood Canal in Washington. They are good steamed, boiled, fried, sautéed, baked, stir-fried, or grilled.

Northern pink shrimp (*Pandalus jordani*), also known as salad, bay, or popcorn shrimp, are harvested in the Gulf of Alaska and on the Washington and Oregon coasts. They fall in the size range of 100 up to 250 per pound and are so small that they are always processed (shelled and cooked) by the time you buy them to create a longer shelf life.

Black tiger shrimp (*Penaeus monodon*) are the most widely distributed and marketed shrimp in the world. About 80 percent of black tiger shrimp on the market are farmed, with the remainder caught in the wild in various Asian countries. Black tiger shrimp are the most common type of shrimp sold in the United States; most are imported from Thailand.

Grown in shallow ponds, black tiger shrimp are fed a fish meal-based diet and reach harvestable size in about $4^1/2$ months.

Available year-round, black tiger shrimp have notably firm-textured meat. They are especially forgiving and easy to work with. You can cook them whole in the shell or remove the shells before cooking. Even though the shells are bluish gray, the shrimp cook to a nice pink color. They are available fresh or frozen raw shell-on tails. Most black tiger shrimp found in U.S. markets are 16/20, which means they number between 16 and 20 per pound, or 21/25.

Rock shrimp (*Sicyonia brevirostris*) is a Gulf of Mexico shrimp with a hard, almost impenetrable shell. Luckily, you won't have to peel them yourself, because they come already shelled. The firm flesh looks like small knobs of lobster tail (white flesh covered by a mottled, brownish red skin) with a flavor somewhat akin to lobster. Like lobster, rock shrimp is sensitive to overcooking, so try not to cook rock shrimp for more than 1 to 2 minutes. Limited cooking time will guarantee you tasty, plump morsels of crustacean. Rock shrimp meat is ideal for stir-frying or broiling with an appropriate sauce. It is available in the Pike Place Market at Jack's Fish Spot.

Raw shrimp range in color from bright pink to reddish brown to shimmery gray, depending on where they were cultivated or harvested. The color should be even, not brownish or yellow at the edges. Quality shrimp are translucent, almost gelatinous, with no black spots on the shells. They should look full with no loose shells. The flesh should feel firm between your fingers; avoid shrimp that

are limp, and discard any that are soft. A clean, briny scent of the sea signals high-quality raw shrimp, whether fresh or frozen; an iodine or ammonia odor is a sign of deterioration.

Cooked shrimp should be firm, full, and pure white inside with the characteristic red coloration on the outside of the meat. It should smell sweet and somewhat briny. Ask your fishmonger to let you sample cooked shrimp, especially pink (salad or bay) shrimp, before you buy them. An ammonia-like smell is a warning sign of less-than-fresh shrimp.

Shrimp are often marketed by size. The cost of shrimp is usually determined by size, ranging from colossal to tiny; the larger the shrimp, the more expensive. For shrimp with the head off and the shell on, the most commonly available categories are jumbo (16/25), large (26/40), and medium (36/50).

Purchase $^1/3$ to $^1/2$ pound of cooked or uncooked shell-on shrimp per person; $^1/4$ to $^1/3$ pound of cooked, peeled, and deveined shrimp per person. A good rule of thumb when buying fresh or frozen raw shell-on shrimp is to allow $1^1/2$ pounds per 4 main-dish servings. When buying by the piece, allow 2 to 10 medium, large, jumbo, or colossal green headless shrimp as an appetizer portion; 5 to 20 as an entrée.

For most recipes, large shrimp averaging 30 to the pound are a useful, all-purpose size. For stuffed shrimp, butterflied shrimp, or a fancy shrimp cocktail, large, jumbo, or colossal shrimp (under 15 per pound) would be a better choice. If you are trying to save money when purchasing shrimp, remember that smaller shrimp usually cost less.

If time is of the essence, remember that

smaller shrimp cook more quickly, although larger shrimp take less time to peel and devein. When buying shrimp that are already peeled, deveined, and cooked, expect to pay a premium price for the convenience and high yield per pound.

A cost-saving measure may be to try a less popular or well-known shrimp variety, which may sell for less even though of the same size and quality as a better-known type. Buying frozen shrimp in bulk (such as a 5-pound box), then defrosting them yourself at home may save even more because it means less work for the fishmonger, who may give you a good deal. Slow thawing in your refrigerator is best; thawing shrimp in hot water is the worst. If you do not want to defrost the whole 5 pounds at once, defrost only what you plan to use quickly under cold running water and return the remaining portion to the freezer for future use.

You can stretch shrimp by adding it to soups, salads, dips, casseroles, or rice or pasta dishes where the starch takes center stage and the shrimp acts as an accent. To make shrimp go further when served in shrimp cocktails or cold on the buffet table for dipping, peel and devein the shrimp, then halve them lengthwise. Steam or boil briefly, and the cooked shrimp will curl into spirals that make for an attractive presentation.

Never overcook shrimp. Because it is low in fat, shrimp is easily overcooked, which turns it rubbery and flavorless. All shrimp, no matter what color when first bought, turn pink when cooked. Whether still in the shell or not, most shrimp is done as soon as the outside changes color to coral pink and white. The shrimp meat changes from translucent to opaque white, loses its glossy appearance, and curls slightly. Never cook shrimp so long that the tails curl tightly. To stop the cooking process (if serving the shrimp cold), immediately rinse shrimp in cold water.

Shrimp cooked in the shell retain more flavor and a brighter color than peeled shrimp. When boiling shrimp, place them in boiling water and cook for 2 to 4 minutes, depending on size, or until shrimp just turn pink. To test, remove a shrimp from the water and cut into the thickest area with the tip of a sharp knife; the meat should be white yet moist. If just barely translucent, remove shrimp from heat and let stand, covered, for a minute or two, then recheck. If the meat is still gray or translucent, continue cooking, checking at 1-minute intervals.

Shrimp can be baked, baked with stuffing, broiled, deep-fried, oven-fried, boiled, sautéed, stir-fried, steamed, grilled, smoked, or microwaved. Do not precook shrimp intended for a slow-cooking sauce or casserole; simply add raw shrimp at the end of the cooking time and heat just until done.

Shrimp should be eaten the day you buy them. However, uncooked shrimp will keep up to 24 hours in the refrigerator if stored properly. Seal shrimp in a plastic bag, put the bag in a pan over ice, drain the water as the ice melts, and replenish the ice as needed. Cooked shrimp lasts no more than 3 days in the refrigerator. Shrimp may also be frozen for up to 3 months if properly wrapped and stored at 0° or colder. To freeze shrimp, wrap tightly in heavy-duty freezer wrap or aluminum foil, place in a heavy-duty freezer bag, expel the air, seal, and store.

The dark thread that runs along a shrimp's back is not actually a vein; it's the lower end of the shrimp's digestive tract. Deveining warm-water shrimp is optional, since it is not harmful if eaten. The sand veins of cold-water shrimp don't need to be removed.

To devein, remove the shell. Using a sharp knife, make a shallow cut (about $1/8$ inch deep) from the head to the tail along the back of each shrimp to expose the vein. Remove the vein with the tip of the knife or with your fingers. Rinse briefly and drain shrimp before cooking. The vein on the inside curve is generally much smaller and does not need to be removed.

To butterfly shrimp, peel the shrimp (use any size larger than medium) and make an incision nearly all the way through the shrimp down the entire length of the back. Leave the tail intact and attached to the shrimp. Then simply lift out the vein, lay the shrimp on the cutting board cut-side up, and press to open and flatten the shrimp.

Shrimp work well with Johannisberg riesling, chenin blanc, sémillon blanc, fumé blanc, sauvignon blanc, and muscat canelli. Shrimp also often pair advantageously with beer, particularly the popular Northwest microbrews. Spanish dry fino sherry paired with spicy shrimp dishes or shrimp dishes flavored with tomatoes or garlic has kept the Iberians happy for hundreds of years, although it is (lamentably) still an undiscovered delight in this country. Light red wines (particularly pinot noir and beaujolais) slightly chilled also work well with tomato-based shrimp dishes. Heavier reds (the zinfandels and merlots) pair advanta-geously with Mediterranean shrimp dishes and hearty shrimp soups and stews.

FUN FACTS

- By weight, the head is 40 percent of the shrimp, but fortunately that's usually gone by the time you're ready to buy.

- A sea fungus called *Phaffia* synthesizes pink pigment, which no other organism is known to do. It's what makes the flesh of shrimp and salmon turn pink.

- Occasionally, you may find shrimp that have paper-thin shells. These are simply shrimp that molted shortly before harvest; they are of the same quality as those with sturdier shells.

- Spot shrimp live about six years. They begin life as males, then change sex to female after about two years as they near spawning age. As adults, they prefer deep waters and rocky habitats.

- Nothing natural is noisier underwater than a bed of shrimp.

All-American Shrimp Boil

~~~
❧
~~~

Nothing beats a good, old-fashioned shrimp boil in which family and friends can get down-and-dirty with America's favorite shellfish. Cover the table with newspaper, pass out the napkins, and dish up the shrimp for peel-and-eat fun. There are almost as many combinations for shrimp boils as there are shrimp in the sea. Try the basic recipe, then sample some of the options for a variety of flavors.

2 QUARTS WATER

1 TABLESPOON SALT

2 POUNDS SHRIMP OR PRAWNS, RINSED,
    SHELLS LEFT ON

1. Bring water and salt to a boil in a large saucepan or Dutch oven. Boil water 10 minutes, uncovered, then add shrimp. Cook 2 to 4 minutes, or until shrimp just turn pink.

2. If eating immediately, drain water and pour shrimp into a large communal bowl and serve. If using later, rinse shrimp in cold water to stop the cooking process, drain well, cover, and refrigerate.

SERVES 4 GENEROUSLY

Variations

• To make a richer stock, try substituting beer or chicken, fish, or vegetable stock for the water. Citrus juices (lemon, lime, or orange) or flavored vinegars (red wine, cider, white wine, or tarragon) can be substituted for part of the water. Try adding a few tablespoons of vinegar or citrus juice to begin with, then increase to taste as desired.

• For a richer flavor, add herbs, spices, and condiments. Fresh flavorings include garlic, shallots, green onions, fresh herbs (tarragon, thyme, parsley, chives, or cilantro), gingerroot, onion slices, celery slices, kaffir lime leaves, citrus slices (lemon, lime, or orange), or fresh jalapeño peppers or other hot peppers. Thinly slice the peppers for lots of added heat or cut slits $1/4$ inch from top to $1/4$ inch from bottom of peppers with the tip of a sharp knife (do not cut all the way through the bottom!) to release heat slowly as shrimp stock boils.

• Prepared flavorings that can be added to shrimp boil include shrimp and crab boil mix (available in the spice section of supermarkets, at specialty seafood stores, or gourmet shops), horseradish, pickling spice, Tabasco sauce, and Worcestershire sauce.

• Dried flavorings include bay leaves, cayenne, seeds (celery, coriander, fennel, or mustard), crushed red pepper flakes, dried thyme, dry mustard, garlic powder, ground ginger, ground white or black pepper, whole peppercorns (green, red, or black), ground or whole allspice, ground or whole cloves, juniper berries, and paprika.

Shrimp Gumbo

— ◆ —

DELCAMBRE'S RAGIN CAJUN, PIKE PLACE MARKET

Danny Delcambre is a native of Louisiana who brings a touch of Cajun magic to the Market, not only because of the spicy food he prepares but because of his personal strength and perseverance. Both deaf and legally blind, chef Delcambre communicates using American Sign Language (ASL). Nevertheless, he's a visionary with his other senses, having interned in New Orleans with renowned Cajun chef, cookbook author, and television personality Paul Prudhomme. Chef Delcambre and wife Holly opened Delcambre's Ragin Cajun in 1993, the first restaurant in the United States owned and run by a deaf and blind person. The employees, most of whom are deaf, also use ASL to communicate. Delcambre's has won recognition from the President's Committee on Employment of People with Disabilities, the State of Washington as Small Employer of the Year, and the City of Seattle as Small Business of the Year.

1/4 CUP VEGETABLE OIL

1/2 CUP ALL-PURPOSE FLOUR

1/4 CUP CHOPPED CELERY

1/4 CUP CHOPPED GREEN BELL PEPPER

1/4 CUP CHOPPED ONION

3 TOMATOES, CORED AND COARSELY CHOPPED

2 CLOVES GARLIC, HALVED

1 TEASPOON SALT

1 TEASPOON MAGIC SEASONING SEAFOOD BLEND

4 CUPS HOT WATER

1 POUND JUMBO PRAWNS, SHELLS REMOVED EXCEPT FOR LAST SECTION OF TAIL, AND DEVEINED

4 CUPS COOKED LONG-GRAIN WHITE RICE

1. To make roux, heat vegetable oil in a large, heavy stockpot or Dutch oven over medium heat. Add flour and stir to combine with oil. Cook, whisking often, about 45 minutes to 1 hour, or until roux turns dark brown. Decrease heat if mixture browns too quickly.

2. In a food process or blender, add celery, green pepper, onion, tomatoes, garlic, salt, and Magic Seasonings Seafood Blend and pulse until smooth. Add puréed vegetables and water to pot and stir well to mix. Simmer for 1 hour, or until mixture reduces by about a third and becomes thicker and darker brown in color.

3. Add prawns. Bring to a boil, then turn down the heat and cook 2 to 4 minutes, or until prawns just turn pink, stirring occasionally.

4. To serve, place 1 cup rice in 4 large soup bowls. Ladle shrimp gumbo over rice and serve immediately.

SERVES 4 AS AN ENTRÉE, 8 AS AN APPETIZER

Note: The Magic Seasoning Seafood Blend is a dried spice mixture blended by Paul Prudhomme and is available at DeLaurenti Specialty Foods in the Market, and in supermarkets.

Herb-Crusted Alaskan Spot Prawns with Warm Mushroom-Potato Salad

———✦———

FULLERS,
SEATTLE, WASHINGTON

I first met chef Monique Barbeau when she led a cooking class at a downtown Seattle department store. Besides the normal flurry of stainless steel bowls, whirling whisks, and savory smells, the image I remember most was the loving way she deseeded a tomato. Instead of chopping it in half and squeezing it to pieces as most people do, she used her pinkie finger to scoop out each gooey pocket of seeds. "It would be disrespectful of the tomato to squeeze it," she explained. "Little things done well make for good food." This Culinary Institute of America graduate and winner of the Best Chef in the Northwest award from the James Beard Foundation does many little things well, placing Fullers restaurant, in the Seattle Sheraton Hotel & Towers, among the most highly lauded restaurants in the region.

Herb-Crusted Prawns

1/4 CUP CHOPPED FRESH MIXED HERBS, SUCH AS PARSLEY, THYME, AND MARJORAM

12 ALASKAN SPOT PRAWNS, SHELLED AND DEVEINED, SHELLS RESERVED

1 EGG WHITE, LIGHTLY BEATEN

2 TABLESPOONS OLIVE OIL

1/4 CUP SHERRY VINEGAR

1 CUP SHRIMP STOCK (RECIPE FOLLOWS)

3 TABLESPOONS TRUFFLE BUTTER (RECIPE FOLLOWS)

SALT AND FRESHLY GROUND WHITE PEPPER TO TASTE

FRESHLY SQUEEZED LEMON JUICE TO TASTE

MUSHROOM-POTATO SALAD (RECIPE FOLLOWS)

1. Line a baking sheet with waxed paper. Place mixed herbs on a small plate or a piece of waxed paper. Dip spot prawns in egg white, allowing excess to drip back into bowl, then dredge prawns in mixed herbs. Place prawns on prepared baking sheet.

2. Heat olive oil in a large skillet over medium heat. Add spot prawns and cook 1 minute on each side, turning only once. Remove prawns to a platter, cover to keep warm, and set aside.

3. Add sherry vinegar to pan used for shrimp and reduce by half. Add shrimp stock and bring to a boil. Swirl in Truffle Butter, then season to taste with salt, pepper, and lemon juice.

4. To serve, place a generous mound of Mushroom-Potato Salad in 4 shallow bowls. Divide sauce over salad and top with 3 prawns.

SERVES 4

Shrimp Stock

2 TABLESPOONS OLIVE OIL

1/4 CUP DICED YELLOW ONIONS

1 MEDIUM CARROT, DICED

1/2 STALK CELERY, DICED

1 CUP RESERVED ALASKAN SPOT PRAWN SHELLS

1/4 CUP DRY WHITE WINE

1 TABLESPOON TOMATO PASTE

2 1/2 CUPS FISH STOCK

1 BAY LEAF

2 SPRIGS OF FRESH THYME

5 BLACK PEPPERCORNS, CRUSHED

1. Heat olive oil in a heavy saucepan over medium heat. Add onions, carrot, and celery and cover with a circle of parchment paper placed directly on vegetables. Cook 5 to 7 minutes, or until vegetables are softened. Remove paper.

2. Add reserved prawn shells and cook 1 to 2 minutes, or until bright pink. Add white wine and reduce until liquid evaporates. Add tomato paste, fish stock, bay leaf, thyme, and peppercorns. Bring mixture to a boil, reduce heat, and simmer 15 to 20 minutes.

3. Strain stock through a fine-meshed sieve into a clean saucepan and place over medium heat. Cook until mixture is reduced to 1 1/2 cups, and reserve.

MAKES 1 1/2 CUPS

Truffle Butter

4 TABLESPOONS UNSALTED BUTTER

1 TABLESPOON TRUFFLE OIL (SEE NOTE)

Add butter to food processor and process just until smooth. Drizzle in truffle oil until incorporated. Transfer to a small bowl, cover, and refrigerate until ready to use.

Mushroom-Potato Salad

6 TABLESPOONS OLIVE OIL

4 CUPS SLICED ASSORTED WILD
    MUSHROOMS (SUCH AS PORTOBELLO,
    SHIITAKE, OYSTER, CÈPE, AND
    CHANTERELLE)

4 TABLESPOONS CHOPPED SHALLOTS

SALT AND FRESHLY GROUND BLACK PEPPER
    TO TASTE

8 FINGERLING POTATOES, CUT IN HALF
    THEN CUT INTO 1/4-INCH SLICES

1. Heat 1 tablespoon of the olive oil in a large skillet over medium heat. Add 1 cup of the mushrooms and cook 7 to 10 minutes, or until browned, stirring occasionally. Add 1 tablespoon of the shallots and cook 3 to 5 minutes, or until golden. Pour mixture into a nonreactive mixing bowl. Repeat cooking procedure three more times using 1 tablespoon of olive oil, 1 cup of the mushrooms, and 1 tablespoon of the shallots each time. Sprinkle mixture with salt and pepper to taste and toss to mix. Remove mushrooms to a large bowl, cover, and set aside.

2. Add the remaining 2 tablespoons olive oil to the skillet and heat over medium heat. Add potatoes and cook 5 to 7 minutes, or until golden. Add mushrooms to skillet and keep warm over very low heat until ready to serve.

MAKES ABOUT 2 CUPS

Note: Although chef Barbeau offers the following recipe for making your own truffle oil, not many home cooks have white or black truffle peelings lying about the kitchen. Therefore, although it is expensive, it is much easier to buy a small bottle of truffle oil, which is imported from Italy and is available at gourmet specialty stores, Italian markets, and larger supermarkets. You can make your own by simmering 1 tablespoon white or black truffle peelings in 1 tablespoon Madeira or dry sherry and adding it to 1 quart extra virgin olive oil. Allow oil to sit overnight, then strain and use as needed. I particularly like just a bit of truffle oil drizzled in at the end of a stir-fry or in vinaigrettes.

Stir-Fried Prawns with Sour Sauce

───❦───

JAPANESE GOURMET, PIKE PLACE MARKET

Located on sloping Stewart Street, just a stone's throw from the hustle and bustle of Pike Place, Japanese Gourmet is a simple but welcoming oasis with hanging paper lanterns, accommodating service, and generous portions. The special sour sauce of this lavish stir-fry, which appears on the menu as Ebi Yasai-itame, is a bracing counterpoint to the richness of the dish. Shredding vegetables for stir-fries was a new technique for me, but the vegetables cook faster, provide an unusual textural context, and look beautiful on the plate. Serve this with mounds of white rice and plenty of sake for sipping.

2 TEASPOONS LOW-SODIUM SOY SAUCE

2 TEASPOONS SUGAR

$1/2$ TEASPOON SALT

2 TEASPOONS VEGETABLE OIL

$1/4$ CUP BUTTER OR MARGARINE

$3/4$ POUND SHELLED AND DEVEINED PRAWNS

4 CUPS SHREDDED CABBAGE

1 CUP SHREDDED EGGPLANT

1 CUP SHREDDED CARROTS

2 CUPS BEAN SPROUTS, RINSED, DRAINED, AND PATTED COMPLETELY DRY

1 CUP THINLY SLICED MUSHROOMS

2 CUPS BROCCOLI FLORETS, CUT IN HALF OR QUARTERS IF LARGE

$1/2$ CUP SNOW PEAS OR SUGAR SNAP PEAS, RINSED, DRAINED, AND WITH STRINGS REMOVED

PINCH OF FRESHLY GROUND WHITE PEPPER

SOUR SAUCE (RECIPE FOLLOWS)

1. In a small bowl, mix soy sauce, sugar, and salt until sugar and salt are dissolved. Set aside.

2. Heat vegetable oil and butter in a large skillet over medium-high heat. Add prawns and stir-fry 1 to 2 minutes, or until prawns just turn pink. Add cabbage, eggplant, carrot, bean sprouts, mushrooms, broccoli, snow peas, and soy sauce mixture and cook, stirring continuously, for 2 to 3 minutes, or until vegetables are tender-crisp. Add white pepper, stir thoroughly to combine and remove from heat.

3. Place stir-fry in a large communal serving plate, put Sour Sauce in a small bowl, and serve family style at the table.

SERVES 4

Sour Sauce

$1/2$ CUP FRESHLY SQUEEZED GRAPEFRUIT JUICE

$1/2$ CUP FRESHLY SQUEEZED ORANGE JUICE

4 TEASPOONS FRESHLY SQUEEZED LIME JUICE

4 TEASPOONS FRESHLY SQUEEZED LEMON JUICE

$1/4$ CUP SOY SAUCE

$1/4$ CUP SUGAR

In a small bowl, mix together all of the ingredients until sugar dissolves. Cover and refrigerate until ready to use.

MAKES ABOUT $1 1/3$ CUPS

Scandinavian Open-Face Bay Shrimp Sandwich

There is no better place to eat Scandinavian food than in the heart of Seattle's Scandinavian district—Ballard—which is also the heart of the city's maritime industry. Northwest Market Street, one of the main thoroughfares, boasts businesses run by shop owners with surnames such as Olsen, Jonssen, and Swensen. A restaurant named Scandies is a good place for first-timers to try authentic Scandinavian food, as well as to catch up on the latest neighborhood gossip. The restaurant is renowned for its lingonberry pancakes, desserts, and traditional open-face sandwiches. This is my version of their bay shrimp sandwich.

1/4 CUP MAYONNAISE

1/4 CUP SOUR CREAM

1/4 CUP SNIPPED FRESH DILL, PLUS FRESH DILL SPRIGS FOR GARNISH

2 TEASPOONS FRESHLY SQUEEZED LEMON JUICE

1/2 ENGLISH HOTHOUSE CUCUMBER, THINLY SLICED

1 POUND COOKED PINK (SALAD OR BAY) SHRIMP, RINSED, DRAINED, AND PATTED DRY

4 SLICES DANISH RYE OR PUMPERNICKEL BREAD OR GOOD-QUALITY WHITE BREAD

1 TOMATO, CUT INTO 4 WEDGES

1/2 LEMON, CUT INTO 4 WEDGES

1. Mix together mayonnaise, sour cream, dill, and lemon juice in a small mixing bowl. Lightly spread bread slices with a couple of tablespoons of the cream mixture.

2. Place cucumber slices on top of cream mixture, pressing to adhere. Add shrimp to the remainder of mixture in bowl and stir to mix well. Spread shrimp salad on top of cucumber layer and place sandwich on small plates. Garnish each plate with tomato wedge, lemon wedge, and dill sprig.

SERVES 4

HOW TO PEEL A SHRIMP

I have found it much easier to peel shrimp with an inexpensive shrimper, a device that loosens the shell and the vein in one step.

To use one of these devices, insert the tip of the shrimper between the back shell and the body of the shrimp. Push the shrimper along the back of the shrimp all the way to the tail. Hold onto the tail shell if you want to save it, while pulling up on the shrimper to release the rest of the shell. Break the shell off at the last section of tail or pull off the shell completely. Rinse shrimp under cold running water to remove any remaining vein.

If you don't have a shrimp peeler, you can shell your shrimp by hand. To accomplish this, hold a shrimp in one hand with the legs up. With the thumb and forefinger of the other hand, start peeling away the shell from the head of the shrimp at the inside curve where the feelers are. Pull the shell around and off the body of the shrimp ("unwrap" the shell from the body) two or three sections at a time. The shell should come away easily. The tail section can be left attached as a decoration or handle for eating, or removed by gently pulling on the tail.

Prawns in Red Lentil Purée

───♦───

Health experts exhort us to eat more legumes—beans, peas, and lentils—because they are high in protein, complex carbohydrates, vitamins, minerals, and fiber. Of the three, lentils are the easiest to prepare because they do not have to be soaked before cooking. And Red Chief lentils, the type called for in this recipe, are the fastest cooking of all at just 15 minutes per cup. The lentils, which are bright orange in the dried state, turn a mustard-gold when cooked, and contrast nicely with the plump, pink, protein-packed prawns. A combination of brightly colored steamed vegetables and crusty sourdough bread would complete the meal.

1 CUP RED CHIEF LENTILS, RINSED AND
    DRAINED

1 TEASPOON YELLOW MUSTARD SEEDS

2 CUPS WATER

1 TABLESPOON BUTTER

1 TABLESPOON MINCED SHALLOT

4 CLOVES GARLIC, MINCED

1/2 YELLOW BELL PEPPER, DICED

1 RED BELL PEPPER, DICED

1/2 CUP SWEET WHITE WINE, SUCH AS
    JOHANNISBERG RIESLING OR
    GEWÜRTZTRAMINER

1/8 TEASPOON TABASCO SAUCE

1/2 TEASPOON SALT

1/8 TEASPOON FRESHLY GROUND WHITE
    PEPPER

1 TABLESPOON MUSTARD OIL OR CANOLA
    OIL

1 1/2 POUNDS PRAWNS, SHELLED AND
    DEVEINED

JUICE OF 1 LIME

1. Place lentils, mustard seeds, and water in a medium saucepan with a lid and bring to a boil. Stir, reduce heat to a simmer, cover pan, and cook 15 minutes, or until lentils are tender. Drain extra water from lentils if any, pour lentils into a bowl, and set aside to cool. Rinse out and dry saucepan for later use.

2. Heat butter in a medium skillet over medium heat. Add shallot and 2 of the garlic cloves and cook, stirring continuously for 30 seconds. Add all of the yellow bell pepper and half of the red bell pepper and cook 3 to 5 minutes, stirring occasionally, or until vegetables are tender.

3. Place reserved lentils, sautéed vegetables, white wine, Tabasco, salt, and pepper in a food processor or blender and process until smooth. Return lentil purée to saucepan and warm over medium-low heat, stirring occasionally.

4. Meanwhile, heat mustard oil in a large skillet. Add the remaining 2 cloves garlic and the prawns and cook 3 to 4 minutes, stirring constantly, until prawns just turn pink. Add lime juice, stir well, and remove from heat.

5. To serve, place several tablespoons of lentil purée on each individual plate and arrange prawns in an appealing pattern within the purée. Garnish with remaining diced red bell pepper.

SERVES 4 AS AN ENTRÉE, 8 AS AN APPETIZER

FUN FACT

- Washington State is the nation's largest grower of lentils.

Alaskan Spot Prawn Wonton Salad

❦

ANTHONY'S HOMEPORT,
VARIOUS LOCATIONS THROUGHOUT THE PUGET SOUND AREA

The Anthony's restaurant chain has made a name for itself among Seattle's top seafood restaurants due in large part to its in-house seafood company. This unique spot prawn salad, developed by former executive chef Sally McArthur, was served at the James Beard House in New York City, where it played to rave reviews.

3 TABLESPOONS VEGETABLE OIL

10 WONTON WRAPPERS, SLICED INTO
   $1/4$-INCH STRIPS

1 TABLESPOON BUTTER

2 CLOVES GARLIC, CUT IN HALF

$3/4$ POUND ALASKAN SPOT PRAWNS,
   SHELLED AND DEVEINED

2 CUPS THINLY SLICED NAPA CABBAGE,
   PLUS 4 TO 8 LARGE, ATTRACTIVE OUTER
   LEAVES

1 CUP THINLY SLICED ROMAINE LETTUCE

$1/4$ CUP SHREDDED CARROT

3 TABLESPOONS CHOPPED CILANTRO, PLUS
   EXTRA CILANTRO SPRIGS, FOR GARNISH

$1/2$ CUP FINELY SLICED CHINESE PEA PODS
   OR SUGAR SNAP PEAS

2 TABLESPOONS THINLY SLICED GREEN
   ONIONS

$1/2$ CUP BEAN SPROUTS, RINSED, DRAINED,
   AND PATTED DRY

2 TEASPOONS BLACK SESAME SEEDS

1 CUP RICE VINEGAR DRESSING
   (RECIPE FOLLOWS)

PICKLED GINGER, FOR GARNISH

1. In a large skillet, heat vegetable oil over medium-high heat. When oil is very hot, add about a third of the wonton strips. Fry 2 to 3 minutes, or until golden brown, turning once, then drain on paper towels. Repeat in batches until all strips are fried, adding more oil if necessary.

2. Heat a large nonstick skillet over medium heat. When pan is hot, add butter. When butter is melted, add garlic and cook 1 minute, stirring continuously. Remove garlic, add prawns, and cook 2 minutes. Turn prawns and cook 2 minutes more, or until prawns just turn pink. Place prawns in a large mixing bowl and add wonton strips, Napa cabbage, romaine lettuce, carrot, cilantro, Chinese pea pods, green onions, bean sprouts, black sesame seeds, and Rice Vinegar Dressing. Toss salad.

3. Line individual plates with Napa cabbage leaves and spoon salad into leaves. Garnish with cilantro sprigs and pickled ginger.

SERVES 4

Rice Vinegar Dressing

$1/2$ CUP UNSEASONED RICE VINEGAR

$1/2$ CUP VEGETABLE OIL

3 TABLESPOONS SUGAR

$1 1/2$ TABLESPOONS SOY SAUCE

1 TABLESPOON TOASTED SESAME OIL

1 TABLESPOON FRESHLY SQUEEZED LIME
   JUICE

$1/8$ TEASPOON DRY MUSTARD

Whisk together all of the ingredients in a large mixing bowl. Use immediately, or cover and refrigerate for up to 1 week.

MAKES ABOUT 1 CUP

Shrimp-n-Vegetable Quiche

LOWELL'S RESTAURANT & BAR, PIKE PLACE MARKET

One of the Market's oldest eating establishments, Lowell's opened for business nearly 90 years ago. Lowell's offers classic American fare that has earned it a reputation as one of the city's most popular family restaurants, and a great place for breakfast. Surrounded by fish stalls, fruit and vegetable stands, and local farmers selling on day tables, Lowell's not only has great views of Elliott Bay and the Olympic Mountains to the west, but the Market's Main Arcade. According to chef Chris Hammett, like the lively area surrounding Lowell's, this quiche has it all! Served with a tossed green salad and a glass of sparkling wine or cider, this seafood pie makes a special lunch, weekend brunch, or a light dinner entrée.

1 PREPARED 9-INCH PIE SHELL, UNBAKED

1 TEASPOON VEGETABLE OIL

1 CUP ASSORTED MIXED CHOPPED VEGETA-
BLES (SUCH AS RED BELL PEPPER, RED
ONIONS, ZUCCHINI, YELLOW SQUASH, OR
BROCCOLI FLORETS)

2 CLOVES GARLIC, MINCED

2 TABLESPOONS SNIPPED FRESH DILL, OR 2
TEASPOONS DRIED DILL, CRUMBLED

$1/2$ POUND PINK (BAY OR SALAD) SHRIMP,
RINSED AND PATTED VERY DRY

$1/4$ CUP GRATED CHEDDAR CHEESE

$1/4$ CUP GRATED PROVOLONE CHEESE

3 EGGS

$3/4$ CUP HALF-AND-HALF

$1/8$ TEASPOON SALT

$1/4$ TEASPOON FRESHLY GROUND WHITE
PEPPER

1. Preheat oven to 400°. Bake pie crust 8 to 10 minutes, or until pale golden in color. Remove to a rack while preparing rest of recipe. Decrease oven to 325°.

2. Heat vegetable oil in a medium nonstick skillet over medium heat. Add vegetables and cook 5 to 7 minutes, stirring often, or until vegetables are tender-crisp. Add garlic and dill and stir to blend. Remove pan from heat and add shrimp, stirring well.

3. Spread shrimp and vegetables evenly over bottom of pie crust and sprinkle with Cheddar and provolone cheeses. In a medium bowl, whisk together eggs, half-and-half, and salt and pepper. Carefully pour egg mixture over shrimp and vegetables. Using the back of a spoon, gently press the vegetables, shrimp, and cheese to below the level of the eggs.

4. Place quiche on center rack in center of oven and bake 40 to 50 minutes, or until a knife inserted in the center comes out clean. Remove from oven and allow to cool at least 20 minutes before cutting and serving.

SERVES 4 AS AN ENTRÉE, 8 AS AN APPETIZER

Shrimp with Porcini Mushroom Glaze

—◦◦◦—

SOSIO'S PRODUCE, PIKE PLACE MARKET

Highstalls are permanent produce stands in the Pike Place Market that sell fresh fruit and vegetables from around the world and also buy from local farmers in season. You know you are at a highstall, as opposed to a farm table, or daystall run by a local farmer, when you see bananas and pineapples on display. Each highstall has its own distinct personality. Sosio's Produce is the highstall to visit for a great, selection of fruits and vegetables as well as the freshest, most exotic assortment of mushrooms in the Market. This recipe was inspired by porcini mushroom season in the fall.

1/4 CUP DRIED PORCINI MUSHROOMS, GROUND TO A FINE DUST IN A FOOD PROCESSOR OR SMALL ELECTRIC COFFEE GRINDER (OPTIONAL)

1 POUND LARGE SHRIMP, SHELLS REMOVED EXCEPT FOR LAST SECTION OF TAIL, AND DEVEINED

1 TABLESPOON OLIVE OIL

2 CLOVES GARLIC, MINCED

1 SHALLOT, MINCED

1/2 POUND FRESH PORCINI MUSHROOMS, STEMS REMOVED AND DISCARDED (OR RESERVED FOR VEGETABLE STOCK), CHOPPED, OR 1/2 POUND FRESH BUTTON MUSHROOMS CUT INTO QUARTERS, OR 1/4 POUND DRIED PORCINI MUSHROOMS

1/4 CUP DEFATTED CHICKEN STOCK

2 TABLESPOONS DRY WHITE WINE OR CHICKEN STOCK

1 TABLESPOON MINCED FRESH BASIL, PLUS ADDITIONAL BASIL LEAVES FOR GARNISH

SALT AND FRESHLY GROUND BLACK PEPPER TO TASTE

WHITE BALSAMIC VINEGAR OR FRESHLY SQUEEZED LEMON JUICE

4 TO 6 CUPS COOKED BASMATI RICE OR BOWTIE PASTA

1. Line a baking sheet and with waxed paper. If using porcini mushroom dust, place dust on a plate or piece of waxed paper. Dip shrimp in dust, lightly coating each side, and place on the prepared baking sheet. If using dried porcini mushrooms in the sauce, cover mushrooms with hot water and soak for 30 minutes, or until soft. Drain well, chop mushrooms coarsely, and set aside. Discard soaking liquid.

2. Heat a large nonstick skillet over medium-low heat. When pan is hot, add oil. When oil is hot, add garlic and shallot and cook 1 minute, stirring continuously. Add shrimp and cook 2 minutes. Turn and cook 2 minutes more, or until shrimp just turn pink. Remove shrimp to a bowl and set aside.

3. Return pan to medium-low heat, add mushrooms, chicken stock, and white wine, and cook 4 to 5 minutes, or until mushrooms soften slightly. Add basil and shrimp, stir gently to combine, and cook just until shrimp are heated through. Remove from heat and season to taste with salt, pepper, and balsamic vinegar.

4. Divide rice or pasta among individual plates, then top with shrimp and sauce. Garnish with basil leaves and serve immediately.

SERVES 4

Vietnamese Shrimp Rolls with Hoisin Dipping Sauce

———◆———

These healthy shrimp rolls epitomize Vietnamese cuisine, which is characterized by the use of raw vegetables and light sauces. They make a great appetizer or even a main dish when accompanied by a filling, Asian-inspired soup such as Coconut Soup with Scallop Medallions (see page 236).

6 TABLESPOONS FRESHLY SQUEEZED LIME
   JUICE

2 TABLESPOONS FISH SAUCE (*NUOC NAM*)

4 CLOVES GARLIC, MINCED

1/4 TEASPOON CRUSHED RED PEPPER
   FLAKES

1 1/2 POUNDS PINK (BAY OR SALAD) SHRIMP,
   RINSED, DRAINED, AND PATTED DRY

16 PIECES RICE PAPER

16 SOFT LETTUCE LEAVES, SUCH AS BIBB,
   RED OR GREEN LEAF, OR ICEBERG

2 CUPS BEAN SPROUTS, RINSED, DRAINED,
   AND PATTED DRY

2 CUPS SHREDDED CARROTS

1/2 CUP CRUSHED UNSALTED PEANUTS

4 GREEN ONIONS, ROOTS AND TIPS
   REMOVED, CUT INTO 1/8-INCH CIRCLES

FRESH BASIL LEAVES OR FRESH MINT
   LEAVES

HOISIN DIPPING SAUCE (RECIPE FOLLOWS)

1. In a medium mixing bowl, stir together lime juice, fish sauce, garlic, and red pepper flakes. Add shrimp and toss well to coat. Cover bowl and refrigerate.

2. Take out 2 large plates and pour 1/4 inch warm water into one of them. Place 1 piece of rice paper in water and soak for 30 seconds to 1 minute, or until pliable. Do not allow to soak too long or rice paper will tear. Remove rice paper to dry plate, then repeat process with remaining rice paper sheets.

3. Place lettuce leaves around the perimeter of a large serving platter. Put shrimp in a serving bowl and place in center of platter. Put bean sprouts, carrots, peanuts, green onions, and basil leaves in separate piles around shrimp.

4. To serve, place rice paper, prepared platter, and Hoisin Dipping Sauce on the table and allow everyone to make their own shrimp rolls by lining a piece of rice paper with a lettuce leaf and adding vegetables, shrimp, peanuts, and basil leaves and folding or rolling to close. The shrimp rolls can then be dipped in the sauce.

SERVES 4 AS AN ENTRÉE, 8 AS AN APPETIZER

Hoisin Dipping Sauce

6 TABLESPOONS HOISIN SAUCE

6 TABLESPOONS SEASONED RICE VINEGAR

2 TABLESPOONS SOY SAUCE OR LOW-SODIUM
   SOY SAUCE

In a small mixing bowl, stir together hoisin sauce, seasoned rice vinegar, and soy sauce. If not using immediately, cover and refrigerate.

MAKES ABOUT 3/4 CUP

Alaskan Spot Prawns with Vanilla Beurre Blanc

~~❦~~

VIRAZON,
SEATTLE, WASHINGTON

Just half a block south of the Pike Place Market, Virazon, which means "changing wind" in Basque, offers traditional French food prepared by chef Astolfo Rueda. This inventive vanilla buerre blanc includes a touch of coconut for a real twist on a classic sauce.

2 TABLESPOONS OLIVE OIL

2 SHALLOTS, DICED

3 WHITE PEPPERCORNS, CRUSHED

1 BAY LEAF

1/4 CUP DICED CARROTS

1/4 CUP DICED CELERY

1 WHOLE VANILLA BEAN, CUT IN HALF
    LENGTHWISE

2 TABLESPOONS CHOPPED FRESH COCONUT
    OR DRIED, UNSWEETENED COCONUT
    (SEE NOTE)

2 CUPS HEAVILY OAKED AND BUTTERY
    WHITE WINE SUCH AS A NORTHWEST OR
    CALIFORNIA CHARDONNAY

1 CUP WHITE DRY VERMOUTH

1/2 CUP SEAFOOD STOCK (SEE PAGE 318)

2 POUNDS ALASKAN SPOT PRAWNS,
    SHELLED AND DEVEINED, SHELLS
    RESERVED

1 CUP UNSALTED BUTTER, CUT INTO PIECES

SALT AND FRESHLY GROUND WHITE PEPPER
    TO TASTE

BRONZE OR GREEN FENNEL, FOR GARNISH

1. Heat 1 tablespoon of the olive oil in a large saucepan over medium-high heat. Add shallots, white peppercorns, bay leaf, carrots, and celery and cook 5 to 7 minutes, or until vegetables are translucent, stirring often. Do not allow vegetables to brown. Add vanilla bean and coconut and stir well. Add chardonnay, stir well, and cook 10 minutes, or until mixture reaches a syrupy consistency, stirring occasionally.

2. Add vermouth and continue to cook 7 to 10 minutes, or until reduced again to a syrupy consistency, stirring occasionally. Add Seafood Stock and reserved prawn shells and reduce liquid by two-thirds.

3. Remove pan from heat and add butter piece by piece, whisking well after each addition, until a smooth, thick sauce forms. Return pan to heat as needed to warm butter.

4. Strain sauce through a fine-meshed sieve into a nonreactive mixing bowl and season to taste with salt and white pepper. Keep warm in the top of a heated double boiler until ready to use.

5. Heat the remaining 1 tablespoon olive oil in a large skillet, add prawns, and cook 2 minutes. Turn and cook 1 to 2 minutes more, or until prawns just turn pink. Remove from heat and keep warm.

6. To serve, divide sauce among 4 individual plates and swirl plate to form a circle of sauce. Arrange prawns on plate, and garnish with bronze fennel.

SERVES 4

Note: Dried unsweetened coconut is available at health food stores and some grocery stores. Do not substitute the sweetened, flaked coconut or the sauce will be too sweet.

Squid

THE SQUID, ALONG WITH its close relations the octopus and the cuttlefish, is a cephalopod mollusk. Unlike shellfish whose shells are located outside their bodies, the shell of the squid is located *inside* the body, in the form of a transparent, plastic-like quill, also called a pen, spine, or sword. This internal quill, the vestige of the squid's primeval molluscan shell, provides stability, although not much protection when compared to the outer shells of the squid's distant bivalve mollusk relatives—clams, mussels, and oysters.

The squid's long, torpedo-shaped body, also called the mantle or tube, is cone-shaped and closed at one end. Two triangular fins, or wings, on the tail end serve as directional rudders in swimming. Eight tentacles and two arms surround the head. Each tentacle is equipped with small suction cups to hold prey. The two arms are longer and thinner than the tentacles, and are used to snare prey. The quill, internal organs, and ink sac are located inside the body.

Because squid have no protective outer shell, they have evolved two major defense mechanisms—deception and flight. Squid jet around backwards and forwards in the water in amazingly fast bursts by alternately inflating their bodies with water like a slender balloon, then contracting to expel the water. When threatened, squid can camouflage themselves by changing their color to appear lighter or darker or can vanish in a puff of ink, which temporarily blinds its attacker, then leaves a "phantom" squid for its predator to attack.

Squid travel through the open water in large schools. They feed at night on the surface of the water, where they are attracted by light. When they come inshore, they can be caught from small boats or docks with jigs or dip nets. Farther out, fishers attract them with lights, then catch them in nets.

There are over 350 species of squid from 25 different families. They are found in every ocean, ranging in size from 1 inch to over 60 feet in length. Squid has lean meat that is firm, yet tender, with a mildly sweet, nutty flavor.

The local variety, *Loligo opalescens*, also known as the **Monterey** or **Pacific squid**, is the variety found up and down the West Coast. It is one of the best types of squid from a culinary standpoint because of its small size (averaging between 4 and 8 inches) and mild flavor. The two other varieties of squid commonly available in the United States are the Atlantic long-finned and short-finned squid.

Squid is available year-round, either fresh or frozen. The frozen product maintains its flavor and texture extremely well and is a very acceptable substitute for fresh. The body or mantle flesh of large squid is commonly sold as steaks—thick, round pieces of snow-white flesh about the diameter of a baseball. Weighing 6 to 8 ounces each, squid steaks are almost always found frozen, and you may have to ask your fishmonger for them if they are not on display. After defrosting overnight in the refrigerator, they are ready to cook, with no pounding or tenderizing necessary.

Smaller squid are usually sold whole or as cleaned tubes, which is the part left after the head (including tentacles) and viscera are removed, leaving the hollow mantle. Bigger tubes can be stuffed whole or sliced at one side, unfolded, and left whole (to form fillets); cut into strips, or sliced on the diagonal partway through to form beautiful squid curls.

When buying squid, the body should be ivory-colored with transparent, violet-spotted skin (if it is still attached), and the tentacles should be white to pinkish purple. The pinker the tentacles, the older the squid since the tentacles are the first to deteriorate. Squid should smell fresh and mildly sweet, never fishy. If you are buying whole squid, the more easily the pen detaches from the body, the fresher the shellfish.

Clean fresh whole squid as soon as possible and store the bodies separately from the tentacles (see page 257). Defrost frozen squid in the refrigerator and do not refreeze. To store thawed or fresh squid, seal it in a plastic bag, set it in a pan of ice (draining the water and replenishing the ice as it melts), and refrigerate to keep it cool. Use within 2 days, and preferably 1 day.

Eighty percent of the squid is edible, a very high percentage for any seafood. As a general rule of thumb, for whole squid, plan on $3^1/_2$ to 5 ounces for each appetizer portion; 6 to 8 ounces per main dish serving. When cooking cleaned tubes and rings, budget $1^1/_2$ to 3 ounces for each appetizer portion; 4 to 6 ounces per entrée serving. However, remember that the way you plan to cook the squid will influence how much to buy. Squid used in quick-cooking dishes such as sautés and stir-fries (1- to 4-minute cooking time) will shrink less than squid used in long-cooking dishes (20 minutes or over), so you may want to increase the amount you buy when planning a long-cooking dish.

Cooked in boiling water for 45 seconds, then drained and rinsed in cold water, blanched squid become tender and are perfect for salads or marinating. Pan- or deep-fried squid need about 2 minutes to cook. For stewed or baked recipes, squid are cooked for at least 20 minutes, at which time they become tender, but shrink in size. Remember to cook squid either very quickly or very slowly—1 to 2 minutes or for over 20 minutes; anywhere in between and squid will be tough and chewy. No matter how you cook it, squid should always be tender enough to cut with a fork.

Squid can be baked, fried, sautéed, braised, steamed, stir-fried, grilled, eaten raw, or used in salads, ceviche, burritos, pasta sauces, stews, and on pizza. Squid lovers consider the tentacles the most flavorful part of the animal, but if you are reluctant to eat them whole, they can be chopped and added to stuffings. Squid ink, or *tinta*, is used in sauces and to color and flavor freshly made pasta.

When planning dishes using squid, remember that squid flesh has a mild, almost bland taste that picks up the flavors of the other ingredients in the recipe. If you want to taste the squid, keep your sauces subtle. If, however, you want to use assertive sauces, then play up the firm texture and playful shape of squid (rings, cross-hatched pieces, steaks), and let the mild flavor of the squid act as a foil.

On its own, squid is a rather bland food, so it may be easier to pair wine (or beer) with the cooking technique and/or sauce used, rather than the squid itself. For example, fried squid, a popular rendition, may work best with sweeter wines, such as Johannisberg riesling and gewürtztraminer, or with a dark beer.

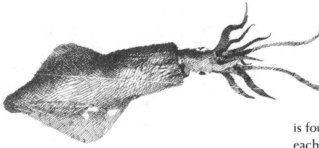

Squid

Squid is often prepared in Asian or Italian recipes, and a spicy zinfandel or merlot would be good with squid dishes cooked in Italian-inspired tomato-based sauces or stocks. Spicy, sweet wines such as Johannisberg riesling, gewürtztraminer, or white zinfandel make good partners with the Asian-leaning dishes. Even a slightly chilled merlot or a light-bodied chardonnay can work with Asian-inspired squid dishes.

FUN FACTS

- Squid consume up to 14 percent of their body weight daily in crustaceans, small fish, and other squid.

- In Japan, squid is called *ika;* in Vietnam *muc,* and in Indonesia, *tjumi-tjumi* ("chew me, chew me"). In the United States, when marketing experts changed the name of squid to its Italian counterpart, *calamari,* the food started to become more popular among the general population.

- *Food & Wine* magazine reports that in Japan, squid is the most popular topping for pizza produced by a major U.S. pizza chain.

- *Calamare en su Tinta,* squid cooked in its own ink, is the national dish of the Basques in Spain.

- The left eye of the squid is four times larger than the right eye because each is used at a different depth. The smaller right eye is used to view objects close to the surface. The bigger left eye is used for deep-water viewing.

HOW TO CLEAN A WHOLE SQUID

1. Place a large cutting board, a small, sharp knife, and your squid close to the kitchen sink. Arrange a single squid lengthwise across the cutting board.

2. Grasp the head and tentacles with one hand and the body with the other and gently pull apart. Set aside the body section while you prepare the tentacles.

3. Cut the tentacles just in front of the eyes and reserve.

4. If it doesn't fall out by itself, squeeze the hard white "beak" from the center of the tentacles and discard. The beak looks and feels like a small garbanzo bean. If the tentacles are large, cut them in half before using, or chop them and add to filling for stuffed squid. I also like to cut the two long tentacles so they are the same length as the other eight. Depending on the recipe, separate the ink sac from the viscera and reserve, or discard along with the remaining viscera and head.

5. To prepare the body meat, pull the pliant, transparent quill out of the body and discard. Squeeze the squid like a tube of toothpaste, starting at the closed end and working your way down to remove any remaining viscera. Alternately, you can insert your index finger inside the squid body and scrape out any remaining viscera.

6. Rub or pull off the skin. If this is difficult, make a small incision beside one of the fins, pull off the fin, and the skin should start coming off, too. Continue pulling off skin until all is removed. Although not usually worth the effort because of their small size, the fins can be chopped and added to stuffing for whole squid, or simply discard them.

7. Thoroughly rinse the body inside and out under cold running water. Drain and pat dry. Slice the body into rings or strips, cut on one side and open into a fillet, cut fillet into a cross-hatch pattern, or leave whole and stuff as desired. To score or cross-hatch the body pine-cone style, cut open a fillet and score on the inside of the body only. Score quite close together or up to $1/4$-inch apart, depending on personal preference. Be careful to avoid cutting through the body. The cross-hatch cut is good to use when marinating or stir-frying squid, or when skewering squid for kebabs.

Boiled Squid

———⚓———

Boiling squid in a stocklike mixture adds flavor to the rather bland shellfish, which can then be used in calamari salads. Just toss boiled squid with one of the vinaigrettes (see pages 321-322) and serve over a bed of fresh greens. Another option is to warm some vinaigrette, pour over spinach leaves and toss until slightly wilted, then top with cooked squid rings.

1 1/2 CUPS WATER

1/2 CUP DRY WHITE WINE OR FRESHLY
   SQUEEZED LEMON JUICE

1 BAY LEAF

8 WHOLE PEPPERCORNS

1 CLOVE GARLIC, CRUSHED

8 SPRIGS OF PARSLEY

1/4 TEASPOON SALT

1 POUND CLEANED SQUID, BODIES CUT INTO
   1/2-INCH RINGS, LARGE TENTACLES CUT
   IN HALF

In a large saucepan, bring water, wine, bay leaf, peppercorns, garlic, parsley, and salt to a boil. Add squid and cook 30 to 60 seconds. Remove from heat, transfer squid to a colander, and immediately rinse squid under cold running water. Drain completely and transfer to a medium bowl. Use immediately, or cover and refrigerate until ready to use, up to 2 or 3 days.

SERVES 4

FUN FACT

• Giant squid are believed to be the largest of all the world's creatures that have no backbones, growing up to 60 or 70 feet in length, longer than a city bus. Its eyes are the largest in the animal kingdom, reaching the size of dinner plates. Some of its nerve fibers are so big they were initially mistaken for blood vessels. Giant squid are inedible, however, because of a high level of ammonia in their bodies.

Calamari Napoli

SHEA'S LOUNGE, PIKE PLACE MARKET

I fell in love with this appetizer the moment I first tried it, and many knowledgeable "foodies" about town consider it one of the best calamari dishes in Seattle. It is served seasonally at Shea's Lounge, the sophisticated Mediterranean-leaning offshoot of Chez Shea. Chef Peter Morrison says that the dish is a variation of a rustic Italian classic and can also be served as an entrée if spooned over cooked pasta or rice.

1/2 CUP ALL-PURPOSE FLOUR

1/2 TEASPOON SWEET PAPRIKA

1/8 TEASPOON SALT

1/8 TEASPOON FRESHLY GROUND BLACK
   PEPPER

2 FROZEN SQUID STEAKS, 6 TO 8 OUNCES
   EACH, THAWED (SEE NOTE), RINSED, AND
   PATTED DRY

1 TABLESPOON VEGETABLE OIL

SALT AND FRESHLY GROUND BLACK PEPPER
   TO TASTE

2 CLOVES GARLIC, MINCED

1/2 RED BELL PEPPER, JULIENNED

1/2 YELLOW BELL PEPPER, JULIENNED

JUICE OF 1/2 LEMON

1/2 TEASPOON MINCED FRESH BASIL, PLUS
   EXTRA LEAVES, FOR GARNISH

1/2 TEASPOON SNIPPED FRESH CHIVES

2 TABLESPOONS DRY WHITE WINE

LEMON SLICES, FOR GARNISH

1. Mix flour, paprika, salt, and pepper in a small bowl. Pour seasoned flour onto a plate or a piece of waxed paper and dust squid steaks on each side, patting off excess.

2. Heat 1 1/2 teaspoons of the vegetable oil in a large skillet over medium-high heat. When oil is hot, add squid steaks, being careful as you place them in the pan, as the oil may pop. Cook 1 minute, or until lightly browned. Do not shake pan or move steaks in pan or browning will be slowed and breading may come off. Turn steaks and cook 1 minute more, or until crust is lightly browned, but squid is still translucent in the middle. Remove squid steaks and place on a cutting board. Cut steaks into 1/2-inch diamond-shaped pieces, sprinkle with salt and pepper, and set aside.

3. Meanwhile, discard any excess oil in pan, return skillet to burner, and add the remaining 1 1/2 teaspoons oil. Add garlic, red bell pepper, and yellow bell pepper to the pan and cook 2 to 3 minutes, stirring frequently, or until vegetables are tender. Scrape up and incorporate browned bits from bottom of pan.

4. Add squid diamonds, lemon juice, basil, and chives to pan. Stir well to mix, then add white wine. Cook 1 to 2 minutes more, or until squid is slightly firm. Divide squid among individual plates and garnish with basil leaves and lemon slices.

SERVES 4 AS AN APPETIZER, 2 AS AN ENTRÉE

Note: Frozen calamari steaks are made from very large squid and are a different texture than the smaller whole squid commonly available. Do not substitute the smaller whole squid. Sources include supermarket seafood departments (you may have to ask for the frozen steaks, as they may not be displayed in the refrigerated case), and Asian grocery stores.

Crisp-Fried Calamari with Three Sauces

———✦———

PARAGON,
SEATTLE, WASHINGTON

Chef Nancy Flume created a name for herself at Adriatica, the venerable Mediterranean restaurant overlooking Lake Union, where she was executive chef for ten years. She served what many people considered the best rendition of calamari fritti (fried squid) in town, accompanied by skordalia, a Greek dipping sauce made of puréed potatoes and copious amounts of garlic. When she became executive chef at Paragon, a popular bar/jazz club/restaurant on top of the Hillclimb in the Queen Anne district of Seattle, chef Flume reinvented her signature dish by adding semolina and white pepper to the breading and pairing the calamari with not one but three accompanying sauces: Green chile aïoli, smoky tomato sauce, and Thai chile sauce.

PEANUT OIL FOR DEEP-FRYING

2 CUPS ALL-PURPOSE FLOUR

$^1/_2$ CUP SEMOLINA

1 TEASPOON SALT

2 TEASPOONS FRESHLY GROUND WHITE
    PEPPER

2 POUNDS WHOLE CLEANED SQUID, BODIES
    CUT INTO $^1/_4$-INCH RINGS, TENTACLES
    LEFT WHOLE

2 LIMES, CUT INTO WEDGES

GREEN CHILE AÏOLI (RECIPE FOLLOWS)

SMOKY TOMATO SAUCE (RECIPE FOLLOWS)

THAI CHILE SAUCE (RECIPE FOLLOWS)

1. Preheat oven to 200°.

2. Fill a large saucepan or wok halfway with peanut oil and heat to 375°. While oil is heating, in a small mixing bowl, combine flour, semolina, salt, and white pepper. Rinse squid in a mixing bowl filled with cold water and ice cubes. While still wet, dredge squid in flour mixture, shake off excess flour; a medium-mesh sieve works well for this. Deep-fry in batches, without crowding, about 1 minute, or until golden. Drain on several layers of paper towels and place on baking sheet in oven to keep warm. When all squid is cooked, serve immediately with lime wedges and dipping sauces.

SERVES 4 AS A LIGHT ENTRÉE, 8 AS AN
APPETIZER

Green Chile Aïoli

1 EGG

1 EGG YOLK

1 (4-OUNCE) CAN MILD GREEN CHILES,
    DRAINED

2 CLOVES GARLIC, CHOPPED

1 BUNCH CILANTRO, RINSED, PATTED VERY
    DRY, STEMS REMOVED (SCANT 2 CUPS
    LOOSELY PACKED)

$^1/_4$ CUP MINCED GREEN ONIONS

$^1/_2$ TEASPOON GROUND CUMIN

$^1/_2$ TEASPOON SALT

1 TEASPOON FRESHLY GROUND BLACK
    PEPPER

2 TEASPOONS RED WINE VINEGAR

2 CUPS CORN OIL

1. Place egg, egg yolk, green chiles, garlic, cilantro, green onions, cumin, salt, pepper, and red wine vinegar in a food processor or blender

and process until smooth. Slowly add corn oil in a thin stream until a smooth, thick sauce forms. Pour into a small mixing bowl or glass jar with a lid and refrigerate until ready to serve.

MAKES ABOUT 3 CUPS

Smoky Tomato Sauce

4 CUPS COARSELY CHOPPED PLUM
   TOMATOES
1 CUP COARSELY CHOPPED ONION
4 CLOVES GARLIC, HALVED
2 JALAPEÑO PEPPERS, STEMS REMOVED,
   SEEDS AND MEMBRANES LEFT INTACT,
   COARSELY CHOPPED
1 TEASPOON SALT
1 TEASPOON FRESHLY GROUND BLACK
   PEPPER
1 TEASPOON CRUSHED RED PEPPER FLAKES
2 TABLESPOONS CANNED CHIPOTLE CHILES
   IN ADOBO
1 TABLESPOON BROWN SUGAR
2 TEASPOONS BALSAMIC VINEGAR

1. Preheat oven to 375°. Oil a baking sheet lightly or spray with nonstick cooking spray. Place tomatoes, onion, garlic, and jalapeños on baking sheet and sprinkle with salt, pepper, and red pepper flakes. Roast 25 to 30 minutes, or until vegetables start to brown.

2. Allow vegetables to cool slightly, then place in food processor or blender. Add chipotle chiles, brown sugar, and balsamic vinegar and process until smooth. Pour into a small mixing bowl or glass jar with a lid and refrigerate until ready to serve.

MAKES ABOUT 2 CUPS

Thai Chile Sauce

1 CUP SUGAR
1/2 CUP WATER
1/2 CUP UNSEASONED RICE VINEGAR
6 CLOVES GARLIC, MINCED
1 TEASPOON SALT
1 TABLESPOON CRUSHED RED PEPPER
   FLAKES
2 TABLESPOONS MINCED CILANTRO

Place sugar, water, rice vinegar, garlic, salt, and red pepper flakes in a small saucepan over medium heat. Bring to a simmer and cook 10 to 15 minutes, or until liquid forms a syrup. Remove from heat and allow to cool. Stir in cilantro, pour into small mixing bowl or glass jar with a lid, and refrigerate until ready to serve.

MAKES ABOUT 1 1/3 CUPS

Note: Semolina is the durum wheat flour from which premium pastas are made, a pale yellow flour ground a bit more coarsely than the all-purpose type. It is available at Ivacco Foods or DeLaurenti Specialty Foods in the Pike Place Market, and in gourmet food stores and supermarkets.

Note: Recent concerns about salmonella poisoning have called into question the use of raw eggs in food preparation. I would encourage the use of the freshest eggs available and a thorough washing and drying of the eggs before use. Individuals with chronic or autoimmune diseases should be informed of the uncooked eggs before eating the Green Chile Aïoli.

Vietnamese-Style Squid

I've always loved the dipping sauce (nuoc cham) *that comes as a condiment with Vietnamese spring rolls. This recipe uses the sauce as a marinade for cooked squid, which soaks up more of the robust flavor the longer it sits. Julienned vegetables and bean sprouts add color and textural contrast. This is a light, easy-to-prepare entrée, great for summertime dining. It also makes a delicious appetizer.*

1 POUND WHOLE CLEANED SQUID, BODIES
   CUT INTO $^1/_2$-INCH RINGS, LARGE TENTA-
   CLES CUT IN HALF

3 TABLESPOONS UNSEASONED RICE
   VINEGAR

1 TABLESPOON VIETNAMESE FISH SAUCE
   (*NUOC NAM*)

$2^1/_2$ TABLESPOONS WATER

$1^1/_2$ TEASPOONS GRATED GINGERROOT

PINCH OF CRUSHED RED PEPPER FLAKES

1 CLOVE GARLIC, MINCED

1 TABLESPOON SUGAR

1 TEASPOON FRESHLY SQUEEZED LIME
   JUICE

4 LARGE, SOFT LETTUCE LEAVES, SUCH AS
   BIBB, RED OR GREEN LEAF, OR ICEBERG

2 CUPS FRESH BEAN SPROUTS, RINSED,
   DRAINED, AND PATTED DRY

2 CARROTS, JULIENNED

1 RED BELL PEPPER, SEEDED AND
   JULIENNED

$^1/_4$ CUP CHOPPED UNSALTED PEANUTS, FOR
   GARNISH

2 TABLESPOONS MINCED CILANTRO OR
   FRESH MINT, FOR GARNISH (OPTIONAL)

1. Bring a large pot of water to a boil. Add squid and cook 1 to 2 minutes, or until squid just turns opaque. Drain into a colander and rinse immediately with cold water to stop the cooking process. Drain well and set aside.

2. In a medium mixing bowl, combine rice vinegar, fish sauce, water, gingerroot, red pepper flakes, garlic, sugar, and lime juice and stir until sugar is dissolved. Add squid and toss to coat evenly with marinade. Cover bowl and refrigerate at least 1 hour and up to 2 days, turning bowl occasionally to redistribute marinade.

3. When ready to serve, place lettuce leaves on 4 individual plates, or arrange on a large platter. Layer bean sprouts, carrots, and red bell pepper over lettuce leaves. Divide squid and place on top of vegetables. Sprinkle with peanuts and cilantro.

SERVES 4

Red Hot Chile Pepper Squid

GARLIC TREE RESTAURANT, PIKE PLACE MARKET

Garlic Tree Restaurant is a friendly family business run by Hong Ja Han (just call her "Mom"), daughter Soo, and son Tony. The restaurant specializes in homestyle Korean food made with cherished family recipes. Soo cautions against overcooking this dish, which should take from 3 to 5 minutes total, to prevent the squid from becoming tough and rubbery.

1 POUND WHOLE CLEANED SQUID, BODIES CUT INTO ³/₄-INCH PIECES, LARGE TENTACLES CUT IN HALF

4 TABLESPOONS SOY SAUCE OR TAMARI SAUCE

1 TEASPOON MINCED GINGERROOT, OR ¹/₂ TEASPOON GROUND GINGER

2 TEASPOONS FRESHLY GROUND BLACK PEPPER

2 TABLESPOONS SUGAR

1 TABLESPOON CORNSTARCH (OPTIONAL)

2 TABLESPOONS VEGETABLE OIL

2 CLOVES GARLIC, MINCED

6 CUPS ASSORTED VEGETABLES, CLEANED AND CUT INTO BITE-SIZED PIECES (SUCH AS BROCCOLI, ONIONS, BELL PEPPERS, MUSHROOMS, GREEN ONIONS, WATER CHESTNUTS, ZUCCHINI, YELLOW SQUASH, CARROTS, SUGAR SNAP PEAS, OR CHINESE PEA PODS)

4 TO 8 WHOLE DRY RED CHILE PEPPERS (DEPENDING ON LEVEL OF HEAT DESIRED)

1 ¹/₂ TEASPOONS TOASTED SESAME OIL

4 CUPS COOKED WHITE LONG-GRAIN OR BROWN RICE

1. Soak squid in a bowl of ice water about 10 minutes, or while preparing rest of recipe.

2. In a small mixing bowl or jar with a lid, mix soy sauce, gingerroot, black pepper, sugar, and cornstarch until sugar is dissolved. Cover and set aside.

3. Before beginning to cook squid, drain well and pat dry thoroughly. Heat a wok or large skillet over medium-high heat and add vegetable oil. When oil is hot, add garlic and cook 1 to 2 minutes, or until golden brown, stirring continuously. Add vegetables and stir-fry 1 to 2 minutes, or until vegetables are tender-crisp. Add squid and red chile peppers and stir-fry 1 minute, or until edges of squid curl. Add reserved sauce and stir-fry 30 seconds. Remove pan from heat, add toasted sesame oil and toss to mix well.

4. To serve, divide rice among individual plates and top with stir-fried squid, red chile peppers, and vegetables.

SERVES 4

Calamari Fillets with Ground Almonds

————— ⌘ —————

CAMPAGNE,
PIKE PLACE MARKET

Award-winning chef Tamara Murphy combines the flavors of sea and earth when she coats calamari fillets with ground almonds and sautés them in fruity olive oil. A sprinkling of fresh thyme completes the simple dish, which offers a tempting alternative to the deep-fried calamari served at many restaurants.

2 POUNDS WHOLE SQUID, CLEANED (SEE
    PAGE 257), BODIES ONLY

SALT AND FRESHLY GROUND BLACK PEPPER

1/2 CUP FRESHLY GROUND RAW ALMONDS

1/4 CUP ALL-PURPOSE FLOUR

4 EGGS

3 TABLESPOONS OLIVE OIL

1 TABLESPOON FRESH THYME LEAVES

1 LEMON, SLICED INTO THIN WEDGES

1. Preheat oven to 200°.

2. Rinse squid bodies under cold running water to remove any traces of viscera or purple skin. Pat dry. Run a sharp knife down one side of squid and open up to form a fillet.

3. Place squid bodies on a large piece of plastic wrap and fold over wrap to cover top of meat. With a meat mallet or tenderizer, pound meat until very thin, just before it threatens to tear. Don't worry if little holes form—the more thinly pounded, the more tender the squid will be. Don't pound too hard, however, or squid will be mushy.

4. Season squid fillets generously on both sides with salt and pepper. Place whole almonds (with skin) in a food processor and process until they become a fine dust. Do not overprocess or they will form a paste. Mix together almonds and flour in a small bowl, then pour onto a plate or a piece of waxed paper. Dust fillets with flour mixture, patting off excess. Place fillets on a large platter until all are dusted. Beat eggs in a medium mixing bowl and place both egg mixture and dusted squid fillets next to stove.

5. In a large skillet, heat 1 to 1 1/2 tablespoons of the olive oil over medium heat. Oil should coat bottom of pan about 1/8-inch deep; if not, add more oil. When oil is hot, dip fillets in beaten eggs, then let excess egg run back into bowl. Cook in batches, placing as many squid fillets into pan as will comfortably fit. Be careful not to crowd fillets.

6. Brown just until egg turns golden, about 6 to 8 seconds per side, decreasing heat or removing skillet from heat if squid cooks too fast. Place squid on paper towels to drain extra oil. Place cooked fillets on baking sheet and keep warm in oven. Repeat with remaining fillets, adding remaining olive oil as needed.

7. When all squid fillets are cooked, divide among 4 individual plates, sprinkle with thyme, and place lemon wedges on side of plate. Serve immediately.

SERVES 4

Florentine Stuffed Squid

Squid tubes make natural receptacles for stuffings, which are often impulsive affairs created with leftovers from the fridge, such as cooked rice, leftover pasta, or bread crumbs; pine nuts, hazelnuts, or almonds; cottage, Parmesan, or feta cheese; and fresh or dried herbs. The squid's tentacles add bulk, and the mixture is bound together by a beaten egg. Stuffed squid dishes look impressive and it's always a surprise for family and friends to cut into the puffy globes and guess what the stuffing contains.

8 LARGE WHOLE SQUID BODIES, ABOUT 5 OR
    6 INCHES LONG, CLEANED AND TENTA-
    CLES RESERVED

1/2 CUP COOKED LONG-GRAIN WHITE OR
    BROWN RICE

1/4 CUP SMALL-CURD COTTAGE CHEESE

1/4 CUP FRESHLY GRATED PARMESAN
    CHEESE

2 TABLESPOONS MINCED FRESH SPINACH

2 TABLESPOONS TOASTED PINE NUTS
    (SEE PAGE 10)

2 CLOVES GARLIC, MINCED

1 EGG, BEATEN

1/4 TEASPOON GROUND NUTMEG

2 TABLESPOONS OLIVE OIL

DASH OF SALT AND FRESHLY GROUND BLACK
    PEPPER

1 CUP MARINARA SAUCE (SEE PAGE 319) OR
    OTHER SPAGHETTI SAUCE

1/2 CUP DRY WHITE OR RED WINE OR
    CHICKEN STOCK

BASIL LEAVES, FOR GARNISH

1. Preheat oven to 325°. Use a baking dish that will hold squid in one layer, and grease lightly with butter or spray with nonstick cooking spray.

2. Leave squid bodies whole. Finely chop tentacles, and combine in a medium bowl with rice, cottage cheese, Parmesan cheese, spinach, pine nuts, garlic, egg, nutmeg, and olive oil until well blended.

3. Spoon stuffing into squid bodies until they are about three-quarters full. Be careful not to overstuff as squid will shrink when cooked and may burst if overstuffed. Close each opening with a toothpick or wooden skewer broken into thirds.

4. In a medium bowl, combine marinara sauce and wine. Spoon 1/4 inch of sauce over bottom of prepared baking dish. Arrange stuffed squid in a single layer over sauce, then pour remaining sauce over top. Cover baking dish and bake for 30 to 35 minutes. Remove cover and bake another 15 minutes, or until squid is tender.

5. Divide stuffed squid among individual plates and garnish with basil leaves.

SERVES 4

Part 4

CANNED AND SMOKED SEAFOOD,
SEAFOOD COMBINATION DISHES,
AND SEAFOOD SIDEKICKS

Canned and Smoked Seafood

Canned Seafood

While the focus of this book is on fresh seafood, a pantry well stocked with canned seafood can provide the remedy for times when you need a quick meal, when unexpected company drops by, or you simply want some seafood but don't have any fresh or frozen on hand. Varieties available in most supermarkets include shrimp (in small and medium sizes), crabmeat (regular or lump), clams (minced, chopped, or whole; regular or smoked), salmon (regular or smoked), oysters (regular or smoked), sardines (in olive oil and various sauces), mussels (in jars, plain, or marinated), anchovies, mackerel, and tuna (regular or smoked).

Canned seafood is thoroughly cooked in the canning process to kill bacteria that can cause food poisoning. Unfortunately, the intense heat and lengthy cooking required for canning diminish the texture, size, and flavor of seafood. For this reason, canned seafood should not be used in recipes where it is the star ingredient, but instead used in a supporting role in robust soups, stews, and pasta sauces where flavor-packed ingredients help compensate for its deficits. Adding canned seafood during the last few minutes of cooking also helps prevent any further loss of quality or flavor.

If you are watching calories, avoid oil-packed products. Canned seafood packed in water, tomato, or mustard sauce, or in its own natural juices is a wise nutritional choice.

Since canned seafood lacks some of the attributes of fresh, buy the best quality you can afford. Avoid dented cans. Store canned fish on a cool, dry shelf for up to one year. Stored longer, the fish is still safe to eat but acquires a strong, salty odor and flavor that many find undesirable. In a pantry that remains warmer than 72° for any length of time, canned fish will lose its quality even more quickly.

After canned fish is opened, store it in a tightly covered glass or plastic container in the refrigerator for 3 to 5 days. Fish salads in dressing can be safely stored for up to 3 days. Frozen at temperatures 0° or lower, properly wrapped fish from cans (either plain or in prepared dishes) keeps 2 to 3 months.

TUNA

Canned tuna is the most popular type of canned seafood. Consumers in the United States purchase over 1 billion cans a year, and the average American eats 3.6 pounds of canned tuna a year. It is one of the three top-selling items in U.S. supermarkets, along with canned soups and boxed macaroni and cheese.

Canned albacore is the highest-quality

tuna and the only variety that can legally be marketed as white meat tuna. Albacore is the best choice for dishes where large chunks and mild flavor are desired. "Chunk light" and "flake" tuna are generally made from yellowfin tuna and are pinkish gray in color. Chunk light and flake work well for casseroles, sandwiches, or soups. The solid-pack, or "fancy" variety consists of large pieces of tuna with no small fragments of meat.

If you buy tuna packed in oil and want to extract as much oil as possible before using the tuna, put the tuna in a sieve and rinse it with cold running water. Gently squeeze the meat to extract all the water, or pat dry, then pass the tuna through a potato ricer.

SALMON

Unlike tuna, which is canned with vegetable oil or water, a can of salmon contains only salmon, plus a pinch of salt. The few tablespoons of juice that pour off a can of salmon are water and oil cooked out of the salmon flesh by the heat and pressure of the canning process. The liquid along with the skin and tiny bones are safe to eat, if not particularly aesthetic. The bones are an excellent source of calcium, while the skin contributes protein and omega-3 oils.

Chinook and sockeye salmon are often sold canned as "red" salmon and are best for any recipe in which appearance counts, such as salads. Pink, chum, or coho are fine for everything else, such as soups, casseroles, and patties. Among canned salmon, color and price generally indicate quality.

SARDINES

Sardines are small fish in the herring family. The fish are thoroughly gutted before processing, are usually canned whole, then packed in olive oil, soybean oil, mustard sauce, or tomato sauce. The preserving process softens the bones, which can safely be eaten. Sardines are used in appetizers and sandwiches.

CRAB

Most canned crabmeat sold in the United States is harvested from blue crabs and comes from China. Lump or backfin is the highest-quality crabmeat. If a can says "white" or "flake" meat, it simply means meat from the body of the crab.

SHRIMP

Canned shrimp should be rinsed thoroughly to remove excess salt before eating. To remove the canned taste, rinse the shrimp in cold water, then soak for 15 minutes in a mixture of 2 tablespoons distilled white vinegar and a splash of sherry. Rinse well before using.

ANCHOVIES

Anchovies are small, very fatty fish with a potent flavor. They are usually filleted, packed in barrels of salt for several months until the flesh is cured to a deep red, then preserved in oil, although they are also available salted in jars. They come flat or rolled and are used in canapés, pizza toppings, salade niçoise, anchovy paste, and anchovy butter.

Caviar

Caviar is one of the world's most celebrated foods, first introduced to European society in the 1920s after the Russian Revolution and eaten by the rich and famous the world over. Yet despite its high-falutin' reputation, caviar is really just uncooked fish eggs, or roe, mixed with salt. Eggs from more than 30 different species of fish are made into caviar, although caviar processed from the roe of female sturgeon caught in the Caspian Sea sets the world standard.

In France, only the processed roe of the female Caspian sturgeon may be called caviar. In the United States, as long as the species of fish is named—such as paddlefish caviar or salmon caviar—the word "caviar" may be used to describe any processed roe.

Of the three types of Caspian sturgeon (beluga, osetra, or sevruga) marketed, none is considered superior to another. Rather, the caviar of each species is prized and revered for its individual characteristics. Caspian caviars labeled "malosso" (Russian for "little salt") signifies the caviars that have been only lightly salted and are of the highest quality.

Caviar is traditionally served in its jar or tin nested in a large shallow bowl of crushed ice. Use a mother-of-pearl, bone, or (in a pinch) plastic spoon to serve it. Sterling silver imparts a metallic taste and discolors when it comes in contact with caviar.

Accompany caviar with fresh toast points, blinis, potatoes, and a touch of fresh lemon juice or crème fraîche. Iced vodka, Champagne, or black tea are favorite accompanying beverages.

Prices range from close to 50 dollars an ounce for Russian beluga caviar to 4 dollars an ounce for domestic golden whitefish caviar.

Caviar is sold fresh, frozen, or pasteurized, in jars or tins in gourmet shops, specialty caviar stores, and some upscale supermarkets. Pasteurized caviar is roe that has been partially cooked, thereby giving the eggs a slightly different taste, consistency, and texture. Because of the way it is processed, pasteurized caviar is less perishable and may not require refrigeration before opening. It is considered of lesser quality, but is also less expensive than the fresh product.

Caviar will keep for only 14 to 21 days unopened in the coldest part of the refrigerator (28° to 32°) and needs to be eaten as soon as it is opened. Never freeze caviar (except for golden caviar). Remove the caviar from the refrigerator no more than 15 minutes before serving, and leave the lid on until the last minute. Once the tin is opened, it should be consumed that day since it deteriorates rapidly.

Caviar should never taste or smell "fishy." Its aroma (if there is one at all) is a faint, clean, fresh sea-air smell. The eggs should be moist, smooth-skinned, and glistening with a light sheen of oil. They should be whole and separate, firm and intact. Dull, broken eggs that are mushy or gummy may reflect improper storage or handling or signify eggs past their prime.

In the mouth, good-quality eggs will hold firm for an instant, "pop" conspicuously when bitten or gently pressed against the palate, then release a subtle, unsalty, "unfishy" flavor containing a suggestion of the eggs' natural oils.

BELUGA CAVIAR

The beluga is the largest sturgeon, weighing up to 2,500 pounds and reaching 20 feet in length, although the fish average between 800 to 900 pounds and about 15 feet in length. The female must reach 18 to 20 years of age before it produces eggs.

With the largest grain and most delicate sturgeon eggs, beluga caviar has a smooth taste considered by connoisseurs to be lightest in flavor. Its color varies from light to dark gray. It is the most expensive caviar, costing twice as much as either osetra or sevruga.

OSETRA CAVIAR

Osetra sturgeons are much smaller than beluga, weighing between 100 and 300 pounds and growing 6 to 7 feet in length. They reach maturation between 12 and 15 years.

Osetra is a large-grain caviar, just a little smaller than beluga and with a firmer, crisper texture. It varies in color from golden yellow to brown, with a flavor often described as nutty or fruity.

SEVRUGA CAVIAR

The sevruga sturgeon is the smallest of the Caspian specimens. It rarely exceeds 4 to 5 feet in length and averages 50 pounds. Sevruga is more abundant than the other caviar sturgeon and matures in 7 years. Its caviar is medium grain, has a strong yet delicate flavor, and ranges in color from dark gray to black. It is the least expensive of the major caviars.

LUMPFISH CAVIAR

Lumpfish caviar is a pasteurized caviar with tiny, hard, black eggs. It is usually imported from Denmark or Iceland.

Lumpfish caviar should be rinsed to remove the dyes and preservatives with which it is processed, as well as some of its salty, fishy taste. After rinsing, drain, cover, and chill thoroughly before serving.

SALMON CAVIAR

Salmon caviar is one of the largest roes prepared as caviar. The eggs have a pleasant taste and a distinct texture. They range in color from pale orange to bright red.

PADDLEFISH CAVIAR

Caviar can be made from the eggs of the paddlefish (*Polyodon spathula*), an ancient and primitive species distinguished by its long paddlelike snout, largely cartilaginous skeleton, and almost scaleless body. The fish is caught on hooks and lines in Montana by sport fishers in the waters of the Yellowstone River. It weighs from 60 to 160 pounds, with 15 years the average age of roe-producing female fish.

Paddlefish eggs are the same size as sevruga caviar and are light to dark gray in color, well separated, and slightly oily. This type of caviar is very mild, smooth, and not salty, perfect for the Northwest palate. It is available fresh late May through early June, and frozen, August through December.

GOLDEN CAVIAR

Golden caviar comes from whitefish found in Montana and the Great Lakes. It is a little smaller than sevruga caviar, is an attractive golden apricot to deep amber color, and has a clean, fresh taste. This type of caviar, like other caviars, must be kept under refrigeration, but unlike sturgeon caviar, may be frozen and even refrozen without loss of flavor and texture.

Smoked Fish

Seafood was once preserved with salt and smoke out of necessity, but today these methods are used mostly to impart distinctive flavors and textures. Because modern smoking techniques rely on much less salt and often no heat, the smoking process alone does not preserve seafood. Just like any other perishable food, smoked seafood needs to be kept in the refrigerator or freezer.

Types of finfish suitable for smoking include salmon, sturgeon, trout, cod, herring, sablefish, tuna, and whitefish. As a general rule, the higher the oil content, the moister the smoked fish will be, although a vigilant cook can successfully smoke lean fish such as halibut and tuna. Most shellfish smoke well, including clams, mussels, shrimp, scallops, and oysters.

COLD-SMOKED VERSUS HOT-SMOKED SEAFOOD

There are two main types of smoke cure: cold-smoking, which smokes but does not cook the fish, and hot-smoking, which smokes and cooks the fish at the same time. In both cases, seafood to be smoked is normally given a preliminary brine bath (a mixture of salt and water or other liquid, sometimes with sugar and spices added) before smoking. The brine draws out moisture, inhibits bacterial growth somewhat, and adds flavor. The fish or shellfish is then rinsed in fresh water and dried before being slowly cooked in indirect heat at a low temperature, with plenty of aromatic smoke. The smoke is supplied by nonresinous woods, such as oak, hickory, maple, beech, apple, cherry, pear, or alder (the Northwest favorite). Differences among the tastes and textures of smoked seafoods come about due to variations in the brine and the length of time the seafood is left in it, the type of smoke and the length of time the seafood is in contact with it, and the type of smoker used.

The internal temperature of a cold-smoked fish never rises above 85° to 90°, so the fish is technically raw even after smoking. The internal temperature of hot-smoked fish rises to 140° or more, which cooks the seafood. In hot smoking, the lower the temperature, the longer the smoking process will take. The longer the smoking process, the more pronounced the flavor.

Hot-smoked seafood (sometimes called "kippered" in the United States) is considered the more versatile of the two because of its firmer, drier texture and less imposing flavor. It may be chunked, flaked, or coarsely puréed.

Cold-smoked seafood remains moister and slightly translucent. Because of their moist and silky texture, cold-smoked fish can be draped, wrapped, layered in one piece, thinly sliced, chopped, or puréed smoothly. Their tender, delicate quality is best enjoyed as is, which is the reason cold-smoked seafoods aren't used in recipes as often as hot-smoked seafoods. Cold-smoked fish should also be used when making mousses that rely on the unset protein of the fish for a silky texture.

SMOKED SALMON

Smoked salmon, the unrivaled king of all smoked fish, comes in many distinct forms. Gravlax is a Scandinavian-style salmon that is always cured using salt, sugar, and dill, and sometimes pepper or other spices. It is weighted down and refrigerated for up to 24 hours, which results in a soft, translucent fish that is served in very thin slices on buttered bread or crackers.

Lox is salmon that has been brined for up to one year, although the terminology is confusing. True lox (the type served on the East Coast) is simply brined and never smoked, while West Coast lox is brined and usually cold-smoked. Nowadays, the definition of lox has been expanded to include almost any type of well-salted and cured salmon, cold-smoked or not, that is served in thin slices.

Nova is short for Nova Scotia style, the process used by North Atlantic fishers in that Canadian province. On the East Coast, nova refers to salt- and water-brined fish that has been cold-smoked. On the West Coast, nova is fish that has been cured in salt and brown sugar for up to 2 weeks, then air-dried and cold-smoked up to 18 hours. Because of its lower salt content, nova is considered of higher quality and more delectable by gourmets; it outsells lox by a wide margin.

Hard-smoked salmon, known as salmon jerky and sometimes sold as "squaw candy," is heavily salted and generally smoked (usually cold-smoked) for a very long time, which draws out most of the moisture in the fish. The moisture loss results in a very chewy product that is easily portable and great to take on camping trips.

Smoked fish should be displayed in a refrigerated case even if it has been vacuum-packed. A good-quality product will look bright and glossy with no signs of mold. All smoked seafood, except that packed in cans or retortable pouches, must be held at 38° or below in the refrigerator. Vacuum packing is no guarantee against bacterial contamination.

Because smoked seafoods are soaked in a salt brine before smoking, they will last longer in the refrigerator than unsmoked seafoods. A whole smoked fish or a large chunk can be stored, tightly wrapped, in the refrigerator for up to 2 weeks. Slices of smoked fish deteriorate much more quickly and should be wrapped in plastic or aluminum foil and refrigerated for no more than a few days. If properly wrapped and stored in a freezer at 0° or below, smoked seafood will keep for 2 to 3 months, although the flesh may be soft when thawed.

Smoked seafood is also often available in bright foil bags called retortable or retort pouches. Smoked products packaged this way do not need to be refrigerated until the package is opened, because they have actually undergone the canning process, which cooks the seafood and kills any bacteria present. The thin pouch, which is made of bonded layers of plastic and metal, simply takes the place of the traditional can. Rules for storage are the same as for standard canned seafood items.

Smoked Salmon Pasta Salad

TOTEM SMOKEHOUSE, PIKE PLACE MARKET

Smoked salmon is one of the traditional foods of the Northwest, which is one reason why Jane and Fred Poole, along with Mark Zenger and Rebecca Petre, are so proud to own Totem Smokehouse, the Market's smoked seafood store. This easy pasta salad show-cases the smokehouse's wonderful product; rich in texture, color, and flavor, it would be great for a summer picnic or to take to a potluck supper.

1 (9-OUNCE) PACKAGE FRESH CHEESE
    TORTELLINI, OR ¹/₂ POUND DRY CHEESE
    TORTELLINI
¹/₄ CUP CHOPPED CELERY
¹/₄ CUP CHOPPED RED BELL PEPPER
1 (8³/₄-OUNCE) CAN GARBANZO BEANS,
    DRAINED
1 (2¹/₄-OUNCE) CAN SLICED BLACK OLIVES,
    DRAINED
1 (6¹/₂-OUNCE) JAR MARINATED ARTICHOKE
    HEARTS, DRAINED OF OIL AND CHOPPED
2 TABLESPOONS CHOPPED FRESH BASIL
DRESSING (RECIPE FOLLOWS)
8 OUNCES HOT-SMOKED SALMON, SKIN AND
    BONES REMOVED, CRUMBLED
FRESHLY GROUND BLACK PEPPER
FRESHLY GRATED PARMESAN CHEESE

1. Cook tortellini according to package instructions. Rinse under cold running water, drain well, and pour into a large mixing bowl. Add celery, red bell pepper, garbanzo beans, olives, artichoke hearts, basil, and dressing and toss to mix. Gently stir smoked salmon into pasta salad.

2. To serve, divide salad among individual plates and sprinkle with pepper and Parmesan cheese.

SERVES 4

Dressing

¹/₂ CUP RED WINE VINEGAR
¹/₄ CUP OLIVE OIL
1 TABLESPOON CHOPPED RED ONION
1 ¹/₂ TEASPOONS SUGAR
1 TEASPOON DRY MUSTARD
1 TEASPOON DRIED BASIL, CRUMBLED
¹/₂ TEASPOON DIJON MUSTARD
¹/₂ TEASPOON DRIED OREGANO, CRUMBLED
2 CLOVES GARLIC, CRUSHED

In a small mixing bowl, whisk together all of the ingredients except the garlic until sugar is dissolved. Add garlic, cover bowl, and place in refrigerator at least 2 hours, and preferably overnight, to allow flavors to blend. Remove crushed garlic cloves before adding dressing to pasta salad.

MAKES ³/₄ CUP

FUN FACTS

- The origins of caviar are sketchy. The early Persians enjoyed fish eggs, known as *chav-jar*, or "cake of strength." The ancient Romans had a fondness for *caviala* and may have carried both the taste and the word with them when they conquered Turkey. The Turkish *khavyar* means "fish eggs."

Smoked Salmon Dutch Baby with Dill Sauce

Dutch babies are puffy pancakes cooked in a skillet in the oven. Although usually served with a sweet lemon sauce, I have turned the dish into a savory one with the addition of smoked salmon and sautéed vegetables. When cut into wedges and served warm or at room temperature, my savory Dutch baby makes an impressive appetizer. For a more down-home brunch item, substitute a small can of red salmon (skin and bones removed) or a cup of leftover cooked salmon for the smoked salmon and add along with the sautéed vegetables. And no peeking while the Dutch baby is cooking; opening the oven door while baking will cause the pancake to fall!

1 TABLESPOON OLIVE OIL

$1/2$ WHITE OR YELLOW ONION, CHOPPED

$1/2$ RED BELL PEPPER, CHOPPED

1 TABLESPOON BUTTER

$3/4$ CUP LOWFAT MILK

$1/3$ CUP ALL-PURPOSE FLOUR

PINCH OF FRESHLY GROUND WHITE PEPPER

4 EGGS OR 1 CUP EGG SUBSTITUTE

$1 1/2$ TEASPOONS GROUND SWEET PAPRIKA

1 (3-OUNCE) PACKAGE THINLY SLICED COLD-
   SMOKED SALMON, SUCH AS NOVA STYLE
   OR LOX

1. Preheat oven to 400°.

2. Heat olive oil in a medium skillet over medium-high heat. Add onion and red bell pepper and cook until vegetables are tender, about 5 to 7 minutes, stirring often. Remove from heat and set aside.

3. Melt butter in a large, nonstick, ovenproof skillet in oven until sizzling. Wrap handle of skillet with aluminum foil if it is not an oven-proof skillet and check skillet frequently to make sure that butter doesn't burn.

4. Meanwhile, add milk, flour, and white pepper to a food processor or blender and blend together. Add egg substitute and process just until blended.

5. Remove skillet from oven and place reserved vegetables into skillet, distributing evenly. Immediately pour in egg batter. Bake, uncovered, in center of oven until Dutch baby is puffed and lightly browned, about 12 to 15 minutes.

6. Remove pan from oven, sprinkle evenly with paprika, and arrange salmon slices evenly over top of pancake. Cut into 8 wedges and serve immediately, or allow to come to room temperature before serving.

7. To serve, place 2 wedges on individual plates and place a dollop of Dill Sauce beside wedges.

SERVES 4 AS AN APPETIZER

Dill Sauce

$1/4$ CUP PLAIN LOWFAT YOGURT

$1/4$ CUP LOWFAT SOUR CREAM

1 TABLESPOON FRESH SNIPPED DILL, OR 1
   TEASPOON DRIED DILL, CRUMBLED

TABASCO SAUCE TO TASTE

SALT TO TASTE

Place yogurt, sour cream, and dill in a small mixing bowl and stir to blend. Season to taste with Tabasco and salt. Cover and refrigerate until ready to use.

MAKES $1/2$ CUP

Smoked Salmon and Wild Rice Cakes with Paprika and Green Onion Aïoli

———

CUCINA FRESCA, PIKE PLACE MARKET

Cucina Fresca, the fresh pasta shop in the Market, is owned by Jessica and Jay Beattie, a hard working, outgoing young couple who have worked in restaurants in the Seattle area and traveled extensively in France, where Jay cooked in Michelin-rated restaurants. At Cucina Fresca, the Beatties offer a wide selection of take-out Italian foods, everything from fresh pastas and pasta sauces to Italian hors d'oeuvres and entrées, along with Italian staples such as olive oil, balsamic vinegar, and hand-crank pasta makers, just in case you get the urge to roll your own! These smoked salmon Cakes, one of their popular take-out items, are a real standout, as is the lusty, rust-colored aïoli sauce that accompanies them.

¼ POUND UNCOOKED WILD RICE (ABOUT ¾ CUP)

½ CUP DICED RED ONION

¼ CUP DICED RED BELL PEPPER

¼ CUP DICED YELLOW BELL PEPPER

1 STALK CELERY, DICED

2 GREEN ONIONS, THINLY SLICED

⅓ CUP CHOPPED FRESH BASIL, LOOSELY PACKED

¼ POUND HOT-SMOKED SALMON, SKIN AND BONES REMOVED, COARSELY CHOPPED AND CRUMBLED

2 TEASPOONS DIJON MUSTARD

1½ TABLESPOONS CAPERS, DRAINED AND MINCED

JUICE OF 1 SMALL LEMON

2 TABLESPOONS CHOPPED FRESH PARSLEY

1½ TEASPOONS EXTRA VIRGIN OLIVE OIL

1 TEASPOON SALT

PINCH OF CAYENNE

¾ TEASPOON DRIED DILL, CRUMBLED

1 SMALL EGG

½ CUP PANKO BREAD CRUMBS OR UNSEASONED DRY BREAD CRUMBS, PLUS EXTRA AS NEEDED

1 TABLESPOON OLIVE OIL OR VEGETABLE OIL

PAPRIKA AND GREEN ONION AÏOLI (RECIPE FOLLOWS)

LEMON WEDGES, FOR GARNISH

1. Cook wild rice according to package directions. Drain well and set aside to cool. Rice should be as dry as possible, so press handfuls of rice between palms of hand or place rice in a fine-meshed sieve and press with the back of a wooden spoon to extract all remaining liquid.

2. In a large bowl, stir together wild rice, red onion, red bell pepper, yellow bell pepper, celery, green onions, basil, smoked salmon, Dijon mustard, capers, lemon juice, parsley, olive oil, salt, cayenne, dill, and egg. Add bread crumbs and stir again. Allow mixture to sit at room temperature for 20 minutes.

3. Ten minutes before cooking, preheat oven to 400°.

4. Divide wild rice mixture into 8 patties. If patties do not stick together, add a bit more of the panko bread crumbs.

5. Heat a large nonstick pan over medium heat. When pan is hot, add olive oil. Before adding salmon cakes, oil should be very hot, but not smoking. Test oil by dropping a small piece of the mixture into pan. Fry cakes for 3 minutes on each side, turning only once. Cook in 2 batches and add additional oil if necessary. Remove patties to baking sheet, place in oven, and bake for 10 minutes, or until golden brown and heated through.

6. To serve, divide patties among individual plates and drizzle with Paprika and Green Onion Aïoli. Garnish with lemon wedges.

SERVES 4

Paprika and Green Onion Aïoli

1 EGG YOLK

1 TEASPOON DIJON MUSTARD

³/₄ CUP OLIVE OIL

1 ¹/₂ TEASPOONS MINCED GARLIC

1 ¹/₂ TEASPOONS GROUND SWEET PAPRIKA

JUICE OF ¹/₂ LEMON

¹/₂ TEASPOON SALT

3 GREEN ONIONS, TOPS ONLY, CUT INTO
    ¹/₈-INCH ROUNDS (ABOUT 2
    TABLESPOONS)

1. In a medium bowl, whisk together the egg yolk and mustard until combined. Continue whisking while adding olive oil a few drops at a time until mixture emulsifies (becomes smooth and thick).

2. Whisk in garlic, paprika, lemon juice, salt, and green onions. Cover and refrigerate for at least 30 minutes before serving to allow flavors to blend.

MAKES ABOUT 1 CUP

Note: Recent concerns about salmonella poisoning have called into question the use of raw eggs in food preparation. I would encourage the use of the freshest eggs available and a thorough washing and drying of the eggs before use. Individuals with chronic or autoimmune diseases should be informed of the uncooked eggs before eating this dish.

FUN FACTS

• The first recorded mention of modern caviar was by Batu Khan, the grandson of Genghis Khan, on a visit outside Moscow around A.D. 1240. About 500 years later, the first private caviar company opened its doors on the northwest shore of the Caspian Sea.

• Fishers in the Caspian Sea have pursued sturgeon, since the thirteenth century. One of the world's most ancient fish species, a large beluga sturgeon can yield 200 pounds of raw caviar.

Smoked Salmon Ravioli with Lemon-Cream Sauce

TULIO RISTORANTE IN THE VINTAGE PARK HOTEL, SEATTLE, WASHINGTON

One Saturday afternoon after a dizzying morning running errands in downtown Seattle, I stopped at Tulio for a leisurely lunch. After a glass of wine and samples of the wonderful focaccia and country breads made in-house, I settled in with a plate of this smoked salmon ravioli and immediately fell in love with its contrasting textures, colors, and tastes. When Executive chef/owner Walter Pisano agreed to share the recipe with me, I was thrilled, particularly when I realized that it is easy enough for the home cook to prepare.

ALL-PURPOSE FLOUR OR SEMOLINA FLOUR

4 (APPROXIMATELY 14 x 6 1/2-INCH) SHEETS
   FRESH PASTA

4 OUNCES THINLY SLICED NOVA-STYLE
   COLD-SMOKED SALMON, SLICED INTO
   1-INCH SQUARES

8 OUNCES MASCARPONE CHEESE

1 EGG

1 TABLESPOON WATER

LEMON-CREAM SAUCE (RECIPE FOLLOWS)

1 TEASPOON SNIPPED FRESH CHIVES,
   FOR GARNISH

1. Lightly flour a large, flat, clean work surface. Sprinkle lightly 2 baking sheets with all-purpose flour or semolina flour and set aside.

2. Lay out 1 sheet of the pasta on a work surface. Place squares of smoked salmon over pasta at 2-inch intervals. Place 1/2 teaspoon mascarpone cheese over each piece of smoked salmon, then top mascarpone with another piece of smoked salmon.

3. In a small mixing bowl, beat together egg and water to form an egg wash. Brush egg wash over salmon pieces and pasta, then press a second sheet of pasta over bottom square of pasta. Press top pasta sheet to seal edges on sides and between pieces of salmon.

4. With a pizza cutter or sharp knife, form ravioli squares, cutting around salmon and pasta. Press edges to tightly seal ravioli, then place individual ravioli on baking sheet. Repeat process with remaining ingredients.

5. When you are ready to cook pasta, bring a large pot of salted water to a boil. Place ravioli in water one at a time to avoid sticking, and stir gently. Do not overcrowd. Cook 3 to 5 minutes, or until pasta is al dente. Drain ravioli well and toss with Lemon-Cream Sauce.

6. To serve, place ravioli on a large serving platter or divide among individual plates and garnish with chives.

SERVES 4

Lemon-Cream Sauce

8 ASPARAGUS STALKS, TOUGH ENDS
   REMOVED

1 TABLESPOON OLIVE OIL

2 TEASPOONS MINCED SHALLOTS

1/4 CUP DRY WHITE WINE

2 1/4 CUPS HEAVY WHIPPING CREAM
1/4 CUP FRESHLY SQUEEZED LEMON JUICE
GRATED ZEST OF 1/2 LEMON
SALT AND FRESHLY GROUND BLACK
    PEPPER TO TASTE

1. In a medium skillet or saucepan, bring 1/2 inch of water to a boil. Add asparagus and cook 2 to 3 minutes, or until tender-crisp. Rinse in cold water, drain well, pat dry, and cut diagonally into 1/4-inch pieces. Set aside.

2. Heat oil in a medium saucepan over medium heat. Add shallots and cook 3 minutes, or until shallots are soft but not brown, stirring occasionally. Add wine and cook 2 to 3 minutes, or until reduced slightly. Add whipping cream, lemon juice, lemon zest, and asparagus and stir well. Season to taste with salt and pepper. Turn off heat, but do not remove saucepan from burner. Sauce should be fairly thin and remain warm until serving.

MAKES 2 1/2 CUPS

Note: Fresh pasta sheets are available in the Pike Place Market at DeLaurenti Specialty Foods and Cucina Fresca and at stores that sell freshly made pasta. Mascarpone, the Italian version of cream cheese, is available at DeLaurenti Specialty Foods and the Pike Place Market Creamery, which sells a Washington-made product that is less expensive than the imported version.

HANDY CHEF'S TIP

Gregg Galushka, chef at McCormick's Fish House in downtown Seattle, is an enthusiastic proponent of what he calls "smoking *à la minute*," or stovetop smoking. Using equipment that is right at his fingertips, he takes a stainless steel hotel pan (available at restaurant supply stores and some kitchenware shops), places it on the burner, adds soaked applewood chips in an even layer, then places another hotel pan with holes in it within the first pan. He turns the heat to medium-high or high and waits for the wood chips to start smoking. When this happens, he places the fish fillets in the perforated pan, then covers it with a tight-fitting lid. He smokes 1-inch-thick salmon fillets for 4 to 5 minutes, then places the salmon in a 400° oven to bake for 2 1/2 to 3 minutes, or until desired doneness. It's easy and fun to try different flavored wood chips and vary the types of fish and shellfish you use when smoking *à la minute*. For the less adventurous, conventional stovetop smokers are available at kitchenware supply stores or via mail order.

Southwestern Smoked Scallop Chowder

TOTEM SMOKEHOUSE,
PIKE PLACE MARKET

As the only store in the Market dedicated solely to smoked seafood, Totem Smokehouse is known far and wide not only for its smoked salmon products, but for the less commonly available smoked oysters, trout, tuna, and scallops. The scallops are lightly seasoned in a preservative-free brine, then slowly smoked over alder fires in the style used by Native Americans. Although they come out of their gold foil pouch a dark chestnut color, they have a surprisingly mild smoke flavor and are tender and flavorful. The scallops are a perfect match for the deep, smoky soup base in this heart-healthy chowder, which is a satisfying blend of Southwest flavors and complex carbohydrates, chock-full of peppers, corn, and black beans.

1 TABLESPOON CANOLA OIL

1 CUP CHOPPED WHITE OR YELLOW ONION

2 CLOVES GARLIC, CHOPPED

1 TABLESPOON DRY SHERRY, CHICKEN
   STOCK, OR WATER

$1/4$ CUP CHOPPED GREEN BELL PEPPER

$1/4$ CUP CHOPPED RED BELL PEPPER

2 ($14^1/2$-OUNCE) CANS DEFATTED CHICKEN
   STOCK PLUS 1 ($14^1/2$-OUNCE) CAN FILLED
   WITH WATER

1 CUP FRESH, FROZEN, OR CANNED CORN

1 (15-OUNCE) CAN BLACK BEANS, DRAINED

1 ($4^1/2$-OUNCE) CAN DICED GREEN CHILES,
   DRAINED

2 TABLESPOONS GROUND CUMIN

1 TABLESPOON DRIED OREGANO, CRUMBLED

1 TABLESPOON GROUND CHILE POWDER

JUICE FROM 1 LIME

$1/2$ CUP CHOPPED CILANTRO, PLUS EXTRA
   FOR GARNISH

2 (4-OUNCE) PACKAGES SMOKED SCALLOPS,
   DRAINED AND CUT IN HALF

$1/4$ CUP NONFAT, LOWFAT, OR REGULAR
   SOUR CREAM

1. Heat canola oil in a large Dutch oven or stockpot (preferably nonstick) over medium heat. Add onion and garlic and cook 2 minutes, stirring occasionally. Add sherry and cook 1 minute more. Add green and red bell peppers and cook 10 minutes, stirring occasionally. Add stock, water, corn, black beans, chiles, cumin, oregano, and chile powder and stir well. Reduce heat and simmer 25 to 30 minutes, stirring occasionally.

2. Add lime juice and the $1/2$ cup cilantro, stir well, and simmer 10 minutes. Add scallops and simmer 5 minutes, or until heated through.

3. To serve, divide soup among individual bowls, top each serving with a dollop of sour cream, and garnish with chopped cilantro.

SERVES 4

HANDY SMOKED FISH TIP

Smoked trout makes a great hors d'oeuvre when placed on small triangles of dark bread (such as pumpernickel or rye) and spread with horseradish cream. To make the horseradish cream, simply mix $1^1/2$ tablespoons grated fresh horseradish with 3 tablespoons good-quality mayonnaise.

Scandinavian Pasta

———✦———

I have been making this ultra-simple pasta dish for years to rave reviews from family and friends and nobody ever guesses how easy it really is.

³/₄ POUND CONCHIGLIE (SEASHELLS),
  ROTINI (SPAGHETTI SPIRALS), OR FAR-
  FALLE (BUTTERFLY OR BOWTIE PASTA)

2 TABLESPOONS UNSALTED BUTTER, AT
  ROOM TEMPERATURE

¹/₄ CUP FRESH SNIPPED DILL, OR 1 TABLE-
  SPOON DRIED DILL, CRUMBLED

2 (3-OUNCE) PACKAGES THINLY SLICED
  COLD-SMOKED SALMON, SUCH AS NOVA
  STYLE OR LOX, CHOPPED

PINCH OF FRESHLY GROUND WHITE PEPPER
  TO TASTE

1. Cook pasta according to package instructions. Drain well, reserving pasta and 1/4 cup of the pasta cooking water.

2. In a large mixing bowl, add butter, dill, smoked salmon, and pepper and toss gently to blend. Add reserved pasta and toss gently until ingredients are thoroughly mixed. If pasta is dry, add reserved pasta water bit by bit, stirring after each addition, until desired consistency is reached. Taste and add additional pepper, if desired.

3. To serve, place pasta on a large serving platter or divide among individual bowls and serve immediately.

SERVES 4

HANDY SMOKED FISH TIP

Eugene Brown is one of my favorite farmers in the Market. From his and wife Ivonne's farm in Puyallup, Washington, this jovial man with the full beard, reading glasses, and jaunty beret brings jewel-hewed jellies and vinegars to the North Arcade most days the Market is operating. The jams, jellies, and vinegars, made by wife Ivonne from 125 different kinds of organically grown herbs, are small indulgences that look beautiful in a pantry, on a windowsill, or as great hostess gifts.

When I asked for suggestions for using Ivonne's lavender jelly, basil-garlic wine vinegar, and blueberry-tarragon jam with seafood, he said one of his favorites was smoked salmon with raspberry-mint jelly. I immediately pictured a crisp whole-grain cracker spread with cream cheese, a pristine slice of lox, a dollop of the pale pink concoction, and a small leaf of mint. He smiled and explained his idea was more basic.

"I like that smoked salmon jerky they sell around the Market. I just stick the end in a jar, scoop up some of the raspberry-mint jelly, and dive in."

The Shinbos' Cherry-Applewood Smoked Salmon

———✦———

Good friends Sharron and Robert Shinbo are hard-working professionals who live in a downtown condominium amid the bustle and bustle of the Market. On the weekends, they head for their boat to relax together and catch fresh salmon. Because salmon can be caught year-round in Puget Sound (a fortunate and felicitous phenomenon), the Shinbos are often able to share fresh blackmouth (an immature Chinook salmon) and home-smoked salmon with their grateful friends. The Shinbos' recipe explains how to smoke salmon using a wet brine and an outdoor smoker. Although the recipe calls for just a pound of salmon, Sharron and Robert normally cook at least a whole side of salmon. They suggest scaling up the recipe in direct proportion to the weight of the fish you are smoking.

1 CUP WOODRING ORCHARDS CHERRY APPLE
    CIDER OR PLAIN APPLE CIDER
1 CUP WATER
2 TO 2 1/2 TABLESPOONS MORTON'S
    PICKLING SALT
APPLEWOOD CHIPS
1 POUND SALMON FILLET, PIN BONES
    REMOVED

1. In a large, shallow nonreactive pan, mix cherry apple cider, water, and pickling salt until salt is dissolved. Add salmon fillet, cover and place in refrigerator for 8 to 12 hours.

2. One to two hours before cooking, rinse salmon and discard brine. Pat the salmon very dry with paper towels, place on smoking rack skin side down, and allow to air-dry or fan-dry 1 to 2 hours.

3. At least 30 minutes before cooking, preheat smoker according to manufacturer's instructions. After smoker has preheated, add the wood chips and place racks with salmon in the smoker. Use 2 pans of chips and smoke the salmon about 3 hours for a moist, mildly smoky product. Smoke longer if you like a drier salmon.

4. To serve, cut salmon into 4 pieces and serve warm with boiled new potatoes and steamed asparagus, or refrigerate and then cut chilled meat into thin slices and serve as an appetizer. Accompaniments might include cream cheese, capers, cucumber slices, Walla Walla onion slices, tomato slices, and good-quality crackers.

SERVES 4 AS AN ENTRÉE, 8 AS AN APPETIZER

Note: Woodring Orchards' cider is available year-round at the Pike Place Market, or a commercial brand can easily be substituted. Applewood chips, a delicate and fruity chip used to smoke salmon, chicken, turkey, and pork, are available in bulk at Totem Smokehouse in the Market, as well as in kitchenware and gourmet shops and many hardware stores.

Tuna and White Bean Salad

───✺───

Sometimes on a warm summer night, the thought of heating up the stove or oven is more than we can bear. On nights such as these, a dinner stirred together in one mixing bowl and made mostly from canned foods that are commonly stocked in the pantry is particularly appealing. Carrot and celery sticks, a platter of fresh fruit, and a loaf of crusty whole-grain bread would keep the menu simple yet accompany this main dish salad in gracious style. The salad is also a perfect item for picnics or the buffet table since the dressing is oil-based rather than mayonnaise-based.

2 (16- TO 19-OUNCE) CANS WHITE ITALIAN KIDNEY BEANS (CANNELLINI) OR AMERICAN NAVY BEANS, DRAINED, 3 TABLESPOONS BEAN JUICE RESERVED

2 (3½-OUNCE) CANS ALBACORE OR CHUNK LIGHT TUNA PACKED IN WATER, DRAINED AND BROKEN INTO CHUNKS, 3 TABLESPOONS TUNA JUICE RESERVED

3 TABLESPOONS EXTRA VIRGIN OLIVE OIL

2 TABLESPOONS RED WINE VINEGAR

1 TABLESPOON BALSAMIC VINEGAR

1 TEASPOON SUGAR

1½ TEASPOON MINCED FRESH BASIL, OR ½ TEASPOON DRIED BASIL, CRUMBLED

1½ TEASPOON MINCED FRESH OREGANO, OR ½ TEASPOON DRIED OREGANO, CRUMBLED

¼ TEASPOON FRESHLY GROUND BLACK PEPPER

4 GHERKINS, DICED, OR 8 CUCUMBER CHIP PICKLES, DICED

¼ CUP MINCED WHITE OR YELLOW ONION, SOAKED IN COLD WATER 10 MINUTES, DRAINED, AND PATTED DRY

4 TO 6 CUPS SPINACH LEAVES, RINSED, DRAINED, AND SPUN DRY

1. In a medium nonreactive mixing bowl, whisk reserved bean juice, reserved tuna juice, olive oil, red wine vinegar, balsamic vinegar, sugar, basil, oregano, black pepper, gherkins, and onion until sugar is dissolved. Add beans and tuna and toss to mix well.

2. To serve, divide spinach leaves among individual plates and top with salad.

SERVES 4

FUN FACT

• Northwest Indians often left their salmon in the smokehouse for two weeks, which resulted in a dark brown, very smoky salmon. They also took smoked salmon, dried and seasoned it, and cut it into thin strips to make "squaw candy," something similar to beef jerky that was eaten between meals as a snack. Salmon jerky is a popular food for modern-day hikers and campers.

Seafood Combination Dishes

A SINGLE SEAFOOD IS magnificent in its pristine simplicity, but when paired with other types of fish and/or shellfish, or mixed with pasta, grains, potatoes, or vegetables, seafood dishes can rise to unparalleled heights. Seafood combinations are also a great way to stretch those precious seafood dollars. When paired with an inexpensive extender, the more expensive seafood acts in a supporting role rather than as the star of the dish, thus providing satisfying and filling meals to greater numbers of family and friends. Most of all, combining seafood with other ingredients is fun; it's a great opportunity to be creative.

Seafood and Noodle Dishes

Seafood and pasta is a classic combination, brought to this country by Italian immigrants to the East Coast. Seafood (especially shellfish) plays a starring role in many dishes that combine it with pasta and cream- or tomato-based sauces.

When pairing pasta shapes and sauces with seafood, keep in mind that pasta strands, ribbons, and tubes (such as angel hair, spaghetti, linguine, or penne) work best with creamy sauces, butter sauces, and light tomato sauces with small pieces of vegetables. These lighter sauces most easily cling to pasta strands, coat ribbons, or flow inside tubes. Pasta formed into shapes (such as bow ties, shells, or little corkscrews) work best with heavy or chunky sauces. Their unusual angles and pockets catch the chunks of seafood and trap the heavy cream for a pleasing feeling in the mouth.

Seafood and noodle dishes have become increasingly popular in recent years, thanks to the influx of Asian immigrants on the West Coast. Some of the favorites that have become standard fare across the United States include shrimp *yakisoba* (Japanese), *pad thai* with shellfish (Thai), or hand-cut noodles and assorted seafood (Chinese).

Seafood Soups and Stews

Cioppino, bouillabaisse, bisques, and chowders are familiar and much loved. More recent additions include the world-renowned Thai and Vietnamese seafood soups. But no matter what their ethnic origin, seafood soups and stews are nutritious, easy to prepare (since the seafood needs only a short cooking period), and especially uplifting on a cold, rainy day.

Most seafood soups start with fish or shellfish, fish stock, and sautéed vegetables, herbs, and flavorings. When preparing seafood soups or stews, be sure to choose fish that are moderately firm so they won't fall apart during cooking. Monkfish, catfish, sea bass, tilapia, and rockfish are some of the best choices.

Seafood with Vegetables, Grains, and Beans

As Americans are encouraged to eat more vegetables and complex carbohydrates, they are finding that these foods pair perfectly with fish and shellfish. Seafood and vegetables are a classic combination in main dish salads (such as salade niçoise, stir-fries), and seafood tacos or enchiladas.

Seafood paired with grains and beans stretches back to childhood favorites such as tuna casserole, seafood hash, and seafood pot pies. Mussels and Millet in Curried Yogurt Sauce (see page 195), Prawns in Red Lentil Purée (see page 248), and Shellfish Risotto (see page 299) are contemporary examples.

Seafood Leftovers

Leftover cooked finfish or shellfish is always a welcome commodity in the kitchen, for it can quickly be transformed into croquettes, added to soups, crumbled into sauces, or sprinkled into main dish salads. Or try combining leftover seafood in quiches, seafood lasagne, shrimp or crab foo yong, or seafood frittatas (a staple at our house, often made with smoked salmon or leftover canned fish or shellfish).

Wines

The possibilities of seafood combination dishes are so myriad that it is difficult to generalize about pairing them with wines. However, in a cioppino and wine-pairing contest held at Elliott's Oyster House & Seafood Restaurant, two merlots, a fumé blanc, and a chardonnay were the winners. Next time you whip up a batch of hearty fisherman's stew, you might try any of these varieties of wine.

Fruity red wines, such as merlot and zinfandel, work well with tomato-based Italian and Mediterranean-influenced dishes. Asian beer or sweet white wines, such as gewürztraminer or riesling, are frequently paired with spicy Asian-inspired seafood combos. Seafoods mixed with vegetables, grains, and beans may pair advantageously with medium-dry white wines, such as pinot gris (pinot grigio in Italian), sémillon, or sauvignon blanc. And don't forget the increasingly popular pinot noir, which many wine experts consider to be one of the most seafood-friendly red wines.

Seafood Chili

———✧———

My friend and fellow foodie, Nancy Sutter, recommends using any firm fleshy whitefish in this recipe, although she admits to a fondness for fresh halibut. For a special New Year's Eve supper, I made the chili with Dungeness crab, Alaska spot prawns, and sea scallops with great results. Unlike many chilis that are souplike, Nancy's rendition, inspired by the late James Beard, is thick and chunky. With the sautéed kidney beans on one side, the seafood chili on the other, and the suggested condiments on top, the dish makes a beautiful presentation.

3 SLICES BACON, PLUS RESERVED BACON
    GREASE, OR 1 1/2 TABLESPOONS
    VEGETABLE OIL

2 LARGE ONIONS, CHOPPED

3 CLOVES GARLIC, MINCED

2 CUPS CHOPPED FRESH TOMATOES OR
    WELL-DRAINED CANNED TOMATOES, PLUS
    ADDITIONAL FOR GARNISH

1 1/2 TEASPOONS GROUND CHILI POWDER

1/2 TEASPOON GROUND CUMIN

1 TEASPOON CHOPPED FRESH OREGANO,
    OR 1/2 TEASPOON DRIED OREGANO,
    CRUMBLED

1 (7-OUNCE) CAN WHOLE MILD GREEN
    CHILES, DRAINED AND CHOPPED, OR 2 (4-
    OUNCE) CANS DICED MILD GREEN
    CHILES, DRAINED

3/4 TEASPOON TABASCO SAUCE

1 TO 1 1/4 CUPS DRY RED WINE OR WATER

1/2 POUND FRESH OR COOKED HALIBUT,
    LINGCOD OR OTHER FIRM, FLESHY WHITE-
    FISH FILLETS, SKIN AND BONES
    REMOVED, CUT INTO 1 1/2-INCH CHUNKS

1 TABLESPOON OLIVE OIL

1 (15 1/4-OUNCE) CAN RED KIDNEY BEANS,
    DRAINED, RINSED, AND DRAINED AGAIN

SOUR CREAM, FOR GARNISH

CHOPPED PARSLEY, FOR GARNISH

1. Cook bacon on medium heat until crisp. Place bacon slices on a paper towel to drain and pour remaining bacon grease (or vegetable oil) into a large saucepan or Dutch oven. Add onions and garlic and cook over medium-high heat until translucent, 5 to 7 minutes, stirring occasionally.

2. Add tomatoes, chili powder, cumin, oregano, mild green chiles, and Tabasco and stir well. Add 1 cup of the red wine, bring to a boil, then decrease heat and simmer 35 minutes, uncovered, stirring occasionally. If mixture becomes too dry, add remaining red wine 1 tablespoon at a time, stirring well after each addition.

3. After the mixture simmers 35 minutes, crumble the bacon and add to the chili. If using fresh fish, add to the chili and stir gently to mix. Cook just until fish is translucent, about 5 to 7 minutes. If using cooked fish, cook bacon 5 minutes after adding, then add fish and cook 2 to 3 minutes, or until fish is warmed through.

4. Meanwhile, heat olive oil in a medium skillet over medium-high heat and sauté kidney beans until warmed through, about 3 minutes.

5. When fish is cooked or warmed through, place chili on individual plates with a spoonful of sautéed beans beside it. Top with a dollop of sour cream, and sprinkle with chopped tomatoes and parsley.

SERVES 4

Mariage Oleronais

MAXIMILIEN-IN-THE-MARKET, PIKE PLACE MARKET

Since 1975, Maximilien's has been serving up authentic French food created from the freshest meats, fish, and produce of the season. A gold medal winner in the 1976 Culinary Olympics in Frankfurt, Germany, chef/owner Francois Kissel was knighted by the French government in 1981. This mariage, or "wedding," of clams, mussels, chicken, and pasta in a light curry-cream sauce comes from L'Île d'Oleron, an island off the coast of France, northwest of Bordeaux. Whether served as an appetizer or entrée, it makes a happy combination when paired with a white Vouvray or an Alsatian white wine.

2 CUPS CHICKEN BROTH

3/4 CUP WHITE WINE

2 1/2 TABLESPOONS UNSALTED BUTTER

1/4 CUP CHOPPED SHALLOTS

1 TABLESPOON ALL-PURPOSE FLOUR

1 1/2 TEASPOONS GROUND CURRY POWDER

1 CUP HEAVY WHIPPING CREAM

SALT AND FRESHLY GROUND WHITE PEPPER
   TO TASTE

12 OUNCES UNCOOKED PASTA (SUCH AS
   FETTUCINE, SPAGHETTI, OR ANGEL HAIR)

3 BONELESS CHICKEN BREASTS, CUT INTO
   BITE-SIZED PIECES

16 MUSSELS, SHELLS SCRUBBED AND DE-
   BEARDED JUST BEFORE COOKING

16 CLAMS, SHELLS SCRUBBED

1/4 CUP CHOPPED WALNUTS, TOASTED, FOR
   GARNISH

CHOPPED FRESH PARSLEY, FOR GARNISH

1. In a medium saucepan, bring chicken broth and 1/2 cup of the wine to a boil. Cook, uncovered, until liquid is reduced by half.

2. To make the curry sauce, in a medium saucepan, melt 1 1/2 tablespoons of butter over medium-high heat. Add shallots and cook 3 to 5 minutes, or until shallots are lightly browned. Add flour and curry powder and whisk until well blended. Add reduced chicken stock mixture a little bit at a time, whisking well after each addition to prevent lumps from forming. Add cream, whisk, and bring to a boil. Decrease heat and simmer 5 to 7 minutes, or until slightly thickened. Season to taste with salt and pepper, and keep warm over very low heat or in the top of a double boiler until ready to use.

3. Cook pasta according to package instructions. Drain and keep warm while preparing rest of dish.

4. While sauce is cooking, heat the remaining 1 tablespoon butter over medium-high heat in a large skillet. Add chicken pieces and cook, stirring often, until chicken is almost cooked throughout, about 5 to 7 minutes. Add mussels and clams and the remaining 1/4 cup wine. Cover skillet and cook 5 to 7 minutes, or until shellfish open, shaking pan occasionally. Pour reserved curry sauce over chicken and shellfish, stir gently to blend, and remove from heat.

5. To serve, divide pasta among individual plates and divide chicken pieces over pasta. Alternate mussels and clams around pasta to form a "necklace." Divide sauce over mounds of pasta and sprinkle with walnuts and parsley.

SERVES 4

Seafood Pasta in Parchment

THE BROOKLYN SEAFOOD, STEAK & OYSTER HOUSE, SEATTLE, WASHINGTON

Whenever we go to The Brooklyn, a high-spirited seafood and steakhouse just a couple of blocks from the Market, I am torn between the dozens of fresh seafood offerings on the menu and this unusual seafood pasta cooked en papillote (in a paper case). Tony Cunio, executive chef and co-owner, loves to watch the guests as the parchment is opened at the table and the wonderful aromas come wafting out.

8 OUNCES UNCOOKED LINGUINI

³/₄ POUND ROCK SHRIMP, RINSED, DRAINED, AND PATTED DRY

³/₄ POUND BAY SCALLOPS, RINSED, DRAINED, AND PATTED DRY

8 LARGE TIGER PRAWNS, PEELED, DEVEINED, AND PATTED DRY

4 CLOVES GARLIC, MINCED

2 TEASPOONS MINCED FRESH BASIL

1 CUP CORED AND DICED PLUM TOMATOES (¹/₂ POUND)

3¹/₂ CUPS THINLY SLICED ASSORTED WILD MUSHROOMS (¹/₂ POUND)

1¹/₂ TO 1³/₄ CUPS DICED ZUCCHINI (¹/₂ POUND)

¹/₂ CUP EXTRA VIRGIN OLIVE OIL

2 TEASPOONS SALT

¹/₄ TEASPOON FRESHLY GROUND WHITE PEPPER

1. Preheat oven to 500°. Cut four 12-inch squares of parchment paper. Fold in half to form four 6-inch squares, then cut each into a half-heart shape. When parchment is opened, you will have symmetrical heart shapes.

2. Cook linguine according to package instructions, drain well, and transfer to a medium mixing bowl. Gently stir together linguine and remaining ingredients until oil is evenly distributed.

3. Open 1 piece of parchment paper so that it forms a full heart. Lay the heart on a baking sheet, then spread the seafood mixture in the center of one side of the parchment paper. Fold the unfilled half of parchment over seafood mixture, then fold and roll the edges of the parchment every inch to seal tightly. It is very important to form a tight seal all around, or the parchment could pop open during baking and the seafood and vegetables will not cook properly.

4. Repeat procedure with remaining parchment paper and seafood mixture, then sprinkle baking sheets with a couple of tablespoons of water so that parchment will not stick or burn. Cook until parchment puffs and browns lightly, about 15 to 20 minutes. To gauge cooking time, look at the prawns through the slightly transparent parchment. The prawns turn orange when fully cooked.

5. To serve, place parchment packets on individual plates and, with a sharp knife or kitchen shears, cut packets open in an X-shaped pattern.

SERVES 4

Sailboat Salmon Pasta

THE INCREDIBLE LINK, PIKE PLACE MARKET

When Jimi Dorsey packed up his family and moved from New Orleans to Seattle to open The Incredible Link in the heart of the Market, reserved Seattleites were a bit skeptical. "Vegetarian's Delight Sausage? Luscious Lamb Sausage? Chi-Chi Chorizo?" they whispered in astonished tones as they watched the family bustling about in their sausage kitchen through a huge glass front window. But Jimi knew better. The secret recipes for his gourmet sausages have been a family tradition for over three generations, and the company received one of the first licenses from the U.S. Department of Agriculture to manufacture sausage with fresh vegetables. Besides, with mom Lorraine Dorsey mixing the spices using formulas passed down by her father, what could go wrong? For a quick and easy dinner, I like to sauté the family's Sailboat Salmon Sausage (a blend of fresh salmon, lightly smoked with herbs and spices, and accented with fresh lemon), then toss it with cooked pasta. And, while I particularly like the Dorseys' sausage because it is chock-full of Cajun and Creole spices, chunks of salmon, and is 98 percent fat free, any good-quality seafood sausage could substitute.

1 1/2 CUPS DEFATTED CHICKEN STOCK

4 SAILBOAT SALMON SAUSAGES OR OTHER
  SEAFOOD SAUSAGE (ABOUT 3/4 TO 1
  POUND)

12 OUNCES UNCOOKED REGULAR OR
  WHOLE-WHEAT SPAGHETTI

1 TABLESPOON OLIVE OIL

1/2 WHITE OR YELLOW ONION, CHOPPED

1 CLOVE GARLIC, MINCED

CHOPPED FRESH PARSLEY OR CILANTRO,
  FOR GARNISH

1. Bring chicken stock to a simmer in a medium skillet. Add salmon sausages and simmer 10 minutes uncovered, turning occasionally. Remove pan from heat, remove sausages to a plate, pour broth into a medium mixing bowl, and reserve. Wipe out skillet and reserve for later use.

2. When sausages are cool enough to handle, slice lengthwise, remove sausage and juices from casings with a spoon, and place meat and juices in the mixing bowl with the broth and reserve. Discard casings.

3. Meanwhile, cook pasta according to package instructions. Drain and keep warm.

4. In the reserved medium skillet, heat olive oil over medium-high heat. Add onion and garlic and cook 5 to 7 minutes, or until translucent, stirring often. Add reserved broth and sausage and increase heat to high. Boil until slightly thickened, then remove from heat, add reserved pasta, and toss to mix well.

5. To serve, divide pasta and sauce among individual bowls. Sprinkle with parsley.

SERVES 4

Pike Place Market Seafood Stew

※

World Class Chili, Pike Place Market

Joe Canavan, owner of World Class Chili, is a character and a half. Born and raised in Butte, Montana, he started cooking at the age of 14 for cowboys on the range. After stints in the Marine Corps and the U.S. Army, he received a degree in economics from Seattle University. But the chili bug bit Joe in 1977, when he discovered chili competitions. In 1981 he helped form the Washington State Chili Society and went on to win the Canadian chili crown. Joe opened World Class Chili in 1986 and since then has dished up his famous fare to Vanna White, Tom Robbins, and George Brett, among others. He and his staff have participated in over 500 chili cook-offs around the world, and Joe is published in international chili publications such as The Old Windbreaker. *The fresh habanero chiles that spike the seafood stew's flavorful broth are among the hottest in the world. They make the back of your throat prickle with heat, a pleasant if unusual sensation.*

3 (7 1/2-OUNCE) CANS CLAM JUICE

2 (7 1/2-OUNCE) CANS LOW-SODIUM CHICKEN STOCK

1/4 CUP FRESHLY SQUEEZED LIME JUICE

1 BUNCH CILANTRO, STEMS TIED TOGETHER WITH KITCHEN STRING, PLUS EXTRA CHOPPED CILANTRO FOR GARNISH

1 TO 4 HABANERO PEPPERS, DEPENDING ON HEAT DESIRED, WHOLE BUT WITH TINY HOLES PIERCED THROUGH SKIN WITH TIP OF A SMALL, SHARP KNIFE

1/2 CUP OLIVE OIL

4 CLOVES GARLIC, CRUSHED

1 ONION, CHOPPED

1 GREEN BELL PEPPER, CHOPPED

1 (2-OUNCE) JAR ROASTED RED BELL PEPPERS, CHOPPED

2 CARROTS, CHOPPED

2 STALKS CELERY, STRINGS AND LEAVES REMOVED AND CHOPPED

1 TEASPOON GROUND SWEET PAPRIKA

1 TEASPOON GROUND CUMIN

1 BAY LEAF

PINCH OF DRIED THYME, CRUMBLED

PINCH OF GROUND NUTMEG

1 POUND WHITEFISH OF YOUR CHOICE, SUCH AS HALIBUT, ROCKFISH, OR COD, WITH SKIN AND BONES REMOVED, RINSED, DRAINED, PATTED DRY, AND CUT INTO BITE-SIZED PIECES

1 POUND SHELLFISH OF YOUR CHOICE, SUCH AS CLAMS (SHELLS SCRUBBED), MUSSELS (SHELLS SCRUBBED AND DE-BEARDED JUST BEFORE COOKING), SHRIMP (PEELED AND DEVEINED), SCALLOPS (RINSED AND DRAINED), CRAWFISH (RINSED), OR OYSTERS (SHUCKED)

SOUR CREAM, FOR GARNISH

1. In a large Dutch oven or stockpot, bring clam juice, chicken stock, lime juice, the tied bunch of cilantro, and the habanero peppers to a very low simmer. Cover and cook 7 to 10 minutes, stirring occasionally.

2. While stock is simmering, in a large skillet, heat olive oil over medium-high heat. Add garlic, onion, green bell pepper, roasted red bell pepper, carrot, celery, paprika, cumin, bay leaf, thyme, and nutmeg and cook, stirring occasionally, 7 to 10 minutes, or until vegetables are tender. Remove from heat and set aside.

3. Remove cilantro and habanero peppers from stock. With your hand, squeeze the cilantro over the stockpot to remove all liquid and discard. Place peppers in a fine-meshed sieve and, with the back of a wooden spoon, squeeze the juice from the peppers into the stock. Discard peppers.

4. Add reserved vegetables to stock and bring stock to a boil, then decrease heat to medium-low. Add seafood in order of length of cooking time needed, from the longest to the shortest amount of time: clams and crawfish (10 minutes); mussels (5 to 7 minutes); whitefish (3 to 5 minutes); and shrimp, scallops, or shucked oysters (1 to 3 minutes). Cover pot while cooking.

5. To serve, divide seafood and stock among individual bowls. Top with dollops of sour cream and a sprinkle of cilantro.

SERVES 4

Note: Habanero chiles are available at El Mercado Latino in the Market and in larger supermarkets and Latin American markets.

Paella à la Navarra

The Spanish Table, Seattle, Washington

When searching for any ingredient with an Iberian flair, if you're in the area of the Pike Place Market, you need go no further than The Spanish Table, a spectacular resource for Spanish and Portuguese olive oils, paella rice and pans (paelleras), saffron, rustic plates and dishes, and take-out foods. The distinctive store also features a wide selection of wines, sherries, and ports.

Paella is a traditional Spanish dish of saffron-flavored rice combined with meats and shellfish, garlic, onions, peas, and/or artichoke hearts and tomatoes. This show stopping paella recipe comes from master cook and pastry chef Joseph E. Jimenez de Jimenez, resident wine expert and catering chef at The Spanish Table and originally from the Navarra province of Spain. When preparing this recipe, do not be intimidated by the specialty ingredients called for; while a more authentic dish results from using the ingredients suggested, I have included readily available substitutes for ease of preparation.

8 GREEN BEANS, RINSED, DRAINED, AND STRINGS REMOVED (2 OUNCES)

1/2 CUP FRESH PEAS, OR FROZEN PEAS, DEFROSTED

2 TABLESPOONS SPANISH OLIVE OIL OR ANY GOOD-QUALITY OLIVE OIL

1/2 CUP DICED YELLOW ONION

1/2 CUP DICED CHORIZO (SPANISH SMOKED PORK SAUSAGE) OR HOT ITALIAN SAUSAGE (IF USING HOT ITALIAN SAUSAGE, REMOVE CASING BEFORE DICING)

1/2 CUP DICED JAMON SERRANO (SPANISH CURED HAM) OR GOOD-QUALITY CURED AMERICAN HAM

2 CHICKEN LEGS, RINSED AND PATTED DRY

2 CHICKEN THIGHS, RINSED AND PATTED DRY

1/2 RED BELL PEPPER, DICED

1/4 GREEN BELL PEPPER, DICED

1 WHOLE TROUT, BONES, HEAD, AND TAIL REMOVED, RINSED, DRAINED, PATTED DRY, AND CUT INTO 1-INCH PIECES, OR 2 TROUT FILLETS, RINSED, DRAINED, PATTED DRY, AND CUT INTO 1-INCH PIECES

6 LARGE OR 12 SMALL CRAWFISH, RINSED (OPTIONAL)

2 CLOVES GARLIC, MINCED

2 CUPS PAELLA RICE (SPANISH SHORT-GRAIN RICE) OR ARBORIO RICE

1 1/2 TEASPOONS SWEET PIMENTON (SWEET SPANISH PAPRIKA) OR SWEET PAPRIKA

1/2 TEASPOON SALT

1/2 CUP CORED AND CHOPPED PLUM TOMATOES

1/4 TEASPOON HOT PIMENTON (HOT SPANISH PAPRIKA) OR HOT PAPRIKA

2 CUPS BOTTLED CLAM JUICE

1 1/4 CUPS WATER

8 SAFFRON THREADS, CRUMBLED

8 SPEARS CANNED WHITE OR GREEN ASPARAGUS

2 CANNED PIQUILLO PEPPERS (MILD SPANISH RED PEPPERS) OR 2 CANNED WHOLE MILD JALAPEÑO PEPPERS, JULIENNED

1 TABLESPOON CHOPPED FRESH PARSLEY, FOR GARNISH

1 LEMON, CUT INTO 8 WEDGES, FOR GARNISH

1. In a small saucepan, bring $1/2$ inch of water to a boil. Add green beans and cook 3 to 5 minutes. Drain, rinse beans in cold water, and drain again. Cut beans into 3 equal-sized pieces, place in a small bowl, cover, and reserve. In same small saucepan, bring $1/2$ inch of water to a boil. Add peas and cook 3 to 5 minutes. Drain, rinse peas in cold water, and drain again. Place peas in a small bowl, cover, and reserve.

2. In a paellera, a 13-inch skillet, or a large shallow roasting pan placed over 2 burners if necessary, heat olive oil over medium-high heat. Add onions, chorizo, jamon Serrano, chicken legs, and chicken thighs, decrease heat to medium, and cook 7 to 10 minutes, turning occasionally, or until chicken turns golden brown on all sides.

3. Add red and green bell pepper, stir well, and cook 3 to 5 minutes more, stirring occasionally.

4. Add trout, crawfish, and garlic, stir well, and cook 3 to 5 minutes more, stirring occasionally.

5. Add rice and stir until rice grains are evenly coated with oil. Reduce heat to low and add the reserved green beans, sweet pimenton, salt, tomatoes, and hot pimenton. Stir well. In a bowl, mix together the clam juice, water, and saffron and add to rice mixture. Stir well. Using tongs, remove crawfish and place around edge of the paellera. Bring to a simmer and cook 20 minutes.

6. Remove pan from heat, and arrange reserved peas, asparagus, and piquillo peppers over top of paella. Cover pan with a clean, damp, hot kitchen towel and let rest for 10 minutes.

7. To serve, sprinkle paella with parsley and top with lemon wedges. Bring paellera to the table and allow family and friends to help themselves.

SERVES 6

HANDY CHEF'S TIP

Brooke Vosika, executive sous chef of the Four Seasons Olympic Hotel in Seattle, offers this great idea when working with lemongrass in soups or stocks: Simply cut off the stem and remove the tough outer leaves of a stalk of lemongrass, then use the lemongrass :wand" to stir the soup or stock. The wand imparts a sublte, lemony flavor to the hot liquid, and does not need to be strained or fished out like chopped pieces of lemongrass.

Country French Fish Soup

SISTERS EUROPEAN SNACKS, PIKE PLACE MARKET

Sisters is one of my favorite places in the Market, not only because the food is prepared with love by three sisters originally from Frankfurt, Germany, but because of its sunny yellow paint job and indoor-outdoor seating along vibrant Post Alley. Nirala, Mariam, and Aruna Jacobi (sometimes ably assisted by mom, Nisha) open at seven each morning, when they begin cooking their soup stocks from scratch, making vegetarian salads laden with heart-healthy grains and vegetables purchased at the Market, and slicing and dicing European meats and cheeses for their famous grilled focaccia sandwiches. This fish soup owes its lightness and freshness to the addition of watercress, dill, and fennel; its beautiful color comes from the diced tomatoes and shrimp floating on top. It pairs with whole-grain bread, a mixed green salad, and a glass of sweet white wine.

8 CUPS SEAFOOD STOCK (SEE PAGE 318)

1 SMALL BULB FENNEL, TOPS REMOVED, COARSELY CHOPPED, AND RESERVED, BULB DICED

1/2 BUNCH FRESH THYME, LEAVES REMOVED AND RESERVED (ABOUT 1/4 CUP FRESH THYME LEAVES), STEMS RESERVED

1/2 LEMON, SLICED

4 CLOVES GARLIC, CRUSHED, PLUS 5 CLOVES GARLIC, MINCED

1 POUND HALIBUT FILLETS, SKIN AND BONES REMOVED, RINSED, DRAINED, PATTED DRY, AND CUT INTO BITE-SIZED PIECES

1/2 POUND LARGE SHRIMP, PEELED, DEVEINED, AND CUT IN HALF LENGTHWISE

3 TABLESPOONS OLIVE OIL

1/2 RED ONION, CHOPPED

1 CARROT, DICED

2 STALKS CELERY, DICED

3 PLUM TOMATOES, CORED AND DICED

1/2 CUP DRY WHITE WINE OR CHICKEN STOCK

1/2 SMALL BUNCH WATERCRESS, CHOPPED (ABOUT 1/2 CUP)

1/2 BUNCH FRESH DILL, SNIPPED (ABOUT 1/3 CUP)

SALT AND FRESHLY GROUND WHITE PEPPER TO TASTE

FRESHLY SQUEEZED LEMON JUICE TO TASTE

4 SLICES CRUSTY BREAD, LIGHTLY BRUSHED WITH OLIVE OIL OR MELTED BUTTER, GRILLED OR TOASTED UNTIL GOLDEN BROWN (OPTIONAL)

1. In a large saucepan or skillet, bring fish stock to a simmer. Add fennel tops, thyme stems, lemon slices, and the 4 cloves crushed garlic and cook 10 minutes, skimming off any foam or impurities that rise to surface. With a slotted spoon, remove all solids and discard.

2. Add halibut pieces and shrimp to stock and poach 3 to 5 minutes, or until fish just turns opaque and shrimp just turn pink. Remove halibut and shrimp from stock, cover, and keep warm while preparing rest of dish. Turn off heat under saucepan, cover pan, and reserve fish stock.

3. Heat 2 tablespoons of the olive oil in a large Dutch oven or stockpot over medium-high heat. Add onion and the remaining minced garlic and

cook 3 to 5 minutes, or until tender-crisp, stir-ring occasionally. Do not allow garlic to brown. Add carrots, celery, and diced fennel bulb, stir well, and cook 5 to 7 minutes, stirring occasion-ally, until vegetables are tender. Add reserved warm fish stock, bring to a simmer, cover, and cook 5 to 8 minutes.

4. Meanwhile, heat the remaining 1 tablespoon olive oil in a small skillet over medium-high heat. Add tomatoes and cook 2 to 3 minutes, stirring often. Add wine and simmer 2 minutes. Add tomato mixture to fish stock and stir well to blend.

5. Just before serving, add watercress, dill, and thyme leaves and stir well to mix. Season to taste with salt, white pepper, and lemon juice. Add re-served halibut and shrimp, and cook 1 to 2 min-utes, or until warmed through, stirring gently.

6. To serve, divide fish, shrimp, stock, and veg-etables among individual soup bowls. If desired, place a slice of grilled or toasted bread into bot-tom of each bowl before adding the soup.

SERVES 4

Fiesta Brew Fish Stew

～⚓～

PIKE PUB AND BREWERY, SEATTLE, WASHINGTON

From its new home just half block south of the Market, the Pike Pub and Brewery has the capacity to make 25,000 barrels of handcrafted beers each year. The 20,000-square-foot facility, nicknamed "Beer Central," also houses a 200-seat pub, a homebrew supply store, and a beer memorabilia museum. With witty names such as Pike Pale Ale, Pike Street Stout, and Old Bawdy Barley Wine, Pike Brewing Company beers have won acclaim the world over. This recipe, developed by food and beer pairing consultant, Melissa Flynn, is a robust, Latin American-inspired seafood stew that is best accompanied with Pike Pale Ale.

8 CUPS SEAFOOD STOCK (SEE PAGE 318)

1/4 CUP CHOPPED FRESH FENNEL

1 TABLESPOON LEMON JUICE

4 WHOLE CLOVES

8 CLOVES ROASTED GARLIC (SEE PAGE 10)

2 TABLESPOONS OLIVE OIL

1 LARGE YELLOW ONION, THINLY SLICED

1 ROASTED GREEN BELL PEPPER, CHOPPED (SEE PAGE 10)

1 ROASTED RED BELL PEPPER, CHOPPED (SEE PAGE 10)

1 ROASTED JALAPEÑO PEPPER, MINCED (SEE PAGE 10)

1 1/2 TEASPOONS FRESH THYME LEAVES, CHOPPED

1 1/2 TEASPOONS FRESH OREGANO LEAVES, CHOPPED

5 KUMQUATS, SEEDS REMOVED AND CUT INTO 1/8-INCH SLICES, OR 1/2 ORANGE, PEELED AND SECTIONED (MEMBRANES REMOVED)

1/4 TO 1/2 CUP PIKE PALE ALE OR GOOD-QUALITY MICROBREWED BEER

1 (14 1/2-OUNCE) CAN PLUM TOMATOES, DRAINED AND COARSELY CHOPPED

SALT AND FRESHLY GROUND BLACK PEPPER TO TASTE

1 POUND FISH OF YOUR CHOICE, SUCH AS HALIBUT, ROCKFISH, OR SALMON, SKIN AND BONES REMOVED, RINSED, DRAINED, PATTED DRY, AND CUT INTO BITE-SIZED PIECES

1 POUND SHELLFISH OF YOUR CHOICE, SUCH AS CLAMS (SHELLS SCRUBBED), MUSSELS (SHELLS SCRUBBED AND DE-BEARDED JUST BEFORE COOKING), SHRIMP (PEELED AND DEVEINED), SCAL-LOPS (RINSED AND DRAINED), CRAWFISH (RINSED), OR OYSTERS (SHUCKED)

CHILE ALE SAUCE (RECIPE FOLLOWS)

CHOPPED CILANTRO, FOR GARNISH

TORTILLA CHIPS, FOR GARNISH

1. In a large saucepan or skillet, bring fish stock to a simmer. Add fennel, lemon juice, and cloves and cook 10 minutes. With a slotted spoon, re-move all solids and discard. In a food processor or blender, process 1 cup of the Seafood Stock with the roasted garlic until mixture is smooth. Add to saucepan with stock, cover, remove from heat, and reserve.

2. Meanwhile, in a large Dutch oven or stock-pot, heat olive oil over medium-high heat and add onions. Stir well, then decrease heat to

medium-low and cook 7 to 10 minutes, or until onions begin to turn brown and caramelize, stirring occasionally.

3. Add green bell pepper, red bell pepper, jalapeño pepper, thyme, oregano, kumquats, and 1/4 cup of the Pike Pale Ale to the pot and stir well.

4. Add reserved fish stock and plum tomatoes and bring to a boil. Cook for 5 minutes, then season to taste with salt, pepper, and additional Pike Pale Ale.

5. Decrease heat to medium-low, and add seafood in order of cooking time needed, from the longest to the shortest amount of time: Clams and crawfish (10 minutes); mussels (5 to 7 minutes); whitefish (3 to 5 minutes); and shrimp, scallops, or shucked oysters (1 to 3 minutes). Cover pot while cooking.

6. To serve, divide seafood and stock among individual bowls. Drizzle with Chile Ale Sauce and sprinkle with cilantro. Arrange tortilla chips around perimeter of bowl.

SERVES 4 AS AN ENTRÉE, 8 AS AN APPETIZER

Chile Ale Sauce

1 OUNCE DRIED NEW MEXICO CHILES

1 OUNCE DRIED PASILLA CHILES

1 OUNCE DRIED ANCHO CHILES

1 1/2 CUPS PIKE PALE ALE OR GOOD-QUALITY
   MICROBREWED BEER

2 OUNCES DRIED SUNDRIED TOMATOES (NOT
   OIL-PACKED)

1 GRANNY SMITH OR OTHER TART APPLE,
   PEELED, CORED, AND COARSELY CHOPPED

PINCH OF GROUND CINNAMON

SALT TO TASTE

1. Break open New Mexico, pasilla, and ancho chiles and remove and discard all seeds and stems. Heat 1 cup of the Pike Pale Ale in a small saucepan over medium heat. When beer comes to a simmer, add chiles and sundried tomatoes. Cover pan, remove from heat and let stand 20 minutes, or until chiles and tomatoes are plumped and soft.

2. Pour chile mixture into a food processor or blender. Add apple and 1/4 cup of the remaining Pike Pale Ale and process until smooth. If mixture is to dry, add remaining 1/4 cup ale in 1 tablespoon increments until mixture reaches a ketchuplike consistency.

3. Pour sauce through a medium-meshed sieve placed over a glass bowl or jar with a lid. Press remaining solids with the back of a wooden spoon to remove any remaining liquid. Discard solids. Add cinnamon to sauce, stir well, and season to taste with salt.

4. Cover sauce and store in refrigerator for up to 3 weeks.

MAKES 1 CUP

No-Bake Seafood Lasagne

This lavish entrée is special enough for company yet saves many steps and lots of time over traditional lasagne recipes because the dish is never baked. The pasta is boiled and the seafood is simply sautéed on the stovetop. Vary the seafood selection depending on what's in season and what appeals to your mood.

8 UNCOOKED PLAIN OR WHOLE-WHEAT
   LASAGNE NOODLES

1 TABLESPOON OLIVE OIL

1/2 WHITE OR YELLOW ONION, DICED

1/4 POUND ASSORTED WILD MUSHROOMS
   (SUCH AS SHIITAKE, CREMINI, OYSTER,
   PORCINI, OR PORTOBELLO), SLICED

1 PLUM TOMATO, CORED AND DICED

1 CUP MARINARA SAUCE (SEE PAGE 319) OR
   GOOD-QUALITY BOTTLED SPAGHETTI
   SAUCE

2 TEASPOONS MINCED FRESH BASIL, OR 1/2
   TEASPOON DRIED BASIL, CRUMBLED

1/2 POUND MONKFISH FILLET, RINSED,
   DRAINED, PATTED DRY, PURPLE
   MEMBRANE REMOVED, AND CUT INTO
   BITE-SIZED PIECES

1/4 POUND BAY SCALLOPS, RINSED,
   DRAINED, AND PATTED DRY

1/4 POUND SHRIMP, PEELED, DEVEINED,
   RINSED, AND PATTED DRY

FRESHLY GROUND BLACK PEPPER TO TASTE

1 OUNCE PARMESAN OR PARMIGIANO-REG-
   GIANO CHEESE (OPTIONAL)

1. Cook lasagne noodles according to package directions. Drain noodles and keep warm while preparing rest of dish.

2. In a large skillet, heat olive oil over medium-high heat. Add onions and mushrooms and cook 5 to 7 minutes, or until onions are tender and mushrooms release their juices. Stir in tomato, marinara sauce, and 1 teaspoon of fresh basil (or all of the dried basil). Stir well and cook 2 minutes.

3. Add monkfish to tomato sauce and cook 4 minutes. Add scallops and shrimp and cook 2 to 3 minutes more, or until scallops just turn opaque and shrimp just turn pink.

4. To serve, arrange 2 lasagne noodles on each plate so that noodles curl over each other and are raised in spots (do not place lasagne noodles flat on plate). Divide sauce and seafood over noodles. Sprinkle with pepper and the remaining 1 teaspoon minced basil. If desired, using a sharp vegetable peeler, shave strips of cheese over pasta and seafood (although Italians consider it blasphemy to mix cheese and seafood!).

SERVES 4

Shellfish Risotto

———⚬———

Risotto is an Italian short-grain rice dish, in which the rice grains must be discrete but loosely bound and cooked al dente. Cooking risotto has taken on a mystique that frightens away many home cooks, but it is really pretty straightforward and more forgiving than many people believe. Simply stir the risotto often and do not allow the stock to ever boil away entirely. The whole process takes just over a half hour and is often very therapeutic and soothing.

4 CUPS HOMEMADE CHICKEN, FISH, OR VEG-
    ETABLE STOCK, OR 1 (14 1/2-OUNCE) CAN
    CHICKEN STOCK PLUS 2 CUPS WATER

1/2 POUND LARGE SHRIMP, PEELED,
    DEVEINED, RINSED, PATTED DRY, AND
    CUT IN HALF LENGTHWISE, SHELLS
    RESERVED

1 TABLESPOON OLIVE OIL

1/2 WHITE OR YELLOW ONION, MINCED

1 CLOVE GARLIC, MINCED

1 1/2 CUPS UNCOOKED ARBORIO RICE

1/2 CUP DRY WHITE WINE OR WHITE DRY
    VERMOUTH

1/2 POUND SEA SCALLOPS, RINSED,
    DRAINED, PATTED DRY, AND CUT IN HALF
    HORIZONTALLY

1/4 POUND CLEANED SQUID, BODIES SLICED
    INTO 1/4-INCH RINGS, TENTACLES CUT IN
    HALF IF LARGE

1 TABLESPOON UNSALTED BUTTER

SALT AND FRESHLY GROUND WHITE PEPPER
    TO TASTE

2 TABLESPOONS MINCED FRESH BASIL, FOR
    GARNISH

1. In a medium saucepan, heat chicken stock until it comes to a simmer. Add reserved shrimp shells and cook 10 minutes. With a slotted spoon, remove shrimp shells and discard. Keep broth warm over low heat, but do not boil or reduce.

2. Heat olive oil in a large saucepan over medium-high heat. Add onion and garlic and cook 2 to 3 minutes, stirring occasionally. Add rice and stir to coat grains evenly with oil. Add wine and cook until wine is almost totally absorbed, stirring often, about 1 to 2 minutes.

3. Stir in 1 cup of the warm broth. Simmer slowly, stirring often, about 6 minutes, or until liquid is almost totally absorbed. Adjust heat if necessary so that liquid does not evaporate too quickly.

4. Continue adding broth in 1/2-cup increments, stirring continuously until almost absorbed. When only about 1 cup of the stock remains, add shrimp and scallops and repeat simmering and stirring procedure with another 1/2 cup of the broth.

5. The rice should now be creamy in consistency and cooked al dente (firm to the bite), and the seafood should be partially cooked. If the rice is too moist, continue cooking. If too dry, add a bit more stock and continue stirring and simmering until the proper consistency is reached. Add squid and cook 1 to 2 minutes more. Remove from heat, add butter, stir well, and season to taste with salt and pepper.

6. Divide risotto among individual bowls and sprinkle with basil. Serve immediately.

SERVES 4

Seafood Sidekicks

URING THE SIXTIES and seventies, a fish dinner meant sautéing a box of frozen fish sticks or dropping by Howard Johnson's restaurant for the Friday night clam fry. Pools of ketchup, mounds of tartar sauce, and (for real sophisticates) a splash of malt vinegar accompanied the deep-fried stuff we knew as seafood.

In the nineties, a fish dinner means poached Copper River salmon fillet with raspberry-mint sauce, grilled mahimahi with a mango salsa, or fresh Alaskan halibut broiled with a soy-sesame glaze. The clean taste of today's seafood surprises the palate and accompanying flavors further delight the senses by adding visual appeal and pleasing texture.

The word "sauce" is used loosely today, for it can mean everything from a glaze to a chutney to a dry rub. The modern cook is fortunate, for today's creative spirit in the kitchen allows and even encourages the pairing of ingredients never before thought complementary to seafood, such as fruits and vegetables or beans and grains. Even sauces traditionally used with other foods, such as vinaigrettes, are now commonly paired with seafood. Since these nontraditional sauces are often lighter in taste and texture than their more conventional counterparts, they allow the essence of the fresh seafood to come shining through.

The sauces in this chapter are tasty enough to stand alone, and many are personal favorites that I make time and again. They range from traditional to less traditional, and each recipe is followed by suggestions of the best finfish and shellfish to pair with its unique flavors. As with selecting wine, pairing seafood and sauce is a matter of personal taste and preference. Remember, there is no "right" sauce for a particular fish dish—it's all a matter of what you like to eat.

Asian Sauces

Chefs in Asian countries have worked with seafood centuries longer than American cooks and have established a rich and distinguished culinary tradition. They prize the freshest seafood, often preferring to keep their fish and shellfish in saltwater tanks until just before cooking.

Because they seek to showcase the flavor and texture of the seafood, many of their sauces are naturally light and healthy. Strong, bright flavors, such as ginger, coconut, curry, or garlic, are paired with salty flavors, provided by soy or tamari sauce, Thai or Vietnamese fish sauce, or fermented black beans. A touch of sweetness is provided by sugar, rice wine, or miso, while a fiery flare from dried red peppers or chile paste completes the perfect balance of flavors.

Due to the large number of Asians who

have made their homes in the Northwest, the growing trade with Pacific Rim countries, and the global exchange of people and ideas, Asian cooking has become part and parcel of the restaurant scene in Seattle, Portland, and British Columbia.

Sake Sauce

Sake, or rice wine, is a clear, slightly sweet beverage made from fermented rice. It has a nutty, sometimes fruity flavor, rich body, satisfying aftertaste, and is slightly more alcoholic than wine made from grapes. It combines with the other ingredients in this recipe to form a sauce that is a pristine blend of sweet and salty, with anise and toasted-nut overtones. This recipe comes from Japan American Beverage Company, importer of Momokawa Premium Saké which is distributed nationwide. Japan America will begin brewing Momokawa Premium Saké at their new brewery in Oregon, where you are invited to sample premium sakes for yourself. I was first introduced to their sake at a dinner at Nikko Restaurant in the Westin Hotel in Seattle. I vividly remember sipping sake with 24-carat gold flakes in it from the traditional masu, *a little wooden box!*

1/2 CUP SAKE

2 TEASPOONS FRESH MINCED TARRAGON LEAVES, OR 1/2 TEASPOON DRIED TARRAGON, CRUMBLED

1 TEASPOON LIGHT SOY SAUCE

4 DROPS HOT CHILE OIL

1 TEASPOON TOASTED SESAME OIL

1 TABLESPOON MIRIN

Bring sake and tarragon leaves to a simmer in a small nonreactive pan. Cook gently for 10 minutes, then add soy sauce, hot chile oil, toasted sesame oil, and mirin and remove from heat. Stir well, pour into a small pitcher, and serve with cooked fish fillets or steak.

MAKES 1/3 CUP

Seafood Suggestions: Golden Rainbow Trout, Salmon, Steelhead Trout

HANDY SAKE TIPS

When working with seafood, sake is a very versatile ingredient. Use it for curing salmon, sort of like an Asian gravlax; mix with fresh lime juice and brush over grilled or baked fish as a glaze; substitute sake for vinegar in chutneys or fruit salsas; add it to fish sauces; mix with rosemary, citrus peel, or lemon grass, then use it as a seafood glaze; pair sake with caviar instead of the traditional vodka or champagne; and use it as a fish marinade when combined with hoisin sauce, sugar, garlic, and ginger.

Black Bean Vinaigrette

Fermented black beans, also known as Chinese black beans and salty black beans, are small, extremely pungent black soybeans that have been preserved in salt. They are added to fish or meat dishes as a flavoring and are available in Asian markets and the Asian section of some supermarkets.

1 TABLESPOON FERMENTED BLACK BEANS

1 SHALLOT, CUT INTO CHUNKS

1 QUARTER-SIZED PIECE OF PEELED GIN-
    GERROOT, CUT IN HALF

1/2 CUP MIRIN

1/4 CUP SEASONED RICE VINEGAR

1 TABLESPOON SESAME OIL

1/4 TEASPOON TOASTED SESAME OIL

ENOKI MUSHROOMS, STEMS REMOVED
    (OPTIONAL)

PICKLED GINGER (OPTIONAL)

1. Place black beans in a small bowl and cover with hot water. Allow to soak for 15 minutes, drain water, and repeat process. Put drained black beans in food processor or blender and add shallot and gingerroot. Process until mixture is finely chopped. Add mirin and seasoned rice vinegar and process until well blended. Add oils and process until well blended.

2. Drizzle dressing over cooked fish fillet, steaks, or shellfish of your choice. If desired, sprinkle with enoki mushrooms and place a few slices of pickled ginger over seafood just before serving.

MAKES 1 CUP

Seafood Suggestions: Any Finfish or Shellfish

Compound Butters

Compound butters, sometimes called flavored or savory butters, are an easy way to add a touch of richness and a lot of flavor to fish fillets or steaks or shellfish. Flavored butters are made by mixing unsalted, softened butter with herbs, spices, raw or sautéed vegetables or fruits, citrus juices, nuts, olives, and/or sweet or hot peppers of your choice.

Mix compound butters by hand with a wooden spoon, or use a food processor or blender. Roll mixture into a 1-inch-thick log shape on a piece of plastic wrap, wrap tightly, and refrigerate for up to 1 week or freeze for up to 3 months. When ready to use, cut off a 1/4-inch slice (about 1 tablespoon per serving) and place on top of seafood before baking or microwaving. Alternately, cut compound butter into 1/4-inch slices and allow slices to come to room temperature, then place slices over broiled, grilled, sautéed, planked, steamed, or poached seafood.

When making compound butters, you are limited only by your imagination. Let your taste buds guide you to new heights of flavor. These are variations you may want to try.

Citrus: Orange, Grapefruit, Kumquat, Lemon, Lemon-Lime, Lime

Condiment: Anchovy, Caper

Fruit: Blueberry, Mango, Papaya

Herb: Basil, Chervil, Chive, Cilantro, Dill, Ginger, Marjoram, Mint, Parsley, Rosemary, Sage, Tarragon, Thyme

Nut: Almond, Chestnut, Hazelnut, Macadamia, Pecan, Pine Nut, Walnut

Olive: Black Olive, Green Olive, Kalamata

Pepper: Chipotle (Canned in Adobo, or Dried), Green, Orange, Red or Yellow Bell Pepper (Fresh or Roasted), Jalapeño, Pasilla

Spice: Cayenne, Chili Powder, Cumin, Curry Powder, Dry Mustard, Paprika, Peppercorns

Vegetable: Asparagus Tip, Fennel, French Green Bean, Fresh Spring Pea, Garlic, Leeks, Onion, Radicchio, Spinach, Tomato, Watercress

Maître d'Hotel Butter

The following recipe is a classic in French cuisine, that pairs perfectly with any type of simply prepared finfish or shellfish.

2 TABLESPOONS MINCED FRESH PARSLEY

1 TABLESPOON FRESHLY SQUEEZED LEMON
    JUICE

1/2 CUP UNSALTED BUTTER, SOFTENED

1. Place parsley, lemon juice, and butter in a medium mixing bowl and stir until well blended.

2. Shape the butter into a 1-inch-thick log on a piece of plastic wrap. Wrap tightly and refrigerate or freeze.

3. To serve, slice off 1/4 inch per serving and place atop fish before baking, grilling, or microwaving. Alternately, let butter soften to room temperature, then spread on hot cooked fish or shellfish.

MAKES 1/2 CUP

Variation: Substitute the fresh herb of your choice for the parsley to make herb butter.

Seafood Suggestions: Any Finfish or Shellfish

Clarified Butter

Clarified, or drawn, butter is unsalted butter that is slowly cooked to evaporate most of the water, thereby separating the milk solids, which fall to the bottom, from the golden liquid on the surface. Clarified butter has a higher smoke point than regular butter and therefore cooks at higher temperatures. It also keeps longer than regular butter because the highly perishable milk solids have been removed. Ghee is the East Indian form of clarified butter.

2 CUPS UNSALTED BUTTER

Melt butter in a heavy saucepan over low heat. As froth rises to the surface, skim off, then carefully pour heavy golden butter from pan into a nonreactive bowl or jar with a lid, leaving behind the milky residue. Discard residue, cover clarified butter, and refrigerate for up to 3 months.

MAKES ABOUT 1 1/3 CUPS

Cream Sauces

Sauces made with heavy whipping cream that is reduced and flavored with herbs, wine, citrus, mushrooms, or nuts can add a soothing note to seafood. Roux-based sauces are also sometimes referred to as cream sauces. These are formed when a mixture of flour and fat (butter, lard, drippings, or pork or beef fat) is slowly cooked over low heat and a liquid is added. The color of the roux can range from white to brown depending on cooking time and designated use. If the high fat content of these sauces is a concern, remember that just a tablespoon or two can greatly enhance almost any simply prepared fish fillet or steak or shellfish.

White Wine (Vin Blanc) Sauce

———— 8 ————

White wine sauce is a traditional building block in French cooking. It can be adapted in so many ways that it is a good addition to any cook's repertoire.

2 CUPS SEAFOOD STOCK (SEE PAGE 318)
$3/4$ CUP DRY WHITE WINE
$1/2$ CUP HEAVY WHIPPING CREAM
SALT AND FRESHLY GROUND WHITE PEPPER
   TO TASTE

In a medium saucepan, boil stock and wine over medium-high heat 20 to 25 minutes, or until reduced to $1/4$ cup. Add cream, reduce heat to medium, and cook 5 to 7 minutes, or until sauce thickens slightly. Season to taste with salt and

pepper. Serve with cooked fish fillets or steaks or shellfish.

MAKES ABOUT $1/2$ CUP

Variation: After sauce is reduced, but before seasoning with salt and pepper, add chopped fresh herbs such as fennel, dill, tarragon, rosemary, sorrel, mint, or lemon balm.

Seafood Suggestions: Flounder/Sole, Monkfish, Salmon, Shrimp

Dr. Doug's Famous Chanterelle Sauce

———— 8 ————

There is a long tradition of dentists in the Market. Dr. Doug Leen recommends this recipe for seafood as tried and true, and says it's also great on steak. If you don't eat pork, omit the bacon and use 1 tablespoon of olive oil to sauté the chanterelles.

2 SLICES BACON
$1/2$ POUND CHANTERELLE MUSHROOMS,
   CLEANED AND CHOPPED
1 LARGE TOMATO, SKINNED, SEEDED, AND
   CHOPPED
1 TABLESPOON HOISIN SAUCE
$1/2$ CUP HALF-AND-HALF
$1/2$ TEASPOON CORNSTARCH (OPTIONAL)
SALT AND FRESHLY GROUND WHITE PEPPER
   TO TASTE

1. In a large skillet, cook bacon over medium to medium-high heat until crisp. Remove bacon, crumble into small pieces, and set aside. Discard

grease and return skillet to medium heat. Add chanterelles and cook 5 to 7 minutes, or until liquid from mushrooms is evaporated, stirring occasionally.

2. Add tomato, hoisin sauce, and half-and-half and cook 3 to 5 minutes, or until mixture thickens. To speed the reduction process, cook the mushroom mixture 3 to 5 minutes, then mix 1 tablespoon of the half-and-half with cornstarch in a small bowl. Remove pan from heat, add cornstarch mixture, stir well, return to heat, and cook 1 to 2 minutes, or until mixture thickens, stirring continuously. Add bacon and stir well to combine. Season to taste with salt and pepper.

3. To serve, spoon sauce over cooked fish fillets or steaks or shellfish.

MAKES 1 1/2 CUPS

Seafood Suggestions: Cod, Sablefish (Fresh or Smoked), Sea Scallops

Beurre Blanc

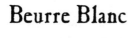

This classic French sauce is composed of a reduction of wine, vinegar, shallots, and whipping cream into which pieces of cold butter are whisked to form a thick, rich consistency. It is a traditional sauce for seafood and becomes even more versatile with the addition of lime or lemon juice, or by varying the type of herbs you add.

1 TABLESPOON FINELY MINCED SHALLOT

1/2 CUP DRY WHITE WINE

2 TEASPOONS WHITE WINE VINEGAR

3/4 CUP HEAVY WHIPPING CREAM

6 TABLESPOONS CHILLED UNSALTED
   BUTTER, CUT INTO CHUNKS

SALT AND FRESHLY GROUND WHITE PEPPER
   TO TASTE

1. In a small saucepan, bring shallot, wine, and white wine vinegar to a boil. Cook 3 to 5 minutes, or until reduced to 3 tablespoons. Add whipping cream, stir well, and cook 10 to 15 minutes, or until reduced to 3 tablespoons. Adjust heat if necessary to keep cream from boiling over.

2. Remove pan from heat and add butter chunks one at a time, whisking constantly, until mixture is thickened. Season to taste with salt and pepper. Keep sauce warm over very low heat or in the top of a double boiler until ready to use. If sauce should separate, whisk in a bit more whipping cream to recombine.

MAKES 2/3 CUP

Variations: At the same time as the butter chunks are being whisked into the sauce, add 2 to 3 tablespoons (or to taste) freshly squeezed lemon or lime juice to make a citrus beurre blanc. Fresh or dried herbs, such as basil, oregano, marjoram, or sage can also be added in lieu of the citrus juice to make an herb beurre blanc.

Seafood Suggestions: Flounder/Sole, Halibut, Salmon, Scallops, Shrimp

Champagne Sauce

———⚬———

Champagne spells romance, and although my favorite way to imbibe it is in a crystal Champagne flute, I am a sucker for bubbly in any form. This is a light, golden-colored cream sauce with a mild Champagne flavor. When paired with that special someone's favorite seafood, this sauce could form the basis for dinner à deux.

2 TABLESPOONS BUTTER
2 TABLESPOONS MINCED SHALLOTS
1/2 CUP SEAFOOD STOCK (SEE PAGE 318),
    BOTTLED CLAM JUICE, OR CHICKEN STOCK
1/2 CUP HEAVY WHIPPING CREAM
1/2 CUP CHAMPAGNE OR SPARKLING WINE
1/8 TEASPOON SALT
1/8 TEASPOON FRESHLY GROUND BLACK
    PEPPER

In a small skillet, melt butter over medium-high heat. Add shallots and cook 2 minutes, or until translucent, stirring occasionally. Add stock, bring to a boil, and cook 5 minutes, or until reduced to 1/4 cup, stirring occasionally. Add whipping cream and Champagne and cook 10 to 15 minutes more, or until thickened, stirring occasionally. Add salt and white pepper, stir well, and serve over cooked fish fillets, fish steaks, or shellfish.

MAKES 2/3 CUP

Seafood Suggestions: Flounder/Sole, Lobster, Monkfish, Salmon, Shrimp

Crusts

Crusts are a fun and creative way to seal in the flavor of fish or shellfish; they also add interesting textures to seafood dishes. Almost anything from ordinary bread crumbs to exotic black mustard seeds to intriguing dried herb and spice blends can be patted onto the outside of fish fillets (skin left on or removed as desired) or shellfish, then sautéed, baked, broiled, oven-fried, or deep-fried until it adheres and turns golden brown and crispy. Another advantage is that many crusts contain very little fat and a maximum of flavor.

Ingredients that can stand alone to form cohesive crusts for seafood include basic fresh or dry bread crumbs (unseasoned or flavored); panko (Japanese) bread crumbs; grains (farina, cornmeal, wheat germ, cooked polenta, rice paper, toasted and finely ground basmati rice); processed foods (crushed potato chips, crushed crackers, crushed unsweetened breakfast cereals); chopped nuts (pecans, almonds, macadamias, hazelnuts); white or black sesame seeds, toasted and crushed coriander seeds, toasted and crushed cumin seeds, yellow or black mustard seeds, or black onion seeds; coarsely crushed peppercorns (black, white, green, pink, or a mixture); and vegetables (grated potatoes or chopped corn).

Certain ingredients can be combined in smaller amounts with a base crust chosen from the ones above to form exotic, often spicy, crust mixtures. These include curry powder, toasted and ground cardamom, star anise, anise seeds, juniper berries, whole cloves, grated lemon or lime zest, fresh thyme leaves or dried thyme, fennel seeds, minced garlic, grated fresh horseradish or prepared horseradish (squeezed dry), grated gingerroot, whole allspice, grated Parmesan cheese, chopped cilantro, and fresh or dried oregano.

Seafood to be cooked in a crust must be patted as dry as possible before adding the breading. If moisture is present when the fish is dipped in the coating, the steam that forms during cooking will resist the coating. Fine, dry crumbs work better than large or damp crumbs, which tend to fall off. If time permits, allow the coated seafood to sit at room temperature for 20 minutes before cooking, which dries the crust and helps it to adhere. When sautéing, oven-frying, or deep-frying, make sure the oil is hot or the crust will absorb oil and be greasy.

Spice rubs and blackening or bronzing mixes are made from dried herbs and spices only (no breading). Fish fillets or shellfish are dredged in these mixtures, then cooked over high heat so that the spices fuse onto the surface. When making spice rubs and blackening and bronzing mixes for seafood, keep in mind that lighter spices or smaller amounts of stronger-flavored spices work best. For example, spices such as ground coriander, cumin, and sweet paprika can be used in large quantities to bulk up a mix; aromatic spices like cloves and cinnamon should be used judiciously.

Spice rubs and blackening and bronzing mixes are often ground to a medium to fine powder in a spice mill or electric coffee grinder. Spices can include kosher salt, peppercorns, coriander seeds, cumin seeds, dried thyme, dried rosemary, lemon pepper, granulated garlic, dried tarragon, dried basil, sweet or hot paprika, dried dill, and white pepper.

Fruit Sauces

While many people would never think of pairing fish and fruit, the two can go together with surprisingly good results. Especially in the Northwest, where our seasonal berries, apples, pears, and stone fruits are of such good quality, it seems a shame not to shed our prejudices, put on our aprons, and get inspired in the kitchen with savory fruit sauces.

Curried Apple Butter

This vibrant, yellow, sweet-hot seafood sauce comes from the Alaska Seafood Marketing Institute, which helps spread the good news about salmon, crab, pollock, and other types of fish and shellfish caught in Alaska. If you don't eat pork, omit the bacon and substitute very finely minced or crushed dried rosemary.

1/2 CUP APPLE BUTTER

1/2 CUP MAYONNAISE

2 TABLESPOONS CRUMBLED, CRISP-COOKED BACON

2 TABLESPOONS MINCED SHALLOTS

1 TEASPOON CURRY POWDER, OR TO TASTE

1. In a small bowl, mix together all of the ingredients.

2. To use sauce, brush mixture on both sides of meaty fish fillets and bake, broil, grill, or sauté fillets, cooking 10 minutes per inch of thickness, measuring fillets at thickest part.

MAKES 1 1/2 CUPS

Seafood Suggestions: Alaska Pollock, Salmon, Sea Scallops

Light Orange Sauce

─────※─────

Reducing fruit juices until they are syrupy, then adding a bit of vinegar and oil creates sauces bursting with flavor, yet light in calories, perfect to pair with fish and shellfish salads. The flavor can be varied depending on the type of fresh herbs added. My favorite is fresh tarragon.

1 CUP FRESHLY SQUEEZED ORANGE JUICE

1 TABLESPOON SEASONED RICE VINEGAR

1 TABLESPOON EXTRA VIRGIN OLIVE OIL OR
   CANOLA OIL

1 TEASPOON MINCED FRESH TARRAGON,
   MARJORAM, ROSEMARY, OR OREGANO,
   OR 1/2 TEASPOON DRIED TARRAGON,
   MARJORAM, ROSEMARY, OR OREGANO,
   CRUMBLED

SALT AND FRESHLY GROUND WHITE PEPPER
   TO TASTE

1. In a small saucepan, bring orange juice to a boil and cook 10 to 15 minutes, or until reduced to 1/4 cup. Adjust heat if necessary to prevent orange juice from boiling over.

2. Remove from heat, pour into a small nonreactive mixing bowl or jar with a lid and allow to cool. Add rice vinegar, olive oil, and tarragon, and whisk or shake well to combine ingredients. Season to taste with salt and white pepper.

3. To serve, drizzle sauce over cooked fish or shellfish, or toss with salad greens and place fish or shellfish on top.

MAKES ABOUT 1/3 CUP

Seafood Suggestions: Crab, Salmon, Shrimp, Tuna

Glazes

A glaze is a thin, glossy coating that may be sweet or savory. Suitable for both hot and cold food, glazes work especially well with seafood because they help lock in the food's natural juices and delicate flavors. Glazes also add an extra flavor boost to fish or shellfish without adding lots of calories.

Lowfat Fish Glaze

─────※─────

ANTHONY'S HOMEPORT,
VARIOUS LOCATIONS THROUGHOUT
THE PUGET SOUND AREA

Sally McArthur, former executive chef of the Anthony's Homeport chain of restaurants, describes this recipe as a multipurpose fish glaze that is healthful and works well on many species of fish. Barbecue, bake, or sauté fish fillets or steaks, then drizzle the sauce over the top. The sauce is complex and fresh, with high notes of lemon and musky-sweet overtones of balsamic vinegar.

2 TABLESPOONS OLIVE OIL

2 TEASPOONS MINCED SHALLOTS

1 TEASPOON MINCED FRESH GARLIC

1/2 TEASPOON FRESHLY GRATED LEMON
   ZEST

2 TABLESPOONS BALSAMIC VINEGAR

3/4 CUP BOTTLED CLAM JUICE

4 TEASPOONS CHOPPED FRESH BASIL

1. Heat olive oil in a medium saucepan over medium heat. Add shallots and garlic and cook 1 to 2 minutes, or until shallots are soft but not

brown, stirring frequently. Add lemon zest, balsamic vinegar, and clam juice and cook 5 to 7 minutes over high heat, or until liquid thickens slightly.

2. Remove saucepan from heat and stir in basil. Drizzle glaze over cooked fish fillets.

MAKES $2/3$ CUP

Seafood Suggestions: Marlin, Sablefish, Salmon, Swordfish, Tuna

Micks' Peppery Fish Glaze

MICKS' PEPPOURI, PIKE PLACE MARKET

During the mid-1970s, Walter Mick was an elementary school principal in eastern Washington. One day as a gift he received a jar of pepper jelly and its accompanying recipe. Walt started tinkering with the recipe and sharing the results with friends, family, and business associates. Over time, more and more people raved about Walt's delicious pepper jelly and encouraged him to market it. The rest, as they say, is history, for in 1982, Walt and wife Ginger formed Micks' Peppouri, which makes pepper jellies using fruits and vegetables raised in the Yakima Valley by the Mick family. The jellies tenderize, season, and glaze in one easy step, and are a boon to the home cook as well as the professional chef. They are available at the Micks' permanent stand in the Market, or by mail (see page 327).

$1/4$ CUP MICKS' PEPPER JELLY OF YOUR
    CHOICE OR JALAPEÑO JELLY

1 TABLESPOON WATER

1. In a small saucepan, heat pepper jelly and water over low heat just until jelly melts, stirring often. Remove from heat.

2. Lightly brush tops of fish fillets, steaks, or shellfish with glaze and broil or bake until seafood is at desired doneness, brushing lightly with glaze every 2 to 3 minutes. Remove seafood to warmed dinner plates and serve immediately.

MAKES $1/4$ CUP

Variations: For a more complex sauce, mix the pepper jelly of your choice with equal parts orange marmalade (I like to use the low-sugar variety for a less sweet taste), then season to taste with Worcestershire sauce. The pepper jellies are also good served alongside crab cakes, added to stir-fry marinades, or thinned with a bit of water and used as a dipping sauce for fried seafood.

Another variation is to make Beurre Blanc (see page 305) and stir in pepper jelly to taste. Serve pepper cream sauce with fish fillets or steaks, or toss with cooked pasta and fish or shellfish for seafood pasta with a spicy cream sauce.

Seafood Suggestions: Chilean Sea Bass, Cod, Halibut, Fresh Oysters on the Half Shell, Rockfish, Salmon, Scallops, Shrimp

Simple Soy Glaze

———∙⧓∙———

I hope this recipe will become one of your favorites because it's so delicious, easy to make, and versatile that you can use it on almost any fish or shellfish you choose.

1 TABLESPOON LIGHT COOKING OIL, SUCH
    AS CANOLA, SAFFLOWER, CORN, SOY, OR
    VEGETABLE
1 TABLESPOON SOY SAUCE OR LOW-SODIUM
    SOY SAUCE
1 TABLESPOON HONEY, BROWN SUGAR, OR
    MAPLE SYRUP
1 TABLESPOON DIJON MUSTARD
1 1/2 TEASPOONS PREPARED HORSERADISH

1. In a small bowl, mix together oil, soy sauce, honey, and mustard. Add horseradish and blend thoroughly.

2. Lightly oil a broiling pan with a rack lightly, spray with nonstick cooking spray. Place fish fillets, steaks, or shellfish on rack and lightly brush with glaze. Broil 3 to 4 inches from heat source for 3 minutes, then brush fillets again. If seafood starts to brown too much, move pan 4 to 6 inches from heat source. Continue brushing at 3-minute intervals and cook until seafood reaches desired doneness.

MAKES 1/4 CUP

Variation: If you don't like horseradish, you can substitute freshly grated gingerroot, Chinese five-spice powder, Japanese seven-spice seasoning (*shichimi togarashi*), or hot chile oil for an Asian flair. Cajun blackening mix creates a Southern touch. Add the alternative seasonings a little at a time, until you reach the level of spiciness or hotness you prefer.

Seafood Suggestions: Halibut, Salmon, Sea Scallops, Shrimp, Swordfish

Marinades

Before modern refrigeration techniques and modes of transportation were invented, marinades were used to preserve foods and even to disguise foods that were a bit past their prime. Today, marinades are used to add flavor and moisture to foods before we cook them. They are especially beneficial for seafood, which cooks quickly, is often low in fat, and may have a mild, delicate natural flavor.

Traditional marinades are made of three distinct parts. These include an acid, such as fruit juice (citrus or apple) or vinegar, soy sauce or fish sauce, yogurt or buttermilk, or wine or beer, which softens the food. The second part is oil, which adds moisture and flavor to the marinated food. Finally come the aromatics, which can include onions, fresh or dry herbs, spices, or liqueurs. These give a marinade its aroma and flavor.

When you work with marinades, several important rules apply:

• Use nonreactive bowls or pans (glass, plastic, stainless steel) to marinate seafood, never aluminum. A plastic bag with a zip-lock top works well and makes cleanup easy, although it is not the most environmentally correct choice since it should not be reused.

• Do not marinate seafood longer than 15 to 30 minutes, unless otherwise specified in the recipe, or the flavor of the fish or shellfish could be overpowered and the acid in the marinade could begin to "cook" the seafood, which will then toughen when heated.

• Marinate seafood, covered, in the refrigerator if not cooking within 15 minutes of placing the seafood in the marinade.

• Turn seafood once or twice during the marinating process to coat all exposed surfaces evenly.

• Do not use liquid in which raw seafood was marinated to baste seafood during the cooking process. Either reserve part of the marinade before adding the seafood, or boil remaining marinade for 2 to 3 minutes to destroy any bacteria before using.

Simple Fish Marinade

Sometimes the simplest preparations are best, as in this easy fish marinade. Immerse fish fillets or steaks for a maximum of 15 to 30 minutes before cooking.

2 TABLESPOONS OLIVE OIL
2 TABLESPOONS FRESHLY SQUEEZED
    LEMON OR LIME JUICE
1/4 CUP DRY WHITE WINE, OR 2
    TABLESPOONS WHITE DRY VERMOUTH
2 TABLESPOONS FRESH MINCED HERB OR
    COMBINATION OF FRESH HERBS, SUCH AS
    BASIL, OREGANO, TARRAGON, MARJORAM,
    LEMON BALM, OR MINT
2 CLOVES GARLIC, MINCED
PINCH OF SALT AND FRESHLY GROUND
    BLACK PEPPER
1 1/2 POUNDS FISH FILLETS OR STEAKS

1. In a nonreactive baking dish large enough to hold fish fillets without crowding, stir together all of the ingredients except fish. Add fish fillets and turn to coat both sides. Cover dish and refrigerate 15 to 30 minutes.

2. When ready to cook, remove fish from marinade and pat dry with paper towels. Discard marinade. Broil, bake, grill, or sauté 10 minutes per inch of thickness when measured at thickest part.

MAKES 1/2 CUP

Seafood Suggestions: Any Finfish

Apple-Chipotle Marinade

———⚬———

This recipe comes from John Sarich, beloved Northwest cookbook author, television chef, and culinary director of Chateau Ste. Michelle Winery in Woodinville, Washington. It is a very flavorful marinade that really sparks up any type of seafood, but my favorites include peeled and deveined shrimp, tuna, swordfish, and marlin. It also works well with chicken.

¼ CUP APPLE JUICE

1 TABLESPOON PEANUT OIL

1 OR 2 CANNED CHIPOTLE PEPPERS IN
    ADOBO, DEPENDING ON HOTNESS
    DESIRED, DRAINED

1 TABLESPOON BALSAMIC VINEGAR

1 TABLESPOON BROWN MUSTARD OR HONEY
    MUSTARD

1 TABLESPOON BROWN SUGAR (OPTIONAL)

¼ CUP FRESHLY SQUEEZED LIME JUICE

2 LARGE CLOVES GARLIC

1 TEASPOON GROUND CUMIN

1 TABLESPOON CHOPPED CILANTRO

½ TEASPOON SALT

¼ TEASPOON FRESHLY GROUND BLACK
    PEPPER

1 ½ POUNDS PEELED AND DEVEINED
    SHRIMP OR MEATY FISH FILLETS, SUCH
    AS TUNA, SWORDFISH, OR MARLIN

1. Place all of the ingredients except the fish in a food processor or blender and process until smooth.

2. Place shrimp or fish fillets in a nonreactive bowl large enough to hold seafood in a single layer and pour marinade over. Turn pieces, cover, and refrigerate 1 to 2 hours, turning occasionally.

3. About 10 minutes before cooking, preheat grill or broiler. Grease grill lightly or spray with nonstick cooking spray, pat seafood dry, and place on grill. If broiling, lightly grease a baking sheet or spray with nonstick spray, pat seafood dry, and place on baking sheet.

4. Place marinade in a small saucepan, bring to a boil, and cook 2 to 3 minutes, stirring occasionally. Remove from heat and reserve.

5. Grill or broil shrimp 3 to 5 minutes, or until shrimp just turn pink, basting with reserved marinade once or twice. For fish fillets, cook 10 minutes per inch of thickness when measured at thickest point, basting with marinade every 2 to 3 minutes. If grilling, turn seafood halfway through cooking time; if broiling, do not turn. Discard marinade.

6. Divide seafood among individual plates and serve immediately.

MAKES 1 CUP

Seafood Suggestions: Marlin, Shrimp, Swordfish, Tuna

Lemongrass Cure for Grilled Seafood

~~❦~~

THE WESTIN HOTEL, SEATTLE, WASHINGTON

Executive chef Marcus Dunbar is a great proponent of Thai food because its clean, vivid flavors and the emphasis on fresh vegetables, noodles, and seafood are right in keeping with our health- and flavor-conscious times. The chef's low-calorie recipe adds a lot of zest to a simple mixed seafood grill with a "cure," a sort of marinade, of distinctively Thai flavors.

1/2 CUP KOSHER SALT

1/2 CUP SUGAR

1/2 CUP CHOPPED CILANTRO

6 STEMS LEMONGRASS, ROOTS AND TOP 2 INCHES REMOVED, REMAINING PORTION COARSELY CHOPPED

1 TABLESPOON FRESHLY GRATED GINGER-ROOT

1/4 CUP SAKE

1 1/2 POUNDS PEELED AND DEVEINED SHRIMP OR PRAWNS, SCALLOPS, SALMON, TUNA, OR MARLIN FILLETS

1. In a small nonreactive mixing bowl, combine all of the ingredients except seafood and stir to mix well.

2. Rub cure into seafood. Cover and refrigerate shrimp or scallops for 2 hours. Cover and refrigerate salmon, tuna, or marlin 2 to 4 hours.

3. About 10 minutes before cooking, preheat grill or broiler. If broiling, oil a baking sheet lightly or spray with nonstick cooking spray. Set aside. If grilling, grease grill lightly or spray with nonstick cooking spray.

4. Just before cooking, remove cure by rinsing seafood and patting dry, or wiping off cure with a damp cloth. Place shrimp or scallops on grill, and cook 3 to 5 minutes, or until shrimp just turn pink or scallops are still slightly translucent in center, turning once halfway through cooking time. If broiling, place shrimp or scallops on baking sheet, position 3 to 4 inches from heat source, and cook 3 to 5 minutes. For fish fillets, place on grill or baking sheet and cook 10 minutes per inch of thickness when measured at thickest point. If grilling, turn fish halfway through cooking time; if broiling, do not turn.

MAKES 1/4 CUP

Seafood Suggestions: Marlin, Salmon, Scallops, Shrimp, Tuna

Asian Marinade

⎯⎯⊱⊰⎯⎯

This Asian-inspired marinade infuses the fish or shell-fish with the flavors of garlic and ginger, while the peanut oil plumps the seafood and imparts a silky texture.

6 TABLESPOONS PEANUT OIL

2 TABLESPOONS LOW-SODIUM SOY SAUCE

1/4 FRESHLY SQUEEZED LIME JUICE

1 CLOVE GARLIC, MINCED

1 GREEN ONION, TOP 2 INCHES REMOVED, REMAINING PORTION CUT INTO 1/8-INCH PIECES

2 QUARTER-SIZED PIECES GINGERROOT, PEELED AND MINCED

1 TEASPOON SUGAR

1 1/2 POUNDS FISH FILLETS OR STEAKS OR PEELED AND DEVEINED SHRIMP, SCALLOPS, OR SQUID

1. In a nonreactive baking dish large enough to hold fish or shellfish without crowding, whisk together all of the ingredients except the fish. Add fish fillets or shellfish and turn to coat completely. Cover and refrigerate 15 to 30 minutes, turning once or twice.

2. Pat seafood dry, and broil, bake, grill, or sauté fish or shellfish until done. Discard marinade. Serve immediately.

MAKES 3/4 CUP

Seafood Suggestions: Any Finfish, Scallops, Shrimp, Squid

Citrus Marinade

⎯⎯⊱⊰⎯⎯

In his enlightening book, Marinades, Jim Tarantino explains that citrus marinades (known as esca-bèche) were brought to Spain by the Moors invading from Africa. Those marinades were later taken by the Spanish to the Caribbean and used by African slaves to create a dish known as escouvitched fish. When Christopher Columbus made his voyages, eating was changed forever on both sides of the Atlantic; Spain got some chiles and the Americas got citrus.

1/3 CUP FRESHLY SQUEEZED LEMON JUICE

1 TABLESPOON OLIVE OIL

1 TEASPOON HONEY

1 TEASPOON FRESHLY GRATED ORANGE ZEST

1 SHALLOT, MINCED

1 TABLESPOON CHOPPED FRESH THYME, OR 1/2 TEASPOON DRIED THYME, CRUMBLED

1/4 TEASPOON SALT

PINCH OF FRESHLY GROUND WHITE PEPPER

1 1/2 POUNDS PEELED AND DEVEINED SHRIMP, SCALLOPS, OR ANY FINFISH FILLETS OR STEAKS

1. In a nonreactive baking dish large enough to hold seafood without crowding, whisk together all of the ingredients except the fish.

2. Add shellfish or finfish and turn to coat completely. Cover and refrigerate 15 to 30 minutes. Remove seafood from marinade, pat dry, and bake, broil, grill, or sauté until done. Discard marinade.

MAKES 1/2 CUP

Seafood Suggestions: Chilean Sea Bass, Scallops, Shrimp, Swordfish, Tuna

Yogurt Marinade

———❦———

The lactic acid in yogurt works much the same way as citrus acid to help soften the food to be marinated. However, yogurt also provides moisture. Yogurt-based marinades are found on all shores of the Mediterranean and in India, the inspiration for this recipe.

1 CUP PLAIN NONFAT OR LOWFAT YOGURT

2 CLOVES GARLIC, CUT IN HALF

2 GREEN ONIONS, TOP 2 INCHES REMOVED, REMAINING PORTION COARSELY CHOPPED

1 QUARTER-SIZED PIECE GINGERROOT, PEELED AND CRUSHED

1 TEASPOON GROUND CURRY POWDER

1 TEASPOON GROUND CHILI POWDER

1 1/2 TEASPOONS GROUND CUMIN

1/8 TEASPOON SALT

PINCH OF FRESHLY GROUND BLACK PEPPER

1 1/2 POUNDS PEELED AND DEVEINED SHRIMP, SCALLOPS, OR ANY FINFISH FILLETS OR STEAKS

1. In a food processor or blender, combine all of the ingredients except the fish until smooth.

2. Place shellfish or finfish in a nonreactive baking dish large enough to hold seafood without crowding, pour in marinade, and turn seafood to coat completely. Cover and place in refrigerator 15 to 30 minutes, turning once or twice. Remove seafood from marinade, pat dry, and bake, broil, grill, or sauté until done. Discard marinade.

MAKES 1 CUP

Seafood Suggestions: Any Finfish, Scallops, Shrimp

Mayonnaise and Mayonnaise-Based Sauces

Homemade mayonnaise is great to have on hand for saucing fish. It can be dressed up or down with the addition of herbs or spices, or thinned with lemon or lime juice or milk for a lighter consistency. It is also the foundation for many other seafood sauces, such as tartar, rémoulade, and aïoli. Homemade mayonnaise can be made by hand, or in a blender, food processor, or electric mixer.

Note: Recent concerns about salmonella poisoning have called into question the use of raw eggs in food preparation. Although I have never experienced any ill effects from using raw eggs when making homemade mayonnaise or any other recipe, I would encourage the use of the freshest eggs available and a thorough washing and drying of the eggs before use. Individuals with chronic or autoimmune diseases should be informed of the uncooked eggs before eating recipes in this section. The use of pasteurized eggs is another alternative for individuals at risk.

Basic Homemade Mayonnaise and Variations

———✦———

Homemade mayonnaise is a cinch to make and tastes much better than storebought versions. Plus, it's fun to experiment with variations on a theme by adding fresh or dried herbs, ground spices, chutneys, salsas, capers—whatever your heart desires.

1 LARGE EGG, AT ROOM TEMPERATURE

1 TEASPOON DIJON MUSTARD

1/8 TEASPOON KOSHER SALT

1/8 TEASPOON FRESHLY GROUND WHITE
   PEPPER

1 CUP VEGETABLE, CANOLA, OR MILD OLIVE
   OIL, OR A MIXTURE OF 1/2 CUP MILD OLIVE
   OIL AND 1/2 CUP VEGETABLE OR CANOLA
   OIL, AT ROOM TEMPERATURE

1 TEASPOON TO 1 TABLESPOON FRESHLY
   SQUEEZED LEMON JUICE, WHITE WINE
   VINEGAR, OR TARRAGON VINEGAR

1. Place egg, mustard, salt, and pepper in a medium nonreactive mixing bowl and whisk until mixture begins to lighten in color. Add the oil drop by drop, whisking constantly, stirring in the same direction and at the same speed.

2. When the mayonnaise begins to thicken, add the oil more quickly, in a thin stream. When oil is incorporated and mayonnaise is thick and smooth, season to taste with lemon juice or vinegar. If mixture is too thick, thin with a bit of hot water to desired consistency.

MAKES 1 CUP

Variations: Add minced fresh herbs, such as tarragon, chives, basil, dill, cilantro, thyme, mint, or garlic. Or cook some curry powder or chili powder in a small amount of oil, allow to cool, then add mayonnaise and stir well to make curry or chili mayonnaise. Citrus juices, such as lime or orange, add another dimension to the mayonnaise. Fresh green, yellow, orange, or red bell peppers, finely diced, add beautiful color, taste, and texture to basic mayonnaise, and roasted peppers add a smoky taste and lush texture. A bit of pesto sauce also works well.

Other additions to flavor mayonnaise include chutneys, salsas, gingerroot or dried ginger, green or black olives, or mustards of all types, including Dijon, honey mustard, or country-style (grainy) mustard.

To make your own homemade tartar sauce, add diced gherkins or sweet pickles, minced capers, a pinch of paprika, minced green olives, and diced parsley to the basic mayonnaise.

A mock aïoli sauce can be made by adding fresh garlic cloves that have been peeled and crushed with a mortar and pestle, or roasted garlic that has been squeezed out of its shell and crushed with the back of a spoon.

A tangy rémoulade sauce is made by adding diced capers, diced dill pickles, Dijon mustard, and chopped green onion to the basic mayonnaise.

Green Goddess dressing is a mixture of mayonnaise and thinly sliced green onions, watercress, or spinach leaves (or fresh parsley, top curly parts only, or fresh dill, feathery parts only), and Worcestershire sauce or anchovy fillets.

Salsa

America is having a love affair with salsa, which recently overtook ketchup as the best-selling condiment in the United States. A native of Mexico, where the word means "sauce," salsa can be mixtures of fruits and vegetables (fresh or cooked) ranging in spiciness from mild to incendiary! As an example of their diversity, the salsas in the book include such varied ingredients as corn (see pages 130-31), blueberries, yogurt (see page 177), Anaheim peppers (see page 50), and honey (see page 177).

Blueberry-Ginger Salsa

RAY'S BOATHOUSE, SEATTLE, WASHINGTON

This salsa packs a wallop of flavor and is best made during the height of the summer blueberry season, when the fruit is at its peak of flavor and least expensive. Serve it with almost any kind of simply grilled, sautéed, baked, or broiled fish fillets or steaks.

2 CUPS FRESH BLUEBERRIES

1 TEASPOON MINCED GINGERROOT

1/2 TEASPOON MINCED GARLIC

2 TABLESPOONS BALSAMIC VINEGAR

1/2 TEASPOON BROWN SUGAR

1/2 RED PEPPER, MINCED

1 TABLESPOON FRESHLY SQUEEZED LIME
   JUICE OR ROSE'S LIME JUICE

1/4 CUP MINCED FRESH MINT

SALT AND FRESHLY GROUND BLACK PEPPER
   TO TASTE

1. In a food processor or blender, process 1 cup of the blueberries until liquefied. Pour into a small nonreactive mixing bowl with a lid, and add the remaining 1 cup blueberries, the gingerroot, garlic, balsamic vinegar, brown sugar, red pepper, lime juice, and fresh mint. Stir to combine ingredients and season to taste with salt and pepper. Allow to sit at least 20 minutes at room temperature for flavors to blend, or cover and refrigerate for up to 2 days.

2. Serve with cooked fish fillets or steaks.

MAKES ABOUT 2 CUPS

Seafood Suggestion: Marlin, Rockfish, Salmon, Steelhead

Seafood Stock

A good fish stock can be used in so many ways—as the base for a seafood soup or stew, as a poaching liquid, or reduced in sauces (see page 133), to name just a few. Use trimmings from mild, lean fish, such as cod, sole, halibut, or rockfish, rather than fatty fish, or the stock will be too oily and strong. Fish stock will keep for a few days refrigerated or up to 3 months frozen. It is also a good idea to pour some of your stock into ice cube trays, freeze, pop out the cubes, and store in freezer-safe plastic bags for times when you feel you need just a bit of stock. However, in a pinch, fish bouillon cubes, bottled clam juice diluted with water, or *dashi-no-moto*, a powdered Japanese soup base, can be substituted for homemade fish stock.

2 POUNDS MILD, LEAN FISH TRIMMINGS
   (BONES, HEADS, AND/OR TAILS),
   COARSELY CHOPPED INTO 3-INCH PIECES,
   OR 2 POUNDS INEXPENSIVE MILD, LEAN
   FISH FILLETS, CUT INTO 3-INCH PIECES

1 ONION, COARSELY CHOPPED

1 STALK CELERY, PLUS LEAVES, COARSELY
   CHOPPED

3 SPRIGS FRESH THYME, OR 1 TEASPOON
   DRIED THYME, CRUMBLED

HANDFUL OF PARSLEY SPRIGS AND STEMS
   (ABOUT 8 SPRIGS)

1 BAY LEAF

1/4 TEASPOON BLACK PEPPERCORNS

2 WHOLE CLOVES

6 CUPS WATER

1. Rinse fish trimmings and make sure no traces of gills or blood remain. Place fish in a large stockpot or Dutch oven and add onion, celery, thyme, parsley, bay leaf, peppercorns, and cloves. Pour water over ingredients in pot, adding a bit more water if necessary so that fish is completely covered.

2. Bring water to a simmer, then cook 20 to 25 minutes (starting from the time the water simmers), uncovered, skimming away any foam that rises to the top. Strain stock through a fine-meshed sieve lined with several layers of dampened cheesecloth and cool to room temperature. Pour into a bowl or jar, and refrigerate or freeze for future use as described above.

MAKES ABOUT 5 CUPS

Note: Two pounds of shrimp shells can be substituted for fish trimmings to make a delicious shrimp stock (see pages 244-45). You can also collect and freeze your shrimp shells for up to 3 months, then simmer. Two pounds of salmon trimmings can be substituted as well. Use salmon stock in strong-flavored or spicy dishes, such as salmon chowders or seafood stews.

Traditional Seafood Sauces

Even though many cooks like to be on the cutting edge of cuisine (no pun intended), tried-and-true seafood sauces have become classics because they taste good and pair well with the fish or shellfish they are designed to enhance. While the sauces that follow have their foundation in the traditional renditions, most of them also feature a twist to bring them in line with modern tastes and, in some cases, health concerns.

Fresh Cocktail Sauce

─────❧─────

Chef Kathy Casey realizes that while oyster purists disdain anything other than a glass of crisp white wine, a loaf of bread, and maybe a squirt of lemon juice before slurping their oysters on the half shell, many people need a little something to wash the oysters down, such as a mignonette sauce (see page 222) or the more traditional cocktail sauce. Her rendition of the often maligned bottled sauce is bright, crunchy, and refreshing and will be appreciated by beginning oyster eaters and seasoned veterans alike. It is also tasty with shrimp or crab cocktails.

2 CUPS $1/4$-INCH DICED RIPE TOMATOES

$1/4$ CUP FRESHLY SQUEEZED LEMON JUICE

2 TABLESPOONS VERY FINELY MINCED
  CELERY

1 SHALLOT, VERY FINELY MINCED (ABOUT
  2 TABLESPOONS)

1 TABLESPOON FINELY CHOPPED FRESH
  PARSLEY

1 TABLESPOON HOT PREPARED HORSE-
  RADISH

$1 1/2$ TEASPOONS SUGAR

$3/4$ TEASPOON SALT

$1/2$ TEASPOON WORCESTERSHIRE SAUCE

$1/2$ TEASPOON TABASCO SAUCE, OR MORE
  TO TASTE

$1/4$ TEASPOON FRESHLY GROUND BLACK
  PEPPER

$1/8$ TEASPOON CELERY SEED

1. In a medium nonreactive mixing bowl, gently stir together all of the ingredients. Taste for seasoning and adjust as desired.

2. To serve, arrange shucked raw oysters on the half shell on a large serving platter covered with crushed ice or rock salt. Set a bowl of cocktail sauce and a small spoon in the center and encourage guests to serve themselves.

MAKES 2 CUPS

Seafood Suggestions: Cold Cooked Crabmeat, Cold Cooked Shrimp, Fresh Oysters on the Half Shell

Marinara Sauce

─────❧─────

A good all-purpose tomato sauce works with everything from grilled fish fillets to seafood pasta. It also forms a hearty base for steaming mussels or clams. Plan on making an extra batch, as it freezes well and comes in handy for last-minute meals.

1 TABLESPOON OLIVE OIL

1 ONION, DICED

2 CLOVES GARLIC, MINCED

1 CARROT, DICED

1 STALK CELERY, DICED

2 POUNDS RIPE PLUM TOMATOES, CHOPPED,
  PLUS ANY JUICE OR 1 (28-OUNCE) CAN
  WHOLE TOMATOES IN PURÉE, CHOPPED,
  AND PURÉE RESERVED

$1/2$ CUP RED WINE OR CHICKEN STOCK

2 TABLESPOONS TOMATO PASTE

2 TABLESPOONS MINCED FRESH BASIL, OR
  $1 1/2$ TEASPOONS DRIED BASIL, CRUMBLED

1 TABLESPOON MINCED FRESH OREGANO,
  OR 1 TEASPOON DRIED OREGANO,
  CRUMBLED

1/2 TEASPOON SUGAR

1/4 TEASPOON SALT

1/4 TEASPOON FRESHLY GROUND BLACK
   PEPPER

1. Heat olive oil in a large skillet or Dutch oven over medium-high heat. Add onion and garlic and cook 3 to 5 minutes, or until onion is tender-crisp, stirring often. Do not allow onion to brown. Add carrot and celery, and cook 3 minutes, stirring often. If vegetables begin to stick, add 1 tablespoon water and stir well. Add tomatoes and juice and cook 2 minutes, stirring often.

2. Add red wine, tomato paste, 1 tablespoon of the fresh basil or all of the dried basil, 1 1/2 teaspoons of the fresh oregano or all of the dried oregano, the sugar, salt, and pepper, stir well, and bring to a boil. Turn down heat, cover partially, and simmer 25 to 30 minutes, or until vegetables are tender and mixture is reduced to sauce consistency, stirring occasionally. Add the remaining 1 tablespoon of basil and 1 1/2 teaspoons of oregano. Allow mixture to cool slightly, then add sauce to a food processor or blender and process until small chunks remain. Season to taste with additional salt, pepper, and sugar. If using sauce immediately, return to skillet and rewarm. If using later, cover and refrigerate for 4 to 5 days, or freeze for up to 2 months.

MAKES 2 1/2 CUPS

Seafood Suggestions: Any Finfish or Shellfish

Crab Louis Dressing

———⊷❈⊷———

MECH APIARIES,
PIKE PLACE MARKET

Crab Louis dressing is traditionally served over cold crab and lettuce salad. Accounts differ on where the dish originated, with some claiming Seattle's Olympic Club or Portland's Bohemian Restaurant, and others recognizing either San Francisco's St. Francis Hotel or Solari's restaurant (long since departed). In this interpretation, beekeeper Doris Mech, author of Joy With Honey, *adds just a bit of the bees' elixir to sweeten up the dressing.*

1/2 CUP MAYONNAISE (SEE PAGE 316)

1/4 CUP KETCHUP

2 TABLESPOONS APPLE CIDER VINEGAR

1 TEASPOON HONEY

1/4 CUP DICED SWEET PICKLES

1 HARD-BOILED EGG, DICED

PINCH OF SALT

In a small mixing bowl, blend together all of the ingredients. Serve over chopped romaine that has been sprinkled with flaked crabmeat or cooked shrimp.

MAKES 3/4 CUP

Seafood Suggestions: Cold Cooked Crab, Cold Poached Salmon Fillet, Shrimp

Romesco Sauce

———◆———

This rich crimson sauce hails from Catalonia, Spain. Traditionally, it is served with grilled or broiled fish; I also like it with shellfish. Be sure to use a good-quality, fruity olive oil—preferably Spanish, of course.

1 VERY RIPE TOMATO, CORED AND COARSELY
   CHOPPED

4 CLOVES GARLIC, CUT IN HALF

1/3 CUP TOASTED WHOLE ALMONDS
   (SEE PAGE 10)

2 SLICES WHITE BREAD, CRUSTS REMOVED,
   CRUMBLED

1/4 TEASPOON CRUSHED RED PEPPER
   FLAKES

1/4 TEASPOON GROUND HOT PAPRIKA

1/4 TEASPOON SALT

1/4 CUP RED WINE VINEGAR

1/4 CUP OLIVE OIL

1. Place tomato, garlic, almonds, bread, red pepper flakes, paprika, salt, and vinegar in food processor or blender and process until only very small pieces remain.

2. Add olive oil in a thin, steady stream until mixture is smooth and thickened. Season to taste with additional salt, paprika, or red wine vinegar, if desired. Serve with simply grilled, broiled, or baked finfish or selected shellfish.

1 1/4 CUPS

Seafood Suggestions: Clams, Cod, Flounder/Sole, Lingcod, Mussels, Rockfish, Scallops, Shrimp, Trout

Vinaigrettes and Dressings

Vinaigrettes and dressings have become the darlings of forward-thinking chefs and home cooks who want to "sauce" their seafood with a flavor-packed yet relatively healthy mixture that enhances, rather than masks, the fish or shellfish.

Another advantage to vinaigrettes and dressings is their ease of preparation, which can be as simple as whisking together good-quality olive oil, vinegar or lemon juice, salt, freshly ground pepper, and fresh or dried herbs. With all of the flavored vinegars and oils that have recently hit supermarket shelves across the nation, the variety of combinations is staggering. Here are just a few: Thai Vinaigrette (see pages 48-49), Ginger Vinaigrette (see page 209), Lightened Caesar Dressing (see page 224), and Rice Vinegar Dressing (see page 249).

To use a vinaigrette or dressing with seafood, simply brush over fish fillets or shellfish just before cooking, use the sauce to marinate the seafood for 15 to 30 minutes before cooking, or use in the traditional manner to dress greens that act as a bed for cooked fish fillets or shellfish.

Cranberry-Walnut Vinaigrette

~⊰⊱~

ERNIE'S GRILL AT THE EDGEWATER, SEATTLE, WASHINGTON

The Edgewater is Seattle's only waterfront hotel. Built in 1962 for the World's Fair, the hotel is known for its distinctive bright-red rooftop "E," which is noted on nautical maps and provides directions for ships navigating in Puget Sound.

1/2 CUP FRESH OR THAWED FROZEN CRAN-
   BERRIES
1/4 CUP WATER
2 TABLESPOONS SUGAR
1/2 CUP RED WINE VINEGAR
2 TABLESPOONS CHOPPED WALNUTS
1 CUP VEGETABLE OIL

1. In a small saucepan, bring cranberries, water, and sugar to a simmer over medium heat. Cook 4 to 5 minutes, or until cranberry skins pop, stirring occasionally.

2. Remove from heat, then place cranberries in refrigerator to cool completely.

3. When chilled, place cranberry mixture in a food processor or blender. Add vinegar and walnuts and process until smooth. With motor running, slowly add oil in a thin stream. When oil is incorporated, turn off machine and season to taste with additional sugar or vinegar, if desired.

MAKES 2 CUPS

Seafood Suggestions: Halibut, Salmon, Scallops

Mustard Seed Dressing

~⊰⊱~

Tiny black mustard seeds provide a piquant crunch to a light dressing that looks beautiful when poured over pristine whitefish fillets.

2 TABLESPOONS BLACK MUSTARD SEEDS
1 TABLESPOON MUSTARD OIL OR CANOLA
   OIL
2 GREEN ONIONS, CUT INTO 1/8-INCH SLICES
1/4 CUP WHITE WINE VINEGAR
1/4 CUP DEFATTED CHICKEN STOCK
1/2 TEASPOON SUGAR
SALT AND FRESHLY GROUND WHITE PEPPER
   TO TASTE

1. In a small skillet, heat mustard seeds over medium heat and cook 3 to 4 minutes, or until mustard seeds begin to pop and release their aroma, shaking pan occasionally. Set aside.

2. Meanwhile, in another small skillet, heat oil over medium-high heat. Add green onions and cook 2 to 3 minutes, or until green onions are tender but not browned, stirring often. Add vinegar, chicken stock, and sugar, and stir to dissolve sugar.

3. Add mustard seeds to green onion mixture and cook 2 to 3 minutes more, or until mixture reduces slightly, stirring occasionally. Season to taste with salt and white pepper. Pour over cooked fish fillets.

MAKES 1/2 CUP

Seafood Suggestions: Cod, Flounder/Sole, Halibut, Lingcod, Skate, Sturgeon

Appendix

Seafood Flavor and Texture Chart

Flavor

	MILD	MODERATE	FULL
DELICATE	**Alaska Pollock** **Cod** **Crabmeat** **Flounder** **Orange Roughy** **Scallops** Sea Trout/Weakfish **Skate** **Sole**	**Gaspergoo** **Catfish** Lake Perch **Lingcod** **Pink Salmon** Whitefish Whiting/Hake	Bluefish Butterfish Eel Herring/Sardine **Mussels** **Oysters** **Smelt**
MEDIUM FIRM	Bream **Crawfish** Croaker Cusk Grouper Haddock **Halibut** Hoki **Lobster** Ocean Pout **Pacific Rockfish** **Sheepshead** **Shrimp** Red Snapper **Tilapia** Tilefish Walleye Pike Wolffish	Atlantic Pollock Black Sea Bass Carp **Canned Tuna** **Chum Salmon** Conch Drum **Mahimahi** Mullet Ocean Perch Pompano Porgy-Scup **Rainbow Trout** **Steelhead** **Shad** Smooth Dory Spanish Mackerel Striped Bass **Surimi Seafood**	Amberjack **Atlantic Salmon** **Canned Salmon** **Canned Sardines** Carp **Coho Salmon** **King Salmon** Mackerel Pomfret **Sablefish (Black Cod)** **Smoked Fish** **Sockeye Salmon** Yellowtail
FIRM	Kingclip **Monkfish** Ocean Catfish Opakapaka Sea Bass **Squid** Tautog (Blackfish) Tilefish	Char **Octopus** **Shark** **Sturgeon**	Bonito **Chilean Sea Bass** **Clams** **Marlin** **Swordfish** **Tuna (Ahi, Yellowfin)**

Texture (row axis label)

Note: The seafood in bold-faced type is available at the Pike Place Market on a seasonal or year-round basis. Seafood not in bold-faced type is available in seafood stores and supermarkets across the United States; these make suitable and delicious substitutes.

Pairing Seafood with Northwest Wines

The following thoughts on Northwest wines and seafood come from Michael Teer, owner of Pike and Western Wine Shop, a favorite haven for local and visiting wine connoisseurs. Pike and Western has been in the Market since 1975; Michael has worked there since 1980 and purchased the business in 1991.

Matching local seafood with local wines is not difficult and there aren't that many rules to follow. Balance is the most basic, hence most important, thing to remember when choosing a wine to go with that great piece of fish. The fish shouldn't overwhelm the wine and the wine shouldn't overwhelm the fish. Of course, you can drink a great big cabernet with your halibut if you want, but you will not be getting the best that either the halibut or the cabernet has to offer.

What follows are wines made from grape varieties grown in the Pacific Northwest that I think work best with seafood. This is by no means a complete list and is only meant to act as a guide. The fun part about food and wine is discovering what combinations *you* like.

Chardonnay—The world's most popular grape variety pairs advantageously with a wide variety of seafood, but be careful of pairing a big, oaky chardonnay with simply prepared fish. Generally, a moderately oaked or un-oaked chardonnay will work with salmon, tuna, or crab (especially a lighter-style wine).

Sauvignon Blanc—This grape variety grows extremely well in Washington, producing wines with bold, bright fruit and crisp acidity. This combination works especially well with meaty white fish like halibut, or with dishes that use herbs or have a bit of heat to them from the use of chiles. If it's a milder version of the wine, fresh trout is a wonderful match. The crisper styles of sauvignon blanc pair well with oysters, clams, and mussels. Please note that this wine can also be called fumé blanc. There is no technical meaning to the name; it is simply a synonym.

Riesling—Many people think that riesling is only a sweet wine, but it is made in styles ranging from bone dry to very sweet. The dry to medium-dry styles are *the* best wine to have with fresh crab. They also pair well with shrimp, scallops, lobster, or other examples of "sweet meat" seafoods. Dry rieslings can also work well with trout or delicate fish like cod or sole.

Pinot Gris—This Oregon grape became a commercial success because it was discovered to go so well with salmon. It still does, but is not just limited to one fish. Since pinot gris is usually not oaked and because of its fresh, clean fruit character, it pairs advantageously with much of what is called "Pacific Rim" cuisine, or dishes that take advantage of the abundance of Asian spices and other products available in the Northwest.

Pinot Noir—You can drink red wine with fish, but you need to be careful in your matchups. For example, red wine with some seafood, such as crab and oysters, just doesn't work. The combination makes both taste bad, giving an almost metallic taste. Pinot noir is one of the most seafood-friendly reds. Its lighter body and soft texture allow it to complement some of the richer fish, especially if they have been grilled. A classic Northwest combination is Oregon pinot noir and grilled salmon.

Mail Order Information

A few of the recipes in this book call for specialty seafood or products available only at the Pike Place Market. To make it easier to try these recipes, or to order seafood from the Market's fishmongers, the following is a list of businesses that will send their products via overnight air service, United Parcel Service, or through the U.S. mail. Some will send fresh seafood, produce, or foodstuffs; others can transport only certain of their products (preserved items, such as herb vinegars, jams, and jellies). The businesses have varying policies on credit cards; some accept them, others will take only a check or money order, so inquire before placing your order.

Alm Hill Gardens
3550 Alm Rd., Everson, WA 98247
(360) 966-4157 (telephone and fax)
Raspberry vinegar, jams and jellies, flowers, berries, vegetables, herbs, evergreen wreaths

Canter-Berry Farms
19102 S.E. Green Valley Rd.,
Auburn, WA 98092
(206) 939-2706
(800) 548-8418
Blueberry vinegar, blueberry chutney, other blueberry products

Chukar Cherry Company
P.O. Box 510, 320 Wine Country Rd.,
Prosser, WA 99350-0510
(509) 786-2055
(800) 624-9544
(509) 786-2591 (fax)
Dried cherries, berries, trail mixes, chocolate-covered dried cherries, fruit preserves and sauces

City Fish
1535 Pike Place, Seattle, WA 98101
(206) 682-9329
(800) 334-2669
(206) 467-5155 (fax)
Fresh fish market

Cucina Fresca
1904 Pike Place, Seattle, WA 98101
(206) 448-4758
(206) 722-7147 (fax)
Italian specialty products, fresh pastas and sauces

DeLaurenti Specialty Food Markets
1435 First Ave., Seattle, WA 98101
(206) 622-0141
(206) 622-3262 (fax)
Italian specialty products, wine, cheeses, deli meats

Duffield Farm
Judy, Dave, and Deanna Duff
P.O. Box 66925, Seattle, WA 98166
(206) 246-8266
Organic vegetables, fruits, herbs, and edible flowers; herbal vinegars

du jour
1919 First Ave., Seattle, WA 98101
(206) 441-3354
(206) 441-5374 (fax)
Gift baskets

El Mercado Latino
1514 Pike Place, Seattle, WA 98101
(206) 623-3240
Latin American, South and Central American, African, Creole, Spanish, and some Asian specialty foods and fresh produce

Frank's Quality Produce
1508 Pike Place, Seattle, WA 98101
(206) 624-5666
Fruit baskets delivered in the Seattle area

Holmquist Hazelnut Orchard
9821 Holmquist Rd., Lynden, WA 98264
(360) 988-9240
(360) 988-6202 (fax)
Raw, roasted, salted, and chocolate-covered hazelnuts

Ivacco Foods
1501 Pike Place, Seattle, WA 98101
(206) 223-9582
Grains, beans, pasta, coffee, tea, olive oil, balsamic vinegar and many other bulk items; health foods; organic produce

Jack's Fish Spot
1514 Pike Place, Seattle, WA 98101
(206) 467-0514
(206) 467-0500 (fax)
Fresh seafood market

Kitchen Basics
1514 Pike Place, #10, Seattle, WA 98101
(206) 622-2014
(800) 233-2014
Kitchenware, kitchen gadgets, Fiesta ware

**Liberty Malt Supply Company/
Pike Pub and Brewery**
1419 First Ave., Seattle, WA 98101
(206) 622-1880
(800) 990-6258
(206) 322-5185 (fax)
Brewing supplies, magazines, books, specialty beers, pub/restaurant

The Market Foundation
85 Pike St., Rm. 500, Seattle, WA 98101
(206) 682-PIKE (682-7453)
(206) 625-0646 (fax)
Market-related merchandise, such as cookbooks, tote bags, notecards, clocks, and jewelry

MarketSpice
P.O. Box 2935, Redmond, WA 98073-2935
(206) 883-1220

(206) 881-5603 (fax)
Dried herbs, spices, coffee, and tea in bulk; a wide array of specialty food products

Mech Apiaries
P.O. Box 452, Maple Valley, WA 98038
(206) 432-3971
Raw honey and honey products

Micks' Peppouri & Cheese
1531 Pike Place, Seattle, WA 98101
(206) 233-0128
(800) 204-5679
P.O. Box 8324, Yakima, WA 98908
(509) 966-6207 (fax)
http://www.wet.net/micks
Pepper jellies and chutneys; cheese

The Perennial Tea Room
1910 Post Alley, Seattle, WA 98101
(206) 448-4054
(206) 448-0113 (fax)
Tea in bulk, tea-making accessories, whimsical teapots

Pike Place Fish Market
86 Pike Place, Seattle, WA 98101
(206) 682-7181
(800) 542-7732
(206) 682-4629 (fax)
Fresh seafood market

The Pike Place Market Creamery
1514 Pike Place, #3, Seattle, WA 98101
(206) 622-5029
Unrefrigerated items only, such as jams, jellies, honey, soy milk; t-shirts

Pike and Western Wine Shop
1934 Pike Place, Seattle, WA 98101
(206) 441-1307
(206) 441-1308 (fax)
Wines and wine accessories

Pure Food Fish Market
> 1515 Pike Place, Seattle, WA 98101
> (206) 622-5765
> (206) 622-2050 (fax)
> (800) 392-3474
> http://www.freshseafood.com
> Fresh seafood market

Quality Cheese
> 1508 Pike Place, Seattle, WA 98101
> (206) 624-4029
> Fresh cheeses from the Northwest, the United
> States, and around the world

Rachel-Dee Herb Farm
> 6311 Stewart Ave., Puyallup, WA 98371
> (360) 825-2797
> (800) 841-7534
> Herbal jellies, jams, and vinegars; dried
> wreaths

Sosio's Fruit & Produce
> 1527 Pike Place, Seattle, WA 98101
> (206) 622-1370
> (206) 622-1540 (fax)
> Local and regional fruits and vegetables in
> season, as well as produce from around the
> world; fruit baskets

The Souk
> 1916 Pike Place, Seattle, WA 98101
> (206) 441-1666
> (206) 367-9360 (fax)
> Indian and Pakistani herbs, spices, and lentils
> in bulk; frozen *halal* meats; chapati bread

The Spanish Table
> 1427 Western Ave., Seattle, WA 98101
> (206) 682-2827
> (206) 682-2814 (fax)
> tablespan@aol.com
> Iberian specialty foods, wines and liqueurs, and
> take-out foods; glassware and porcelain; paella
> pans (*paelleras*); cookbooks

Stackhouse Brothers' Orchards
> 13501 Cogswell Rd., Hickman, CA 95323
> (209) 883-2663
> (800) 382-7654
> Raw, roasted, and flavored almonds; dried fruits

Sur La Table
> 84 Pine St., Seattle, WA 98101-1573
> (206) 448-2244
> (800) 240-0853 (Pike Place Market store)
> (800) 243-0852 (catalog division)
> (206) 448-2245 (fax)
> Kitchenware, kitchen gadgets, French copper-
> ware, table settings, cookbooks

Totem Smokehouse
> 1906 Pike Place, Seattle, WA 98101
> (206) 443-1710
> (800) 972-5666
> (206) 441-8166 (fax)
> http://www.totemsmokehouse.com
> Smoked salmon, oysters, scallops, trout, and
> tuna; wood chips for grilling; cookbooks

Verdi's Farm-Fresh Produce
> 1033 S. Director St., Seattle, WA 98108
> (206) 763-7162
> Fresh produce with an Italian flair, particularly
> well known for fresh basil in season

Woodring Orchards
> 5420 Woodring Canyon Rd., Cashmere, WA
> 98815
> (509) 782-2868
> (800) 548-5740
> (509) 782-4811 (fax)
> jtrankin@nwi.net
> Apples and apple cider; specialty foods made
> from apples and other fruits

Several other businesses noted within this book, while not in the Market, deserve special mention for their wonderful products:

Chandler's Fresh Fish Market
901 Fairview Ave. N., Bldg. B-101, Seattle, WA 98109
(206) 223-2722
Fresh seafood market

Jensen's Old-Fashioned Smokehouse, Inc.
10520 Greenwood Ave. N., Seattle, WA 98133
(206) 364-5569
(206) 364-0880 (fax)
Smoked seafood; also smokes and vacuum-packs salmon caught by fishers

Mutual Fish
2335 Rainier Ave. S., Seattle, WA 98144
(206) 322-4368
(206) 328-5889 (fax)
Fresh seafood market

Pacific Northwest Fine Wood Products
E-520 Twanoh Falls Drive, Belfair, WA 98528
(360) 275-5397
Cedar planks and planking cookbook

Port Chatham Smoked Seafood (main store)
632 N.W. 46th St., Seattle, WA 98107
(206) 783-8200
(800) 872-5666
(206) 281-4484 (fax)
Smoked seafood, including smoked sablefish (page xx); also smokes and vacuum-packs salmon caught by fishers; specialty foods; cookbooks

Seattle Caviar Co.
3147 Fairview Ave. E., Seattle, WA 98102
(206) 323-3005
(206) 726-9603 (fax)
http://www.caviar.com
Imported caviar; domestic paddlefish and whitefish caviar

Simply Seafood
5305 Shilshole Ave. N.W., Ste. 200, Seattle, WA 98107
(206) 789-6506
(800) 835-2722
Magazine subscriptions

University Seafood & Poultry Co.
1317 N.E. 47th St., Seattle, WA 98105
(206) 632-3900 or (206) 632-3700
(206) 632-3800 (fax)
Fresh seafood market

Uwajimaya, Inc.
519 6th Ave. S., Seattle, WA 98104
(206) 624-6248
Fresh seafood and produce market, Asian specialty items, kitchenware, cookbooks

Seafood Festivals

Annual Crab Races and Crab Feed, Westport, Washington, third Saturday in April. Watch live Dungeness crab claw their way to victory as they race (and sometimes crawl or slide) down a 6-foot ramp. Afterwards, enjoy a crab boil complete with salad, garlic bread, and baked beans. Contact the Westport Chamber of Commerce, (800) 345-6223.

Annual Wine and Oyster Fest, Joe Fortes Seafood House, 777 Thurlow St., Vancouver, British Columbia, January. The city's largest oyster bar features a stand-up buffet with a wide array of oysters and matching wines. Contact the restaurant at (604) 669-1940.

Ballard SeafoodFest, downtown Ballard (just north of downtown Seattle), last weekend in July. An alder-smoked salmon feed, lutefisk eating contest, two concert stages, and an array of food booths highlight this festival held in the Scandinavian section of Seattle. Contact the Ballard Chamber of Commerce, (206) 784-9705.

Crabfest, Chandler's Crabhouse and Fresh Fish Market, Seattle, Washington, spring (late March to mid-May). This celebration of crab from around the world features a wide variety of appetizers, entrées, and even ice cream made with crabmeat. Contact the restaurant at (206) 223-2722.

Elliott's Oyster Festival, Elliott's Oyster House & Seafood Restaurant, Seattle, Washington, third Friday in October. See page 220 for complete details about Seattle's largest oyster festival. Contact the restaurant at (206) 623-4340.

Great Astoria Crab Feed and Seafood Festival, Astoria, Oregon, fourth full weekend in April. This festival highlights every concoction made from the famed Dungeness crab, accompanied by Oregon wines. Fresh scallops and fish are also on the menu, as are activities such as crabbing, water taxi rides, and charter fishing. Contact the Astoria Chamber of Commerce, (503) 325-6311.

Hood Canal ShrimpFest, Brinnon, Washington, opening weekend of shrimp season on Hood Canal (May). Celebrate the largest shrimp in Washington, the giant spot, which may grow to 9 inches (not including the antennae), with a food fair, shrimp cooking contest, live music, and a shrimp gear display. Contact the Greater Quilcene Chamber of Commerce, (360) 765-4999.

Issaquah Salmon Days Festival, Issaquah, Washington, first full weekend in October. Watch the salmon return to the hatchery while you feast on all-you-can-eat baked salmon, as well as salmon burgers, pesto salmon, and salmon skewers. Contact the Issaquah Chamber of Commerce, (206) 270-2532.

Jazz and Oysters Festival, Oysterville, Washington, third weekend in August. Grilled oysters bathed in fennel butter with an optional splash of Tabasco sauce pair perfectly with the unmistakable sounds of live jazz. Contact the Long Beach Peninsula Visitors Bureau, (800) 451-2542.

Kodiak Crab Festival, Kodiak, Alaska, Memorial Day weekend (Thursday through Monday). This family-oriented festival honors the crab with cuisine from the Philippines, Mexico, and China, along with a marathon and the "Blessing of the Fleet" parade. Contact the Kodiak Chamber of Commerce, (907) 486-5557.

Newport Seafood and Wine Festival, Newport, Oregon, third weekend in February. Salmon and Dungeness crab are showcased, along with more exotic seafood such as squid, eel, abalone, and smoked tuna, as well as more than 100 Northwest wineries. Contact the Newport Chamber of Commerce, (541) 265-5883.

Oyster Olympics, Anthony's Homeport, 6135 Seaview Ave. N.W., Seattle, Washington, last Tuesday in March. This lively event, considered to be the most challenging bivalve competition in the world, features restaurants competing in oyster shucking and identification contests, a celebrity oyster slurp, and numerous Northwest oysters on the half shell and hors d'oeuvres paired with oyster wines and micro-brewed beers. It benefits the Puget Soundkeeper Alliance, which works to preserve and protect the waters of Puget Sound. Contact the Alliance at (206) 286-1309.

Oyster Stampede, South Bend, Washington, Memorial Day weekend (Friday night, Saturday, Sunday). Every spring, Willapa Bay oysters "stampede" from one bed to another looking for a mate—or so the legend goes. To celebrate the gutsy mollusk's rite of passage, South Bend, which claims to be the "oyster capital of the world," celebrates with a seven-course seafood and wine dinner. Booths stocked with oysters cooked in every conceivable manner, as well as oyster burgers, shooters, clam chowder, fish-and-chips, and smoked salmon offer other tempting treats. Contact the South Bend Chamber of Commerce, (360) 875-5231.

Penn Cove Mussel Festival, Captain Whidbey Inn, Coupeville, Washington, first weekend in March. This popular event held on scenic Whidbey Island in Puget Sound features activities such as tours of the mussel beds aboard the *Cutty Sark,* a restored tall ship; lectures by aquaculture experts and cooking demonstrations by celebrity chefs; a mussel chowder-off, mussel-eating contest, and mussel beach party; and special winemaker's and brewmaster's dinners. Contact the inn at (800) 366-4097.

Salmon Homecoming, Seattle Aquarium and Waterfront Park, Piers 62/63, Seattle, Washington, third weekend in September. This four-day event salutes the return of Chinook, coho, and chum salmon to Puget Sound with numerous cultural, musical, and arts-and-crafts presentations by Native American tribal communities (including a lavish powwow). A salmon bake highlights the festivities. Contact the Aquarium, (206) 386-4320.

The Great Monterey Squid Festival, Monterey Fairgrounds, Monterey, California, Memorial Day weekend (Friday, Saturday, Sunday). Here is your chance to try squid cooked in every way imaginable, including Squid Cordon Bleu, squid blintzes, squid pie, and even squid donuts. Contact the Monterey Chamber of Commerce, (408) 649-1770.

The World's Only Smelt Derby, La Conner, Washington, first Saturday in February. Each winter, as millions of smelt run through the Swinomish Slough, hundreds of kids of all ages march to the shoreline, attach small fish hooks to fishing poles and jig for smelt. Catches are large in number even if the fish themselves are small in size, and prizes are awarded. Contact the La Conner Chamber of Commerce, (360) 466-4778.

West Coast Oyster Shucking Championship and Washington State Seafood Festival (Shelton OysterFest), Mason County Fairgrounds, Shelton, Washington, first full weekend in October. See page 227 for a full description of the festival. Contact Shelton Chamber of Commerce, (360) 426-2021.

Westport Seafood Festival and Craft Show, Westport, Washington, Labor Day weekend (Saturday). Enjoy a seafood extravaganza featuring grilled oysters, salmon, and cod, then stroll through the crafts displays while enjoying live music. Contact the Westport Chamber of Commerce, (800) 345-6223.

Index

A Celebration of Seafood from Ten Speed Press and Celestial Arts:

PACIFICA BLUE PLATES
by Neil Stuart

Where *is* the Pacific Southwest? It's where salsa meets satay, where jalapeño meets hoisin, where burritos meet banana leaves. The hundred-plus recipes in this book feature innovative combinations of Southwestern and Pacific Rim elements, brought together with a California touch. But these dishes are also healthful, mostly low-fat, and simple enough for any home chef. 164 pages.

THE STREAMLINER DINER COOKBOOK
by Alexandra Rust, Elizabeth Matteson, Judith Weinstock, and Irene Clark

Diner food as you've never had it before from a small café near Seattle which has gained a reputation for honest, fresh, made-from-scratch American food. 192 pages.

TOTALLY SHRIMP, TOTALLY CRAB, TOTALLY LOBSTER, AND TOTALLY SALMON
by Helene Siegel

Helene Siegel casts her culinary net once again and hauls in a huge catch with the Totally Seafood series. Seafood restaurants have spawned all over the country, and why not? With some twelve thousand miles of coastline to choose from—the Eastern Seaboard, the Gulf Coast, and the Pacific Coast—Americans have a wealth of seafood to choose from. 96 pages each.

EDIBLE CRUSTACEANS AND EDIBLE MOLLUSKS POSTERS
by Bill Marinelli

Celebrate the bounty of the sea with these two lavish, full-color posters. Over 60 gorgeous species are beautifully displayed—perfect for home, office, or restaurant decor. 24 x 36.

Available from your local bookstore, or call 1-800-841-BOOK for information on how to order direct from the publisher. Write for our free complete catalog of over 500 books, posters, and tapes.

Ten Speed Press
P.O. Box 7123
Berkeley, California 94707